A GUIDE TO WELSH LITERATURE

D0872817

A GUIDE TO WELSH LITERATURE

VOLUME VII

Welsh Writing in English

Edited by

M. WYNN THOMAS

UNIVERSITY OF WALES PRESS
CARDIFF
2003

British Library Cataloguing in Publication Data

A catalogue record for this book is available from the British Library

ISBN 0-7083-1679-4

Published with the financial support of the Arts Council of Wales

THE *A*SSOCIATION FOR
*W*ELSH *W*RITING IN *E*NGLISH
*C*YMDEITHAS *L*LÊN *S*AESNEG *C*YMRU

Cover illustration: Ceri Richards, *The Force that through the Green Fuse Drives the Flower*, lithograph, 1945. Reproduced by permission of the City and County of Swansea: Glynn Vivian Art Gallery Collection. © Estate of Ceri Richards 2003. All Rights Reserved, DACS.

Cover design by Olwen Fowler
Typeset at the University of Wales Press
Printed in by MPG Books Ltd, Bodmin, Cornwall

CONTENTS

ACKNOWLEDGEMENTS

Commissioned in 1994, this volume has been a long time in preparation and sincere thanks for their patience is due both to those contributors who completed their work many years ago and to the University of Wales Press for enduring such a long wait before its authoritative series of guides to the entire literature of Wales could be brought to a conclusion. During the long interval between the initiation and the completion of the project, the commissioning editor, Ned Thomas, was succeeded as Director of the Press by Susan Jenkins and my gratitude to both of them for their belief in this undertaking and their determination to see it through is heartfelt. In the latter stages, Ruth Dennis-Jones and Liz Powell have attended to the production of the book with their customary tact, insight and good-natured rigour. Dr Claire Powell, at *CREW*, has assisted me with the proofing of the text, and my daughter, Elin Manahan Thomas, has again assiduously prepared an index. Diolch o galon ichi i gyd.

M. Wynn Thomas
CREW (Centre for Research into the English Literature and
Language of Wales)
University of Wales Swansea
January 2003

A NOTE ON CONTRIBUTORS

Jane Aaron is a Professor of English at the University of Glamorgan and author of a study of nineteenth-century women's writing in Wales, *Pur fel y Dur*. She also co-edited the volumes *Out of the Margins: Women's Studies in the Nineties*, and *Our Sisters' Land: The Changing Identities of Women in Wales*, prepared a Honno anthology of Welsh women's short stories, *A View across the Valley*, and has most recently edited Hilda Vaughan's novel, *Iron and Gold*.

Tony Brown is Reader in English at the University of Wales, Bangor, where he is also co-director of the R. S. Thomas Study Centre. He has published extensively on Welsh writing in English and has edited *Pe Medrwn yr Iaith: Detholiad o Ryddiaith R. S. Thomas* (with Bedwyr Lewis Jones), *The Collected Stories of Glyn Jones*, and Glyn Jones's *The Dragon has Two Tongues*. He is editor of the journal *Welsh Writing in English: A Yearbook of Critical Essays*.

Born in Bengal in 1931, Tony Conran was educated at Colwyn Bay and University College, Bangor, where he tutored until 1980. He has published over a dozen books of poetry, and is editor and translator of *The Penguin Book of Welsh Verse* and a selection of Waldo Williams's poems. His *Collected Poems* are to appear this year. He is the author of two critical books and many articles on Anglo-Welsh poetry, and a volume of appreciation of his work, *Thirteen Ways of Looking at Tony Conran*, was published in his honour by the Welsh Union of Writers in 1995.

James A. Davies is Honorary Research Fellow in the Centre for Research into the English Literature and Language of Wales, University of Wales Swansea. His publications include *John Foster:*

A Literary Life; *The Textual Life of Dickens's Characters*; *Leslie Norris*; *Dylan Thomas's Places*; *A Reference Companion to Dylan Thomas*; and *Dylan Thomas's Swansea, Gower and Laugharne*. He has edited Dannie's Abse's plays and two anthologies, *The Heart of Wales* and *A Swansea Anthology*.

Katie Gramich is a Staff Tutor with the Open University. A native of Ceredigion, she was educated at the Universities of Wales, London and Alberta. Recent publications include an edition of Allen Raine's *Queen of the Rushes*, Amy Dillwyn's *The Rebecca Rioter* and book chapters on Dylan Thomas, Rhys Davies, and D. H. Lawrence. She has also written on Nadine Gordimer for the Open University course A430, 'Post-colonial Literatures in English'.

Formerly a lecturer in bibliographical studies at Aberystwyth, John Harris has edited numerous works by Caradoc Evans and written on Anglo-Welsh literary and publishing history. The compiler of *A Bibliographical Guide to Twenty-four Anglo-Welsh Authors*, he has more recently edited *Goronwy Rees: Sketches in Autobiography* and published the Writers of Wales monograph on Rees.

Formerly Senior Lecturer in English and Head of Department at St David's College, Lampeter, Belinda Humfrey has published studies of authors including John Cowper Powys, Henry Vaughan and John Dyer. She is the editor of a collection of essays on twentieth-century Welsh writers, *Fire Green as Grass*, and of Glyn Jones's novel *The Island of Apples*. She was the founding editor of *The New Welsh Review* and is editor of *The Powys Review*.

Stephen Knight is a Professor of English Literature at Cardiff University. Belonging to a family scattered through south Wales, he was educated mostly in England and spent over twenty years working in Australia. Author of many essays on literature medieval and modern, canonical and popular, he has written and edited books on Chaucer, crime fiction, industrial fiction, the myth of king Arthur and the tradition of Robin Hood.

M. Wynn Thomas is a Professor of English and Director of CREW (the Centre for Research into the English Literature and Language of Wales), University of Wales Swansea, and has been a Visiting Professor at Harvard University. He is author/editor of twenty books, in both Welsh and English, on American literature and on the two literatures of modern Wales. He is a Fellow of the British Academy.

Ned Thomas is academic director of the Mercator Centre at University of Wales, Aberystwyth, where he taught for many years in the English department and founded the cultural magazine *Planet*, before becoming director of the University of Wales Press. He has taught at the Universities of Salamanca and Moscow and his published work includes *The Welsh Extremist – A Culture in Crisis*, and studies of George Orwell, Derek Walcott and Waldo Williams.

John Powell Ward was educated at Hereford Cathedral School and the Universities of Toronto, Cambridge and Wales and is now Honorary Research Fellow in the Department of English at University of Wales Swansea. He is editor of the Seren *Borderlines* series and his critical studies include *Poetry and the Sociological Idea*, *As You Like It* and works on Wordsworth, Raymond Williams and R. S. Thomas. Collections of poetry by him include *The Clearing* (Welsh Arts Council prize for 1985) and most recently *Late Thoughts in March*.

INTRODUCTION

Asked to name one Welsh writer, the majority of people would no doubt mention the English-language writer Dylan Thomas. But when could Welsh writing in English be said to have begun? Did it begin around 1470 with 'Ei sik, ei sing, ei siak, ei sae', Ieuan ap Hywel Swrdwal's defiantly mocking hybrid text, 'The hymn to the virgin', an extraordinary document of colonization? Or was it in 1915, with 'On the banks of Avon Bern there lived a man who was a Father in Sion', the prelude to Caradoc Evans's Oedipal onslaught in *My People* on the Welsh-language culture that was his patrimony? Do we have in Wales one of the youngest literatures in Europe, a post-colonial 'English' literature, alongside one of the oldest literatures in Europe, still written in a Romano-Celtic language? Or do we have two almost equally venerable literatures?

Well into the nineteenth century, English had been spoken, and therefore written, by only a small minority in a Wales whose population was otherwise Welsh speaking. The English-language literature of this pre-modern period was consequently produced almost entirely by the gentry, the clergy, the professional classes and the tiny urban bourgeoisie, and many of the writers were English incomers. Virtually the only exceptions were those few intellectuals and religious leaders whose first language was Welsh but who nevertheless turned to English on occasions. The great seventeenth-century Puritan mystical writer, Morgan Llwyd, wrote doggerel verse and religious tracts in English, and there are many hymns by the eighteenth-century Methodist William Williams, Pantycelyn, considered by some to be the major poet of Welsh-language culture. Apart from the poetry of Henry Vaughan and John Dyer, the bulk of the writing before the twentieth century can seem little more than an inferior, provincial version of the mainstream English literature of the day. It has, consequently, been considered to be of only very limited, historical, interest, but recent researchers have become increasingly fascinated with this whole field of pre-twentieth century writing as a rich source of materials for those interested in, for example, women's writing (many of the significant figures were women) and in the textual products of a colonial subculture.

During the second half of the nineteenth century the situation began to change, as the processes of industrialization set in train the mass inward migration that was to transform the cultural scene in Wales, and a developing education system played a decisive part in assimilating even the indigenous Welsh population to an intolerantly anglophone British culture. A typical product of this period was Lewis Morris, a patriotic poet in the fulsome Victorian style. It was to be many decades before the new, anglophone society of Wales (largely concentrated in the south Wales coalfield) began to produce, especially in the 1930s, a distinctive body of work (much of it proletarian in sympathy, socialist in conviction and internationalist in outlook). And many of the most prominent writers of this era naturally came from the south Wales valleys, the crucible in which modern Wales could be said to have been fashioned. That it was the new, cosmopolitan and predominantly anglophone culture produced there that eventually made a new literature necessary, and thus inevitable, is a truth that has been limned and hymned both by historians and by cultural critics. It is a truth reaffirmed in the present volume. But if every valley (at least in the south-east) has been exalted, there is then a corresponding danger that the hills may be brought low. The literary, as well as the geographical, map of Wales would become strangely deformed were that to happen and it is perhaps the tendency in that direction that has been partly responsible for the slighting of such geographically marginal figures as that man of the hills, the mid-Wales border-country writer Geraint Goodwin, and the Llanybri-based Lynette Roberts. The rivalries between the regions of Wales – rural west and industrial south-east; coalfield south and quarry-district north; heartland Wales and border country – that give rise to the mental, or symbolic, geography of the country as revealed in its literature and that produce the dynamic of Welsh politics, can all too easily distort the discussion and evaluation of the literature as well. The present study therefore tries to avoid that trap by viewing Welsh writing in English in a wide geographical and cultural perspective. After all, from a narrow, valleys, perspective even Swansea jacks like Vernon Watkins and Dylan Thomas become resident aliens.

'If Wales were to be flattened out it would be bigger than England' runs the legend on a popular postcard. It would also, inevitably, cease to be Wales, and that flattening-out of Welsh experience to approximate to an Anglocentric norm was the charge levelled at modern Welsh writers in English by powerful representatives of Welsh-language culture during much of the twentieth century. A variation on that charge is the accusation, heard latterly, that, in contrast to the writing of the culturally turbulent 1960s, poetry and fiction from the 1970s onwards have lacked any significant markers of Welshness. This is the sort of cultural bickering that can seem tiresome to outsiders, but it should be remembered that, in the case of a stateless nation whose separate identity was for centuries substantially maintained by its writers, a failure to reproduce itself through literary texts quickly becomes a serious matter. Whether the token powers granted a fledgling National Assembly are sufficient to ensure the full institutionalization of identity that other nations take so much for granted that they are largely unconscious of it, remains to be seen. But the legend on the card can also be read as a parable of a different kind. Why Wales's obsession with viewing itself in terms of England? This, too, is a question often asked with reference not only to Welsh writing in English itself but also to the critical discussion of it, with the result that emphasis is, for instance, coming to be placed, as some of the contributors to this volume duly note, on viewing the literature in the context of other non-English anglophone literatures worldwide. However, such a necessary concentration on exploring the distinctive Welshness of the writing will itself need to be carefully monitored, as it could result in an underestimating of its British dimensions.

While the present volume has been designed primarily as a layperson's guide, it will also doubtless function as a sourcebook for scholars. That is because, whatever its omissions and limitations, it can reasonably claim to be the most inclusive study of its subject that has been published to date. To state that no authoritative study of Welsh writing in English so far exists is to intend no disrespect to those excellent pioneering writers, critics and scholars – notably including Gwyn Jones, Glyn Jones, Raymond Garlick,

Roland Mathias, not to mention some of the contributors to the
present study – who have been at work for so long in this field. It is
simply that, for political reasons at bottom, the materials and
opportunities necessary for such a major undertaking are still only
slowly being made available. With the exception of the distinguished poet and translator Tony Conran (whose chapter on
the sixties is written from the perspective of a participating figure),
the contributors to this volume are (or have been) university
scholars, several of whom came together in the early 1980s to form
a kind of mutual support group initially cumbersomely labelled
The Universities of Wales Association for the Study of Welsh
Writing in English (subsequently AWE – the Association for
Welsh Writing in English). Almost all of them were, and are,
specialists in other fields (from medieval literature to American
literature) who were moonlighting, so to speak, by venturing on
additional work in this academically suspect area of study. It was,
after all, the case in Wales that no scholar could establish her or
his credentials by specializing in Welsh writing in English. And has
the situation changed? Not much, it is to be feared. It is still the
case that young scholars have to be advised by their seniors that
they will only risk their careers if they confine themselves to this
'backward' and 'provincial' subject. It is remarkable that any
persist. But they do, and the last few years have seen the emergence
of a constellation of younger talents. Whether there is a future for
them must be uncertain, given the present state of the academic
world in Wales. But if they are allowed to mature, it is already
plain to see that they are likely to make an exhilarating difference
to the way in which Welsh writing in English is construed and
constructed through scholarly discussion, not least by reinforcing
the recent welcome trend to introduce sophisticated contemporary
discourses to what has for too long been a somewhat old-
fashioned field of study. Through operating with the more relaxed
concept of 'writing' they are likely to bring currently marginalized
figures into the frame: fiction writers such as Dorothy Edwards;
'travel writers' such as Jan Morris and Robert Minhinnick; 'nature
writers' like Jim Perrin; autobiographers of note, from Goronwy
Rees to Barbara Hardy, Mavis Nicholson, John Cale, Lorna Sage
and Charlotte Williams; political writers from the eighteenth-
century Richard Price through great nineteenth-century radical
Nonconformist thinkers like Samuel Roberts ('S.R.') to Roy

Jenkins; journalists such as John Morgan, Russell Davies and
Alan Watkins; 'popular writers' such as Dick Francis, Bernard
Knight, Ken Follett or Leslie Thomas; children's writers galore;
historians of oral culture such as George Ewart Evans. They also
seem certain to be better equipped to do justice to subaltern
groups – Jewish Welsh writers for instance, including the recently
rediscovered Lily Tobias – and to culturally ambiguous figures
such as James Hanley and John Cowper Powys. Art forms are
likely to seem altogether more porous to them, so that the work
of writer-painters such as Brenda Chamberlain will become more
accessible. And it is difficult to believe that they will perpetuate the
unfortunate Welsh practice (not completely avoided in this volume)
of relegating drama to some imperfectly defined category distinct
from 'literature'. The impact of Welsh drama in English – and most
notably of the plays of J. O. Francis – on the cultural scene during
the first decades of the twentieth century, for example, deserves
very careful consideration.

There has been no attempt at uniformity of approach in this
volume. Each contributor has been encouraged to operate on
terms of her and his own choosing. Consequently, traditional
modes of evaluation are employed in some chapters; popular
culture is honoured elsewhere; a thematic history is preferred in a
few discussions; convinced polemic powers others. Such an eclectic
array of approaches has been deliberately encouraged, as this book
is intended to be read not so much as an 'objective' account of the
anglophone literary culture of Wales but as an active contribution
to the very culture it seeks to describe, interpret and evaluate. For
the same reason, occasional overlap of treatment of some authors
has been allowed. The decision to organize the volume on a
thematic basis, rather than by adopting a chronological and/or
generic structure, was entirely that of the editor, as was to suggest
themes – a decision that has, no doubt, resulted in the strait-
jacketing on occasions of both contributors and authors, and in
the relative slighting of some key writers. The reason for this
approach was to demonstrate the kinds of shapes it is possible
(and indeed necessary) to make out of Welsh culture in an attempt
to comprehend the phenomenon of 'Wales'. The analogy is
therefore with the work of the artists of the Beca group, who, from
Paul Davies to Iwan Bala, have toyed very productively with the
map of Wales to similar purpose. And, of course, in engaging in

this kind of activity many of the contributors to this volume are trying to make illuminating shapes out of that which has shaped them, to paraphrase David Jones.

This *Guide* is therefore intended to be an intervention in the ongoing discussion between texts that constitutes the world of writing. And it is also a contribution to the ongoing process of 'producing' Welsh identity by textual means. In his study of Italian democracy, Joseph LaPolambara has remarked that 'a country that seems to lean into the void but never really falls into it may actually be firmly anchored there, like the Tower of Pisa'. Wales is a bit like that. But it will be remembered that recently the tower needed jacking up just a few cautious millimetres to prevent it from toppling over. Perhaps a 'critical' study like this volume, through the gentle counter-pressures it applies to at least some Welsh literary and historical leanings, may perform a similar mildly corrective service for Wales.

CHAPTER 1

PRELUDE TO THE TWENTIETH CENTURY

BELINDA HUMFREY

There is no advantage in attempting to disguise the fact that, as such eminent literary historians as Raymond Garlick and Roland Mathias have diligently discovered, although there are Anglo-Welsh writers aplenty between the age of Shakespeare and the advent of the First World War (or Caradoc Evans's *My People*), only two writers can be described conscientiously as great Anglo-Welsh writers (and for a small, sparsely populated country, that is an achievement). They are both poets: Henry Vaughan (1621–95) and John Dyer (1699–1757). Each is very much a creative writer of his own century; each giving us a substantial and varied body of work; each experimental in subjects and style, and innovative, that is producing poetry which is new, distinct and inimitable within the body of English literature. Vaughan and Dyer are both Welshmen with a Welsh pedigree of many generations, both from south mid-Wales, both bilingual from their parentage, both from versions of the lesser Welsh landed gentry, so that to a sound Welsh classical education they added further education – Vaughan in Oxford, both in London – for a few years. Both read extensively throughout their writing lives and could justly be called bookish. This youthful experience of England, bringing contacts with lively literary, scholarly and political circles outside Wales, seems to have given them extra stimulus, perhaps confidence in their writing, but, as they developed, also to have given each his sense of his special identity, experience and voice as a Welsh writer belonging to a distinct Welsh rural landscape; sense of place and sense of self are merged in their work; from this harmony emerges their memorable poetry.

In literary histories, Henry Vaughan is usually recognized as a late, but major metaphysical lyric poet, of the seventeenth-century school of John Donne (1572–1631), possibly of the 'strong lines' of Ben Jonson (1572–1637) and of George Herbert (1593–1633). This label is of limited use. It suggests a poetry of intellectual twists and turns of argument, using incongruous images yoked together, as strong emotion is suspended and often finally projected from them; it suggests the influence of theatre, with an initial plunging into a personal scene, at its grandest helped by the choice of some personal form of poem like ode or elegy, with a flow of spoken or conversational language, often with some witty word-play. These characteristics can be found in many of Vaughan's poems. What most obviously, if partly, differentiates the Metaphysicals from one another is their driving forces – from erotic love to Christian devotion – and their distinctive imagery – Donne, say, liking images of measurement, Herbert domestic and church architectural imagery. Obviously, Vaughan's dominant imagery is from the natural world ('I walked the other day . . . Into a field'), which makes him utterly distinct from his predecessors. Other thematic concerns also remove him from them.

Vaughan put himself with the Metaphysicals by a few echoes of Donne (among other poets, such as Shakespeare) and by his declaration, at the point at which he began to write with clear distinction, that he was inspired by his 'cousin' Herbert 'whose holy life and verse gained many pious *converts*'. Indeed, at this stage, in *Silex Scintillans* I (1650) Vaughan echoes or borrows many of Herbert's phrases. Yet, as a shaper of poems, Vaughan is the opposite of Herbert at his most characteristic. Herbert's lyrics, even of narrative, are architecturally tightly strictured, enjoy symmetry and employ staccato endings; and although more of his poems than Vaughan's have been later employed as hymns, they are not, like Vaughan's poems, hymning in the sense of flowing. The spiritual tone and movement and the physical structure of Vaughan's poetry tends to be expansionist and centrifugal, contrasted with Herbert's which is centripetal. (And Vaughan's poetry is rooted in Wales, as, despite his elements of Welsh blood, Herbert's is not.) Vaughan's poetry is never an exhibitionist, virtuoso performance, like Donne's in the experimental theatre of himself. He is usually prompted to write by an event or by the observation of something (a bird, a tree, a waterfall) outside himself. And whereas, as we shall see, he had more cause than Herbert to be preachy, and wished to preach because he was living in an area and time deficient in preaching and teaching, unlike Herbert in his collection of 'solitary devotions', *The Temple* (1633), even when Vaughan moves through ordered church occasions, his Christian poems are truly solitary, scattered with indicative words like 'hid', 'secret', 'unseen'; even as he writes primarily from promptings of biblical texts his poems record private spiritual longings, powerful in their impact.

Vaughan's distinctive version of *hiraeth*, the longing of his 'love-sick heart' for union with God, is expressed within the poetry as the feeling that he can only move forward by moving backward to an early, unpolluted life: to unfallen pre-existence, to the state of Adam in Eden, to the Old Testament prophets who conversed with angels, to the state of Primitive Christians, to 'Angel-infancy', his own childhood, or to the unpolluted vegetable life around 'the fair stream of Usk'. As a regenerative writer, paradoxically for one who expresses tender love and admiration for the 'small innocent' fellow creatures of the natural world, both animal and vegetable, in many poems he is apocalyptic on a drastic scale, looking for a time of judgement when the earth shall be made 'all new'.

Explanation of Vaughan's spiritual inclination and the recurrent devotional metaphors of his *hiraeth* may be found in his Welsh biography. Throughout his writing career (which he seems to have ended in the mid-1650s), Vaughan lived in disturbing, turbulent times. As a Welshman, and from family and education, he was a Royalist and Churchman writing throughout the length of the Civil War. The 'Brecknock' countryside, the place of his peaceful childhood, became a place of strife and repression so that he frequently looked back and saw his holding-on to that which was good, his Christian 'striving' for Heaven, as 'retreat'.

> Fair, shining *mountains* of my pilgrimage,
> And flowery *vales* whose flowers were stars:
> Those *days* and *nights* of my first, happy age;
> An age without distaste and wars[.]

Vaughan's grandfather (d.1617) was William Vaughan of Tretower, Breconshire, which the family had acquired in 1450. Henry Vaughan and his younger twin brother Thomas (clergyman, scientist and prolific prose-writer) were born in 'Newton by Usk' (now on the A40, a few miles east of Brecon), a house in the parish of Llansanffraid, which had become the home of their father Thomas (d.1658), when in 1611 he married the eighteen-year-old heiress daughter of David Morgan of that parish. Except for about four years in Oxford and London, it appears that Henry Vaughan spent his life in this home. His mother, if not both parents, would have been Welsh speaking. In his *Anthroposophia Theomagica* (1650), Thomas Vaughan writes: 'I profess I am no Englishman' and 'English is a Language the Author was not *born* to.' Eventually, as the local doctor, Henry would have conversed in Welsh.

The twins were educated locally, nine miles west along the Usk, at Llangattock, for six years, by the quite affluent 'noted Schoolmaster' Matthew Herbert, rector of Llangattock and other parishes. Whereas his twin Thomas (rector of Llansanffraid, *c*.1645, until his ejection in 1650) stayed in Oxford for ten to twelve years, after two years at Jesus College, Henry, to get a knowledge of law, was in London from late summer 1640 until the outbreak of the Civil War in 1642 (when he was aged twenty-one). This meant that, although his first volume of occasional *Poems* (1646) shows him spending a merry life with literary friends, he would have been aware of the Long Parliament's impeachment of Strafford and Laud in December 1640, Strafford's execution in May 1641 and the related mob violence (which probably caused Vaughan's otherwise surprising writing against 'the populacy' throughout his verse).

In Wales, from 1642 to 1645, Vaughan appears to have been secretary to Sir Marmaduke Lloyd, Chief Justice of the Brecon circuit from 1636, who was an active royalist and churchman and was taken prisoner at the siege of Hereford in December 1645. There is evidence that Vaughan himself and his brother served as soldiers in the Royalist cause late in 1645 at Rowston Heath, Chester. (It is possible that Vaughan's younger brother, William (d.1648), died of wounds.)

By November 1645, Breconshire had been taken over by Parliamentary soldiers. By the close of the first Civil War in 1646, Puritan rule was established universally in south Wales. Charles I was executed in January 1649 and the Church was threatened with eclipse. Vaughan's schoolmaster, Matthew Herbert, was displaced as rector in 1646, although, despite times in jail, he continued to preach until 1655. With the Act for the Propagation of the Gospel in Wales of February 1650, numerous Royalist clergy were evicted with little replacement, Llansanffraid being without ministry until December 1657. Vaughan, in his prose, describes himself as writing 'out of a land of darkness' where 'God's Ministers are trodden down, and the basest of the people are set up in [his] holy places'. There is actual and spiritual meaning in the last words of 'L'Envoy' to *Silex Scintillans* (1655), a prayer for redemption from 'our sad captivity'.

Contemporary events in Wales no doubt projected Vaughan into his distinctive poetry which is, for the large part, discovered in his two *Silex Scintillans* volumes of 1650 and 1655, subtitled *Sacred Poems*. It is difficult to read the shocking (and some would say visionary) opening to the poem 'The World' – 'I saw Eternity the other night/ Like a great *Ring* of pure and endless light' – as by the 'Silurist' of *Olor Iscanus* (1651, largely written by 1647). Contemporary life and opinion, political and social, is interestingly pictured in *Olor Iscanus*, published by a friend, and in *Thalia Rediviva* (1678), a retrospective collection.

This trail of autobiographical, topical poems would have made Vaughan a noticeable but not an astonishing poet. Some of the London- and Oxford-based poems show Vaughan's later useful inclinations as a writer, such as his play with conceits. Early bold, Royalist poems appeared in both these secular volumes. But the outstanding autobiographical poems are Wales-based, ranging from highly comic satire on Brecon residents, and another on himself as a soldier in a too-large borrowed cloak, to an elegy on a friend killed in battle and several poems to local Brecon rectors expelled from their livings. The latter employ metaphor for the Welsh clergy's silenced teaching, drawn from natural observation, such as,

> a deep snow
> *Candies* our country's woody brow.
> The yielding branch his load scarce bears
> Oppressed with snow, and *frozen tears*,
> While the *dumb* rivers slowly float,
> All bound up in an *icy coat.*

In *Thalia Rediviva* comes a poem showing a subtle understanding of the heart, 'Man's secret region', 'To the Pious Memory of C.W. . . . [died] 1653' – Charles Walbeoffe being Vaughan's first cousin, a Royalist who constructively collaborated briefly with Parliamentarians; by natural analogy he is interpreted as a glow-worm glittering in the dark.

Vaughan's first collection, *Poems* (1646), has no apparent

location in Wales, except in the title 'Upon the Priory Grove, His Usual Retirement', which only the informed would recognize as referring to a green area below Brecon cathedral. This is a charming poem, invoking sweet, 'amorous' emblems from the natural universe, from woodbine to 'gentlest showers', and banishing any 'hoarse bird of night' and 'poisonous ivy' from the Grove, using the rhythm of fairy enchantments within Shakespeare's *A Midsummer Night's Dream*, because here it was that Vaughan first met and also made 'vows' to his 'love'. Presumably this 'love' was his first wife Catherine Wise, the Amoret of several poems in *Poems.* Vaughan's wife next appears in *Silex Scintillans* (1655), after her death (1653 or 1654), as a guiding star. She is the 'Fair and young light' of the poem's first line, and Vaughan, 'the surviving turtle [dove]', says that he in her lifetime, but for his own 'foolish fire', might have been brought by her to regenerative 'holy/ Grief and soul-curing melancholy'. Its use of argument through chains of imagery, its theatrical moods and direct, conversational style ('I did once read in an old book' etc.) relate the poem to the Metaphysical school rather than the con-current world of Cavalier poets. The choice of imagery, such as light versus dark, pre-existence and Paradise and the poem's sense of local landscape imbued with holy light, stamp this as a poem by Vaughan.

Within *Silex Scintillans*, the hills or mountains of the Usk valley are transformed frequently to the 'eternal hills' of the Holy Land, hills which Vaughan also explored through every possible biblical association, story or interpretation, his favourite being the Mount of Olives. Actual and literary hills both merged for him with a landscape of Heaven. The collection is also clearly marked by Vaughan's interest in hermeticism, an interest which Thomas took further in his interpretation of chemical (physical) experimental science as alchemy. It is a delight probably derived from their boyhood education but also 'intuitive' in their shared concern with process, especially transformation. Henry's realization throughout his poems of the living communion or exchange between visible and invisible worlds is clearly set out, for example, in his occasional use of the hermetic doctrine of 'correspondences' as metaphor for his own 'celestial pure desire', the would-be 'exalted flight' of a 'love-sick soul' in whole poems like 'Cock-Crowing', or as here in 'The Favour'.

> Some kind herbs here, though low & far,
> Watch for, and know their loving star.
> O let no star compare with thee!
> Nor any herb out-duty me!

However, Vaughan's visible world is Wales and the living imagery he selects from his meditative walks in the Usk valley subtly describe even more than that 'quick' world 'full of spirit'.

In the first poem of *Olor Iscanus* (1651), 'To the River Isca', completed before 1647, Vaughan is setting himself up importantly and for the future, even after his death, as *the* poet of the Usk valley, as celebrative of the genius of the place, possibly as the genius itself. In its first paragraph, 'To the River Isca' is derivative from one of the early Vaughan's favourite poets, William Habington (of *Castara* (1634–40)); the poem also picks up ideas and echoes from Milton's 'Lycidas'; but the poet is describing an identity. With older predecessors Ovid, Petrarch and Ausonius celebrating their local streams, Vaughan joins three English poets, Sidney, Milton and Habington, who haunt the Thames and Severn. He asserts that poets who have 'sat and sung' on happy river banks bless them before passing 'from this sickly air' to immortal regions of 'youthful green'. Thus it is that, as '*Poets* (like *Angels*) where they once appear/ *Hallow* the *place*', Vaughan himself speaks to the Usk:

> But *Isca* . . .
> When I am lay'd to *rest* hard by thy *streams* . . .
> I'lle leave behind me such a *large, kind light,*
> As shall *redeem* thee from *oblivious night*[.]

He calls upon real successive bards to produce '*vocal groves*' in which their readers shall 'more *fair truths* see/ Than *fictions* were of *Thessaly*'. He wishes local people and the river to experience, 'Mild, dewie *nights*, and Sun-shine *dayes*,/ The *Turtle's voice, Joy* without *fear*', and ends his poem with a prayer for the land to be '*redeem'd from all disorders*', a place of life and peace, not woken to 'a new war'. Vaughan has moved from myth (Apollo and Daphne; Orpheus) and literary allusion to his local and contemporary social and political concerns; he has moved softly to a universal and non-strident pacifism in which he is aided by a (sparsely detailed) evocation of the Usk valley's 'wandering crystal', over which he presides as a present and future inspirational genius. This poem is important in its dedication to a new poetic art based on the place of his birth, life and death, and in its vowed bestowal of 'a large kind light' to his people – 'kind' meaning 'native' and 'natural', in addition to sympathetic.

> ... *O quis me gelidis in vallibus ISCAE*
> *Sistat, et ingenti ramorum protegat umbra!*

(O who will set me down in the cool valleys of the Usk, and protect me with the ample shadow of his branches!)

(Rudrum's translation)

So Vaughan exclaims briefly and memorably at the opening of *Olor Iscanus* (1651). In contrast, the ponderous dedication to *Silex Scintillans* (1655) is confessional; here we find the poet begging to 'communicate [his] poor talent to the Church'. Yet the 'sacred poems' of *Silex Scintillans* could be argued as set substantially in 'the cool valleys of the Usk'.

With the fuller Welsh location comes a noticeably increased feeling for Welsh poetic form. That Vaughan was aware of what he called, in a letter to Aubrey, 'several sorts of measures and a kind of Lyric poetry' practised by 'the later Bards', such as he learned from the *Welsh Grammar* of John David Rhys (or 'Rhesus') and from conversations with Welsh poets about their inspired 'poetic furor', is noted by F. E. Hutchinson. He also points to Vaughan's translation of three lines of *englyn* attributed to Aneirin, in his prose work *The Mount of Olives*. Hutchinson, his major biographer, shows examples galore of Vaughan writing and rhyming English with a Welsh accent, Welsh stresses, writing extravagantly with assonance and alliteration, often using sharp antitheses in the manner of Welsh-language poets and practising *dyfalu* (definition by stringing together fantastic similes). But, however Welsh his craft, it is Vaughan's 'true' natural flow of English which contributes to making him outstanding, the more paradoxically so as he is expressing obviously unfeigned spiritual experience, like Wordsworth so much later, able to write in 'the real language of men' even 'when the light of sense/ Goes out, but with a flash that has revealed/ The invisible world'.

Within his poems, Vaughan, like the later Romantics, insists on his presence in the present. One fine example of this is the poem chosen to open *Silex* II (1665), 'Ascension-Day'. Here the shining 'fields of Bethany', which Vaughan walks, are transformed to a full, springtime, Welsh landscape. The story is punctuated with the poet's glad activity: 'I greet thy Sepulchre . . . I smell her spices . . . As rich a scent as the now primrosed fields . . . I see them, hear them . . . and move/ Amongst them.' In many poems Vaughan grasps his reader because he stresses his use of all the senses, even as he conveys spiritual aspiration or ascension.

Not only the large-scale events of the Civil War seem responsible for the content and poetic achievement of *Silex Scintillans*, but also the death of his brother William, mid-1648, probably aged only twenty. Hence the numerous elegies and related poems in *Silex Scintillans* expressing a wish to be with the dead in their 'air of glory'. One of the most famous begins,

> Joy of my life! while left me here,
> And still my love!
> How in thy absence thou dost steer
> Me from above!

– a starkly simple, visually shaped poem, building upon the image of a dead 'saint' as being like a star in the cloudy night when the road is 'foul'.

Vaughan's poems on grief and loss all provide movement towards comfort and aspiration; he writes from a 'quick world'. In a wide variety of poems he progresses structurally through opposites to some form of life. The brilliant poem 'The Night', an invocation to darkness, 'The day of Spirits; my soul's calm retreat', is built on contrasts: of temple and field, of man's noise and God's silence, of spiritual illumination and worldly darkness, of worldly ill-guiding light and solitary 'deep but dazzling' darkness. It is built, too, on the objective New Testament story of 'Wise *Nicodemus*' who knew 'his God by night', yet also subjectively on the poet's current, questioning search ('O who will tell me where/ He found thee at that dead and silent hour!'). And it moves gradually from the universal to a final three stanzas expressing the longing of 'I', the poet. Midway through the poem, the fourth stanza's contrast is the most emphatic of life:

> No mercy-seat of gold,
> No dead and dusty *Cherub*, nor carved stone,
> But his own living works did my Lord hold
>   And lodge alone;
> Where *trees* and *herbs* did watch and peep
> And wonder, while the *Jews* did sleep.

The idea of Christ in the fields, appreciated more by excited vegetable life than by men, is sustained throughout *Silex Scintillans*. The natural world produces the ideal state, the 'virgin', the un-corrupted, 'dear secret *greenness*' of 'The Seed Growing/ Secretly', the affirmation that 'all unseen/ The blade grows up, alive and green'. Vaughan, who wishes 'O that I were all soul', can easily wish he were some 'poor highway herb'.

This is the idiosyncratic created world of Vaughan's most remarkable poetry. It is a world of created beings, which move upwards; the poet's aspiration matches a landscape full of vertical movement; shadows of divinity are in the creatures of Eden more than Adam, creatures which rise upwards: growing seeds, grass, plants, trees, birds, bees, moths, mists, evaporating rain and fountains. Vaughan may be seen at his best when describing naturally aspiring 'fellow-creatures', like a bird singing in the rain or a 'drowsy silk-worm' emerging with 'weak, infant hummings'. This may be why 'The Morning-Watch' is so much anthologized. It is exclamatory, like so much of Vaughan's poetry; it opens with exultant spirit, expressed through the imagery of leaf and flower: 'O joys! Infinite sweetness! with what flowers/ And shoots of glory, my soul breaks, and buds!' But the visual shape of the poem on paper describes the '*hymning circulations*' of an ascending lark so clearly that it is surprising to find the name 'lark' missing; instead, we read the rhyming word 'hark':

>   . . . In what rings,
>   And *hymning circulations* the quick world
>   Awakes, and sings;
>   The rising winds,
>   And falling springs,
>   Birds, beasts, all things
>   Adore him in their kinds.

This is a world of 'heaven's' music, in a poem which celebrates outstandingly Vaughan's sustained delight in music, especially as it celebrates an ideal universal harmony. The early world is whirled, or as he says, 'hurled'

> In sacred *hymns*, and *order*, the great *chime*
> And *symphony* of nature. Prayer is
>   The world in tune,
>   A spirit-voice . . .

Vaughan's poems are full of pressure upwards, to 'eternity', but therefore also refer constantly to that which they work with and against: time, the time of the seasons, day and night, the hours of the clock (''tis now/ Since thou art gone,/ Twelve hundred hours . . .'). Time also takes the poet out of the quiet and innocence of early childhood, and, with his effort, will take him back to it. Here again we find a subject peculiarly Vaughan's – though Thomas Traherne, living on the margins of Wales as a child amid the horrors of the Civil War, not much later in the century, remembered his celestial vision when as a child he looked out of the Widemarsh Gate of Hereford at 'orient and immortal wheat', trees and people: 'I cannot reach it; and my striving eye/ Dazzles at it, as at eternity.' These opening words of 'Child-hood' suggest that Vaughan, the adult man, cannot be converted and reach back to the child's 'white designs' and 'the thoughts of each harmless hour'. And this poem ends with the admission that despite long 'study' of childhood, Vaughan can 'only see' the margins of this angel-guarded 'age'; he can 'only see through a long night/ Thy edges, and thy bordering light!' Vaughan's 'The Retreat' gathers up easily the distinguishing ideas and imagery of his most famous poems. Within it he talks naturally, albeit confidently, about the pre-existent life in sight not of Brecon but of a heavenly Jerusalem, 'That shady city of palm trees', a state of life of shining 'Angel-infancy' in which he would wish to be at his death. The grass of the Usk valley, unseen or in various stages of sunlight, is only apparent within a general picture of childhood vision: 'When on some *gilded cloud*, or *flower*/ My gazing soul would dwell an hour.' For this poem of longing quest, sustained by the metaphor of travel, in its pursuit of an uncorrupted, unconditioned self, centrally debates some subtly divided elements of identity. The prominent 'I' of the poem is separate from 'my soul' of 'white celestial thought(s)'. This 'I'

> taught my tongue to wound
> My conscience with a sinful sound,

when, ideally, every bodily 'sense', 'this fleshly dress', 'felt . . . Bright *shoots* of everlastingness'. Vaughan's inclination to move beyond the natural world 'To search my self', to find the integrated 'I' of 'the enlightened spirit', also increases the power of *Silex Scintillans*.

* * *

If contemporary events in Wales projected Vaughan into writing about the ideal valley of his childhood nurture, it seems to have been the place alone, and his sense of identity within that place, which stimulated Dyer to 'paint' it, from at least the age of 16. A joyous sense of his home place, the house and gardens of Aberglasney, below Grongar Hill, in Carmarthenshire's Tywi (Towy) valley, made Dyer a revolutionary poet! When Dyer, in his early fifties (December 1751), via fortune and misfortune, was living in the 'squalid' regions of Lincolnshire writing his ambitious long poem, *The Fleece* (1757), he portrayed the place of his birth and his family nurture as especially 'soft' and peaceful: 'that soft tract/ Of Cambria deep embay'd Dimetian land.' At the very end of *The Fleece*, with a conclusion which is triumphant and typically upbeat, Dyer places his inspiration and 'exulting Muse' in the same area as Vaughan's: in 'Siluria's flow'ry vales', those 'first springs' of a harmonious 'globe'. The tribe of the Silures are taken to have inhabited the south-eastern area of Wales between the Severn and mid-Carmarthenshire. Early in *The Fleece* Dyer locates them in present-day Monmouthshire and Herefordshire, the land of hops and apples, where he farmed from 1730 to 1738. Apparently the Silures resisted the Romans of the first century and the Normans a millennium later. However, the tribe of Dimetians, that is the Demetae, a tribe of pre-Roman and Roman Wales, occupying the south-western part of Wales between the rivers Teifi and Tywi, appear to have been passive in their encounters with the invading Romans and, subsequently, with the invading Irish tribes of the fourth to sixth centuries. By identifying with the Demetae, Dyer enhances his presentation of his Welsh birthplace as a gentle, protected, 'fenced' haven, not only peaceful but 'lulled', 'nodding', sleepy:

>   that soft tract,
>   Of Cambria deep embay'd, Dimetian land,
>   By green hills fenc'd, by ocean's murmur lull'd;
>   Nurse of the rustic bard who now resounds
>   The fortunes of the Fleece; whose ancestors
>   Were fugitives from Superstition's rage,
>   And erst from Devon thither brought the loom,
>   Where ivy'd walls of old Kidwelly's tow'rs,
>   Nodding, still on their gloomy brows project
> Lancastria's arms, emboss'd on mould'ring stone.

But Dyer's poetry, while often celebrating quiet, even silence, is never sleepy. It is characterized usually by energy, a sense of activity, a pleasure in movement. 'Grongar Hill' and the other two poems in which he figures visibly as the poet, 'The Country Walk' and 'The Ruins of Rome', describe walks. In his twenties, as he polished versions of 'Grongar Hill' and wrote 'The Country Walk', apparently in the summer of 1725, his style expresses a sprightly confidence based on his possessing his Cambrian house. In 'The Country Walk', the named house and grounds of Aberglasney, his 'home', is the focus of the poem. It is his place of beginning and return, regarded from the point of view of 'Nature', the landscape prospect from Grongar Hill which rises above the house:

>   Up Grongar Hill I labour now,
>   And catch at last his bushy brow.
>   Oh! how fresh, how pure, the air!
>   Let me breathe a little here;
>   Where am I, Nature? I descry
>   Thy magazine before me lie.
>   Temples! – and towns! – and towers! – and woods! –
>   And hills! – and vales! – and fields! – and floods!
>   Crowding before me, edged around
>   With naked wilds, and barren ground.
>   See, below, the pleasant dome,
>   The poet's pride, the poet's home,
>   Which the sunbeams shine upon.
>   To the even from the dawn.
>   See her woods, where Echo talks,
>   Her gardens trim, her terrace walks,

Her wildernesses, fragrant brakes,
Her gloomy bow'rs, and shining lakes.
Keep, ye gods! this humble seat
For ever pleasant, private, neat.

The Dyer's 'seat' of Aberglasney, in the small village of Llangathen, some twenty miles from Kidwelly, is not 'humble' but
substantial. It was bought in 1710 as part of the Manor and Lord-
ship of Kidwelly, by Dyer's father Robert, a successful lawyer.
Robert Dyer was rebuilding it even at his death in 1720. John
Dyer's Welsh descent on his father's side began with certainty with
a David Dyer, mayor of Kidwelly in 1531–2. His mother's parents
were from Worcestershire and Herefordshire. Dyer himself was
born only five miles from Llangathen, still in the Tywi valley, in
Llanfynydd where his grandfather was churchwarden. From a
local education, possibly including Queen Elizabeth Grammar
School, Carmarthen, at thirteen or fourteen Dyer went to Westminster School, staying there long enough (one to three years) to
make significant London-based friendships with future anti-
quarians and scholars supportive of him later. One friend, David
Lewis from Pembrokeshire, the publisher of the authorized version
of 'Grongar Hill' in 1726, and to whom Dyer wrote verses, was an
usher at Westminster School. Dyer was the second of four sons.
Two, probably all three others, went up to Oxford, but Dyer
remained at Aberglasney to study law.

Several months after Dyer's father's death in 1720, Dyer's
brother Robert, executor and chief beneficiary, arrived to manage
the estates. John then, released or ejected, went to London to
study painting, as apprentice to Jonathan Richardson (1665–
1745), portrait painter and author of books on the theory of
painting. Here, according to Dyer's 'Epistle to a Famous Painter',
Richardson was his mentor. The 'Epistle' was possibly written a
few years before its publication in 1726, as Dyer declares 'As yet I
but in verse can paint'. Richardson encouraged Dyer's love of
Milton, the 'Epistle' being written in the octosyllabic couplets of
Milton's 'L'Allegro' and 'Il Penseroso' as, by 1726, was the most
famous version of 'Grongar Hill'.

London's human company for Dyer in the 1720s was composed
of two groups. The first was of painters and scholars, including
long-lasting friends mentioned in *The Fleece*. The second group,

all writers, was flamboyant, even shocking, including Richard Savage, Aaron Hill and Mrs Martha Fowke Sansom ('Clio'), whose portrait Dyer painted, and who all provided an exchange of epistolary poems; James Thomson of *The Seasons* was on the fringe. Clearly Dyer was sociable, and from the 1720s to 1750s could sometimes describe himself as 'melancholy for want of society'. However, even in London years he would have alternated seasons with Wales, and his major poetry is composed from a love of rural solitude and solitary observation.

Before Dyer's first poems were published, he spent a year in Italy, 1724–5, studying art and architecture in Rome, Florence, Naples and elsewhere, gathering, as he wrote to his mother, 'enough of knowledge in painting to live well in the busiest part of the world, if I should happen to prefer it to retirement'. However, letters also show his mind on poetry and indicate how his mind will work in composition, to evoke responses in his readers.

The longest poem to emerge from the Italian year was 'The Ruins of Rome' (1740), a philosophic/moralistic, sonorous, descriptive and dramatic poem of 545 lines. It is intricately wrought and Dyer was to go on working on it until 1737. The poem is developed through a narrative of the poet-as-tourist's climb up the Palatine hill of ruined Rome, surveying buildings and scenery and reflecting on the history of the people who inhabited them, both destructively vicious (the warmongering, idolatrous and lascivious) and creatively virtuous (including the poets). The poem opens with an identification with Wales, even as Wales is dismissed for travel to Italy for 'the love of arts,/ And what in metal or in stone remains/ Of proud antiquity':

> Enough of Grongar, and the shady dales
> Of winding Towy, Merlin's fabled haunt.

Comparison and contrast with Britain, especially Wales, runs slenderly throughout the poet's examination of Roman history and scenes. Even the once 'stately pines' of the baths of Caracalla are:

> Rent of their graces; as Britannia's oaks
> On Merlin's mount, or Snowdon's rugged sides,
> Stand in the clouds, their branches scattered round
> After the tempest.

The poem, with high moral tone, beloved of eighteenth-century descriptive poets later in the century and often sounding forced, in an address to his countrymen is anticipatory of the Coleridge of 'Fears in Solitude . . . 1798'. But the preaching, though strong, is not a primary force in Dyer's poem. It is a virtuoso performance by an artist, a luxurious poem full of delight in the sounds of its feast of language – it asks to be read aloud as well as silently – and full of pleasure in the senses its description calls forth, especially *via* texture, colours and noises in amazing but subtle variety. Its imagining is intense, the condensation of imagery, from the architectural to the historic, dependent on an abundance of adjectives. Foamy, globose, pendant, shrouded, plaintive-echoing, spiry, caverned, mossy, airy, crystal, glittering, sleeky, cerulian, intermingling, wide-embowering, crooked, lingering, are only some of the adjectives which stand out within fifty early lines. The representative, painterly effects in 'The Ruins', mixed with a conveyance of drama ('The sunk ground startles me with dreadful chasm', for example), show Dyer choosing this intricate style as appropriate for his subject. If we compare it with 'The Country Walk' and 'Grongar Hill', they, juxtaposed, appear impressionistic, minimalist, at least simple, in style, vocabulary and metre.

The flight into 'The Ruins of Rome' is especially memorable. In the poem's first paragraph, 'the shady dales/ Of winding Towy' are contrasted with the 'forlorn and waste' 'wide' plains of Rome, 'Where yellow Tiber his neglected wave/ Mournfully rolls'. Dyer's Muse sweeps across France, the 'cloud-piercing Alps', 'the Umbrian and Etruscan hills', and is bidden to 'soar a loftier flight' in viewing 'imperial Rome'. In the second, highly dramatic, oratorical paragraph, part-echoing the Tiber's movement, the idea of 'rolls' and 'rolling' is taken up in an imagery of falling and rising which introduces two major themes of the poem; man's creative response to the spectacle of life, even in its decay ('the solemn scene/ *Elates the soul*, while now the *rising* sun/ Flames on the ruins') and the leveling revolutions, or rolls of time. This paragraph has a certain circularity *via* its verbal repetition, alliteration and its beginning and its end-pictures of fallen heaps, the 'urns' and 'tombs' of death and obscurity.

> Fall'n, fall'n, a silent heap! her heroes all
> Sunk in their urns; behold the pride of pomp,

The throne of nations, fall'n! obscur'd in dust;
Ev'n yet majestical: the solemn scene
Elates the soul, while now the rising sun
Flames on the ruins in the purer air
Tow'ring aloft upon the glittering plain,
Like broken rocks, a vast circumference!
Rent palaces, crush'd columns, rifled moles,
Fanes roll'd on fanes, and tombs on bury'd tombs!

There is all the confidence of a great poet here, especially in
the tricks of contrast and verbal repetition, close to refrain, which
appear fresh and new, and were claimed as new, by the Wordsworth
of 'Tintern Abbey' (1798).

A simile and an image later come the lines which some of Dyer's
eighteenth-century critics (even Dr Johnson) found outstanding
and which Wordsworth in the nineteenth century pointed to as 'a
beautiful instance of the modifying and investive power of
imagination':

At dead of night, the pilgrim oft, mid his oraison hears
Aghast the voice of Time, disparting tow'rs,
Tumbling all precipitate down-dash'd,
Rattling around, loud thund'ring to the moon[.]

There is something bizarre or at least incongruous in this mixture
of sounds, all of them within the hearing of the silent night and
moon: the pilgrim's prayers, 'the voice of Time', the rattling,
thundering towers. Through the four lines there is an accelerating
movement as we move from the motionless pilgrim, through
'tumbling', and 'down-dashed' to the crash of 'thundering'; the
swift fall is heightened by the odd Latinate word 'precipitate' amid
so many descriptive words of Old and Middle English origin,
including even 'Aghast' which is the dominant word in concept
and force, played against the four words ending in '-ing' to convey
noise and the movement of fall: disparting, tumbling, rattling,
thundering.

'The Ruins of Rome' continues Dyer's dedication to the poetry
of place which was being explored also in 'Grongar Hill' during
the year of exile in Italy. Lines expressing self-dedication, probably
composed in 1724–5, appear in 'The Ruins of Rome'. They come

after musings on virtuous Romans, including Cicero whom
'Eloquence arrays':

> . . . Me now, of these
> Deep musing, high ambitious thoughts inflame
> Greatly to serve my country, distant land,
> And build me virtuous fame[.]

Did Dyer at this time mean service as a poet, as a painter? Poets'
written self-dedications are rare; one thinks mainly of young
Milton. Wordsworth, in *The Prelude*, found a time when 'vows/
Were . . . made for (him)' when he knew that 'else sinning greatly'
he would be 'A dedicated spirit'. As Wordsworth in *The Prelude*
was tracing the 'growth of a poet's mind', his dedication is
obviously to poetry. Earlier, in 1795, Coleridge, in a poem
describing a climb to a hilltop in Somerset, dedicated himself to
Freedom and Christianity. Whereas Wordsworth addressed a
sonnet to Dyer deeply appreciative of the 'Bard of the Fleece' and
of 'Grongar Hill' as fit to be appreciated by 'pure and powerful
minds', it is Coleridge who praises him in several poems by means
of modified imitations of the structure of 'Grongar Hill'. It is
Dyer's poetry which makes possible the achievements of these two
great 'Romantic' poets in their astonishing transitions in some of
their poems from general musings to the personal, because their
musings are located in the domestic, in the landscapes of home.

It appears that from Italy Dyer retired to his mother's home in
Carmarthenshire, continued to work on 'Grongar Hill', and wrote
'The Country Walk'. First publication of his poems began in 1726.
There were three versions of 'Grongar Hill' in three miscellanies,
though in two forms. It appeared as a Pindaric ode in Richard
Savage's *Miscellaneous Poems* together with 'The Country Walk'.
'Grongar Hill invites my song;/ Draw the landscape bright and
strong': the two Grongar Hill poems aspire to landscape or
prospect painting. Dyer would expect his readers to know the
admired styles of the light Claude, the learned Poussin and the
savage Salvator Rosa. Possibly Dyer blends all three styles but he
is aware of the added advantages of 'song', the word-painting of a
moving spectator, able to extend the range of view beyond a single
frame. The ode with its longer lines sometimes achieves broad
painterly effects with more detail. Both poems in their theoretic

openings suggest that painting is the servant of poetry. The much anthologized 'Grongar Hill' of octosyllabic couplets, summoning Painting as a 'Silent Nymph' to 'Come and aid thy sister Muse', obviously the unsilent Poetry, mixes colours immediately with sounds: 'the purple evening' with the 'yellow linnet' (yellow-hammer?) and 'tuneful nightingale'. Grongar from the beginning is claimed to be the dwelling of 'Sweetly-musing Quiet' which in one of the last few lines of the poem we discover to be its primary subject. However, the jaunty style, 'bright and strong', together with a series of commands, opens the poem to a breadth of expectancy and breathes excitement. This dual command of peacefulness and vitality is achieved as the poet places himself in the scene, at the end of this very first paragraph. The Muse of Painting, the nymph who 'loves to lye' observing a scene, is replaced by the poet:

> So oft I have, the ev'ning still,
> At the fountain of a rill
> Sat upon a flow'ry bed,
> With my hand beneath my head,
> While stray'd my eyes o'er Towy's flood,
> Over mead and over wood,
> From house to house, from hill to hill,
> 'Till Contemplation had her fill.

This is the picture which attracted the artist who provided the frontispiece to *The Poems of John Dyer* in 1761: the poet-painter is the figure inside the landscape giving perspective to that which he paints from outside. The thinking, looking poet, straying with his eyes from his 'flow'ry bed', holds the views for us. In the 'Grongar Hill' ode there is no walk up the hill but, instead, a concentration on the view from the top. The version in couplets provides the 'winding' ascent of the hill's chequered sides, the poet noticing the 'changing', widening 'prospect' which moves as he does, for example, mountain or hill ranges changing height. Again there's counterpoint in the poem. We have been captured by a bold simplicity of language: 'Over mead . . . over wood . . . house to house . . . hill to hill.' This simplicity is aided by what appears to be sometimes the galloping metre of the Welsh long *cywydd* couplet with seven syllables ('Grongar Hill invites my song'). Yet, with

this, there is a sense of rippling mental and emotional as well as
visual expansion, caught in the octosyllabic simile 'As circles on a
smooth canal'.

In 'Grongar Hill', Dyer does 'draw the landscape bright and
strong', especially for anyone who knows it. He doesn't load the
poem with place names, as do numerous Welsh poets of the mid-
twentieth century to assert their nationality. Even the most evident
of the neighbouring castles, Dinevawr (Dinefwr) on its 'dark hill,
steep and high' is not named:

> Deep are his feet in Towy's flood,
> His sides are cloath'd with waving wood,
> And ancient towers crown his brow.

Only Grongar Hill and Towy (Tywi) are named in the poem, but
experiment such as changing the Welsh river name for any of the
rare English rivers of two syllables does not remove the scene from
Dyer's beloved home. This is the first really *local* descriptive
poetry in the English language, highly personal in tone. It opens
up poetry to the detail of observation combined with emotional/
spiritual response explored by the later 'Romantics'. Yet it is
always balanced, moved towards shared human experience, like
previous and contemporary 'philosophic', moral poetry, while
being new and inventive, asking the reader for involvement in its
poet's feeling.

At the end of 'Grongar Hill', even Dyer's generalizations, such
as the final contrast of 'courts', 'the domes of Care', with the
country 'Quiet' become his own discovery. The almost allegorical
'Quiet', here, is Dyer himself above the Towy valley; except that he
is not an allegorical figure, but a man in time and place who 'Hears
the thrush, while all is still/ Within the groves of Grongar Hill'.
The song of the thrush rightly closes the poem because the poem
has been in praise of harmony within the poet ('O may I with
myself agree' matches the Towy valley's 'music' of 'waters' and
'birds' so that his 'joys run high').

'Grongar Hill' is designed to sound dashed-off, a walking
soliloquy, but it cannot be read as anything but a careful work of
'skilful genius'. The easier 'The Country Walk' can be read as
more careless, a rough sketchbook. It is a variation on 'Grongar
Hill', perhaps complementary to it. For example, while 'Grongar

Hill' is about ascent, in 'The Country Walk' the descent is significant. In fact, 'The Country Walk' is equally experimental, possibly more daring. Even more than 'Grongar Hill', it sets up an appearance of spontaneity, provides *random* scenes of country life, but this in accord with its aim. The speaker, the poet, is straightforward, active, honest: 'I am resolved, this charming Day/ In the open fields to stray.' He contrasts impoverished country life and wealthy courts, but casually. The drawn landscape around Grongar Hill is broad but generalized, making a concentration on Aberglasney. A major difference is in the noting of figures in the landscape, the 'wearied swain' with his food scrip open, the shepherd 'All careless with his legs across' piping to his crowding sheep, the fisherman in a willow's shade who 'Sways the nibbling fry to land', the ploughman unbinding his oxen at sunset, and the fuller, sympathetic picture of an old man in his cottage garden who 'digs up cabbage in the shade'. The figure and the person of the poet himself with a 'busy brain' dominates the poem. He enters early and is always present. As he lies on green moss, his 'numerous thoughts', 'Like moles, whene'er the coast is clear/ . . . range in parties here and there'.

The description of 'The poet's pride, the poet's home' from the top of Grongar, strong as it is, is only a prelude to the poem's important conclusion, the poet's descent to the named house. Deceptively, until this ending, the poem could almost read like an anticipation of many a John Clare poem, as it exultantly lists the experiences of a country walk. The poet erupts into a farmyard full of poultry and rustics, watches a smoking chimney, sniffs honey-suckle, leans on an aged tree, and so on. This listing is strengthened by reference to movement through one day, a movement from having 'no roof' at sunrise to returning home at sunset. The casual encounters of the day gain resolution by tending homeward.

This is not a poem about retirement, not about 'quiet [in] the soul' like 'Grongar Hill', because the poet makes a communal return home. The figures in the landscape have meaning. Love and affection are hinted as 'the descending sun/ Kisses the streams' and 'vocal mountains' re-echo the lowing of the unbound oxen:

> The jocund shepherds piping come,
> And drive the herd before them home;
> And now begin to light their fires,

> Which send up smoke in curling spires:
> While with light heart all homeward tend,
> To Aberglasney I descend.

The nearest achievement to this ending is over seventy years later in Coleridge's 'Fears in Solitude . . . 1798', which ends with the poet on a hill above his village, looking down to his 'beloved Stowey' where his family 'dwell in peace' and then returning with sentiments which gather up much of Dyer's creation in 'Grongar Hill' and 'The Country Walk'. Yet the endings of the two Dyer poems are also more cheerful, unpriggish and full of music. The poet of 'Grongar Hill', by realizing quiet in himself, a consciousness of himself and his 'joys' in solitary musings, is at peace and in tune with the natural world. The poet of 'The Country Walk', by solitary musings, has moved, as does Coleridge in some of his conversation poems, from some awareness of suffering in others to a lightness of heart through recognition of shared experience of home. But he is acutely self-assertive, emphatic that he is the poet, even as he joins in the music of the natural and country world. Dyer's distinctive character, art and achievement in this ending is celebrated in its counter movement. Though he ends with darkness and descent, his imagery also moves upward; his 'light heart' is anticipated as villagers 'light their fires' and the suggested flames 'send up smoke in curling spires'.

Dyer was still in his Welsh home through 1726–7, in the first part because of illness, probably malaria. However, Aberglasney probably became closed to him from November 1727 when he made an appeal to the Court of Chancery against his brother Robert. Robert had not passed their inheritance to the three younger brothers, due to each at the age of twenty-four, under the terms of their father's will. John obtained receipt of money for them by March 1729. Poems and records show him in north and mid-Wales as well as in London until 1730, when he began to farm a forty-eight-acre smallholding for his mother's sister at Mapleton, fourteen miles from Worcester – hops, grain, cattle and pigs (no sheep). This was a useful place for itinerant painting incursions to Wales, though we know of only two: in 1735 when he wrote a fragment of a poem about the ideal man, 'The Cambro-Briton' ('far withdrawn . . . / Through the green reed he sends the voice of

Love') and 1737 to friends including Nicholas Clagget, bishop of St Davids. On this last visit he was collecting subscriptions, probably towards a projected commercial map – a map of rivers, roads, canals, manufacturing towns, minerals and 'chiefest curiosities ancient and modern'. This prose work, to 'augment the public good', was not completed but furnished knowledge for the forthcoming *The Fleece*. If *The Fleece* was a fulfilment of young Dyer's 'high ambitious thought . . . greatly to serve [his] country', then his journey towards it was long, complex in unexpected exile, though not out of the personal character shown in the poems, nor the concentrated study revealed in 'The Ruins of Rome' some twenty-five years earlier.

In 1738 Dyer bought two farms for himself near Nuneaton, and married a local widow. In 1740 he painted the portrait of his friend, 91-year-old Bishop Hough of Worcester, and spent time with a Dr MacKenzie (praised in two poems) who both restored him from illness (probably the start of consumption) and 'renovate[d] the Muse' after the death of Dyer's first and infant son. In autumn 1741, Dyer was ordained as a priest, to serve in south Leicestershire, as rector of Catthorpe until 1751. Here he farmed thirty-six acres of glebeland, learning sheep-farming thoroughly. As a shepherd, traditional image of the poet-priest, utilizing his large range of experience and reading, he worked on *The Fleece*. The first book was completed in 1750 (the year of a surviving painting of the Vale of Neath; so he continued to visit Wales). In 1751 (the year when he was awarded the degree of Bachelor of Laws, Cambridge) friends helped him move to supposedly better livings in Lincolnshire, Coningsby and Belchford, wishing to remove him from the necessity of sheep-farming so that he could complete *The Fleece*. The last of its four books reached the publisher in November 1756, a year before his death.

In form, *The Fleece* is an eighteenth-century poem, in contrast with his early inventive lyric narratives. To write a usefully instructive poem, modelled on Virgil's *Georgics*, which describe and celebrate farming, was not original in eighteenth-century Britain. Dyer probably read John Philips's *Cyder* (1706) but not John Gay's *Rural Sports* (1718) or William Somerville's *The Chase* (1735); Christopher Smart's *The Hop Garden* also appeared in 1757. Philips, not Welsh, includes some Welsh landscape in his poem, but his tone is light and witty compared with Dyer's. None of these Georgic poets wrote with the great length (2,700 lines) nor the ambition – including its intricate detail – of Dyer's poem. Nor did they write on Dyer's subject, announced in Book I: 'The care of sheep, the labours of the loom,/ And arts of trade.'

The Fleece is an astonishing work, thoroughly detailed in its conscientious instruction in British sheep-rearing (Book I), wool and dye-making (II), weaving and transportation to ports for export (III) and world trade in wool, to bring 'universal good' (IV):

> What bales, what wealth, what industry, what fleets!
> Lo, from the simple fleece, how much proceeds.

And what a challenging subject for a poet!

To some extent (and unlike 'Grongar Hill'), The Fleece is a historic document and requires a determined reader. But its lasting power is in its cumulative, detailed descriptions of scenes and activities in named places throughout England and Wales, capturing their character and differences with great verbal skill. In these descriptions Dyer is clearly a poet enjoying himself, displaying them with ingenious variety, with occasional irony, especially in quiet literary allusion, with flights of fancy, with free associative imaginings, often leading to far-fetched similes or images which move the poem out of its own realm or provide a blaze of colour or music; and, with evident enthusiasm, Dyer concentrates on those areas he knows best, extensively in Wales and Leicestershire, to create a 'living landscape'. But he provides an impressionistic portrait of the British landscape fuller than any other poet's, including Thomson's. He is still writing poetry of place of a kind new in English literature. Autobiography slips in and out of the poem with easy freedom, including tributes to friends and inessential memorable experiences (such as viewing tapestries at Blenheim). Siluria's sheep and vales get frequent reference until the Muse, 'with weary wing', returns to them, 'where the first springs arise/ Of Britain's happy trade', in the very last lines of the poem. In this poem, the poet is no longer concerned with self-realization but has a philanthropic aim. He has his eye on the subject, the utility of sheep, the perfection of farming and wool production whatever the regional conditions. He is fulfilling a 'sacred charge'.

It is noticeable how few named birds there are in this poem,
despite Dyer's apt reference to his 'lark-winged Muse', unless, say,
it is a bird like a circling kite threatening the lambs. But there are
named wild flowers aplenty. Dyer is concerned with the sheep's
eye-view!

> . . . If verdant elder spreads
> Her silver flowers; if humble daisies yield
> To yellow crow-foot, and luxuriant grass,
> Gay shearing-time approaches. First, howe'er,
> Drive to the double-fold, upon the brim
> Of a clear river, gently drive the flock,
> And plunge them one by one into the flood:
> Plunged in the flood, not long the struggler sinks,
> With his white flakes, that glisten through the tide;
> The sturdy rustic, in the middle wave,
> Awaits to seize him rising; one arm bears
> His lifted head above the limpid stream,
> While the full clammy Fleece the other laves
> Around, laborious, with repeated toil;
> And then resigns him to the sunny bank,
> Where, bleating loud, he shakes his dripping locks.

The mature Dyer *sees* more detail in the human and natural world
as they interact. This passage, like others, anticipates descriptive
verse on villagers and animals by William Cowper in *The Task*
(1785), such as on the woodman and his dog in 'A Winter
Morning Walk'. Dyer had already studied animal behaviour with
affection as in his short poem, 'My Ox Duke', written at
Mapleton; in Book I of *The Fleece*, for example, there is the 'new
dropt lamb/ Tottering with weakness by his mother's side': 'each
thorn,/ Hillock, or furrow, trips his feeble feet'. The mature Dyer is
more aware of everyday drama affecting others, as in the Welsh
incident pictured soon after the plain account of sheep-dipping:

> . . . Sometimes among the steeps
> Of Cambrian glades (pity the Cambrian glades!)
> Fast tumbling brooks on brooks enormous swell,
> And sudden overwhelm their vanish'd fields:
> Down with the flood away the naked sheep,
> Bleating in vain, are borne, and straw-built huts,

> And rifted trees, and heavy enormous rocks,
> Down with the rapid torrent to the deep.

Man-made music recurs throughout *The Fleece*, heralded by a
lengthy musical display at the end of Book I. This long concluding
passage is typical of the technique throughout the poem: steadily
instructive but full of surprises, with free associative imaginings.
Here, unusually, the poet, as 'I', enters the poem, with reverie-like
lines attempting to remember inspiring songs:

> Could I recall those notes which once the Muse
> Heard at a shearing, near the woody sides
> Of the blue-topp'd Wreakin! Yet the carols sweet
> Throu' the deep maze of the memorial cell
> Faintly remurmur.

Dyer then produces the song, though not 'faintly'. It is a dialogue
between two shepherds from the area between Montgomeryshire
and 'Plynlymmon's brow', part traditional pastoral, part an
echoing of his own experience in 'Grongar Hill', but more realistic-
ally developed and argued. Overall, this is an elevating and jolly
celebration of country festival, with dancing and feasting, set in a
dreamy haze by a rewriting of Milton's invocation of British myth
(in *Comus*) involving Sabrina, guardian of the Severn. It is
profoundly musical in its language, such as in the alliterative use of
river names:

> . . . lov'd
> Vaga, profuse of graces, Ryddol rough,
> Blithe Ystwith, and Clevedoc, swift of foot;

until it reaches an orchestral climax, closed and lifted by the juxta-
position of an image of the river and its ships delaying to listen:

> . . . while the mountain-woods,
> And winding valleys, with the various notes
> Of pipe, sheep, kine, and birds and liquid brooks,
> Unite their echoes: near at hand the wide
> Majestic wave of Severn slowly rolls
> Along the deep-divided glebe: the flood,

And trading bark with low contracted sail,
Linger among the reeds and copsy banks
To listen; and to view the joyous scene.

* * *

Noteworthy Welsh writing in English between John Dyer's time and Caradoc Evans in the early twentieth century is extremely varied in nature but is mainly prose. Except in one outstanding nineteenth-century novelist, views of life are not sunny, like Dyer's. A concern with childhood experience as distinct and valuable, such as we find in Vaughan, is suspended until mid-twentieth-century literature. Vaughan's gilded flowers and Dyer's gilded sheep are forgotten. With this forgetting seems to go, too, a loss of dedication to a high quality of writing or to innovation, although this could be a matter of accidental inability. As I have indicated, the great successors to those highly original and skilful Welsh poets, Vaughan and Dyer, rooted creatively in the Welsh countryside of their birth, appear to be the English 'Romantics', especially Coleridge and Wordsworth – for whom travel in Wales had literary impact and who used Welsh locations to convey spiritual transformations and creative revelations. Of course Coleridge and Wordsworth have had a profound influence on all poetry since, even in reactions against their assumptions.

Those impressive, scholarly historians of Anglo-Welsh literature, Raymond Garlick and Roland Mathias (themselves unique as poets) have given immense wealth to scholars and readers. However, in assembling long descriptive lists of writers and works, they have struggled to make the majority of the works sound worthy of attention, have had to include much non-fiction and, in the wish to be inclusive, have perhaps had too levelling an effect, so that, of the many writers discussed, even the better appear mediocre or worse in achievement. The fact is that although distinctly Welsh material on antiquities, history, myth and landscapes was being discovered in writing throughout the eighteenth and nineteenth centuries, opportunities to use it, creatively or even entertainingly, were not seized, except by a marginal few.

For example, the Welsh, using their Welshness, could have contributed towards, or made something extraordinary of the Welsh tourist literature which sprang up in the late eighteenth

century when Europe was closed by wars and young gentlemen
needed a substitute for the Alps; these works flowed into the first
half of the nineteenth century. Since the attractive work of Gerald
de Barri (Giraldus Cambrensis; 1146–1223), born at Manorbier –
the *Itinerary* (which, importantly, was translated into English by
Richard Colt Hoare in 1806) – literary tours of Wales, usually with
a *historic* interest in landscape, had been written by outsiders. Yet
there was interesting antiquarian material available for the Welsh
writers, particularly from the *Britannia* of William Camden
(1551–1623), translated into English in 1610, revised and added to
in 1695 and 1789. (Vaughan and Dyer knew its material on the
three tribal areas of Wales.)

The fashion for entertaining accounts of journeys in Wales
seems to have been started by Henry Penruddocke Wyndham
(1736–1819), born in Wiltshire, whose illustrated *Gentleman's Tour
through Monmouthshire and Wales*, 1775, was published in en-
larged editions in 1777 and 1781. Although he saw the effects of
Wesley's teaching as pernicious and St Davids cathedral as 'very
dirty and slovenly', Wyndham gave flattering accounts of the
people throughout Wales, encouraged tourists to explore the good
roads and inns and to see the picturesque and 'romantic beauties
of nature' of an extravagant kind unique to Britain. And so they
did, as witnessed by some hundred or more such published Tours.

One Welshman, an antiquarian, naturalist and the greatest
British zoologist since Ray and before Darwin, who took Tours
seriously was Thomas Pennant (1726–98). He was from the same
sort of class as Wales's two great pre-twentieth century English-
language poets, was born in Flintshire, spoke some Welsh, was
educated in London and Oxford, and, well travelled on horseback
throughout the British Isles and the Continent, was a man of great
energy and ambition, like Dyer. (His writings, which he con-
templated in his *Literary Life* (1793), include twenty-two manuscript volumes of *Outlines of the Globe* – imaginary tours.)
Pennant's *Tours of Wales* (1778 and 81), covering only the north,
are not in the fairly usual journal form, but are in sustained, clear
and highly readable narrative, concerned with his primary interests
together with topography (illustrated by the fine Moses Griffith).
Wales did have a couple of other native tourists. One was a young
Welshman, cashing in on the demand for useful guidebooks to
his 'native country', a Thomas Evans of Radnorshire, of *The*

Cambrian Itinerary, or Welsh Tourist (1801). He is admittedly partly derivative from Pennant and some English books – where they are accurate, he deliberately ignores his people, keeping to his own confident terse descriptions of landscape, county by county, and adding a useful English–Welsh colloquial vocabulary. It is a neat book. Richard Fenton (1747–1821), a St David's lawyer and miscellaneous writer, author of *Poems* (1773), who liked amusing anecdotes, as in his *Memoirs of an Old Wig* (1815), is however mainly serious and topographical in his *A Historical Tour through Pembrokeshire* (1810). His *Tours in Wales, 1804–13* was not published until 1917. However, Wales's only really literary tourist, with a creative appreciation of the form, was a painter, an exhibitionist at the Royal Academy for fifteen years, Edward Pugh (*c*.1761–1813), born at Ruthin. His *Cambria Depicta: A Tour through North Wales* (1816), descriptive of landscape between Chester and Shrewsbury, is perhaps not as rich in amusing anecdotes as the work of one of the English tourists, Richard Warner, to which he refers with Pennant's; but it is vigorous, often funny, exploiting his knowledge of the language, the people, their poetry and their customs as he walked through his country, some three thousand miles over nine years. His seventy illustrations, full of life and variety, memorably reflect his writing and style.

Many novels in the eighteenth and nineteenth centuries, using the strange foreign setting of Wales, have been written by the English, a few of them with Welsh connections or antecedents; there are very few Anglo-Welsh novels. *The True Anti-Pamela* (1741) by James Parry, the story of a man as victim of a breach of promise, purporting to show a reversal of Richardson's novel, and pre-dating Fielding's *Shamela* and *Joseph Andrews*, is interesting historically. However, as the coarse, viciously directed auto-biography of a rogue, it is better forgotten as an Anglo-Welsh work. This, as a work of hate, without art, is by no means a fore-runner of Caradoc Evans. But the novel, *Elisa Powell, or the Trials of Sensibility* (1795) is pleasingly claimed as the first Welsh novel rather than the picaresque *Twm Shon Catti* (1828) by T. J. Llewelyn Prichard which is of local west-Wales interest but of no literary merit. *Elisa Powell* is the one novel by the energetic Edward 'Celtic' Davies (1756–1831), who tried verse and plays, too, but is famous for his collection of old Welsh poetry, for his *Celtic Researches* (1804) and for *The Mythology and Rites of the*

British Druids (1809). *Elisa Powell* is located at the Builth Wells of Davies's childhood. But the Welsh are seen from the outside by an English tourist, the epistolary narrator who is in love with the generally unfortunate and dying heroine. Their plight, the trials of sensibility, forms the second half and least enjoyable section of the novel. The Englishman writes vividly, particularly in drawing other characters, especially the two main, eccentric, larger-than-life characters, mock-heroic portraits of aspects of Edward 'Celtic' Davies himself. One is Dewi Morgan, a 'Cambrian Ossian', an old soldier who wears 'the sky-blue of the ancient bards', plays an 'enormous treble harp' (and has one eye and one leg, rather like Davies), and provides verse interludes in the novel. The other, Dr Pemberton, excited by Welsh ancient history and literature, is described in face and dress as a grotesque giant by a local lawyer, in a torrent of similes, including:

> a brown cloak that would have covered a haystack . . . an antique periwig swelled out like a thunder pillar . . . a nose of unconscionable length, like the bowsprit of a man of war . . . eyes, large and piercing, beneath two shaggy brows, like clear springs in the shade of a forest.

This is not a great novel (though how few are), but it is an interesting attempt to mix comedy (where the subject is dear to the novelist) and sentiment (where he is following fashion for the sake of publication), and it has Welsh originality because of the author's knowledge of place and the injection of his special interests.

At the end of the nineteenth century however (and notice the hundred years' gap), west Wales produced a deservedly best-selling novelist, trading on the area, intimately and affectionately known to her, as an exotic setting. The eleven novels of Allen Raine (Mrs Puddicombe; 1836–1908), written and published in her last twelve years, have titles which declare their location, especially *A Welsh Singer* (1896), *By Berwen Banks* (1899), *Garthowen* (1900), *A Welsh Witch* (1902) and *Hearts of Wales* (1905). Allen Raine, born in Newcastle Emlyn, sets her works on the rural coast of Cardigan Bay, based on the village of Tresaith, her home from her youth to her retirement, except for seven years in her teens and twenty-eight years of married life in London; she began writing them with the clear sight of exile. The fully idealized topography and fine details of sea, land and houses contribute to her plots. Her love stories are never simple, involving mistaken choice, trial and slow awakening, all eventually rectified like any chivalric romance. Whereas her young heroes and heroines from poor fishing and farming families (their dress usually 'faded' or 'frayed') are idealized, usually by their social responsibility and 'brave spirit', they are surrounded by villagers who may be prejudiced, superstitious, limited by old feuds, social pretensions and social distractions, which may even affect their own thinking.

The Welsh Witch, for example, is built around the litigated rivalry of two farms, and with two teenage-love stories intertwined – the four strongly drawn and developed characters hedged by different backgrounds and expectations. The central youth (though the girls are wiser than the boys) runs his father's farm smoothly, at home cheers a grandmother with lost memory, and is a virtuous leader of the local boys. But he makes some wrong choices, almost wrecking the three other young lives, not discovering the truth of his emotions until he has suffered in a Glamorgan coal-mine, has rescued a friend from death on the sea (though the two young women are rather more heroic and sensible in this than he is) and (in a final trial) made a journey to the foothills of Snowdon to recover almost-lost love.

Interwoven, the ugliness of life in this 'out of the way corner of the world' is all too clear. The 'Witch' is a fifteen-year-old girl, the 'untaught' Catrin Rees, a 'simple child of nature', usually sweet-tempered, who lives in the open air of fields, whose only witchery is to disappear over a cliff (by means of a hidden tree) to hide in an invisible and nasty cave. Her mother is dead (but had good gypsy relatives who arrive at one time in her story to help her). Her father, whom she loves and protects, is lazy and drunken, though able to get to church on Sundays, and beats her, even to the extent of breaking her arm; in this he is unopposed by his two farm servants. Village boys cruelly torment her, and adults too easily condemn her: there are thoughts of taking her to an asylum. But this is not a forerunner of Caradoc Evans's portraits of rural west Wales. One of the many, usually more dramatic, high points of the novel is the confrontation of the witch and the vicar, whose sermons she has listened to from outside the church, by 'the old leper window'. The kindly vicar is disconcerted by her confidence in God's closeness to her, her question 'Where is heaven?', her assertion that, as God has told her, her dog, drowned by the boys, is not dead, and so on. Eventually, she prays for the vicar:

> Dear God! I ask you to bless this poor man, and to teach him as You teach me. He doesn't know much, and he wants to feel You near him in the close house and the dark church. Near as You are here on the hillside.

Of course, the female noble savage marries the hero, as we guessed she might from the beginning, he having taught her to read – the Bible, *Robinson Crusoe*, *The Pilgrim's Progress*! – and able to be unashamed finally of his ability to enjoy a childlike friendship with her. But we cannot fore-guess the multiple events of the well-paced plot crowded with country life, the fair, the market and the like, with the entry into so many characters' thoughts.

There is no authorial introspection in Allen Raine's novels, no thought about their fictionality; there's plain authorial narrative command with ample, vivid description of landscape scenes, and of people in convincing conversation; sophistication goes little beyond techniques where one character can spy on another from a height or through a window, or tenses can change from past to present for immediacy. The novels are painstaking attempts to bring west Wales fully before us in all its life and variety. The moral stance and sympathies of the author are plain to see; she is only comically satirical on social pretensions to gentility (which are shown mainly by degrees of good use of English). The novels are well scattered with untranslated Welsh phrases, no doubt to put a stamp on their alien setting for puzzled English readers.

The other best-seller at the end of the nineteenth century was a poet, Lewis Morris (1833–1907) of Carmarthen, whose *Collected Works* (1891) sold 11,000 copies in five years. A distinguished academic, with his initial education reaching from Queen Elizabeth Grammar School, Carmarthen, to Jesus College, Oxford, he did much for Welsh university education. However, his prolific verse is largely unmemorable, often not even metrically acceptable, gliding like cut-up prose. Morris used some Welsh settings, especially Carmarthen and the Tywi valley, as in the tale of doomed love 'Gwen', and he used Welsh local history, as in 'The Physicians of Myddfai', but was not as Welsh in style or subject as might be expected from such a popular writer, dedicated to Wales. This curiously repeats the failure of Iolo Morganwg (Edward Williams; 1747–1826) of Glamorgan a hundred years earlier. Iolo Morganwg was devoted to Wales as the first nation of Britain, forging additional medieval Welsh poetry, and inventing the *Gorsedd* which first met on Primrose Hill, London in 1792 and became linked with the eisteddfod movement in the Ivy Bush, Carmarthen in 1819. Yet, when he wrote in his first language in *Poems Lyric and Pastoral* (2 vols., 1794), despite some simple charm, his creation is dull, especially if read beside Blake's *Songs of Innocence and Experience* of the same year.

In 1895, the year of Oscar Wilde's trial, Lewis Morris was knighted and apparently was half-expected to succeed his friend Tennyson (d.1892) as Poet Laureate. It is noticeable that Tennyson bought Lady Charlotte Guest's *Mabinogion* (1846) which influenced his writing of the vigorous *Idylls of the King* (1895). *The Mabinogion* is perhaps the most powerful Anglo-Welsh work to emerge from Wales in the nineteenth century. It is interesting itself in the consistent style of the translation, an imitation of the antique, somewhat in the style of the Old Testament:

> And the green of the caparison of the horse, and of his rider, was as green as the leaves of the fir-tree, and the yellow was as yellow as the blossom of the broom. So fierce was the aspect of the knight, that fear seized upon them, and they began to flee. And the knight pursued them.

It is surprising that material inspired by *The Mabinogion* did not emerge until the twentieth century, for many lyric poets, and of course for the major Anglo-Welsh poet (other than R. S. Thomas), David Jones (1895–1974), and the major novelist John Cowper Powys (1872–1963) – neither having been born in Wales, but both profoundly Welsh. John Rhŷs (1840–1915), first professor of Celtic at Oxford, 1877, produced further inspirational material in his numerous pioneering works on mythology and folk literature. His *Studies in Arthurian Literature* (1891) was of primary importance for Powys from his twenties to his seventies.

It is ironic that in the 'Celtic Twilight' of the 1890s, Welsh writing in English was scarce, and that Ernest Rhys (1859–1946) was then and now seen as the 'most noteworthy' of the writers. O. M. Edwards, in the first number of his *Wales* in 1894, announced a 'literary awakening', 'a strong desire for a literature that

will be English in language but Welsh in spirit'; in 1891, Ernest
Rhys founded the Rhymers' Club with Yeats, six years younger,
who was to declare that Rhys's Welsh translations and original
poems had 'often moved [him] greatly'. But Rhys's loyalty was half
to London (*Wales England Wed*, 1940) where he was employed as
editor of Dent's Everyman library. His *Welsh Ballads* (1898), which
include his successful free translations, has nothing of the quality of
Yeats's *The Wind Among the Reeds* (1899) or *In the Seven Woods*
(1904), though both poets were gently exploring local heroic Celtic
myth and legend.

As we move from the rosy and/or ineffectual patriotism at the
turn of the century to the shock-horror of Caradoc Evans's full
frontal attack on *y werin*, his rural people of west Wales, as the
First World War began, two modest writers, both from Gwent,
somewhat quirky and dark in spirit, concerned mainly with making
a living, give Wales some interesting literature. Arthur Machen
(1863–1947) was born in Caerleon, for which place of his childhood
he expressed a longing in his autobiographical volumes *Far Off
Things* (1922) and *Things Near and Far* (1923). However, his
imagination and much of his work rises in the Celtic Twilight and a
High Anglican fascination with the occult, shown at its most
distinctive in short stories of the supernatural/mythical breaking
into the natural. The ironically titled *Hill of Dreams* (1907) –
previously *Garden of Avallaunius* – written in the mid-1890s, is the
very antithesis of Glyn Jones's *The Island of Apples* (1965), though
both include a youth perishing through his mental heroics.
Machen's novel, set in the vale of Usk, with visions of Roman
Siluria and Arthurian Avalon, is the story of a youth for whom
sunset is a glow 'as if great furnace doors were open' and who dies
in that imagined furnace by means of a hallucinatory drug. When,
in 1908, Machen wrote a novel, 'a mysterious Celtic tale, with a
touch of the Holy Graal', which became *The Secret Glory* (1922),
mixing youthful autobiography with the legend of the Nanteos cup,
his hero, Ambrose Meyrick, was crucified in the Far East, where he
had carried that healing vessel. His short stories, his strongest form,
may be set in soft Welsh landscape, but they involve beatific vision
or, more often, horror, from the time of *The Great God Pan* (1894)
to the *Shining Pyramid* (1925) – its much anthologized title-story
about the little people having been composed in 1895.

The paradoxical simplicities of the poet W. H. Davies

(1871–1940), born in Newport, are perhaps explained by the mixed blessing of his childhood in Gwent, which provided an idealizing love of the natural world, blended with his adult down-and-out life in America (from which came his popular narrative *The Autobiography of a Super-Tramp* (1908)) and in London doss-houses. W. H. Davies is famous for his poem 'Leisure' ('What is this life if, full of care,/ We have no time to stand and stare'); he could celebrate the bliss of transience – 'A rainbow and a cuckoo's song/ May never come together again' ('A Great Time') – and declare himself inspired by the song of birds. Yet, also, in one poem a robin sings of his patricide; in another, 'The Inquest', Davies, as a member of a jury, mocks the ballad-style and sympathy of Wordsworth's 'The Thorn', when a dead baby ('I judged it was seven pounds in weight,/ And little more than one foot long') seems to laugh with one eye and say, 'Perhaps my mother murdered me'. He is a poet for whom 'the harlot's curse' is often at his back, so that he can describe a country-world with bizarre similes: butterflies can 'stagger' and, in 'The Villain':

> While joy gave clouds the light of stars,
>   That beamed where'er they looked;
> And calves and lambs had tottering knees,
>   Excited, while they sucked;
> While every bird enjoyed his song,

the poet (with a disturbance of metre) turns and sees the wind,

> . . . Dragging the corn by her golden hair,
>   Into a dark and lonely wood.

* * *

The creative imagination of Caradoc Evans (1878–1945) gilds nothing and is not even balanced. He claims a Welsh identity which overturns all concepts of nobility in the Welsh character. He presents a claustrophobic rural west Wales without landscape, history or myth, and inhabited by a people incapable of emotion, exploitative of one another – family and neighbours alike – filled with lust, greed, extreme meanness, lies and hypocrisy. Anyone with a glimpse of goodness is a victim, usually a woman in this patriarchal society. Evans's savage satire, which erupted in the short stories *My People* (1915) is apparently motivated by a reforming wish. It is an attack on the Carmarthenshire and Cardiganshire of his childhood in the 1880s and 1890s. This 'ill-condition' he still described non-fictionally in the 1930s:

> I wrote down our ill-condition to the tyranny of the preachers and the liberal politicians. They have not only robbed us and given us a god of their own likeness – a god who imparts neither charity nor love – but they have dominated us for so many generations that they have fashioned our mind . . . The chief offender is Methodism, which of all denominations is the most anti-democratic in Wales. She is the hand-maid of Liberalism . . . ; they have deadened more spirits than a famine . . .

It is also held that Evans's literary violence was a response to villagers' ill-treatment of his widowed mother in the Rhydlewis of his childhood, which became the oppressed 'Manteg' of all the stories in *My People*, the oppressors being the ministers and deacons of the chapel. The stories in themselves are horrific, more and more as they unfold. The first introduces Sadrach, the title's 'A Father in Sion', whose thoughts we are told 'were continually employed upon sacred subjects. He began the day and ended the day with the words of a chapter from the Book and a prayer on his lips. The Sabbath he observed from first to last . . .' and, when 'entreated to deliver a message to the congregation' of Capel Sion, 'he often prefaced his remarks with, "Dear people, on my way to Sion I asked God what He meant".' The story shows this Father imprison in the hayloft his once rich, good wife Achsah, mother of eight children, his senior by ten years. She is aired at night in the fields with a cow's halter over her shoulders. He soon imports a younger substitute named, aptly, Martha, and, by bribery, is promoted to the chapel's *Sedd Fawr* ('Big Seat'). Six children die, one by one. The first, Rachel, fell while hoeing turnips in the twilight of an afternoon, her head resting in a ditch of water. At first her father thought her lazy; when he discovered otherwise he emptied his manure cart,

> cast Rachel's body into the cart, and covered it with a sack, and drove home, singing the hymn which begins:

'Safely, safely gathered in,
Far from sorrow, far from sin[.]'

The story ends with the so-called 'mad Achsah' breaking out to watch the wedding procession of her youngest son from behind a hedge and discovering that the children who are not there are dead in the graveyard. The hint is that the vile cruelty of this 'Father in Sion' will continue in his son, for as the new bride crosses the farm threshold, 'the door of the parlour was opened and a lunatic embraced her'.

And so on. Marriage is often, when not robbery, a commercial transaction. In the next, simpler story, the new wife, viewed at market, is more swiftly chosen than 'A Heifer without Blemish'. If someone like the untaught Eben of 'The Talent Thou Gavest' glimpses the truth of Christianity, he is eventually brought back again to the chapel rule of 'the Respected Bryn-Bevan', the major villain of *My People*. The most anthologized story, 'This Be Her Memorial', is obviously a memorial to all those duplicates of the horribly poor and aged Nanni who in 'search for God . . . fell down and worshipped at the feet of a god'. This god is 'the Respected Josiah Bryn-Bevan' whom she actually nursed as a baby. Hearing that he is to move to Aberystwyth, she prays to the 'Dear little Big Man' to let her 'live to hear the boy's farewell words', and she gives all she has to buy an illustrated bible for him as a farewell present. Because of sores on her face, she gives the bible to (the vile) Sadrach, the 'Father in Sion', to present; and Bryn-Bevan gives it back to him. As so often in Caradoc Evans's stories, the overwhelming lacerating revelation is in the last paragraph. Bryn-Bevan does cross the fields to Nanni's wood and straw cottage, and finds her on the floor:

'Nanni, Nanni!' he said. 'Why for you do not reply to me? Am I not your shepherd?'

There was no movement from Nanni. Mishtir Bryn-Bevan went on his knees and peered at her. Her hands were clasped tightly together, as though guarding some great treasure. The minister raised himself and prised them apart with the ferrule of his walking-stick. A roasted rat revealed itself. Mishtir Bryn-Bevan stood for several moments spellbound and silent; and in the stillness the rats crept boldly out of their hiding places and resumed their attack on Nanni's face. The minister, startled and horrified, fled from the house of sacrifice.

It is noticeable that when Caradoc Evans is intent upon us not
missing his view, he writes in a succinct but fairly normal flow of
narrative English. But why is he so powerfully original and moral
(and more so than the preacherly writer of short stories, T. F.
Powys, who was simultaneously revealing from elsewhere the
soullessness and cruelty of country people in works like *Mr
Tasker's Gods*)? His strength is in his style; overall he blends the
cadence of the Old Testament and Marie Lloyd's music-hall
storytelling skill through what she did not say. The simple,
ponderous biblical style is, of course, ironic, given its evil usage in
Caradoc's peasant community. It is destructive because it is mixed
with an atmospheric, caricatured rendering of Welsh-English and
its idiomatic inversions, together with Evans's grotesque
translations of the Welsh. The latter reveal Manteg's mental
reduction of divinity: as heaven becomes a place of 'white shirts'
and God is the 'Great Male' or 'Big Man'.

Caradoc Evans's *My People* sold well outside Wales: five
editions in two years. Two subsequent collections of short stories
and a play follow the same formula. In *My Neighbours* (1919) he
lashed the London-Welsh small-business families who had taken
rural manners to the city; here he is more starkly ferocious but not
so creatively forceful. His outstanding tour de force is in the
autobiographically founded novel, *Nothing to Pay* (1930),
motivated by the same rage against the effects of Liberal Nonconformity but with more subtle interpretations. The novel provides
more leisurely pace, which Evans uses brilliantly to alternate it
with brief, understated revelations of the disgusting. *Nothing to
Pay* provides space for a new, ample characterization, including
those who escape shackles, which is vivid and fascinating,
especially in his portrayal of Carmarthen town and its varied
society. The novel is a historical document of 'brutal thorough-
ness', finely detailing the lives of drapers'-shop assistants in south
Wales and London. Caradoc Evans, forced into this life as a boy,
initially in Carmarthen, escaped by twenty-five into London
journalism. The novel's central character, Amos Morgan, likes and
prospers in drapery-shop life. The novel traces his gradual
corruption to total degeneration, and moves beyond satire to
imply questions about the relativity of genetic inheritance and
conditioning. We watch Amos from when, as a country child, he is
lifted into his grandfather's coffin – which is so skimped in wood

and varnish that the dead man's legs are bent – to when he dies thanking God for death, because for death there is 'nothing to pay', and when his wife, embittered and made avaricious like himself, kicks his bible and discovers notes, to the high value of £5,000, pinned within its pages.

A moral satirist is usually a thwarted idealist; but, in his literary vision of Wales and his people, Caradoc would seem to be in a different world from the Anglo-Welsh writers of the three centuries before him and even from his near-contemporaries. His work makes difficult a coherent appraisal of Anglo-Welsh literary portrayal of Wales (mainly, south and west Wales) in this long period. *My People* is often interpreted as kick-starting the birth of the twentieth-century Welsh writing in English which followed it; but Caradoc Evans's work is different, too, from what followed it, so I cannot see why this is observed as one of his merits.

FURTHER READING

Jane Aaron, 'The hoydens of wild Wales: representations of Welsh women in Edwardian and Victorian fiction', *Welsh Writing in English* 1 (1995), 23–39.

Sam Adams, *Thomas Jeffery Llewelyn Prichard* (Cardiff, 2000).

Kirsti Bohata, 'Apes and cannibals in Cambria: images of the racial and gendered other in Gothic writing in Wales', *Welsh Writing in English* 6 (2000), 119–43.

Anthony Conran, *The Cost of Strangeness* (Llandysul, 1982).

Moira Dearnley, *Distant Fields: Eighteenth-century Fiction of Wales* (Cardiff, 2001).

Caradoc Evans, *My People*, ed. John Harris (Bridgend, 1987).

Raymond Garlick, *An Introduction to Anglo-Welsh Literature* (Cardiff, 1970).

Katie Gramich and Andrew Hiscock (eds), *Dangerous Diversity: The Changing Faces of Wales* (Cardiff, 1998).

L. W. Hockey, *W. H. Davies* (Cardiff, 1971).

Belinda Humfrey, *John Dyer* (Cardiff, 1980).

F. E. Hutchinson, *Henry Vaughan: A Life and Interpretation* (Oxford, 1947).

Sally Roberts Jones, *Allen Raine* (Cardiff, 1979).

Roland Mathias, *A Ride Through the Wood* (Bridgend, 1985).

Roland Mathias, *Anglo-Welsh Literature: An Illustrated History* (Bridgend, 1987).

Catherine Messem, 'Gender, class and the Welsh question in the poetry of Jane Cave (*c*.1754–1813)', *Welsh Writing in English* 2 (1996), 1–21.

D. P. M. Michael, *Arthur Machen* (Cardiff, 1971).

E. C. Pettet, *Of Paradise and Light* (Cambridge, 1960).

J. Kimberley Roberts, *Ernest Rhys* (Cardiff, 1983).

Alan Rudrum, *Henry Vaughan* (Cardiff, 1981).

J. H. Summers, *The Heirs of Donne and Jonson* (London, 1970).

M. Wynn Thomas, *Internal Difference: Writing in Twentieth-century Wales* (Cardiff, 1992).

M. Wynn Thomas, *Corresponding Cultures: The Two Literatures of Wales* (Cardiff, 1999).

William Tydeman (ed.), *The Welsh Connection* (Llandysul, 1986).

CHAPTER 2

'A NEW ENORMOUS MUSIC': INDUSTRIAL FICTION IN WALES

STEPHEN KNIGHT

I

> Night had fallen completely when I began the climb of Arthur's Crown, walking up the same path as I had descended on my way into Moonlea. In its summit I looked down. There below me was the house of Penbury, big, smiling and living with light. I turned away, walking away from Moonlea, yet eternally towards Moonlea, full of a strong, ripening, unanswerable bitterness, feeling in my fingers the promise of a new enormous music.

So Gwyn Thomas concludes his freehand treatment of the Merthyr Rising of 1831 in *All Things Betray Thee* (1949), intermingled with references to other conflicts through recent Welsh history. In this passage he realizes a dialectic central to industrial fiction, and especially the Welsh version of it. The conditions of life are dire enough to make anyone want to leave: and yet they are also humanly empowering in complex ways. A tormented industrial town like Moonlea is for an artist a source of both political anger and creative fascination. Wales, in several areas, was a major contributor to the productive dissonance of British industrial history, and Welsh writers, working in both of the country's languages, created fictions of abiding importance and value, expressing, as Thomas puts it, both bitterness and music.

Welsh writers of industrial fiction were less early in the field than English colleagues, as H. Gustav Klaus has noted, but their productivity was both strong and richly varied, especially in the 1930s. It concentrated on the major activity of coal-mining in the south, but also dealt with the north-western industry of slate-mining, to a minor extent with the north-eastern coalfield, and also to some degree with the initially more important southern activities in iron- and steel-production. In recent years writers have worked mostly in the past tense, reflecting on the demise of heavy industry in the country and the losses and problems that are now visible.

The Welsh material is notable both for the substantial number of writers and for their widely differing treatments of the industrial experience, ranging from strongly political analyses, through re-creations of the social context, to almost entirely domestic representations of the impact of arduous industrial labour. But before exploring these riches, some definitions seem important. The 'industrial' novel is here taken to be one that focuses on the social, political and economic issues and consequences of the industrialized life. That excludes from consideration novels that use industry as a context for a humanly focused narrative, Welsh parallels to D. H. Lawrence's *Sons and Lovers* like Rhys Davies's *Jubilee Blues* (1938), Glyn Jones's *The Valley, The City, The Village* (1956) – even though its 1980 reprint has a pithead on the jacket – Emlyn Williams's play, and later film, *The Corn is Green* (1938), a work notable for both its Anglocentric conservatism and its rare status as a fiction connected to, if not in fact delineating, the Flintshire coalfield. If Emlyn Williams's play is excluded as non-industrial though Welsh in topic and authorial origin, the reverse case is James Hanley: though he lived for some thirty years in Wales as an adult, his powerful industrial fictions, whether set on sea or land, do not undertake in any significant way a treatment of Welsh-related matters, and so are not discussed here.

The industrial element of this definition also of necessity excludes the substantial amount written about farming, even though in many respects the strains and issues involved are not unlike those found in early forms of industrial production. The bitter experiences of hill farmers in the fiction of Caradoc Evans or the earlier poetry of R. S. Thomas are in many ways like those of home-based weavers and frame-knitters, if not of industrial workers en masse, but it would seem a strained definition to include them in this discussion. The new and dramatic tensions of the industrial situation are the major features of Welsh industrial fiction, though, as will be seen, rural structures, and especially rural values, remain a strong element in the texts to be discussed.

The industrial novel in Wales had a considerable handicap to its emergence, because, as is well known, the novel itself as a genre was for long alien to the country and both its languages. Yet even when Wales did adopt the novel form, there remained difficulties about industrial fiction arising from inherent features of the genre itself. The form of the classic novel has frequently been described as inherently middle class, shaping an aesthetic that is deeply involved with the individual, with moralized choice and with many kinds of accepted hierarchy, social and discursive. That assembly of implications must present writers of industrial fiction with something of a problem, both literary and political, and the result- ant strains are clear throughout the tradition – and no more so than at its beginning. Is the focus of the fiction the sentient individual, as in classic realism, or the politically understood social grouping? Does the reader in terms of personal response empathize with people or, as in Brecht, come to comprehend the sociopolitical patterns that are laid bare by the text? This kind of structural tension between humanist and socialist writing tech- niques will be evident in many of the novels to be discussed.

Another problem for industrial writers is simply mechanical. How would someone fully aware of and deeply involved in the processes of industrialization find the time and energy, let alone the technical skill, to produce some hundred thousand words of writing polished enough for acceptance in commercial publishing? The same pressure also militates against other forms of dissemin- ation like *zamisdat* or serial mode, and must make even short-story writing difficult. The novel's generic form, that is, conspires in terms of both production and consumption to make industrial fiction inherently marginal to the literary mainstream of the novel, unless there are strong contradictory forces at work in either the writer's self and circumstances, or in the publishing environment, to enable its success. These mechanical negative forces must be especially strong when, as Raymond Williams comments, the fictions are in the Welsh case largely written from inside the industrial community itself .

Nevertheless, each Welsh industrial writer found, in different ways, time and an audience, and some of their processes are on the record. Jack Jones and Gwyn Thomas were out of work when they started serious writing – the cyclic nature of industrial profit helped to generate its own critique. Ill health provided time for T. Rowland Hughes to write. Rhys Davies, Gwyn Jones and Kate Roberts were more directly committed as writers, though their varied social and economic contexts inflected their commitment in

different ways, with different results in their work. Lewis Jones just
seems to have found the time somehow in his hectic working and
political life, but he comments on the difficulties in his preface to
Cwmardy.

In terms of audience the industrial working class itself is not
normally likely to provide enough readers for the quite substantial
and sophisticated genre of fiction to be a commercial success.
There was in general a lack of interest among committed leftist
publishers in fiction until Martin Lawrence took up the form in
the mid-1930s. A feature of the Welsh novels is their concentration
in the mid to late 1930s, and access to a sympathetic audience
seems a major reason for that short but intense period of
flourishing. This was when several commercial London publishers
found a market for leftist surveys of life in what were called the
'regions', by no means only Welsh ones, as severe economic conditions and vigorous local responses had the power to prod some
consciences among at least some of the English middle-class
reading public.

In addition to Martin Lawrence (later of Lawrence and
Wishart), Cape was early in the publishing field, and became the
leader in numbers, with at least ten industrial titles in the 1930s.
Gollancz and Faber followed the trend, and so to some degree
did other major fiction houses – Dent, Chatto and Windus,
Hutchinson, Collins. With interesting exceptions (such as the real
success of James C. Welsh's Scotland-based *The Underworld* in
1920), sales of firmly radical texts were not large, rarely more than
a few thousand. However, the more popular and distinctly less
radical texts could gain very large sales like the Lancashire-set
Love on the Dole (1933) and, among the Welsh novels, the
inherently romantic *How Green Was My Valley* (1939) and, to a
lesser degree, *Bidden to the Feast* (1938). There were also strong
segments of readership among those who were more directly
involved in industrial activities, as was the case with Tressell's *The
Ragged Trousered Philanthropists* (1914), a novel famously supported by the union movement, and Lewis Jones in particular had
a committed left-wing audience in Wales and elsewhere.

However, the possibility of London outlets for industrial fiction
faded after the Second World War, perhaps because of growing
familiarity with socialism in practice, perhaps because the drama
of world politics seemed to overwhelm the semi-touristic interest in

'regional' affairs which had always been a partial appeal of the industrial novel: from the 1930s, London reviews of Welsh novels, or indeed fiction from any of the non-metropolitan British regions, can have the flavour of a *National Geographic* journey among intriguing and pitiable savages. A more positive element likely to have reduced interest in industrial fiction was the alleviation of extreme distress and reflexive resistance by the working class in an improved working economy. For varied reasons, by about 1950 the industrial world had become simply less dramatic as a fictional topic.

In the period of post-war prosperity, although Menna Gallie successfully retained the industrial focus in two of her first three books – *Strike for a Kingdom* (1959) and *The Small Mine* (1962) – and Gwyn Thomas continued to publish his Rhondda-based fables, the impact of Welsh industrial fiction was significantly reduced among the reading public, and critics seem to have largely forgotten it: in Stuart Laing's book *Representations of Working-Class Life 1957–1964* (1984), Raymond Williams is the only Welsh writer to be included, and that with reference to his almost entirely England-set novel, *Second Generation* (1964); in Ian Haywood's recent survey of the genre in Britain, Williams and Lewis Jones are the only Welsh writers discussed. As a result of the post-war lack of interest in the more radical kinds of text that flourished in the 1930s, the dominant and critically admired Welsh voice of the post-war period was the conservative regionalism of Richard Llewellyn, which can be interpreted as bringing the Welsh industrial novel back to a position close to its distinctly conservative point of origin half a century before.

II

A well-known early writer who touched on the industrial world is Allen Raine in *The Welsh Witch* (1902), but coalfield realism is not a major thread of the novel nor a feature that recurs in Raine's work. She may have been briefly influenced by a novel by Joseph Keating, a Mountain Ash miner who turned to journalism. His *Son of Judith* (1900) includes a substantial amount of mining material, yet its focus is outside working-class life in both personnel and concerns. The illegitimate son of the title works in a south Wales pit because his mother is so poor, abandoned by a mining surveyor who does not even know his son. Early on there is a minor pit-disaster in which the brave young man leads to safety both a distressed lady visitor and the man who is, unknown to him, his father. This is highly reminiscent of *Germinal* (1885): from Zola on, the dramatic encounter in the mine disaster has been a leading motif in the more melodramatic and action-oriented examples of industrial fiction set far underground, but Keating's endangered characters are all gentry of some kind.

While Keating's second book to deal with mining, *Maurice* (1905), is subtitled *A Romance of Light and Darkness*, the romance between Jethro and Olwen is secondary to the focus on Maurice, a child who grows up just as his part of south Wales is reached by the growing coal industry. Much of the novel is to do with family and place, but Chapter XVI is a powerful version of the 'boy's first day down a coal-mine' theme – it would seem the first example of that recurrent feature to appear in Wales. Though there is some Zola-esque realism, romance dominates. Another romantic element lies in Maurice's being finally revealed as the long-lost son of an Irish aristocrat, and this element of somewhat dirt-streaked silver-spoon romance emerges from the hectic plot just as the love of Jethro and Olwen ends with him dead underground and her following him, a mining Romeo and Juliet.

The pit is also a context for melodramatic romance in Keating's other industrially based novel *Flower of the Dark* (1917) – the title itself seems like a reference to the symbolic final sequence of *Germinal*. As in *Son of Judith* we move among the ownership and managerial class – a group of workers in the mining industry who are rarely discussed in the novels except with automatically dismissive gestures, though Gwyn Jones's *Times Like These* (1936) does offer something of an exception, as James A. Davies has noted. The hero himself belongs to this group: he is a skilful manager risen from the ranks, called Osla Silvertop. The bizarre name has the effect, if not the intention, of caricature, seeming to disown, as if in embarrassment, the author's quite sympathetic realization of this humbly originated figure.

It is clear that Keating values the mining world mostly as a way of giving weight and context to family dramas of various sorts, but he was not alone in both noting and eliding the conditions on the coalfield. Irene Saunderson, the wife of a south Wales doctor, gave a demotic voice and a sympathetic representation to the travails of colliers in *A Welsh Heroine* (1911), but her brave working-class girl finally marries the noble English officer who leads his troops against the striking miners. A more complex withdrawal from political confrontations can be found in the work of Rhys Davies. As I have discussed elsewhere, many of his short stories use the mining world as a contest for emotional and familiar dramas, a *Sons and Lovers*-like movement away from mining itself into the fiction of feeling – and Davies became friendly with Lawrence, who admired his work. This movement clearly relates to some degree to Davies's upbringing, as the son of a shopkeeper in Blaenclydach in the Rhondda. His work frequently refers to the degrading and disabling aspects of life in the coalfield, and in both his autobiography *Print of a Hare's Foot* (1969) and the auto-biographical novel *Tomorrow to Fresh Woods* (1941) he writes with a distinctly negative tone of the violence he saw in the strikes of 1910–11.

A displaced version of the autobiographical negativity dominates his first novel *The Withered Root* (1927). This offers in grim tones a miner, his alcoholic wife and their son. As is common in Welsh tradition, family is in the foreground, but here not as a positive force. Whereas in Keating familial relations were fragmented, in Davies's novel they are firmly negative. The son is a miner and, familiarly enough in this genre, he moves out from home and industrial work. But unlike most who do that, this social traveller moves not into management, education or writing – he escapes into that alternative Welsh craft, preaching. This displace-ment of working-class energy is confirmed by the resolution of the plot, which focuses on personal tragedy, not political critique. As Davies said in his autobiography, *Print of a Hare's Foot*, the novel has a 'highflown theme . . . warfare between religious spirit and carnal flesh, with spirit a heavy loser'.

After he was established as a writer in London, widely noted for his sensitive stories of emotional realism, Davies nevertheless kept returning to the industrial world: in fact he wrote more stories and novels set in the coalfield than any other Welsh writer, and he obviously felt some value in the resistance of the workers to their difficulties and oppressions, though he did not take the clearly political line of other industrial novelists. His next engagements with this context are inherently displaced. In *Count Your Blessings*

(1932) the central figure is a girl who leaves a mining village and finally returns, to mixed success and happiness, after earning both money and experience in a Cardiff brothel. A less extreme displacement, but also capable of being read as showing the author's own interest in a marginal engagement with the world of his origin, is in *The Red Hills* (also 1932) where a somewhat romantic hero mines in old-world fashion a simple coal-bearing level in the hills just away from a new-style deep mine and its village: only his own Lawrentian vigour, and his passionate women, rescue him from what is represented as the mean-minded vengeance of the industrial villagers.

These stories all use an individual focus to distance the realities of industrial life, but Davies took a more wide-ranging, even communal approach in the trilogy which told the history of 'Glan Ystrad', clearly a version of his own Blaenclydach, from its rural peace to the turbulent 1930s. The first novel, *Honey and Bread* (1935), recounts the coming of industry into an innocent world and landowning family, an arrival that is brusque and besmirching rather than stimulating. *A Time to Laugh* (1937) is Rhys Davies's strongest engagement with Welsh social conditions. It responded to the worsening industrial conditions of the 1930s (and presumably to the London saleability of novels about them), but is set back at the turn of the century. A greater sidestep yet is that the primary consciousness of the political agitation is focused through a doctor who not only sides with the miners but also remains among them, not moving on to Harley Street like the hero of A. J. Cronin's initially Welsh-set *The Citadel* (1937).

A Time to Laugh realizes – at about the same time as Lewis Jones did in *Cwmardy* – the conflict on the coalfield at the end of the nineteenth century, with wage cuts, the sliding scale, the miners' battle to construct a multi-company union. Men march over the hills to address strike meetings by flaring torchlight, there are scenes of exploitation, conflict, violence on both sides, by coal-owners against miners and by miners against scabs. For all this social activity, largely positively treated, Davies does still, unlike Lewis Jones, locate the focal intelligence of the book outside the industrial workers, in the doctor, one of the family who once owned the pastoral valley. He sympathizes strongly with the workers, speaks at their meetings, yet is never one of them and he can, finally, see an improbable positivity in their appalling circumstances. At the end of the novel, he watches the unemployed from a distance while they are capering around a bonfire on the hill, and tells his wife, with her Lawrentian dark eyes and full lips, that it *is* ultimately 'a time to laugh', 'with all this wealth'. He appears to mean a wealth of human interrelations, not his medical income: the moment of idealism creates a drastically personalized foreclosure to this sometimes searching presentation of the conflicts in the mining world.

Another and in many ways more persuasive form of distancing by Rhys Davies operates in the last of the trilogy, *Jubilee Blues* (1938). The focus this time – as in many of Davies's short stories and later novels – is a woman, Cassie, a rural domestic worker who inherits from her master and marries a chancer who opens a pub in the valleys with her money. Her own exploitation is in some ways a parallel to that of the miners, but this is all seen at a distance – if an often horrified one, as injuries and starvation cross the deeply sympathetic Cassie's gaze. Yet she will eventually return to the country; this is where Davies's ultimate idea of value lies, not in the committed politics of the industrial world, and though the landowning family has now provided, in the doctor's son, a communist, Davies had his own, essentially apolitical, position on the rights and wrongs of coalfield politics. He frequently wrote about the way in which the miners' resistance was, at its most earnest, and not simply violent, a modern version of the old Welsh spirit of resistance to invaders. This decidedly simplistic notion was, with some spirit, artistically focused on the figure of Dr William Price of Llantrisant, who clearly fascinated Davies. In his autobiographical novel *Tomorrow to Fresh Woods* which, for all its escapological title and its individualistic hero-focus, is another close look at the coalfield, Dr Price stalks in all his exotic grandeur, with his fox-hat, women and children, through Glan Ystrad, just as he had, in Davies's mother's memory, through Blaenclydach, as is recorded in *Print of a Hare's Foot*. Price, Davies feels, was

> a descendant of the warrior-bards who were always at the side of those Welsh kings and leaders incensed by the attempts of invaders to obliterate the ancient heritage of their race. Instead of foreign soldiers he had coal-owners and iron-masters to grapple with – more subtle invaders. His task was to ensure that they should not utterly possess the spirit of his people.

Davies's politics could slip off easily into personalization and romanticism, but he nevertheless paid recurring attention to the industrial world, and saw in its conflicts and its people something that was essentially Welsh and, so long as they were not unseemly violent, inherently admirable.

The opposite of that position in many ways is *Sorrow for Thy Sons* (1986), written by Gwyn Thomas by 1937 and entered in a competition Gollancz was holding for a novel about the depression – apparently meant to produce something like a sequel to Gwyn Jones's *Times Like These* (1936), which brought the story of Welsh conditions up to 1929. *Sorrow for Thy Sons* is a very powerful, even bitter, novel of working-class conditions – too much so for publication at that time.

When he wrote *Sorrow for Thy Sons*, Thomas was down from Oxford, and down indeed. Involved in the anti-means-test action as, he said, 'a committee man and refulgent orator', he wrote a bleak and powerfully ironic book about three brothers and a desperate Rhondda community, based on Cymer, his village of origin. There is no trace of an upbeat conclusion; Hugh, a central figure, simply leaves the valley at the hope-starved end of the novel. His brother Alf is a deeply radical mischief-maker; a second brother is devoted to the values of the shop where he works. The political satire is savage and it is comprehensible – if regrettable – that Victor Gollancz rejected *Sorrow for Thy Sons*. Thomas reported in his autobiography, *A Few Selected Exits*, that the publisher's readers found the writing impressive but unduly negative, yearning for some of the novelistic poetry of Rhys Davies, not to mention a more positive form of socialism. The transmitter of the bad news about his rejection to Thomas was Norman Collins, who obviously understood the advice well, as he went on to great success with sentimental novels about the English proletariat like *London Belongs to Me* (1945).

Thomas never wrote again in the consciously political and substantially realistic mode of *Sorrow for Thy Sons*, and he became famous for a fluent, witty, word-spinning kind of writing, similar to the brilliant and compelling talks on radio and television and the many journalistic pieces he produced from the mid-1950s on. The general view of his work seems to be that the best is closest to the industrial world and the workers' direct resistance. Many would agree with Dai Smith that 'Oscar', a novella published in the collection *Where Did I Put My Pity?* in 1946, is his finest writing. It certainly has a political edge: it ends with the hero arranging the death of the brutal coal-tip owner Oscar. Others would, like Raymond Williams, in his Introduction to the 1988 reprint, praise highly *All Things Betray Thee*, a romanticized, if still political, historical novel. The later work, a number of novels and many short stories, tend to be dismissed as crowd-pleasing lightweight material, stripped of the leftist passion that informs the fluent and committed writing of those favoured early texts.

But this view of Thomas as a failed leftist is as limited – and as comprehensible – as the hostility shown to him by those who found intolerable the many sarcastic and negative remarks Thomas made in the 1960s and 1970s about the activities of the Welsh-language movement. Thomas was the youngest of ten brothers, the first five of whom spoke Welsh: he always disavowed the language and its culture, in part because he found oppressive the discipline of the Welsh chapel he attended, but also because, as Glyn Jones noted in *The Dragon Has Two Tongues*, Thomas was one of those who saw 'nationalism as a threat to the international unity and strength of the working class'. But the waspish tone of Thomas's comments on the language go further than political purity – they are reminiscent of the biting tone of Caradoc Evans's satires, and may well also partly derive from a sense of guilt at separation from the native culture.

This is what would be expected if Thomas were read in the light of post-colonial criticism, as I have proposed elsewhere. The two most realist-socialist novels, *Sorrow for Thy Sons* and *All Things Betray Thee*, can be read as having that form because they were attuned for the London publishing market – the first because it was written for a Gollancz prize, the second because the publishers Michael Joseph were making with it a push to establish Thomas as an international success in the Richard Llewellyn mould. Neither project succeeded, and in his later work Thomas used a different approach, not the realist voice of classic English fiction but what post-colonial critics call a hybrid voice, combining native Welsh themes such as ogres and sovereignty-symbolizing women with a satiric awareness of colonizing oppressions, and creating a style that challengingly combines the imaginative rhetoric of the Welsh tradition with the actual structures of the colonizing language. The texts that achieve this complex hybridity most successfully are not so much industrial as post-industrial: in *The World Cannot Hear You* (1951) and *The Thinker and the Thrush* (written by 1948 but not published until 1988), the sage, witty group of friends who observe the world of south Wales, its dreams, its ironies and its complicities, no longer work in productive industry.

This post-colonial reading helps to explain the elements of unrealism which are central to the earlier texts. *All Things Betray Thee* is unquestionably an industrial novel, but it is generalized: while it deals in a distanced and symbolized way with the events of Merthyr in 1831 and Newport in 1839, it is set in a place with the English, even ironic, name Moonlea, and is overall imbued with a tone close to sentimentality and nostalgia. James A. Davies sees 'an uneasy mixture of modes', and Christopher Meredith, reviewing the 1986 reprint, described it as 'a sort of Ruritania with class war'. But this movement away from realism is not necessarily a retreat: Raymond Williams admired Gwyn Thomas's capacity to allegorize the industrial struggle and felt in his Introduction to the reprint that, by resisting the English pressure towards 'a fiction of private lives' and so 'writing at an effectively legendary distance', Thomas had created the capacity to 'write the inner experience of that historical moment which is always more than depression and protest'.

As Michael Parnell has charted in his biography of Gwyn Thomas, there is, in his work in the later 1940s and afterwards, a clear withdrawal from directly radical topics, just as there is an increasing tendency for the narrators of Thomas's stories to be distanced from the action. A pivotal figure in this development is the young, strong Lewis in the powerful novella 'Oscar'. Lewis, unlike his relatives – his father was 'a great man for strikes' – and his deeply, even desperately radicalized friends on the Terraces, has regular work, being the faithful, even servile, man of all work for Oscar, who owns a hill but makes his living by forcing the unemployed to scrape for useable coal on the tip which is all the hill now holds. Complicit with Oscar in almost all ways, Lewis eventually undergoes some internal conflict (described by Golightly), and as a result he then sides with the Terracers, and murders his master. If Thomas is, as Smith asserts and Williams implies, essentially a symbolist, it is not hard to see a self-projection of the author in Lewis: curiously, Thomas had an uncle called Oscar – 'a cantankerous jeweller' from Mountain Ash.

James A. Davies has also seen 'Oscar' as one of Thomas's best works, combining both political commitment and more literary control than he shows elsewhere, but Davies would select the early novel *The Dark Philosophers* as Thomas's finest, seeing there a stronger plot, with clearer and more separated characterization and an overall moral meaning both better focused and more symbolically realized than are normal in Thomas's later and more discursive works. Even when Thomas's own position is less directly revealed than in 'Oscar', there is always ironic sympathy for the verbally self-propelling people of the Rhondda, and there remain political depths to his later, primarily entertaining, books.

Gwyn Thomas's personal politics clearly remained close to the fierce leftism of *Sorrow for Thy Sons* and several critics have detected this throughout his work: Glyn Jones felt that no one could miss 'the powerful underthrob of compassion' in the stories; Katie Jones sees a consistent background of 'the underlying struggle of landlord/coal owner against worker'. Howard Fast, the American Marxist novelist, was a great admirer of Thomas's work; as Golightly has recorded, they maintained a warm, and distinctly left-wing, correspondence through the worst Cold War years and, in *Literature and Reality*, Fast described *All Things Betray Thee* (under its American title *Leaves in the Wind*) as 'one of the best achievements in socialist realism that we know in modern Western literature'. Thomas himself seems to have valued this connection, in spite of the considerable and increasing stylistic differences between his work and the social realists: Roger Stephens Jones's argument that his work moved steadily towards Absurdism is one way of explaining this tension, but a fuller explanation may derive, as argued above, from understanding Thomas and his complexities, including his hostility to the native culture from which he came, as being those of a writer engaging with difficulty and dynamism with his colonized situation.

Glyn Jones called Gwyn Thomas 'the *cyfarwydd* of the working class' and this term, meaning 'traditional story-teller', no doubt refers both to his compelling verbal skills and his volatile imagination. By far the most verbally gifted of the writers to realize the industrial context, Gwyn Thomas seems to have been basically unsuited to realist fiction, too subtle and multiple in his responses to accept the inherent political and moral directness of the form. As he said, 'my bardic name was ambivalence'. The

continuing audience for his work – in reprints and in lively public
interest in talks about him – suggests that the anti-colonial tensions
he generated, for the spirit but against the form of traditional
industrial fiction, gave his work a dynamic hybridized quality that
will ensure its survival.

Fictional flexibility of a quite different kind is evident in the
career of Jack Jones. A miner from Merthyr Tydfil, but mobile
around south Wales as so many people then were, he turned to
writing when out of work. But unlike Joseph Keating, he did not,
then at least, use middle-class models. His first books are only just
describable as novels; *Rhondda Roundabout* (1934) and *Black
Parade* (1935) in title and form suggest circus or theatre, and the
texts are cavalcades of local life, cutting across time and conventional narration, like a free-form or perhaps music-hall version of
Dos Passos's modernist textual verity, as Keri Edwards suggests.

Jones not only has a clear sense of radical politics, he also gives
a substantial role to strong women characters – Glyn Jones notes
that the original title for *Black Parade* was 'Saran'. Jones also
speaks warmly of these texts as evoking a powerful sense of the life
and history of the south-eastern coalfield and Raymond Williams
has seen *Black Parade* as 'a novel of the making, the struggles, the
defeats of a class'. It was written before *Rhondda Roundabout*,
though published after it, and the two together were in many ways
forerunners of the Welsh industrial tradition: later texts tended to
vary or redirect the structure that Jones worked out through his
first two books. *Black Parade* might seem overladen with a
journalistic history of the Merthyr district (though it was once far
heavier in this respect: Jones cut it from 250,000 words to its
present 80,000), but its power is to offer both a strong narrative-
and-character structure and a trenchant realization of the violence,
both physical and psychological, of social life in the emerging
industrial districts: Edwards sees the book as offering 'lantern
slides of industrialism'. The central figure develops from a
reasonably promising young man into a less than courageous
figure, as if Scott's Waverley were transplanted to south Wales,
and his wife's endurance through great difficulties is neither
sentimentalized nor represented in sadomasochistic terms, those
two poles of proletarian romance of later years.

Black Parade spans the years from the early 1870s up to the first
real intimation of the socio-economic disaster that was gathering

as trade began to weaken and conflict began to flare on the coalfield in the years before the First World War. Jack Jones has the capacity to write in an almost Dickensian voice, locating social tension firmly within the strains felt by the characters, whether they are tough men turned religious, nervous people staying respectable, the weak of both sexes being consumed by the violence of their world and their work, or, a central point of value in Jones's work, strong and enduring women who go on fighting for those closest to them. The novel vigorously expresses both strains and collaborations as grand economic narratives are imposed on intimate lives, and the viewpoint and intimately detailed technique of *Black Parade* retain a position on the side of the distinctly small battalions of struggling workers.

It may well be that his later conservatism in politics and fictional technique have helped to obscure Jack Jones's achievement and influence in the early novels. His original fictional context is fully industrial, with miners, mining families and all the associated culture of chapel, pub and sport. Jones also has no hesitation in establishing the family rather than a central male figure as the social location of the narrative: his novels, like the most fully and formally radical of the working-class texts around the world, do not depend on a single focalizing male narrator; they move among a large group of people to realize and evaluate aspects of the culture. *Bidden to the Feast* (1938), like a fully developed version of the often sketched-in *Black Parade*, is the first of Jones's early texts to approach the overarching narrative of the long novel but it still retains substantial sequences of information – about mining, sanitation, immigration, the Merthyr district in general. Politics proper enters the text through the hauliers' strike of the 1890s and the deteriorating structure of economic life after the boom of the early days in the valleys. But Jones's attention also moves on to other themes – emigration, mercantile activity, the family in general and especially its emotional possibilities: the signs of his later populist sentimentality are certainly present but that, as with Gwyn Thomas's comedy, may have had stimuli in the processes of commercial publishing. Glyn Jones, who knew Jack Jones well, reports that in the mid-1930s an English publisher rejected the manuscript of 'Behold They Live' as too gloomy. This may well also have shaped Jack Jones's humorous and conservative approach in later texts, which are technically and politically weaker, with rather predictable technicolour novels about the Welsh diaspora (*Off to Philadelphia in the Morning*, 1947), Cardiff social and business life (*River out of Eden*, 1951), or little more than cartoon-like valley nostalgia (*Choral Symphony*, 1955).

Bidden to the Feast was well received, with many reprints and readers, and it has been widely followed as an emotional saga of Welsh working folk by writers like Alexander Cordell and Iris Gower. It is not easy to decide whether the novel's commercial success came because Jones balances the political and the human, aesthetically resolving the essential tension between industrial theme and bourgeois form, or simply because he ultimately elided any real radical thrust into a sentimentalized family fable. The latter seems the more common view among critics, but it is important to note the positive features of the text, both in terms of a fully credible and energetic account of working-class life in the industrial valleys and also in terms of his representation of the central and dynamic role of women, which is fairly unusual in the international working-class novel and a distinct feature of the Welsh tradition. Upton Sinclair's *The Jungle* (1906) was a strongly male text, so was *The Ragged Trousered Philanthropists* (1914): in both, women were represented as troublesome appendages or tragic victims. *Germinal*, as in many other aspects, was more complex and larger-minded than that; the most determined revolutionary is Maheude, mother of a large family; her daughter Catherine may be a victim but also has distinct agency; and Zola's other women represent a whole range of social engagement, though it is true that they rarely act as the viewpoint for events and ideas. Jack Jones does however treat women, in terms of form at least, as capable of focusing the narrative and thematically as having some capacity to wield power well. While this may in some sense derive from a sentimental idea of matriarchy, it also makes possible a varied if still gendered representation of women that is in some degree parallel to the treatment of men.

Dai Smith, writing as David Smith, has offered a somewhat negative account of Jones's achievement, even in his early works. He is sceptical about the socio-historical value of the 'authenticity' of the novels as 'often no more than a compilation of the "Hundred Best Known Facts about South Wales" whose clichéd epithets are a specious fumbling rather than the agents of rooted particularity'; Smith also sees political naivety, and worse, sentimentality, at the heart of the books. Speaking of the end of *Rhondda Roundabout* as the communist anti-means-test march winds through the Rhondda and Dan Price as a result commits himself to God, he judges that:

> The appeal of this writing lies in the hand-wringing, heart-rending simplicity of the analysis and of its implied solution. The message is that radical political action derives from the bitterness caused by unwarranted poverty: so intellectual decision, anger, self-consciousness, class-consciousness even, the education of work itself, are all shunted to the sidelines. The universality of the South Walian story is given us in a guise that only stresses its limited, transitory, almost parochial, significance.

This is by no means unfair, but however sentimental and naively communal Jones's work may be, however diminished his later work, and however far he moved from the industrial heartland of the early fiction, his writing had immediacy and conveyed a sense of authenticity: the *Daily Worker* reviewer urged that *Black Parade* should be 'widely read by all who seek to find the basis of the great social unrest in the British coalfields today'. It is clear from reminiscences by those who read him as he was being published that Jack Jones meant a great deal to readers in south-east Wales in that period: his work sounded as if it belonged to them and their region; it gave a credible account of the strange world in which they found themselves. His autobiography, *Unfinished Journey* (1937), struck an especially strong chord among a people aware both of their past mobility and their uncertain present direction. Jack Jones created a fictional voice that was not falsely conscious like Keating's or mediated through idealized romanticism like that of Rhys Davies, but one that naturalized a type of colloquial prose, created a recognizable, if sometimes close to caricature, 'valley voice', and also presented a dynamic and loosely structured narrative form which was credible to Welsh readers and also – presumably as a sign of an intriguing Celtic other – had success in the English market.

Jack Jones's work, with its colour and sentiment, is a striking contrast to the work of a writer who preferred to give a factual-seeming account of the situation on the coalfield. Bert Coombes's *These Poor Hands* (1939) is a plainly told and searching account of a miner's life, and he gave more detail in *Those Clouded Hills* (1944); the often anthologized short story 'Twenty tons of coal' is widely recognized as a masterly revelation, both quiet and deep, of the dark experience of industrial life. Coombes has in the past been taken basically as a factual writer whose work strayed into fiction, but recent research on his newly discovered manuscripts by Bill Jones, Chris Williams and, particularly, Barbara Prys Williams indicates that there is considerable art in *These Poor Hands* and that Coombes completed, but never published, a good deal of other fiction, some of which has been made available in *With Dust Still in His Throat* (1999). Through the account of his work given in their 1999 book in the Writers of Wales series, Jones and Williams have established Coombes as someone who felt he had a major contribution to make to Welsh industrial fiction, but the nature of the unpublished work does not change his position. His restrained realism had little parallel in Wales; the only similar piece of work is *Stay Down Miner* (1936), a short but powerful account of the miners' resistance of the mid-1930s by the English Marxist Montagu Slater. Historically important as he is and politically effective as he may have been in presenting the situation on the coalfield in a way difficult to dismiss as sentimental or nostalgic, Coombes's adoption of a quiet, even recessive authorial voice, makes him very different from the characteristically powerful, even flamboyant voice of the Welsh writers, typified by Jack Jones

III

Work, family and woman's role: Jack Jones brought those issues forward in the south Wales industrial novel; Kate Roberts developed further their interconnections in a north Wales version different in language but also quite separate in tone, context and sense of narrative discipline. A famous exponent, indeed a shaper, of the Welsh-language short story, her great contribution in the industrial context is *Traed mewn Cyffion* (1936). *Feet in Chains* is the title used for the English translation (1977), but 'fetters' or even 'stocks' might be closer to the 'immobilizing' sense of *cyffion*. This novel deals only at a distance with the slate-quarrying which was male industrial work in Gwynedd, but it powerfully realizes one central aspect of working-class experience, the impact on the family of modern capitalist development. Roberts, herself a classic case of the educated working-class person, turns back to the origins of her own world in this short, powerful novel, at once epigraphic and epic.

Jane Gruffydd marries into the quarrying world; she produces and tends her children. Then she experiences a steady dissipation of the family unit. One daughter drifts off into town life, to become part of the shopocracy. The sons are educated away from home in various ways: Owen and Twm to be teachers, Wil to be political – he goes to south Wales and never returns. Twm joins the army and is killed: Owen is left with a sense of the need to resist these destructive circumstances, rather than construct a family for himself. But for all his intent that is an untold story, lying in the future: political actions, like the work of slate-mining, are on the margins of the text and its focal concerns. As R. Gerallt Jones has commented: 'A deep sympathy enriches a book which might well have been an historical exercise.' The theme of *Traed mewn Cyffion* is more than a male career, and the tragic impact of the war is seen as a development of the destructive modernism of the industrial disaster of the great strike in the slate-field, overturning as it did a secure world of Welsh language, religion, work-customs and the social culture of the *gwerin*, the traditionally oriented folk of Welsh Wales. Roberts represents, in Ned Thomas's view, 'the crystallizing anger of an exploited class, the dissociation of a minority from the political aims of the State'. At the same time as expressing this sense of anger, even betrayal, at the hands of modernity, the novel outlines with brief but telling clarity the paths available to young Welsh men and women at the turn of the century through the varied careers of the older Gruffydd children: into the limited and introspective world of teaching (Owen), into bourgeois Anglophilia (Sioned, or Janet as she becomes), into industrial politics north and south (Wil), into faithful domesticity (Elin) and into dysfunction at home and death in the war for the passionate Welsh teacher Twm.

Against this powerful political overview, at once leftist and Cymric, the filiated personal politics of a woman in the modern world are brought centrally to light: industrial disasters are only one of the problems observed from this familial and female viewpoint. As Ned Thomas comments, Roberts 'shows the social forces converging on the domestic situation'. The positioning is closer to that of Walter Greenwood's *Love on the Dole* (1933) or Ellen Wilkinson's *Clash* (1929) than to the work of Jack Jones or Gwyn Thomas, but Roberts requires neither the theatricality of Greenwood nor the formal leftism of Wilkinson to establish her position, one emphasized in technique through the highly effective condensation of a long saga into narrative vignettes mediating strong feeling. Noragh Jones has seen Roberts as an example of 'conservative feminism' by a writer who values fully 'fruitful domestic experiences' and also shows that 'true grit is not a male monopoly'. Roberts deals with some aspects of this theme in some of her sparely forceful short stories, especially those dealing with a young girl's growing up in the Nantlle valley of the slate-field in *Te yn y Grug* (1959), translated as *Tea in the Heather* (1968). Here she not only sees the slate industry from a woman's viewpoint, but also appropriates to women's writing the structure, much loved among male Welsh writers past and present, of the *Bildungsroman*. In addition to this innovative element, *Te yn y Grug* is, like *Traed mewn Cyffion*, a country story. Through the recurrent combination of rural and industrial life in the novels focused on working lives, the Welsh tradition had asserted itself as internationally unusual and having its own national character: Roberts writes with definitive clarity and confidence in this respect.

A later novel which has some similarities of origin at least to *Traed mewn Cyffion* and which also is devoted to tracing the emotive impact of the north-western industrial context is Caradog Prichard's *Un Nos Ola Leuad* (1961), translated as *Full Moon* by Menna Gallie in 1973 and as *One Moonlit Night* by Philip Mitchell in 1995. Prichard came from Bethesda in the heart of the slate-quarrying area, but worked for most of his life as an English-language journalist in Cardiff and London, while also writing poetry in Welsh, for which he gained the crown at the Eisteddfod three years in succession – a unique achievement – and later the chair. He was, as Harri Pritchard Jones says in his Introduction to Mitchell's translation, 'a tortured soul', tormented by his mother's mental instability and, it seems, by the notion that his father had been a *bradwr*, a 'traitor' or scab, in the great slate-field strike.

Un Nos Ola Leuad is generically that common Welsh form, in both languages, the young man's biography, but it is written with such intensity of feeling and implicational power that it communicates the sense of personal and social instability generated on the slate-field with the imaginative force associated with Joyce and Kafka. Events and feelings are both remembered by the narrator and realized in a desperate present, and his own isolative degeneration is a potent metonym for the disintegrating social and ethical structures of the world of the slate industry. Frequently described as the finest of all Welsh novels, in both languages, *Un Nos Ola Leuad* clearly transcends the usual political context of the industrial novel and is difficult to compare with most of the other texts in the area, apart from Roberts's equally intense but socially less isolative account, but it also indicates just what, at its most intense and poetic, the industrial-novel form can produce.

Not only geography and language suggest that T. Rowland Hughes's *Chwalfa* (1943, translated as *Out of Their Night*, 1954, though *chwalfa* means something like 'dispersal', 'disaster' even 'total defeat') should be considered together with the work of Roberts and Prichard. Born in the north Wales slate-quarrying district and eventually a broadcaster-writer in south Wales, Hughes wrote about his origins when he was ill in the 1940s. His third novel, *William Jones* (1944), translated as *William Jones* (1953), has an industrial context, firstly in the northern quarries and then in the southern valleys, but it is 1935 when William moves south, and the miners in his sister's village are locked out. The novel stresses, with rich and humorous description, the communal and religious life of the valleys and finally, with William beginning to work for the BBC, becomes an ironic version of T. Rowland Hughes's own biography. Two other novels, *O Law i Law* (1943), translated as *From Hand to Hand* (1950), and *Y Cychwyn* (1947), translated as *The Beginning* (1967), used the slate-quarrying context, but it is little more than a backdrop for closely observed personal and familial narratives.

Rowland Hughes's *Chwalfa*, however, is in the full sense industrial. It covers the years 1900 to 1903, the time of the great strike in the northern slate quarries, and focuses on a family, with its head, Edward Evans, acting as the central character. The book is not in itself notably radical in formal terms, though the narration does to some degree challenge the norms of the novel: speeches and summaries are given verbatim at times. Basically this is a historical novel of heroic but failed labour resistance. Hughes reports on and implies judgements about courage, oppression and

the complex human reasons for what was called *brad* (treachery).
In its coherent narrative and contained emotion, it resembles
another under-noticed piece of elegiac realism, Harold Wells's
account of a defeated Australian coal strike, *The Earth Cries Out*
(1952).

None of *Traed mewn Cyffion, Un Nos Ola Leuad* nor *Chwalfa*
had an English market – though the London Welsh certainly read
them in some numbers. The audience for these novels was both less
large and also less distracting than that enjoyed by writers like
Jack Jones and Gwyn Thomas. By being published in Welsh, and
therefore largely within Wales, there is an authorial authenticity, a
non-hybridized character to the work of Roberts, Prichard and
Rowland Hughes that gives them a focused power that tends to be
dissipated through the more multiple and reception-conscious
aims of the English-language writers – at least until recent years,
when they, too, have been published within, and largely for,
Wales. Less well-known still than the Welsh-language industrial
novelists is the Welsh-language tradition of representing 'the good
collier', as described by Hywel Teifi Edwards: in many tracts,
poems and even novels of the later nineteenth and early twentieth
century a sober, religious, hard-working and uncomplaining figure
is presented on a continuum between the real heroics of the
rescuers of Tynewydd in 1877 and the bardic sonority of Mabon,
the Liberal leader of the miners. Edwards shows that the Welsh
language rejected as firmly as the conservative press the radical
miner of the twentieth century, and did not represent this
challenging figure, with the exception of the much criticized play
by J. Kitchener Davies *Cwm Glo* ('Valley of Coal', 1934). Edwards
regrets that Davies did not pursue this vein. He suggests that this
might not have been caused simply by the hostility aroused by the
play in many Welsh-speaking contexts, including the Eisteddfod,
but that the dramatic, inherently foreign world of the turbulent
pits might have 'overcome' Kitchener Davies; he adds the striking
comment that this was like 'Kate Roberts, who failed to write that
novel about the Rhondda which she had in mind'. It is perhaps
not surprising, seeing the distance between a traditional Welsh-
language culture and the world of the southern valleys, both alien
and alienated, that it is only in north Wales contexts that the
Welsh-language texts confront in any depth the industrial
experience.

By charting the bitter history of industrial conflict from inside a community, and especially from within a language resistant to external influence, novelists like Roberts, Prichard and Rowland Hughes can be said to realize, in however sombre a form, the consciousness of working people and their capacity to cherish certain values and identify the enemy with an unconfused eye. However, although the political battle was always severe, whether it was for north Wales slate or south Wales coal, not all resistant treatments of the conflict were as negative as those pressed upon Roberts, Prichard and Rowland Hughes by the conditions on the slate-field. A polemically positive version of the drama of industrial labour was produced by Lewis Jones; his remarkable novel sequence *Cwmardy* (1937) and *We Live* (1939) has a prominent place in any history of consciously political fiction. Writing at just the time when Wales was most gripped with radical action, after resistance to the means test and during the agitation over threats to unionism itself, Jones also wrote for a 1930s English audience who were now aware of what was happening in Wales and sympathetic to hear more. Or some at least: Storm Jameson called it 'the finest socialist novel I have ever read', but on the previous day *The Spectator* reviewer had found it 'laborious and conscientious propaganda'.

Family is the centre of *Cwmardy*, with an emotionally strong mother and a father who is big, honest and somewhat *twp* (simple). The son is influenced towards politics partly by instinct, partly by the incomplete family of a slightly outdated union leader and his daughter. Jones gives women a strong role, though not an entirely positive one; as Pamela Fox remarks, 'women bear the brunt of Jones's anxieties about class difference'. He provides a striking instance of a curiously repetitive feature of many of these novels that needs considering – the motif of the lost sister. She might marry a wastrel (*Chwalfa*), join a shop (*Traed mewn Cyffion*), disappear to London (*Times Like These*), become an opera singer (*Bidden to the Feast* – but there one other sister stays at home) or, as in *Cwmardy*, be made pregnant and die in childbirth. Only F. J. Child's collection of the traditional English and Scottish ballads has so many mislaid maidens. There are some resemblances here to the treatment of Catherine in *Germinal* and Jurgis's wife in Upton Sinclair's *The Jungle*, but the feature seems more likely to be a complex response to a real context than a mere literary tradition; it is a response which recognizes the crucial role played by women in industrial society, yet finds it impossible to relocate the novel away from the dominance of male gender issues – as Dorothy Hewett was able to do in *Bobbin Up* (1959), where the setting is a Sydney textile factory in which almost all the workers are women. Presumably, the inability to dispense with a male-gendered focus is the reason for the contradictory way in which many industrial writers recognize the reality of an active female presence but also dispose of it by narrative devices to concentrate on the men. Even though Kate Roberts focuses her novel firmly in the home and makes the female relationships very important, there is still a thread of masculine authority, of recurrent narrative interest, that runs in *Traed mewn Cyffion* from the dying father through to the surviving son.

The political events in and around Tonypandy from about 1900 to the mid-1930s are recounted through *Cwmardy* and *We Live*, though the thrust is general rather than specific: the miners join the union after the major strike and this is not historically true, but a way of asserting that only the radical and combative union of the post-1912 period was in Jones's eyes the proper kind of federation for fighting the workers' cause. Len Roberts, the hero, is similarly constructed as an ideal figure: physically weak and studious, he is able to master the necessary political literature, but he is also an instinctive leader and speaker, realizing in this the concept that true revolution comes from the rank and file's instinctive political awakening and their workplace combination. This idea is much closer to the syndicalism that was widespread in the south Wales coalfield, and that inspired the crucial statement *The Miners' Next Step* in 1912, than to the idea of the centralized power of the Communist Party line that both Jones and *We Live* officially espoused.

Local as its tendencies might sometimes be, the text is not only about the situation in Wales: socialism is international in this context and an important moment is when Len, with very little support in the valley, resists the call to support the war. In *We Live*, the story moves on to deal with Spain, where Len himself dies – a moving prediction of Jones's own death from a heart attack after giving many speeches to street-meetings on behalf of the Spanish government and against the right-wing insurgents there (as described by Dai Smith in his Introduction to the 1978 reprint of *Cwmardy*). Jones did not live to complete the text, though apparently his notes were the basis of the conclusion, where a political collective, prominent among them the surviving Roberts family, realizes its continuing vitality by a march of 'common unity' and the singing of the Red Flag – a conclusion that might seem rosy rather than red, and less dialectic than Jones himself might have written.

Reprinted as a leftist classic, and the most directly activist of all the proletarian texts apart from the later works of 'Mikhail Sholokov', the book has been criticized by Frank Kermode in *History and Value* (1988) for its alleged naivety and formal clumsiness; from a different political viewpoint, Ian Haywood has found *We Live* 'less satisfactory' than *Cwmardy* because 'its structure is virtually cleansed of contradiction'. Carole Snee has taken the opposite line, charging *Cwmardy* with being complicit with the bourgeoisie through its family basis, and finding *We Live* a more satisfactorily collective work. John Pikoulis, however, has commented that the family scenes create a powerful imaginative counterpart to the political sequences. Whatever a literary critical judgement might be on Lewis Jones – and even an enthusiast like Pikoulis feels that 'Not all the writing convinces equally' – it is clear that his novels have survived to the present as texts with a conscious sense of radical weight. Harold Heslop in England and Lewis Grassic Gibbon in Scotland shared Jones's leftist convictions, but he is more directly and industrially politicized than Gibbon and more humanly interesting than Heslop. For those who are not put off by overt politics, Lewis Jones must remain one of the hero-workers of the industrial novel.

A less excitably positive account of the possibilities of the sociopolitical context appeared in Gwyn Jones's *Times Like These* (1936), a realistic account of life in the southern valleys from 1920 to the Labour government collapse in 1929. Luke, the protagonist, experiences unemployment and the death of his wife, themes that dominate the evanescent hopes and prosperities of that stark period. But this is ultimately not a politically focused story: Raymond Williams has commented that, in this novel, 'the family, always important in the Welsh tradition, becomes the only structure of real value, but it is more a refuge than a means of rectifying the situation'. This breadth also enables Gwyn Jones, as James A. Davies has noted, to produce 'one of the few Welsh

industrial novels to move beyond a relentless concern with
working-class life to the sympathetic portrayal of middle-class
characters, such as Shelton, the colliery agent, and Broddam, the
self-made Newport businessman'.

Overall this is a sombre and somewhat passive account, a novel
of exposition rather than engagement, and in that respect Jones
is like most of the contemporary leftist authors of industrial
fiction in England such as Walter Brierley or, a little later, Jack
Lindsay. Though there is something about early Merthyr and
Tredegar in his later novel *The Walk Home* (1962), Gwyn Jones
did not return to the industrial theme; he went on to a distinguished
literary and scholarly career, but there are few flourishes of art
in the solid, capable *Times Like These*. Its politics were admired:
Ralph Wright recommended it in the *Daily Worker* as 'just and
unexaggerated', yet by being so faithful to the novel form, so
full in its characterization, so cautiously judicious in its judgements, *Times Like These* seems to lack the vigour of other Welsh
industrial novels. The enthusiasms of *Black Parade*, the colloquial
intensity of *Traed mewn Cyffion* and the focused force of *We Live*
seem to escape the aesthetic limits and needs of the bourgeois-
novel form and stake out a new ground of passionately engaged
sociopolitical writing in fiction.

IV

The end of the 1930s brought an end to peace, unemployment and,
ultimately, the separately self-conscious mass working class. After
the war, welfarism, new media and growing prosperity drew the
sting of the protest novel. It seems therefore darkly appropriate
that the last Welsh working-class novel of the 1930s was that
thoroughgoing sentimentalization of a national image, Richard
Llewellyn's *How Green Was My Valley* (1939). Its title privileges
both individualism and nostalgia; personally owned in imagination, fertile in the past and the literary future, both the valley and
the story smoothly digest the motifs of the Welsh industrial
tradition, eschewing the hard elements of politics and pain for the
tasteful pleasures of nostalgia.

There can be no doubt this is a highly skilled piece of bookmaking, just as John Ford's film of the novel was brilliantly

effective – if facile stereotype and personalized sentiment are what you want. Ford's model was essentially his romanticized memory of an Irish past, and a similar displacement helped the novel's success in England, in part because it exploited a sense of quaint regionality, and in part because the real political dramas of the pre-war period were absorbed in terms of Welsh stereotypes and personal achievement, from mournful songsters to handsome young schoolboys. Raymond Williams pithily called the novel 'the export version of the Welsh industrial experience', and two recent essays by Ian A. Bell and John Harris have well described its inner speciousness and its highly skilful placing in the market by its publisher.

The fullest critique of the book has been offered by Dai Smith, writing as David Smith in 'Myth and meaning in the literature of the South Wales Coalfield'. Having contrasted the rave reviews from England with the sharper response in Wales – led by Keidrych Rhys's trenchant headline in *Wales* 'Ignore this Trash' – Smith notes the fact that little about work or actual union activity is represented in the novel and that, while it does offer 'an acknowledgement of injustice, a desire to see this rectified', it also insists on 'a rejection of any action beyond conciliatory dealings'. As a result, the novel becomes 'a homily on extremism, as reasonable methods of redressing grievances are spurned'. Smith notes the 'skill in presenting its imagery' and its power in 'myth-spinning', but argues that: 'Community is lauded only so long as it steers clear of that collectivity of spirit and of action which, in reality, proved the sole defence of coalfield society.' The climactic scene where the men of the Morgan family combine to act as strikebreakers to protect the mine-owner's equipment seems to support Smith's position with some force. His final judgement is firmly negative:

> As economics this is infantile, as history a falsification, as literature concerned with uncovering human dilemma on a societal whirligig, it is feeble, but as Romance, dealing in comforting stereotypes and concerned to tease out a thematic explanation of social disaster, it is perfect. The novel is not 'a dream' superimposed upon 'the South Wales Valleys' but a gargantuan con-trick that parcels out guilt and reduces human history to the emotional level of any tawdry Hollywood 'B' picture.

The novel is not so much apolitical as political against the struggles of the Welsh working class: it basically created a stereotype that could be said to have done significant harm to Wales over the years as a land of 'Black and White Taffy minstrels'. Peter Stead has argued against this view, suggesting the novel's romantic naivety is appropriate for the viewpoint of a child, and that it reworks the past in the light of the new prosperity of the very late 1930s, but most Welsh-based readings are a good deal more critical that Stead's, seeing the novel as more or less meretricious, more or less exploitative. No doubt the publisher's packaging had much to do with that effect: Llewellyn apparently wanted to call the book 'Slag', a title which would have cast a different light on the overall meaning of the narrative – yet it is also true that the saccharine title finally chosen does mesh with a good deal of the stereotypes and sentimental rhetoric in the text itself. Llewellyn went on to merchandise his technique more fully, especially in the book that appeared to relish the industrial emptiness of modern Wales, *Green, Green, My Valley Now* (1975).

Another writer in the same genre of regional nostalgia, Michael Gareth Llewelyn, produced in *The Aleppo Merchant* (1945) a highly successful post-war and more considered version of south Wales soap opera that is, with its rural images, village pubs and off-stage coal-mining, a strain-free version of Rhys Davies's *Jubilee Blues*. Michael Gareth Llewelyn also produced a more traditional mining saga with a focus on politics and education, *Far From Honour* (1949), a serious novel written in a tone much like that of *Times Like These*, but it was less well received, apparently not suiting the times and audience as well as the more whimsical and sentimental *The Aleppo Merchant*. Against the primarily tourist tracts of Llewellyn and Llewelyn, the slightly later historical industrial novels of Alexander Cordell, starting with *Rape of the Fair Country* (1959), seem at least related, if indirectly and in a highly coloured way, to the historical dramas of the Welsh working class. Cordell has been seen as 'a more than competent historian' by Chris Williams, himself a historian, and is also praised by the same scholar for being the first to argue, in fiction or in historical writing, that the Chartist disturbances at Newport in 1839 were in fact organized resistance rather than mere reaction to oppression. Cordell's knowledge of and sympathy with his topic are not in question, but the remorselessly hyperbolic tone of the novels and the consistent use of cartoonish Welsh clichés in language and stereotype cut them off from the stark and painful actuality of real industrial experiences: the father is inevitably both morally admirable and a superman at fighting; the daughters are richly stereotypical in both emotionality and bosom. Though Raymond Williams praised Cordell's sense of 'a history both wide and intense', he was surely right also to call them 'headline novels', notable for their simplicity. While Cordell's novels may disseminate some of the fantasized past of Welsh industry they have little to do with its challenging present at any time – though they have stimulated similar fictions, historical romances by women writers, like *The Smouldering Hills* (1996) by Celia Jones, set in Dowlais, *A Fierce Flame* by Tydfil Thomas (1997), set in Merthyr, or the highly successful Swansea-based series by Iris Gower, beginning with *Copper Kingdom* (1983), on the development of the metallic industries in the late nineteenth century and extending through six novels to *Black Gold* (1988), set during the General Strike of 1926. Melodramatic as Gower's series is both in terms of events and the characters' responses to them, it also combines the familiar masculine industrial dramas with an unusual and often strongly credible, if also highly coloured, account of the way women lived, survived and sometimes triumphed in the difficult industrial world.

English reviewers tended to read all post-war Welsh fiction as quaint, whether in fact nostalgia or not. That reaction notably belittled Menna Gallie's novel *Strike for a Kingdom* (1959), published, like Gwyn Thomas's works, by Gollancz. The *Times Literary Supplement*, at its most condescending, felt that she was 'Fresh and beguiling from the land of her fathers', and would 'delight all those who take pleasure in the seedy skylarks of Mr Gwyn Thomas's voters or who kindle to the elfland music of *bach* and *bachgen i*'. The condescension, as usual, combines with ignorance, as is indicated in the unmutated form of 'bachgen': *The Times* does not show such cultural discourtesy towards more highly valued European languages.

Strike for a Kingdom is an account of 1926, set in Cilhendre (a fictionally named version of Gallie's native Ystradgynlais), and mediated through village lives, especially those of women; it also, as if having limited confidence in the political genre itself, shapes itself around a mysterious death. Humour and gossip are central to the style, and while there is a continuity with Jack Jones's communal and familial approach, and also with his male-centred ideology, Gallie's novels are less politically unfocused and a good deal more formally structured than are Jones's. They interpret the effects of political action in social contexts and, while one of her strengths is her representation of a range of credible women characters who are involved in social and political life, she also realizes clearly the forces of the material world that act upon them: the mine-manager, it is remarked, 'has been murdered by economic conditions'. In her later book *The Small Mine* (1962), Gallie concentrates more on human relations in the context of a pit village, and though both humour and politics are reduced in impact, she thought this was her best work. Jane Aaron, in her 'Foreword' to the reprint, has argued persuasively that Gallie represents the past and the present of mining in the private 'small mine' and the nationalized large pit, both in the same village, and that she uses the central incident, the death of a miner, as the focus for a broad and sensitive sociocultural study: 'this is the story not so much of an individual death as of a representative Valley community, and in particular its womenfolk, as they struggle to come to terms with the sudden catastrophic loss.'

Gallie's other Welsh-related novel, *Man's Desiring* (1960), withdraws from the industrial tradition into another area of characteristically Welsh labour, offering a saga of a collier lad who becomes a young academic. A major strength of Gallie's writing in her industrial fiction is her power of intimate realization: as Raymond Stephens noted in an essay on her work: 'Her miners have elements in common with the faces and figures of Josef Herman's miners, but more energetic and fluid, less monumental and grim, the contours relaxing'. Stephens also notes Gallie's social rather than simply political values, commenting that 'Menna Gallie is, both in private life and in her novels, haunted by the desire for the good community'. In spite of seeing these strong points, Stephens feels she does not pursue far enough the ethical centre of her work, and thinks she avoids this, for example, by killing off before the end her focal character Joe in *The Small Mine*, and using comic names and wry ironies that verge close to what Stephens considers as 'the sad case of Gwyn Thomas'. However, as I have argued, these features may well now seem dynamic, ways in which Gallie tends to resist the simplistic closures of the conventional novel of character and uses means of constructing novels that operate both as sociopolitical statements and as that unusual phenomenon, industrially based work by a woman writer.

Gallie wrote these books and her later, often very amusing, novels outside Wales as she moved about with her academic husband. This mobility out of the industrial areas was common enough among well-educated Welsh women and men, but Menna Gallie casts her fiction, at least at first, strongly back to the area of her first political experiences. The different viewpoint of an outsider gives an equally powerful, but more fully analytic vigour to Margot Heinemann's unjustly forgotten *The Adventurers* (1960). A Cambridge English graduate and committed leftist, she used her long experience of journalism, unions and left politics in a novel which starts by tracing the movements of Dan Owen, who resists conscription into the mines during the Second World War, as he – and especially his mother – have higher aspirations. Dan becomes a successful and somewhat cynical journalist in London, but the book increasingly revisits Abergoch to explore the increasing problems both of the coal industry and of the left. It ends with the men of Abergoch – without Dan – facing a doubtful future with their values intact: they, it seems, may be the true 'adventurers' of the title – and Heinemann is evidently aware of the implications of *coch* (red), in the place name. Andy Croft has shown how Heinemann uses the mining industry as both a reality and an evaluative focus to trace the downward course of the British left from 1943, the height of the second-front agitation, to the difficult post-Krushchev and post-Hungary years. *The Adventurers*, in one sense a novel which is not about industrial Wales but rather uses it as a point of narrative departure and evaluative reference, as I have discussed elsewhere, also displays considerable political weight and expertise, and has a rare perspective in its capacity to deal convincingly with political perceptions about and influences on the mining industry in Wales.

As retrospective as Gallie and as political as Heinemann, but based in traditional discourses – male, political and Welsh language – is a sequence of emotive historical treatments by Rhydwen Williams, whose novels revisit dramas of the past with the eye and ear of a poet. He wrote mostly in Welsh, and is very little known outside the country, though *The Angry Vineyard*

(1975) appeared first in English. In this powerful book, Williams mixes the media of fact and fiction to realize the dramatic events and political contexts of the Merthyr Rising of 1831. Donald Evans described the book in positive terms: 'Wholehearted imaginative sympathy is shown with the close-knitted common people in scene after scene of strife, extreme distress and heart-rending deaths.' Williams focuses in particular on the execution of Dic Penderyn. This is, he says in his foreword,

> not a requiem for a dead man of a bygone century, but a testimony to certain values that have outlived the ironmasters and their industries and most of the acrid wastes they left behind.

Williams refers warmly to the work of Gwyn Alf Williams as a 'people's remembrancer' in this foreword, and has himself also fulfilled that role in his Welsh-language writing, dealing with the Rhondda in the *Cwm Hiraeth* ('Valley of Longing') series (1970–3) and, most potent of all, with the Senghennydd disaster of 1913 in *Amser i Wylo* ('A Time to Weep'; 1986). What in sentimentalized terms can be nostalgia – a marketable commodity as Llewellyn, Cordell and Gower have shown – can in more rigorous forms be the construction of race memory, a form of radical stimulation to which Rhydwen Williams devoted himself with impressive impact. This was a mode towards which Raymond Williams moved in his last years – his unfinished *Black Mountains* novels, while tracing Welsh history forward from the first inhabitation, would have in finished form contained extensive material realizing the industrial communities, in something of the spirit of Rhydwen Williams.

In both criticism and fiction, Raymond Williams has spoken on the modern Welsh situation of declining heavy industry and rapidly changing politics. Two essays deal with the topic – 'The Welsh industrial novel' (1979) and 'Working-class, proletarian, socialist: problems in some Welsh novels' (1982). He has also dealt with the theme, in varying degrees, in five novels. Three are a sequence, *Border Country* (1960), *Second Generation* (1964) and *The Fight for Manod* (1979), in which, with some overlap of characters and themes, but no constraining sequential plot, Williams deals with the major issues of the 1926 strike, the Welsh diaspora into English industry, and the possibility of new-style industries and social forces in Wales – all the time using his narrator's voice to locate these dramas in the context of European political and cultural thought, that discourse so familiar from Williams's scholarly writing. Two other novels deal to a considerable degree with Welsh politics and people, but in different time-frame: in *The Volunteers* (1978) Williams writes of a dystopic near future, but in *Loyalties* (1985) his focus is firmly on the past.

The style of Williams's novels has seemed to some critics deliberately repressed in emotional terms, and sometimes, as in *Loyalties*, it can seem clumsy, but at basis Williams's plain style is itself a comment on and a contribution to the tradition of Welsh industrial writing. Smith reports that Williams 'took a deliberate decision to avoid the rhetorical excesses often seen as marking out an "Anglo-Welsh" school'. All of Williams's novels have a recurrent concern with an increasingly dispossessed Welsh working class, from the defeated railway strikers of *Border Country* and the expatriate car-workers of *Second Generation*, to the noble but sidelined artisans of *Loyalties*. These figures retain the traditions of resistance and political comprehension that were developed in the industrial cauldron of south Wales, but the ineffective nature of their action responds both to the growing conservatism of the period in which Williams wrote these books and also, it might seem, to his own theory-pure but politically distant situation in Cambridge. Another feature which makes the novels, particularly *Loyalties*, seem somewhat outdated is what Gwyneth Roberts has identified as the fact that for Williams, '"community" as portrayed in his novels is a gender-specific concept, in that it rests upon the twin pillars of masculine work and close involvement in socialist politics'. The effort in *Second Generation* to write a substantial part for a woman, who is both intellectually active and moving towards emotional independence, seems neither fully successful in terms of the novel – Kate never seems to be more than a male projection of a dissident voice, rather than a credibly female representation – nor a new orientation in Williams's approach to gender. It should, though, be noted that H. Gustav Klaus considers that in *People of the Black Mountains*, Williams 'displays a far greater sensitivity to the subordinate position of women in history and the imperatives of gender'.

If the novel of traditional politics and male community seemed to become decreasingly potent in Williams's hands, in later life he both physically and conceptually returned to Wales and Welsh themes, and such a movement by an inquiring intellectual is basic to the structure of his fullest statement about post-industrial Wales, *The Fight for Manod*. This novel looks forward with concern to a world where Wales is subject to European-monitored, Whitehall-condoned international exploitation – a world that is now clearly visible along the M4. In *The Fight for Manod*, industry is based in electronics and information, and old structures of political organization seem irrelevant; the novel traces with acuity and honesty both the difficulty and the seriousness of Williams's effort to describe the complexity and the dangers of the modern Wales, much changed from the world of the Great Strike, that world which both he and his narrator left behind in *Border Country*.

Williams renewed his inquiry in a different genre in *The Volunteers*; while this is primarily a politically chilling piece of near-futurism, it both looks back for value to past political struggles and also suggests that future politics may need to be outside traditional forms. The novel vests its only positive hope in a political and even violent resistance that runs very close to terrorism, validated by the stand of south Wales miners against Whitehall manipulation: a crucial scene takes place as miners picket a coal-depot and troops move in. This is a modernized but still traditional Welsh drama that Williams finds much more compelling and dialectically valuable than what he sees as the quasi-communal fictionality of the Welsh Folk Museum at St Fagans (now the Museum of Welsh Life): as a whole the novel asserts that, through the mazes of modern mediation, there is a source of value in traditional politics of the left.

The Volunteers, by using the thriller genre as its structure, seems able to be both more mobile in its imagination and sharper in its political critique than the more realist texts and it is notably more effective and nimble than *Loyalties*, which reviews various forms of leftism but seems, like the strikers of 1984 (when it was being written), to come to no more than a dead end. It may be that *Loyalties* suffers from not having been rewritten and rethought as much as was normal with Williams's fiction, or it may simply share the deep pessimism on the left in the mid-1980s. Its strongest points are the elegiac treatment of the past, and this points forward to Williams's unfinished project, the 'Black Mountains

Trilogy', a historical survey of human life in his own part of Wales, from the earliest inhabitants to the present, a treatment that confirms Williams's movement away from realist fictions, like the path taken by both Gwyn Thomas and Menna Gallie.

V

That sense that realism alone cannot give a true enough account of the present situation is also evident in Welsh writers who deal with the post-industrial scene. Widely perceived as contemporary threats are the anomie and violence that rise from de-skilling and worklessness in areas long dependent on heavy and well-paid labour to support the ideals of social coherence and masculine self-fulfilment. A number of recent novels have realized this disturbing world. The sense of alienation that is archetypally expressed in Alan Sillitoe's *Saturday Night and Sunday Morning* (1958) is found in Christopher Meredith's account of the collapsing south Wales steel industry, *Shifts* (1988), by an author who also has considerable standing as a poet. One of the two central male characters is a hedonistic man between youth and middle age, lacking now any affiliation to place or person; but the friend with whom he stays on his return to Wales encounters aspects of past community in his rediscovery of local history and possible renewal in Welsh-language culture. Powerful emphasis falls on a sense of negative change in the area: between the steelworks scenes and a disjointed social and domestic life (where neither man manages to satisfy the amateur historian's wife), the novel realizes a state of industrial, social, and therefore personal, disintegration, asking, as Ioan Williams put it in a review of the novel, 'How do people cope who are caught up in one of these incomprehensible historical shifts which topple economic superstructures and distort the emotional patterns which shape their inner experience?'

John L. Hughes's *Before the Crying Stops* (1986) has some relationship with *Shifts*, being a sharp-edged account of life without work in Pontypridd, a novel modernist both in its technique and its nihilist themes, but both more materialistic and more clearly a reversal of collier heroics is Duncan Bush's *Glass Shot* (1991), a novel that can be described variously as urban realism, dark romance and an ultra-modern thriller. It certainly makes use of some of the forms of the criminal-focused psycho-thriller, but it is also conscious of its position as a negative reflex of industrial fiction. The anti-hero is a strong-willed, strong-bodied young man who can only find trivial manual work as a tyre-fitter. His derailed energies flow over into violence and malice and, in a fine scene, as he roars around south Wales in his large car, he passes a pit where the miners, some of the last left now, are on strike. But his glance at them is distant; the connection between male vigour and industrial work has been broken, to the detriment of both.

A further stage in post-industrial writing, now only symbolically linked to the world of communal work and struggle, is to be seen in some recent novels that explore, through notably powerful plots and language, the isolation of young people in modern Welsh towns, and their attempts to reconstruct social contacts and networks. It is striking that two of these novels, Lewis Davies's *My Piece of Happiness* (2000) and Richard Evans's *Entertainment* (2001), both focus on a character who is disabled: the literal problems of a mentally handicapped youth and a young man in a wheelchair are symbolic nodes of meaning for the incapacities of modern Wales – and yet in neither story has character or text given up: these are challenges that a life might be made and a community reassembled in the wake of the industrial holocaust of the 1980s. Other treatments are more fully negative, like Ed Thomas's play, and then film, *The House of America* (1994), which explores together a set of modern transitions: from communal pit into mechanized open-cut mine, from productive work into drug-drenched idleness, and from operative nuclear family into distressed mutual aggression. At the end of the film, one character, his youth symbolized in the name Boyo, leaves to work in England as so many fictional characters, and indeed real people, did in the past, and much the same negative spirit pervades Rachel Trezise's austere girl's-eye view of the modern valleys *In and Out of the Goldfish Bowl* (2000) and Desmond Barry's myth-inspired *A Bloody Good Friday* (2002).

Other post-industrial writers continue to honour the memory, and celebrate the surviving values, of the industrial world now lost. As time passes, and tips have become almost green, and writers like Jack Jones and Gwyn Thomas seem themselves to have been levelled from literary memory, there continue to appear fictions that refer in memorial reverence and retrospective anger to the industrial reality of the past, that rue both the absence and the aftermath of the dramatic, dangerous but also vibrant world of industrial Wales. Until his death in 1997, Ron Berry continued to write short stories about the coalfield, and some directly about mining itself, like the ironic reminiscences of 'Comrades in Arms' (1995). In much of his work he, like Alun Richards, uses an industrial backdrop for male self-discovery, as in *Hunters and Hunted* (1960) or *Flame and Slag* (1968), but, not long before he died, he published his major industrial novel *This Bygone* (1996).

Like many others in the genre, this is a pit-village *Bildungs-roman*, but instead of deploying the overfleshed fathers, domestic-ally labouring madonnas and dust-spattered temptresses of the usual valleys saga, Berry makes his hero a somewhat self-seeking young man who, in vividly realized wartime, goes by way of a love affair with an older woman on to a minor success in small-time mine ownership. John Pikoulis has spoken in very positive terms of the book, saying that 'only in Lewis Jones' *Cwmardy* has pit life been so authentically realised', and Berry's work in general, in both its unsentimental themes and his potently colloquial style, shapes one of the strongest contributions, if an inevitably retro-spective one, to Welsh industrial fiction: Alun Richards, himself a chronicler of the social life of the post-industrial world, in reviewing Berry's posthumously published autobiography, says that it was 'his dedication to the truth in relating the history of broken lives which made him unique'.

Less energetic but still effective versions of this approach have been offered by other recent writers. In *The Drift* (1974), Aldryd Haines looks back to the early 1950s to interweave evenly the story of a young man's interest in mining, sport and girls with his awakening, and eventually dominating, interest in politics and education. Robert Morgan has published several collections of retrospective mining stories, and his novel *In the Dark* (1994) is notable for its calm but also biting effect in conveying vignettes of valley life. Other writers have addressed quite directly the dramatic circumstances under which the coalfield was effectively silenced in 1984. Tom Davies's *Black Sunlight* (1986) is a Jack Jones-esque saga of valleys life updated to the 1980s with delinquent youths, women moving towards independence, and a sense of growing crisis for an upper Rhondda community, modelled on Maerdy.

The miners' strike of 1984 is the climax of the drama, and no way forward is envisaged for characters or community, in spite of a somewhat mystical element focusing on the modern motif of a charismatic disabled character. A later treatment of the strike is less emotional, though no more positive. In *Dark Edge* (1997), Roger Granelli deals directly with the confrontation of working-men in pits and police-lines by making his hero, the thinking collier Edwin, half-brother to a thuggish, even sociopathic, policeman, Elliott. The encounter is well developed in personal and social terms, and Elliott's wife plays an important role as a participant in the political action and also as an interpreter of the situation – which ends in something like personal stalemate as well as industrial decay. A less direct treatment of a strike is offered in Russell Celyn Jones's well-received novel *An Interference of Light* (1995), which transposes the spirit of the earlier Great Strike on the slate-field to the late 1930s. In an essentially post-modern mode, Jones uses history as a lens for examining memory, human interaction and the disturbing presence of the writer as spy; industry is not a primary topic and, in fact, is most important as a source of metaphor, as in the title, which emotionally generalizes a slate-miner's technique for judging rock.

The male dominance of industrial writing is evident from the authors' names, but just as a few women like Kate Roberts, Menna Gallie and Margot Heinemann realized the industrial world while it thrived, women's voices are still heard in fiction in the aftermath – indeed some have been a good deal closer to the old spirit of resistance than the somewhat gloomy and accusatory tone of Granelli, Davies and, in his more distanced way, Meredith. Catherine Merriman's *State of Desire* (1996) is in part about a woman's emotional and sexual reawakening after her husband's death, but Merriman makes it quite clear by the way she inter-weaves the narrative strands that a major element of Jenny's new life is her dedicated and successful engagement in fighting an environmentally destructive plan for open-cast mining in the southern uplands. With something of the vigour that surges through Jill Miller's powerful account of the women's support groups of 1984 in *You Can't Kill the Spirit* (1986), and with a less romanticized sense of women's contribution than Iris Gower, Merriman imagines a world where women take a lead in assess -ing and containing the powers of industrialization; the male characters, whether sexually exciting or bloodlessly contemptible, are allotted a second place. Where male authors often end with a single male figure who leaves the valley or stays there feeling defeated, Merriman, like Roberts and Gallie, suggests that lives, commitment, resistance, must continue. That position may well signal the future of a new kind of post-industrial fiction, similar to the renovation of the private-eye novel in recent years and seen in many of the recent women-only short-story collections, as women writers – not unlike the mothers and sisters of the foregrounded men in the classic texts – combine human sensitivity with a stronger sense of political endurance than their male counterparts have sometimes shown.

VI

The industrial novel in Wales, and indeed around the world, has always had an odd, uneasy status, in substantial part negotiating between difficult writing conditions and the tastes of middle-class readers. Now that productive industry itself has largely gone, a position has emerged from which the types and the functions of the industrial novel can be identified and assessed. Among the international versions there can be little doubt that the Welsh contribution is one of the fullest, most varied and most forcefully creative of a consciousness both national and political, a point noted by David Bell when he speaks of 'the predominance of Welsh writers among the miner novelists'.

Apart from its substantial size, the Welsh tradition is notable for a number of things – its radical vigour; the unusual extent to which it internalizes the viewpoint within the class without Zolaesque outsiders as interpreters; the distinct emphasis – within some limits – on the role of women in proletarian life; the marked and unusual degree to which rural themes are often involved. The formal problems of the industrial novel were explored boldly by the Welsh writers and some interesting resolutions were offered, ranging from programmatic politics, through complex hybridized texts, to an inward personal response. The themes involved also appeared, in nationally characteristic mode, in idea-oriented poetry. Idris Davies's poem sequence *The Angry Summer* (1943) is one of the finest narrative texts of the period, representing the responses of ordinary people in subtly and firmly heightened form, with the poet's power to go straight to the distilled thematic summary – it is for this reason that Dafydd Johnston (1993) has likened the poem's effect to that of Gwyn Thomas's *All Things Betray Thee*.

Some major Welsh-language poets dealt with the industrial theme. 'Gwenallt' (David Gwenallt Jones), whose father was splashed to death in a Pontardawe steelworks, produced a number of lyrics both angry and anguished about the impact of the modernized world on human and spiritual life. J. Kitchener Davies wrote – as well as the controversial play *Cwm Glo*, referred to above – the major poem sequence *Sŵn y Gwynt sy'n Chwythu* (The Sound of the Wind that is Blowing), which uses industrial Wales as the context for its moral and religious themes, as does Saunders Lewis in his deeply negative 'Y Dilyw, 1939' (1941). This grim mood is shared by the considerable number of English-language poets who have written about the industrial aftermath in recent years; John Gurney's *Coal: A Sonnet Sequence* (1994) is a major statement, and poems looking back at the industrial world, its pains and also its values, have come from Duncan Bush, Chris Meredith, Leslie Norris, Huw Watkins and Harri Webb.

In the context of these poetic voices, it is appropriate and also comprehensible to note that in comparison with the product of other nations in this genre, the Welsh industrial novels in both languages provide a sense of literary, even poetic, spirit and conscious idealism stronger than that found in most of the other national cultures (though the Russians are a challenge here); and, perhaps the deepest-seated feature of all – and without any real parallel elsewhere – they are in almost all cases outstanding in humour, both broad and ironic.

Dai Smith has implicitly asked why industrial Wales did not produce a great novelist, the equivalent of Tolstoy or Conrad. Considering the short history of the context, and its lack of leisured practices of reading and writing, such a writer or novel would be hard to conceive, or even to see as appropriate. The achievement of the Welsh industrial novel is – with an authentic touch of democracy and social spirit – communally broad and mobile, not individualistically deep and static. Of about twenty major landmarks in the international working-class novel, that is novels that define the possibilities and test the limits of the form, the Welsh writers have provided about a quarter. They could also claim, if shame permitted, to have produced some major examples of the selling-out of the working-class novel to commercial interests in writing about this distant world in comfortingly touristic and quaintly delightful terms.

I would judge those leading radical texts to be *Black Parade*, *Cwmardy*, *Traed mewn Cyffion*, *Sorrow for Thy Sons* and *The Angry Vineyard*, with *The Fight for Manod* as a possible addition and *This Bygone* as a remarkable retrospective creation. In the category of melodramatic and England-oriented commercial reworking of the tradition – or, as a Gwyn Thomas character might put it, saleable sell-out – I would nominate as leading examples *How Green Was My Valley*, *The Aleppo Merchant*, *Rape of the Fair Country* and their authors' later works; I would feel that the inherent commitment to country and people rescues *Bidden to the Feast* and *Copper Kingdom* from that negative judgement. And there are other, more complex successes: I would see *All Things Betray Thee*, *The World Cannot Hear You*, *A Time to Laugh*, *Strike for a Kingdom* and *Chwalfa* as novels that transmit the intensity and vigour of the industrial situation in spite of some formal, generic and, to some extent, thematic distancing from the primary industrial focus.

The Welsh writers have also produced fine examples of genuinely post-industrial fiction, with *Shifts*, *Glass Shot* and *House of America* as major achievements. But their authors are not alone: in poetry, film and fiction, including new perspectives in women's writing, Welsh authors continue to revisit and to revalue the dramas of a century of major industrialization. Against the productivity and the achievement of the Welsh writers, English and Scottish industrial novels appear a good deal less varied in kind and less vigorous in style, and the American and Australian repertoires, while full of intriguing books, are not as coherent in theme, as experimental in form nor as recurrently and determinedly radical as the industrial fictions generated in and about Wales.

The tradition of the Welsh working-class novel is one worth honouring and remembering, and one with values that remain potent. The valleys may indeed be grassy again, but their story was often vividly red, and the values of the fictional achievement remain evergreen. Nearly a century after industrial fiction appeared in Wales, it is proper and, in some nationally conscious sense, crucial to recall that in fiction at least, the Welsh were able to release their feet from the stocks of history and, in spite of a sense that all things betray thee, were able to strike for their kingdom, responding in a black parade to the upheaval that came upon them at the dialectical feast to which they were unwittingly bidden; in times like these, full of sorrow for their sons, and indeed their daughters too, telling the story of communities like Cwmardy, the achievement of the Welsh industrial writers is to have asserted that, in spite of the darkness of the world of industrial Wales and its social and human oppressions, through the resistance of art and politics, we live.

NOTE

This chapter is written in memory of my three great-uncles who died at Senghennydd, 14 October 1913.

Warm thanks are due to James A. Davies, Katie Gramich, H. Gustav Klaus and M. Wynn Thomas for their generous contribution to the process of producing it.

FURTHER READING

David Bell, *Ardent Propaganda: Miners' Novels and Class Conflict* (Umea, 1995).

Ian A. Bell, 'How green *was* my valley?' *Planet*, 73 (1992), 3–9.

Tony Brown, Review of Christopher Meredith, *Shifts*, *New Welsh Review*, 3 (1988), 77–8.

James A. Davies, 'Kinds of relating: Gwyn Thomas (Jack Jones, Lewis Jones, Gwyn Jones) and the Welsh industrial experience', *Anglo-Welsh Review*, 86 (1987), 72–86.

James A. Davies, '"Two Strikes and You're Out": 1926 and 1984 in Welsh industrial fiction', in H. Gustav Klaus and Stephen Knight (eds), *British Industrial Fictions* (Cardiff, 2000), 137–47.

Hywel Teifi Edwards, 'The Welsh collier as hero: 1850–1950', *Welsh Writing in English*, 2 (1996), 22–48.

Keri Edwards, *Jack Jones* (Cardiff, 1974).

Donald Evans, *Rhydwen Williams* (Cardiff, 1991).

Howard Fast, *Literature and Reality* (New York, 1950).

Pamela Fox, *Class Fictions: Shame and Resistance in the British Working-Class Novel, 1890–1945* (Durham, 1994).

Victor Golightly, 'Gwyn Thomas's American "Oscar"', *New Welsh Review*, 22 (1993), 26–31.

Victor Golightly, '"We, Who Speak for the Workers": the correspondence of Gwyn Thomas and Howard Fast', *Welsh Writing in English*, 6 (2000), 67–88.

Katie Gramich, 'Introduction' to *Queen of the Rushes* (repr. Dinas Powys, 1998).

John Harris, 'Not only a place in Wales', *Planet*, 73 (1992), 10–15.

Ian Haywood, *Working-Class Fiction* (Plymouth, 1997).

Dafydd Johnston, Review of Idris Davies, *The Angry Summer: A Poem of 1926*, ed. Tony Conran, *New Welsh Review*, 21 (1993), 16–18.

Bill Jones and Chris Williams, *B. L. Coombes* (Cardiff, 1999).

Glyn Jones, *The Dragon Has Two Tongues* (London, 1968).

Katie Jones, Review of Gwyn Thomas, *Selected Stories*, *New Welsh Review*, 3 (1988), 75–7.

Noragh Jones, 'Comforts and discomforts of home', *Planet*, 107 (1994), 75–82.

R. Gerallt Jones, 'An introduction to the work of Kate Roberts', *Anglo-Welsh Review*, 9 (1958), 10–21.

Roger Stephens Jones, 'Absurdity in the novels of Gwyn Thomas', *Anglo-Welsh Review*, 25 (1975), 43–52.

Frank Kermode, *History and Value* (Oxford, 1988).

H. Gustav Klaus, 'The border fiction of Raymond Williams', in *Literature of Region and Nation: Proceedings of the 6th International Literature of Region and Nation Conference* (Saint John, Canada, 1998), Vol. I, 329–43.

Stephen Knight, '". . . the hesitations and uncertainties that were the truth": three women writers of Welsh industrial fiction', in H. Gustav Klaus and Stephen Knight (eds), *British Industrial Fictions* (Cardiff, 2000), 163–80.

Stephen Knight, '"Not a place for me": Rhys Davies's fictions and the coal industry', in Meic Stephens (ed.), *Decoding the Hare* (Cardiff, 2001), pp. 54–70.

Stephen Knight, 'The voices of Glamorgan: Gwyn Thomas's colonial fiction', *Welsh Writing in English*, 7 (2001), 16–34.

Chris Meredith, 'Two from the heart', *Planet*, 59 (1986), 98–9.

Ian Michael, *Gwyn Thomas* (Cardiff, 1977).

Michael Parnell, *Laughter in the Dark: A Life of Gwyn Thomas* (London, 1988; repr. Bridgend, 1997).

John Pikoulis, 'Lewis Jones', *Anglo-Welsh Review*, 74 (1983), 62–71.

John Pikoulis, 'The wounded bard,' *New Welsh Review*, 26 (1994), 22–34.

John Pikoulis, 'Word-of-mouth cultures cease in cemeteries', *New Welsh Review* 34 (1996), 9–15.

Alun Richards, Review of Ron Berry, *History Is What You Live*, *New Welsh Review*, 41 (1998), 78–9.

Gwyneth Roberts, 'The cost of community: women in Raymond Williams's fiction', in Jane Aaron et al. (eds), *Our Sisters' Land: The Changing Identities of Women in Wales* (Cardiff, 1994), pp. 214–27.

Dai Smith, 'Introduction' to *Cwmardy* (repr., London, 1978).

Dai Smith, 'Myth and meaning in the literature of the South Wales coalfield', *Anglo-Welsh Review*, 25 (1975), 21–42.

Dai Smith, 'The Welsh Identity of Raymond Williams', *Planet* 76 (1989), 88–98.

Dai Smith, 'The Early Gwyn Thomas', *Transactions of the Honourable Society of Cymmrodorion* (1985), 71–89.

Carole Snee, 'Working-Class Literature or Proletarian Writing?', in Jon Clark et al. (eds), *Culture and Crisis in Britain in the Thirties* (London, 1979), pp. 165–91.

Peter Stead, 'How green is my valley now?', *New Welsh Review*, 15 (1991–2), 4–9.

Raymond Stephens, 'The novelist and community: Menna Gallie', *Anglo-Welsh Review*, 14 (1964–5), 52–63.

M. Wynn Thomas, *Internal Difference: Writing in Twentieth-Century Wales* (Cardiff, 1992).

Ned Thomas, *The Welsh Extremist* (2nd edn, Talybont, 1991).

Chris Williams, 'Master of a lost past', *Planet*, 121 (1997), 12–18.

Ioan Williams, 'Forms of Living', *Planet*, 73 (1988), 95.

Raymond Williams, *The Welsh Industrial Novel* (Cardiff, 1979).

Raymond Williams, 'Working class, proletarian, socialist: problems in some Welsh novels', in H. Gustav Klaus (ed.), *The Socialist Novel in Britain* (Brighton, 1982), pp. 110–21.

Raymond Williams, 'Introduction' to Gwyn Thomas, *All Things Betray Thee* (repr. London, 1986).

CHAPTER 3

BORDERERS AND BORDERLINE CASES

JOHN POWELL WARD

Literature came out of the England–Wales border strip long before the twentieth century. If some scholars are correct, it was in the Wirral that Gawain met his adversary the Green Knight, making that anonymous poem an early border classic. During the civil wars of the seventeenth century, when Wales was largely pro-monarchist, the twins Henry and Thomas Vaughan fought side by side in a bloody battle at Rowton Heath outside Chester, and the mystic Thomas Traherne virtually certainly resided in or very near Hereford when that city was besieged and changed hands. The nineteenth-century English, Matthew Arnold and Lionel Johnson prominently, discovered or invented the Celtic Twilight in the same era as the National Eisteddfod rebuilt itself in a new resurgence; and the same period, of course, yields up familiar names like Gerard Manley Hopkins and Francis Kilvert. Before all this came the Roman occupation, an event to which more than one border writer attends.

But as to the literary imagination, within Britain as a whole, the England–Wales border is a special case. From the Welsh point of view we are the Celts crammed in and up front; the English neighbour is large and the border near. It is a long way, even by today's standards, from Hadrian's Wall to the English heartland, while close to the boundary itself the terrain is much the same both sides. And Dublin sits away across a sizeable sea. Indeed, it is ironic that Ulster loyalists are separated from England by water while Welsh nationalists are a short car-drive away. Scotland and Ireland, in short, can still feel distant geographically.

Yet the England–Wales border terrain itself slightly compounds this picture. In the twentieth century, with real military activity (the Norman castles and Roundheads–Cavaliers) long over, and in contrast to the distractions of Scottish oil-based aspirations north and the Irish 'troubles' west, we have come to project a certain vision on the land which stretches from the Severn to the Dee. Its topography still changes sharply, in that short distance from bleak infertile uplands to open pastures and wooded plains, and that depends on which country you are in. But that meant, all the more, that in the terms of the Irishman Edmund Burke, you could have the sublimity without the pain. This is the land of Housman's 'blue remembered hills', the paintings of Turner and Wilson Steer, and the pastoral song-settings of Edward Elgar and Ralph Vaughan Williams. In fact, all that is already changing somewhat too. Two massive single-span Severn bridges to the south, the huge Connah's Quay power station at the northern tip, and every kind of electronic technology buzzing quietly away in between, in small border towns and outlying converted barns. But of course, the twentieth-century English–Welsh border literature was already more mixed than its pastoral reputation suggests. The relative proximity, already mentioned, of this terrain to the big English cities, and even to the capital, led, in hindsight, to a hidden yet febrile sense of possibilities nearby, a mutual fertility and anxiety which could go into reverse as necessary, at any time. The English poet, painter or composer in the Black Mountains was just near enough home to incorporate the scenery as not too exotic, while the Welsh person could become Birmingham teacher or London journalist within a weekend's fairly easy distance. Put perhaps too simply: all England–Wales border writers are borderline cases, some merely more so than others. But the literary results from so unpopulous an area, and sometimes by however indirect a route, are rich and surprising.

The nineteenth century ended with even Victorian Wordsworthianism in abeyance. Rather, we were into the (strictly) Decadent orientations of Pater, Wilde and Beardsley, the chattering observations of Shaw and the non-naturalistic vision of Yeats. To an aspiring border writer the options might seem mixed if not confused. This was the starting point, certainly, for Arthur Machen (1863–1947), who was born in Caerleon, Gwent. Machen became a successful Fleet Street journalist and wrote a stream of novels, stories and essays in the Decadent mode. Yet he did this without really letting go of his Gwent roots or his memories of the countryside round the rectory at Llanddewi Fach, his childhood home where his father held the living. Machen was born Arthur Llewellyn Jones, and later took his mother's maiden name for professional purposes. In *The Hill of Dreams* (1907), his main border novel and perhaps the best of all his novels, the stunning naturalistic evocations of that landscape are revealing:

> He walked smartly down the hill; the air was all glimmering and indistinct, transmuting trees and hedges into ghostly shapes, and the walls of the White house farm flickered on the hillside, as if they were moving towards him. Then a change came. First, a little breath of wind brushed with a dry whispering sound through the hedges, the few leaves left on the boughs began to stir, and one or two danced madly, and as the wind freshened and came up from a new quarter, the sapless branches above rattled against one another like bones.

A countryside scene, yet we suddenly remember that this writer invented single-handed the myth of the Angels of Mons, those heavenly figures who appeared in the sky over the Allied troops in the First World War there. The atmosphere seems filled with living spirits. These furthermore are not a diffusion of nature, but ghosts of a sedimented past: with Machen, a past literary and martial, going back to the Roman. The layering is informative. Machen's original Mons story was actually called 'The Bowmen', and Machen himself explicitly notes that 'the bowmen of Agincourt were mostly mercenaries from Gwent'. Yet in the accompanying illustration when the story was first published, these supposed archers are Roman legionaries, and it is hard to suppress the notion that, by whatever route from writer to illustrator, this expresses the great influence on Machen of the Roman fort at Caerleon, to which he frequently refers elsewhere, including in this same novel. Machen was to become one of the century's best-known writers of Gothic fiction, with *The Great God Pan* (1894) among the most pre-eminent.

The Hill of Dreams is a single-character novel. The protagonist is Lucian Taylor, recognizably close to Machen himself, and son of a Welsh rural rector who goes to London to write. As boy and man he has friends, but they do not grow into full-bodied characters in the book. The story is essentially an exploration of Lucian's growing apprehensions of the merger he feels between the dream-world of literature and the real worlds of both country and city. References to literature, usually the naming of his own reading, litter all Machen's writing. Indeed his one substantial volume of literary criticism *Hieroglyphics* (1902) – rather oddly described by Godfrey Brangham as Machen's 'one serious work' – is a touch shrill and excessive, and is actually fictionalized as the story of a literary hermit. It does demonstrate the overt compulsion in *The Hill of Dreams* we have just referred to.

Soon after the passage just cited, the boy is exploring the old Roman fort at Machen's birthplace Caerleon, which has one of the largest, most famous and best-preserved encampments on the border, and its grip on Lucian's imagination is seen to pick up, or itself enhance, his own interests in the ancient and medieval worlds. At school, Latin and Greek are Lucian's preferred subjects, and then and later he revels in the garden of Avallaunius and Apuleius' *The Golden Ass*. His reading in fact is not romantic but exotic: 'He would only read what was uncouth and useless. The strange pomp and symbolism of the Cabala, with its hint of more terrible things; the Rosicrucian mysteries of Fludd, the enigmas of Vaughan, dreams of alchemists – all these were his delight.' The absorption in things Roman may well tie Machen back to Walter Pater, and the improbable name of the book's hero recalls that writer's novel *Marius the Epicurean*. As did Edward Thomas a little later, Machen overtly rejected the Pateresque mode (in the Introduction to *The Hill of Dreams*), but this change never went as far as it did with Thomas. Machen's style remains, not ornate, but certainly finely shaped and 'cadenced' (Machen's term) with a sybaritic quality which repeatedly surfaces: 'He was wet with heat; the sweat streamed off his face, and he could feel it trickling all over his body.' Lucian loves not so much women's bodies in themselves, as the proximity of their jewels and clothes to the flesh they hang upon. He relishes descriptions of sumptuous meals. Thomas de Quincey's opium is a frequent reference. Even the ordinary scenes of afternoon tea and evening fireside in the rectory – that central 'big house' of so many classic border novels – are caressed for their artefactual texture.

Yet the Gwent background never entirely vanishes. Even in London Lucian is never far from the city's edge, and the trail of the road out into the foggy fields beyond the last lamp enables the young writer always to regain contact with those scenes. Near the end of the book Lucian longs for home in Gwent, and then recalls that, with his father's death the year before, it is gone. The outcome, as in all Machen's work, is a rich mix of three ingredients:

London streets and the Decadence; the border countryside; and, as hinted already and like David Jones and indeed Anthony Powell later, the dimension of the Roman settlements, the Caerleon fort which had impressed the Gwent boy so powerfully. If Machen had been Scottish or Irish this mix would have worked out very differently. The proximity of Wales to the English heartland is as we outlined above, but the Roman occupation of Wales, which did not much happen in other parts of what later became known as Celtic Britain, is a resource available to any border writer who is open to it. Its many aspects surface in the border literature in various ways and, in different writers, go in different directions.

The importance to Machen himself of the material from which *The Hill of Dreams* was worked, is underlined by the non-fictional yet near-parallel work, the autobiographical *Far Off Things* (1922). In whimsical and self-mocking vein, but nonetheless deeply serious for all that, the same material is recovered – in two senses. Now nearly sixty, in *Far Off Things* Machen wrote that:

> . . . in my boyhood and youth I was a deep and learned student of the country about my home, and that I always saw it as a kind of fairyland . . . I came into a strange country, and strange it ever remained to me, so that when I left it for ever there were still hills within sight and yet untrodden, lanes and paths of which I knew the beginning but not the end. Everything to me was wonderful, everything was the veil of an invisible secret.

This passage, of which all but the first sentence could be Thomas Traherne without one word altered, suggests how Gwent was always present to Machen. With its spiritually populated heavens the passage offers a way in to the curious imagination that led to his Gothic fiction. With Machen the border, knowingly or otherwise, is a matter of England and Wales, but it is not only that. It lies also between topography and books; between the Roman and the Celtic; between this world and that of the departed; between the body beautiful and what grows wild like nettles and brambles. In this theme of the edge, a central character so often crosses a crucial boundary, or has one enticingly or threateningly nearby, or feels a clash of two polities in his or her own day-to-day existence. It is a feature of all the novels of this region that have emerged in the twentieth century. The multi-layered nature of all Machen's writing finds testimony in the varied list of those who have spoken of his influence on their own lives; John Betjeman, Siegfried Sassoon, the composer John Ireland (who said that his music and his life were revolutionized by Machen's work), cellist Julian Lloyd Webber and television personality Barry Humphries. Yet it is *The Hill of Dreams* which seems like a small classic overdue for rediscovery.

Other border novelists produced an altogether more singular texture. Like Machen, Geraint Goodwin (1903–41) was a border Welshman who went to London to pursue a career in journalism. But there the similarity ends. Goodwin's affinity is with the unsentimental and (sometimes) sex-powered pure realism of D. H. Lawrence and contemporary Irish writers like J. M. Synge and Sean O'Casey. Unlike most England–Wales border writers, who tend either to leave permanently in their early twenties or only much later under duress if at all, Goodwin deliberately returned to the border region after fifteen years in Fleet Street, when he was thirty-five. He was born and raised near Newtown, Montgomery-shire – about seven miles from the edge of Shropshire – and in 1938 he took his family back to Merioneth. Since he died only three years later in his late thirties, it is not entirely clear whether his undoubted (and documented) commitment to Wales and things Welsh were the prime motive force, or whether he really returned home to die. A compromise view, that he returned home perhaps precisely to extend his precarious life, seems fair enough. He may well have felt that the surroundings that most mattered to him would be most conducive to that end.

Not that Goodwin's journalistic career lacked a cosmopolitan dimension. His reports on military manoeuvres in the Rhineland, sent from Germany, were published in newspapers like *Empire News* and the *Daily Mail*, and his non-fiction work *Conversations with George Moore* came out of numerous talks and growing friendship with the great man in Ebury Street. It was a success in its own right – as indeed were most of Goodwin's books at the time of their publication, a fact which contrasts starkly with his near-total neglect now. (Interestingly Arthur Machen had also interviewed Moore, though not for a whole book.) But Goodwin's most successful and best-remembered novel, *The Heyday in the Blood* (1936), requires a mention in any examination of twentieth-century border writing.

Goodwin was what is sometimes called a 'natural storyteller'. But as Sam Adams strongly brings out in his short study of the writer, the novels too are sometimes assemblages of self-contained incidents united by an overall setting rather than a single storyline. In *The Heyday in the Blood* however this setting is not just the rural landscape, even though from early journalism with the *Montgomery Express* Goodwin knew the area thoroughly. Rather, it stems from an unspoken though deeply present political orientation via the indirect encounter, not of the Welsh with the English, but of border folk with 'pure' Welsh. The novel centres, topographically as well as thematically, on the plan for a new arterial road through the area. Yet what stands out is the immediacy of the separate incidents. We remember the revenge-fight in the upstairs barn, complete with rounds and seconds; the technically exact catching of a salmon at night under torchlight; the old man's exasperation with his ear-trumpet; and the parson wading the brook Sunday after Sunday to avoid going to church the long way round – this last incidentally a scene strongly reminiscent of the work of Richard Jefferies. The characters are numerous, and less dominated by a central one than in so many novels: Turni the publican, his eighteen-year-old daughter Beti and her friend Gweno, Beti's swaggering cousin Llew who fancies her, and the young bankrupt poet Evan the Mill whom she herself fancies.

As with Raymond Williams but seldom with Machen, there is little of what is superficially called wit or humour. But the aim of both writers to leave their characters' dignity paramount closes down that possibility, and none such is intended. Phrases like 'the complexion of an autumn sunset' and 'they shared the companionship of the earth' jar less than they might; this is the era of between-wars Britain when everyone everywhere longed for peace. The characters do come over with a certain strain. But the book's integrity and unity emerge from a total-control commitment that never wavers. Goodwin's lack, no doubt, is that his novels don't reach out beyond themselves. *Watch for the Morning* (1938) was certainly more ambitious, but in general there is little room for authorial comment, or reader's inference, or general implication – a danger which Williams, unsurprisingly, was to offset in quite other ways. Goodwin's mode is thus disconcerting for a critical age like our own, in which historicism – both as to the author's background and the work's overt content – has come to seem indispensable. Goodwin's sense of history, like that of nature, is of something distilled and away from the mess of actual surrounding circumstance. He studied Welsh history in detail with great care; but in the novels, it is somehow another thing. Yet, for these very reasons, *The Heyday in the Blood* is the prototypical poetic novel. Dialogue abounds, but the book's limits are close to a certain vision that where one lives and has one's immediacy of being matters more than anything else. These novels found real favour with the London press, with *The Heyday in the Blood* chosen 'Book of the Month' for the *Evening Standard* by the writer Howard Spring (1936) and *Come Michaelmas* nominated 'first choice for fiction' by the *Times Literary Supplement* (1939). *Watch for the Morning* (1938) also received a highly favourable review in the *Times Literary Supplement*.

Margiad Evans (1909–58) is a most remarkable transplant. She had Goodwin's intensity but for quite different reasons. She was born in Uxbridge, Middlesex as Peggy Eileen Whistler. Aged only nine, she underwent some kind of quite extraordinary, maybe mystical experience on the banks of the river Wye when taken to Ross in Herefordshire for holidays. She stayed there on her uncle's farm for an entire year soon afterwards, and she and one of her sisters then took their grandmother's surname and used the Welsh forms of their first names (Margiad and Sian) as writers' pseudonyms. Their parents took the family to live near Ross permanently and the girls attended Ross Grammar School. Later Margiad spent a year teaching in France; but virtually all her adult life was spent in the border country, until illness took her back to Sussex in great and sardonic sadness for the last few years of her life.

For in 1950, when she was forty-one, Margiad discovered that she was an epileptic. *A Ray of Darkness* (1952) – unlike the *Autobiography* of nearly ten years earlier – is her true story. It is highly revealing, if in hindsight, about the forces that had already long made her a writer. In this book she made the explicit attempt to relate her creative impulses to the nature and deep-rooted sources of the epileptic experience. She consults the clinical diagnoses of the several specialists who attended her, but her main aim is to enter the experiences direct. The chapter describing the wholly unexpected and extremely frightening first fit has a stronger and more compelling narrative line than do most of her novels. She is reading and writing by the hearth, but then suddenly sees that the clock has gone forward an hour and three-quarters apparently in a single minute. She is lying on the floor, tea-stains have appeared all over the poem she is writing (which the book gives complete with gaps), and she is dangerously close to having fallen on the fire. She goes out down the lane – this is after one o'clock in the morning – and rouses neighbours. They take her into the hospital immediately. The book ends tying the whole experience to the border; and this is crucial, for Margiad explicitly sees epilepsy as border experience.

Writing in *Poetry Nation Review* in 1988, Idris Parry perceptively noted that Margiad 'was the kind of writer who did not need a plot . . . Her last prose work, *A Ray of Darkness*, contains the plot she has been looking for'. Without wanting to straitjacket the argument, one can suggest that Margiad Evans's fiction depends for its tension less on the normal sequences of complex narrative than on a series of clear splits between opposed forces; darkness and light, self and other, England and Wales. The oxymoronic title *A Ray of Darkness* itself declares the starkness of the line between the disparate parts of all she encounters. The brilliant and visionary if strangely named prose work *Autobiography* depicts in astonishing detail one side of this dark–light experience.

Autobiography is almost pure experience. It is sustained without lapse. Near the end we find the only case in the book of an image repeated (a moorhen cutting a V of light in the water), and there is an intensity and electrifying charge of Evans's own throughout which makes 'description' an inadequate word for it. She is one with nature and the landscape, which is far away and at her hands and feet; on hills and in fields; in farmyards; in her garden and in the lane; and indoors in kitchens and bedrooms too. She presents her feelings and responses undiluted, and this bears out her claim to be elaborating a theory of solitude itself.

> I got up at a quarter to six. When M—— was gone I went to the door and lifted the latch and listened. The plovers were awake and wheeling but the rooks making a sleepy nestling sound under the hill. Down there it was darker. Blackbirds in the hedge. I went and fetched a fork. The shed let light in through the tiles and under the eaves revealing the belly of the roof. So softly, slyly the morning came without a sunrise.
>
> I watched [this raindrop] collect over Garway hill, half a dozen miles away, looming and glooming nearer the sun and me. Now like bubbles

in ice they cling to the pane, seeming to be neither on one side nor another, but inside the glass, so instantly *still* are they. But slowly the weight in them drags them downward; they elongate and sag, holding by a rim of iridescent water, but dark in the middle with a clear seed of light, like a bird's eye. Then suddenly they shoot down the pane, leaving a more transparent track than glass.

Such perceptions were hard earned. There is a daily direct encounter with the elements – dripping rain in the hair, dirty and freezing cold hands, hard manual labour in the fields for trifling wages, and complete absence of television, telephone, central heating and labour-saving devices. It leaves the fitted-kitchen and fast-food age pallid before it. It is not clear whether such communion with nature is even possible today, with our ecologically saturated awareness, our map of motorways, our second-home vision and our carve-up of all terrain into systematic areas. But Margiad's mysticism is authentic because it is concentrated and not effusive; it always enquires. Nature appears before us close up; actual birds and their cries and colours; shapes of clouds and leaves; twirls of stream water; phases of seasons, crops, moon and stars; yet never didactically; the apprehension is optical and staring. The experience gives rise to heights of reflection on such experience's quality and significance. Margiad wonders incessantly what we are, how we know it, and how she herself is somehow inside it.

These considerations are the background for looking at what most critics consider her best, maybe her only lasting novel, *Country Dance* (1932), which seems to have the perennial border light playing all over it. Here the dark side of Margiad's vision finds equal and opposite presence in the lyrical expression of the stark and unabated rivalry of England and Wales in the words and emotions of most of the book's speaking characters. The symptom of the book's lyrical darkness lies in the overtness of its human structure. There are two lead characters, 'Gabriel Ford and Evan ap Evans, shepherd and farmer, Englishman and Welshman', as Margiad puts it herself in the book's introduction. The symmetry of this equation is mirrored throughout; but the incessant taunts and anger from Welsh to English and back again do not drag, mainly because of the lilting rhythms of the writing and the mass of authentic detail about the processes of work, farming and household in country life.

The book purports to be the diary of the middle character, the woman both men love, Ann Goodman. She is English but was brought up on a Welsh farm, and this formula comes as near to a compromise arrangement as could reasonably be expected. The rivalry starts in the Introduction itself, and the taunts never let up. 'He has a Welsh voice that sings in speaking English'; 'Why does he always speak to me in Welsh? I wish Gabriel would come!'; 'Get away, you little bitch, and find your Welshman!'; 'I hate the Welsh and all their shifty ways of dealing'; 'I am riding into Wales, Ann Goodman. What message have you for your sweetheart?'; 'Mine is not fit for fodder. The Welsh hog!'; 'He will never go where the Welsh tongue is spoken'; 'Ah, it is good to hear English again!'; 'Her father is fair furious at the marriage, being a true Welshman that would have his daughter marry one of her own country'; 'There is something in having an English boy about the place, even if he is thick-headed'; 'If you are an Englishman, Gabriel Ford, then from this day I'll count myself as Welsh'; 'I think the Welsh are fanciful folk that frighten none but themselves by their tales'; 'Your mother was Welsh and was kind to me, while shepherd will never give me a word.' There are dozens more.

As so often in her books, this relentlessness is deliberate and it works. Margiad Evans is a unique phenomenon in border-country writing, and pretty rare in any writing. But the final issue relates to the sharp dualities already mentioned. This issue is gender. For the question arises of how far these black–white divisions in Margiad's thought are suppressions of this deepest unspoken distinction, particularly bearing in mind the evidence of bisexuality that is sometimes hinted at in her unpublished writings. Ann Goodman's placing as inert cipher between two clashing males and two antag-onistic nations may be projection from an inner sexual division which, for whatever reason, Margiad did not address overtly. The feminist critic Cora Kaplan has written that 'masculinity and femininity . . . are always, already, broken, ordered, and broken up again through other social and cultural terms, other categories of difference'. Margiad Evans is a main case for the argument that writers of border experience as terrain invariably find, or are using, correlatives within their own psychic border condition and wider experience, however seemingly far removed. In the current burgeoning of interest in women's writing in Wales, Margiad is at last being restored to her rightful place.

A different case again emerges with Raymond Williams
(1921–88). Williams was born and raised in Pandy near Abergavenny, four miles from the border itself. His forty-year career as
a humanist left-wing don at Cambridge was what normally drew
attention to him in the intellectual world. He attained massive
success with *Culture and Society* and *The Long Revolution* in the
early 1960s, followed by a kind of second wave which included
Keywords, Writing in Society and *Marxism and Literature* twenty
years afterwards. But these achievements can easily lead us to
overlook his closely wrought and deeply serious novels, which he
himself laid great store by. We are most concerned here with the
'border trilogy' consisting of *Border Country* (1960), *Second
Generation* (1964) and *The Fight for Manod* (1979). There are also
the first two volumes of the late novel *People of the Black
Mountains* (1989 and 1990), a vast and very different project
Williams did not live to finish, though these two volumes were
published posthumously.

It took Williams twenty years and numerous rewritings to
complete the border trilogy. Yet he put it on record that it was
indeed conceived as a trilogy from the start. This is despite that, as
he said in *Politics and Letters*, he was not originally aware of the
exact shape the whole narrative would take. The breadth and
spread of the work are great, and we can only offer here a brief
summary of each novel's action along with some small comment in
the context of a border-literature survey. In the first novel of the
trilogy, *Border Country*, Matthew Price is a lecturer in London
who returns to the border region on hearing that his father Harry,
a railway signalman, has had a stroke. The subsequent story, set
largely in that region, centres on flashbacks to the General Strike
of 1926, culminating in a confrontational scene when the signal
box is closed by the local stationmaster. Meanwhile another
railwayman turns a strike-support delivery service into a private
and profitable enterprise. In *Second Generation* the scene shifts to
(presumably) Oxford, and the action turns on the idealism of an
intense young student Peter Owen and his politically active mother
Kate. The setting is the local major motor works, the university –
both students and dons – and more briefly the border country
where Peter returns, in effect, for support and counsel during the
action. The third novel *The Fight for Manod* then retrospectively
unites the trilogy through the meeting and mutual assistance of

Matthew and Peter, now both some years older. They cooperate in gradually unearthing a covert intrigue by high-level business interests to site a new town in central Wales, not only against the wishes of the inhabitants but, to the last possible moment, without their knowledge.

Like Arthur Machen and Margiad Evans in their different ways, Williams was an explicitly autobiographical writer. This appeared not just in his novels' choice of narrative and setting, but in his own external comments about them as indeed about most of his work. Talking at substantial length to the staff of the *New Left Review* – understandably somewhat specialist interlocutors – Williams gave the strong impression that his concerns in the border trilogy ran along class rather than national or regional lines. He spoke of the shaping of the nineteenth-century realist novel within the bourgeois world; later attempts by working-class novelists to reuse that form but from their own perspective; the 'novel of escape' from the restraining proletarian background; and so on. These remarks are interwoven with comments about Williams's own political activity during those two decades of roughly 1960 to 1980, his ambivalent relationship with the Labour Party and the large part he played in the long period of Marxist attitudes behind much post-war literary criticism. These dimensions, of course, informed all Williams's work for that period, before the wider alignments of race, ecology, feminism, Europe and the rest somewhat changed the traditional working-class agenda, finally in the 1980s. True, the explicit solidarity and corporate loyalty of official trades union activity, central to the first two novels, has departed by the time of *The Fight for Manod*. But this still leaves the encounter between political power-groups as that novel's energizing force, even if in a somewhat wider sense.

Yet, beyond a doubt, the terrain of Raymond Williams's childhood and youth, and to which he returned all his life, is a sine qua non of the entire trilogy. It allows the extraordinary calm, the sense of graded space, in which the human stresses of so deeply contentious a topic can be worked out. As early as page two of the first novel, Matthew, in London, reflects to himself just who he really is: 'The man on the bus, the man in the street, but I am Price from Glynmawr, and here understandably that means very little. Yes, they say the gateway of Wales, Yes, border country.' It is seldom explicitly denoted again. Yet scenes in all three novels –

though mainly the first and third – unforgettably underwrite the
sense of land being fought over, on both domestic and class lines.
The fullness of one's identity is inseparable from the free creative
and responsible working of the territory where one lives and
breathes. The close bonds of a rural community are embedded in
its small population and its occupation of its terrain.

Chapter 4 of *Border Country* begins vividly:

> In the spring of 1926, in Glynmawr, the green of the meadows was fresh
> and cool, and the blossom was white in the orchards, and on the thorns
> and crabs in the hedges. Along the banks of the roads the violets were
> hidden in overgrowing leaves, but the primroses were out, though not
> so thickly as on the banks of the railway, where they flowered most
> richly as if the cuttings and embankments had been made for them.

It is so very typically the border writer's evocation of nature, as so
frequently found in Machen, Margiad Evans, Hopkins and
Kilvert. Yet here it comes with a touch which quietly points to
Williams's own concerns. The first and last phrases of this passage
interlock the processes of nature and organized labour in single
focus and as a single process. Nearly twenty years later in *The
Fight for Manod*, the opening chapter's setting in Whitehall turns
out to be prelude to the second chapter's breathtaking invocation
of the Welsh valley at Bryndu at night. Glynmawr in spring and
Bryndu at night; they are so different on the surface, but it still
seems the one precious, mysterious land that – in the later novel –
is under the manipulative eye of the ministerial mandarins who
have already incorporated it into the developmental planning
intended to change it for ever. But the implication of this profound
merger between nature, planning and work is germane not merely
to rural life but to border life. This happens in ways Williams
seldom names on the surface but which are to be found in a deeper
sense of the relation between the entire work, Williams's other
strand of social commentary in his non-fictional work, and the
man himself.

The link between these matters in Williams's writing is his
frequently invoked concept of the 'knowable community'. The
knowable community of the village, small town or wider array of
smallholdings and hill farms is particularly intensified when it
is set on the edge between two much vaster and national

communities. The deliberately cognitive adjective underlines Williams's lifelong reflection on the nature of human relations in shared settlements. Yet this does not mean that 'border' is merely a metaphor for the interface between worker and boss, youth and older parent, or indeed England and Wales, which focus Williams's wider political concerns. Rather the *border* community is perennially in receipt of a gentle pressure to define itself – know itself – as against the larger entities on either side. These bigger entities may, with equally tacit yet unremitting insistence, claim the small border community's allegiance exactly while they are also in larger rivalry with each other. In such a situation, to be able to focus on your own patch and – if you are lucky – its sustaining beauty too, but also its small vital processes of work, is an establishing of living itself. This living defines identity by contrast to that of groups with a fuller nationalist outline. William's border novels are littered with these small daily practices: growing vege-tables; getting and laying afternoon tea; teaching a new recruit the leverage system of the signal box; grooming and saddling a horse (when you had no car); repelling floodwater when a small river bursts its banks. And in his posthumously published work *People of the Black Mountains* he attempted a fictional but imaginatively true account of Black Mountain life for no less than the past twenty thousand years of human habitation of that region. As such, it is unlike anything previously undertaken in the twentieth century from this border literature. It enters deep time, at least by human scales, and, as more than one commentator has noted, it will require considerable assimilation for some years to come.

The two or three main interventions by English border writers over the same long period ask for brief comment here too, consorting as they do with what has been achieved by Welsh writers in English. It is mildly ironic that *Gone To Earth* (1917) and *Precious Bane* (1924) by Mary Webb (1881–1927) are effectively pure Shropshire, despite that she was born Meredith of a Welsh line and enjoyed a close and lasting friendship with Geraint Goodwin. For, by contrast, Francis Brett Young's *The House Under the Water* (1932, one of his 'Mercian' novels) and Bruce Chatwin's *On The Black Hill* (1982) both take stabs into the Welsh border heartland and so raise questions of some importance in our context. Both authors were Englishmen – West Midlanders, but still Englishmen with no Welsh connection. Brett Young (1884–1954) and Chatwin (1940–89) recognizably enter the terrain of *The Fight for Manod* and even *Country Dance*. Little need be said here, but the political and structural similarity between Brett Young's story of the flooding of a Welsh valley – along with the 'big house' in it – to supply England with water is clearly cognate with the Manod story, and they would repay comparison. Brett Young's fascination was with water and its technology; he made more than one pilgrimage, on bicycle and on foot, along the real-life pipeline itself from the Midlands right through to the Elan valley in Wales where the novel is recognizably situated. Chatwin's saga covers three generations, but its central characters, the twins Benjamin and Lewis Jones, serve to turn the usual border-novel structure on its side. The twins' infertile cloning (neither marries nor procreates) perhaps implies that there is productive value in encounter between groups of different origin and culture. Different again is Edith Pargeter (Ellis Peters; 1913–98), a genuinely popular writer of some Welsh descent. Her medieval monk-sleuth Brother Cadfael lives in Shrewsbury as did his author, constantly notices what ordinary mortals overlook, and several times helps innocent victims of official persecution across the border into Wales and freedom, or retrieves villains therefrom. Pargeter was a published historian as well as novelist. Whatever else, her research is authentic and of importance in the stories she creates.

Finally there are other novelists who might seem to have no great connection – though some – with the border itself, but claim some kind of dual English–Welsh allegiance. The novels of John Cowper Powys (1872–1963), weird mixes of hallucination, water-imagery and sadistic evil like *Wolf Solent* (1929) and massive cosmic-symbolist time-space visions such as *A Glastonbury Romance* (1932), render their speculations via day-to-day description and dialogue in a disconcertingly readable fashion. It is reasonable therefore to think of Powys as drawing from the same inspirations as led to the main border novels already considered. Richard Hughes (1900–76) was a complex personality, and his strongly claimed Welsh ancestry, his English public school and Home Counties background, his love of Morocco and his intellectual interests in Darwin and Freud led him to write a range of powerful but oddly assorted works. *A High Wind in Jamaica* (1929) is not obviously concerned with either Wales or England, but the curiously structured (and never completed) big work *The*

Fox in the Attic (1961) opens with a Welsh-estuary setting which achieves one of the most powerfully evoked natural scenes in the cognate literature. It then goes on to a depiction of Hitler which has been equally highly praised yet seems not to belong in the same book. Hughes published some poetry, acknowledging Gerard Manley Hopkins and Robert Graves as among his mentors.

With the England–Wales novel then, we have a twentieth-century genre of what may be called the small border classic. The rural landscape is static, realist and named, and the narrative does depend on central characters who either confront a cross-cultural interface or, precisely, knowingly live out an insulation from that, by inhabiting a kind of non-national self-defining community with the advantages and difficulties which that entails. In describing his childhood in the border country in an interview with the present writer in 1977, Raymond Williams stated that at home 'we talked about "the English" who were not us, and "the Welsh" who were not us'. With the poets we encounter larger difficulties. It is partly a matter of recognition. Since, at least until recently, they have received notably greater attention than the corresponding novel-ists, any status they may have as 'border poets' has been partly overshadowed by their full stature as central figures in the full British tradition; and this is of course understandable enough.

With the poet, even the lyrical and/or nature poet, the real or imagined world gestured at can be felt on the pulse as both intensely inner and fully planetary at once, and there is room for expropriation by the reader to his or her own scene of life. Equally the poets too may be drawn to transplant their sense of life to anywhere they imaginatively find themselves. I will argue that this was partly true of Wilfred Owen, Edward Thomas, W. H. Davies and others. Our attention to these poets has to be incomplete, and there is already much major work on all these poets elsewhere. We depart here from strict chronology too. The very early deaths in battle of some of them puts their life-centre of gravity far earlier than their dates of birth would suggest. Wilfred Owen (1893–1918) is a case in point. The poet gets no entry in *The New Companion to the Literature of Wales* (1998), and his early editor Cecil Day-Lewis stated firmly that Owen's parents 'were both English and he was born in England'. True enough, and Owen didn't always do much to discourage this view, clamping down on his younger sister's attempts at the presumably unworthy Welsh language,

although admittedly Owen himself was still a gauche and somewhat over-solemn young man at this time. Yet there is another side
to this picture. Owen's biographer Dominic Hibberd has written
that:

> Owen was Welsh by descent on both sides, a fact which he valued
> because he held the Victorian view that imagination and strong, often
> melancholy emotions were Celtic endowments . . . Even during the
> action in which he won the Military Cross in 1918 he remembered those
> earlier soldier poets, 'my forefathers the agile Welshmen of the
> mountains'.

If this seems to ring rather dubiously from the other side –
making the present writer clearly hard to please – perhaps that
itself merely highlights the borderline-ness, the difficulty of definition, we always encounter with these writers, as already implied.
But it still remains that Owen was born at Oswestry, a stone's
throw from the border, and, after a decade in Birkenhead, was
finally moved back to Shrewsbury. There he stayed until he went
to the war, never to return other than when invalided out for brief
periods. Birkenhead itself is, of course, only seven miles from the
border's northern end. Certainly its ambience is of a different
nature, yet Birkenhead has played a curious and interesting role in
Welsh literary life, and is in particular associated with the National
Eisteddfod held there in 1917 at which the presentation Chair was
draped in black throughout. The winner, Ellis Evans (the *Hedd
Wyn* – his eisteddfod pseudonym – of a recent Oscar-nominated
film), had been killed in France only five weeks earlier. Wilfred
Owen, also prematurely killed in the First World War, spent
virtually the whole of his short civilian life within close reach of the
boundary between England and Wales.

Two matters may be raised about Owen in this context. The first
concerns the truth or otherwise of whether Owen employed
traditional Welsh forms in his poetry. Alan Llwyd, himself twice
winner of both Crown and Chair at the National Eisteddfod, has
left no doubt that he believes in the influence of Welsh forms on
Owen's poetry, although he concedes that this has never been
substantiated by strict documentary evidence. More important it
would seem is the transposition, by Owen and others, of a certain
imaginative and perhaps mysterious sense of borderland terrain to

the No Man's Land between the trench-bound British and German armies on the First World War front. Some lines are occasionally cited in this regard:

> Hour after hour they ponder the warm field
> And the far valley behind, where buttercups
> Had blessed with gold their slow boots coming up;
> Where even the little brambles would not yield
> But clutched and clung to them like sorrowing arms:
> They breathe like trees unstirred.
> . . .
> Marvelling they stood, and watched the long grass swirled
> By the May breeze, murmurous with wasp and midge;
> And though the summer oozed into their veins
> Like an injected drug for their bodies' pains,
> Sharp on their souls hung the imminent ridge of grass,
> Fearfully flashed the sky's mysterious glass . . .
> . . .
> So, soon they topped the hill, and raced together
> Over an open stretch of herb and heather
> Exposed . . .

This is from 'Spring Offensive', one of Owen's most famous poems. Here, surely, we witness a terrain typical of the work of Geraint Goodwin or Margiad Evans. But also, the heightened emotion and tense anxiety, out of context, might as easily have been an evocation of troubled young love projecting itself on to the sublimity of nature. It is as far from the mud, twisted gun-metal and broken tree-stumps of Beaumont Hamel and Savy Wood as could be imagined. It is pure Shropshire. Yet it is space and non-space, a clear ground between two contrastingly positive entities as border territory so often must be anywhere. 'So, soon they topped the hill, and raced together/ Over an open stretch of herb and heather/ Exposed . . .' – hardly the cumbersome dash through a mish-mash of slurry and corpses. Rather it is Machen's Lucian Taylor discovering the Roman fort, or Margiad Evans herself during one of her all-day walks or more extreme ecstasies.

The first stanza of Owen's poem ended with a line that became renowned as an aphorism of that front-line experience: 'Knowing their feet had come to the end of the world.' Border writers, poets or novelists, Welsh or English, hardly see the relevant other

country as 'the end of the world'. Yet the deeper sense of something unknown and beyond seems to have gripped some of these
poets as imaginative counter-strategy to the novelists' attempt, as
suggested, to present a small but total community which belongs
to neither place. It is certainly remarkable how many major First
World War poets – Edward Thomas, David Jones, Wilfred Owen
and (if we may cheat and briefly borrow him) the Gloucestershire
poet Ivor Gurney – were born in, lived in, or were strongly
associated with, the England–Wales border region. Edward
Thomas (1878–1917) was born fifteen years before Owen and died
from an exploding shell a year before Owen did. He therefore had
more time to put down markers on the Welsh and London literary
scenes so that a wider influence can be felt spreading later. Thomas
was born of fully Welsh parents, but in London, and he never lived
in Wales. But he went to Wales frequently, sometimes summer
after summer, and wrote a book about his ancestors' homeland
Beautiful Wales (1905). This was admittedly one of the many travel
books he produced about many parts of Britain, indeed mainly
England. Yet Edward also once wrote in a letter that 'I am reading
O.M.E.'s "Wales". At every page I am filled with admiration of
the author and love of his subject.' The reference is to Owen M.
Edwards, one of the most celebrated and influential of Welsh
historians and educationalists, who had been Thomas's tutor at
Lincoln College, Oxford.

Thomas spent a brief but, in literary terms, highly important
period in the Gloucestershire village of Dymock. Here blossomed
his friendship with the American poet Robert Frost. Between them
they elaborated – if this is not to oversimplify matters – their
general approach to the writing of poetry. It was based on simple
language, the cadence of the natural voice rather than a formal
diction, and response to the general, if tamed, world of nature. The
record does not suggest that the nearby interface of Wales with
England was especially important at this time, nor does Thomas's
poetry show him identifying that landscape with the battlefield in
any but the most general terms. Rather one needs to look at the
strange sense of peace, surprising as it may seem, which apparently
came over the poet after his enlistment and when he was at the
front line. It is as though Thomas's depressive nervous tension,
which always sought alleviation in some unknown country beyond
the familiar, found it there. Two of his editors have commented on

this. The poet R. S. Thomas once wrote that somewhere beyond Edward Thomas's mind was 'a world he never could quite come at' (the context clearly implies Wales), while Edna Longley believed that Edward Thomas 'failed to become a poet of 1900, because the literary time was as much out of joint as he was . . . he became inevitably a poet of 1914'. These interesting observations suggest, if indirectly, that the longed-for otherness of Wales and the empty space of the farmlands round Arras may have met and been mutually sublimated.

The dual presence of England and Wales in the life and work of David Jones (1895–1974) takes different form. It bears an interesting relationship to *Mercian Hymns*, the notable volume of poetry by the contemporary Warwickshire poet Geoffrey Hill. It is based on a wider archaeology of understanding of the still relevant place of Wales as epicentre of the ancient Kingdom of Britain itself, from its Britonesque and Celtic origins. It was sedimented later and crucially by the Roman invasion, and ended only at the level of official political settlement with the final conquest of Wales in AD 1282. In this sense of the archaeological, Jones can be seen legitimately, if somewhat improbably, as poetic parallel to some aspects of the ideas of Michel Foucault. Foucault turned round major historical readings of what has occurred in Europe in the last few centuries. He achieved this by unearthing patterns of orientation to reality, at various stages, which themselves derived from something deeper than just one more scientific discovery or advance in economic perception. But Jones's 'unearthing' is, of course, more literal. He poetically excavates the Roman walls and roads, and also the strata of language, almost as though its words, too, are chips of earthenware, old bones or weapons, left lying below the surface of communities, farms and battlefields long since vanished.

David Jones was born in Brockley in south London and he passed much of his life in the capital. His father however had come to London from Holywell in Flintshire, north Wales; he was a printer's overseer, and David's mother was the daughter of a Thames-side shipbuilding artisan. This merger of two strains of tangible craftsmanship stayed with David Jones his whole life, and his work as painter, poet and essayist never ceased to refer back to this essential theme. Yet the equal duality of the two lines, England and Wales – or as it sometimes seems, London and Wales – is just as clear-cut. It took the massive architectonic work, in a series of paintings and two huge poems as well as shorter fragments, to see these traditions as belonging to an even greater overall historic unity and continuity while keeping the profile of each clear. Jones's formal membership of and dependence on the liturgy and life of the Catholic Church is cognate with this. His sense of continuity of the Roman Church from the Roman empire and its Europe-wide influence is never far from his concerns.

This clarity of difference between English and Welsh is, perhaps, where David Jones finds his 'border'. As has often been pointed out, the soldiers in the war epic *In Parenthesis* (1937) are clearly London cockney and, as clearly, Welsh boyo: they do not (except incidentally) clash, for that isn't the point, but they don't merge either:

> and the Royal Welsh sing:
> Jesu
>   lover of me soul . . . to *Aberystwyth.*
> But that was on the right with
> the genuine Taffies
>   but we are rash levied
> from Islington and Hackney
> and the purlieus of Walworth
> flashers from Surbiton
> men of the stock of Abraham
> from Bromley-by-Bow
> Anglo-Welsh from Queens Ferry

Jones's boundary therefore is as likely to be a wall – Hadrian's Wall or the wall of Roman Jerusalem – as a landscape with horizons blurred in the mist. Such boundaries are not just barrier, they are also artefact. Yet the 'space' we referred to above in context of other First World War poets comes out in Jones too, if in rather different fashion. Perhaps, pursuing the earlier line of thought, we still should not make too much of the fact that it was precisely when he was spending his four-year spell from 1924 to 1928 in the Black Mountains of the border country with the sculptor Eric Gill that Jones first put pen to paper to sketch this epic war poem. But the presentation of the genealogy of the troops, their relationship with each other, and their gradual movement up to the battle lines toward the end, leads to an evocation of that battle which seems to focus Jones's whole poetic, his voice, in one of its fullest forms. As the soldiers gather to go over the top, the last countdown moments are ticked off by the regimental sergeant major with eerie slowness. There are some mutterings, but mainly total silence. When the battle comes, it is experienced with an elusiveness and indeed an invisibility which is deeply uncanny. Strange as it may sound, the operative word is gentleness. Goodness, futility and acceptance dissolve into a single dimension. We sense a soldier's name, a voice is heard and, later, we sense that the same soldier is dead; this is actually said at times, yet somehow obliquely. Terror and forgiveness seem hardly separable.

The mode continues into Jones's later poetry. Indeed Neil Corcoran has written of the equally monumental *Anathémata* (1952) that 'there is no other poem in the language that so clearly surrounds its individual words with space and silence'. In the same poem though, as Corcoran also points out, that stance toward history is purposeful: 'a stubborn will towards keeping, hoarding, re-discovering, conserving'. Again the mode is archaeological. It is in parts 'a relentless barrage of interrogatives . . . a poetry of *enquiry* – searching out, examining, speculating on its own trad-ition and cultural history' (Corcoran's emphasis). This is the Angle-Land section of *Anathémata* and is also found in *The Sleeping Lord* (1974).

The suggestion is only that this sense of space will come up, in one form or another, in any writer who hangs between two cultures and feels them in their own ancestry and inheritance. This will happen whether or not the writer dwells in the narrow terrain where two lands meet. In David Jones's case he tends rather to inhabit one *or* the other, or to sojourn in many – Sussex, Llanthony, Palestine, Caldey Island, France and finally Harrow – for definite periods. Jones's impulse was often then to fill the space he had created for himself, with everything it had once contained; the Latin liturgy, the Arthurian legend, the block-and-tackle work-manship of the London docks, the bantering swear-words, the several languages and the archaeological masonry. Even the land itself may be alive with the sleeping lord on the Gower peninsula, who either occupies it or is synonymous with its geology. But on this one occasion, in the (in one sense) emptiness of the war zone, there was an analogy with what Wilfred Owen and Edward

Thomas felt more regularly – Owen from his life-residence in the border area, Thomas from his more inward and melancholy yearning.

Of course, the war is not the provenance of all the border poets. While Wilfred Owen's poems found a home as libretto in Benjamin Britten's *War Requiem*, another poet later had the rock group Supertramp named after him, its record-sleeves authenticating the name's source. This differential in cultural recognition is underlined by the truly remarkable story of the poet concerned, W. H. Davies (1871–1940), about whom misunderstandings as to both poetry and life may now be dispersing. Davies was born and raised in impecunious and familially difficult circumstances in Newport, Monmouthshire. His father already dead, he was raised by a loyal but temperamental mother, a chapel-pushing grandmother and a sailor-turned-publican grandfather notable for kindness and bouts of heavy drinking. In childhood, Davies became leader of a schoolboy gang which committed several criminal exploits and, in 1884, he got birched by magistrate's order for shoplifting. By his early twenties, drinking and whoring were seemingly routine. Although his six later years in America and Canada were not spent entirely as a hobo, he did certainly mix arduous manual labour with periods of full-time begging and unemployment, in the company of the tramp population whom he was permanently to christen 'true travellers'. At twenty-seven he was run over by a train and lost his right leg below the knee. It changed his attitude entirely; yet the next six years were also passed on the social fringe in London, largely it seems in doss-houses, though now with firm motive of becoming a poet. According to his archivist, the late Sybil Hollindrake, Davies's friends – whom he dearly loved – included Scotty Bill, One-eyed Jim, Rags, Monkey Sam and The Dodger. Until the last period of his life he was more or less without property and usually penniless. W. H. Davies's *The Autobiography of a Supertramp* (1908) drew enormous praise and is still read as a classic of vagrant literature.

Next to all this, the later picture, given equally one-sided selection of facts, might seem unlikely. When Davies's poetry gained acceptance he entered the society of Lady Asquith, Lady Ottoline Morell and Nancy Cunard. He received a Civil List Pension for his last thirty years with the support of the then prime minister, and was a central figure in London literary life,

befriended by Bernard Shaw, Edward Thomas (who gave him
house-room in Kent for some years), D. H. Lawrence, the Sitwells,
Robert Graves and numerous others. He also got himself painted
by Augustus John, Jacob Epstein, Walter Sickert (another long-
time friend), William Rothenstein and several more. By our own
classless standards this new-celeb status may not seem so unusual,
but it does seem rather as though Vernon Watkins or John
Betjeman latterly turned out to have spent an early decade in
Cardboard City. Davies married late and finally settled in at least
relative tranquillity in Gloucestershire. From there, he could stare
across the Severn to the far side where he had been raised. It is this
last pairing which led Sybil Hollindrake to style him a 'borderer',
although certainly his failure to relate to what he may have
regarded as the true Welsh – on somewhat unsuccessful visits to
relatives in Neath – was another factor.

But this over-journalistic picture does at least point away from
Davies the 'nature poet', a tag he held for many years. Lawrence
Normand and Jonathan Barker, among others, have done much to
adjust this view in a more realistic direction. This nature-poet
designation of Davies is often held to have come from James
Reeves's Penguin anthology *Georgian Poetry* (1962), where
Davies's twenty-two poems were a higher number than any other
contributor received. However, Davies's major editor Jonathan
Barker does see Reeves as a highly perceptive critic of Davies's
poems, and he adds, too, that Reeves was as aware as anyone of
Davies's propensity to use deliberate archaism here and there for
popular consumption.

It was to be expected that words like truth, freshness, simplicity,
sincerity and the like should appear in the plaudits of the time, but
not least from Edward Thomas, who was sensitive to both the
nuances and the dangers in such descriptions. Davies's poems,
after all, have by and large natural settings. And, it has to be said,
Davies was at times extremely naive and indeed ignorant of the
traps laid by the various sophistications around him. His contrastingly enormous experience of raw life in earlier quite different
circumstances provided, then, the unique mix from which his
'simple' poems emerged. But they were pieces which not so much
shed the complexities of social institutions and conventions, as
never had them in the first place. Similarity with ordinary
Georgian poetry is only apparent. In poem after poem, for

example 'Money', 'The Best Friend', 'The Dark Hour', 'Now', 'Fancy's Home', 'Treasures', 'Christ, The Man', 'Thunderstorms' and 'Till I Went Out', the resonances are certainly not W. W. Gibson or Lascelles Abercrombie. Rather, we hear William Blake and George Herbert, Ben Jonson and Shakespeare's songs, and the anonymous traditional ballad. We also hear Emily Dickinson, whose poems had first appeared in America in 1890, to reappear with additions during the following decades. That period included Davies's years there, though it is hard to envisage when and where he might have come across Dickinson's work. But one can see why Ezra Pound, no less, recognized the real significance of Davies's lyrical cutting-edge and pared-down achievement.

Finally, going as far north, border-wise, as Davies was south, we find the actor and playwright Emlyn Williams (1905–87), who was born in Mostyn, Flintshire. Williams was a well-known and much-travelled figure, not unconnected with sleaze and one who, in the words of his first biographer James Harding, thrived on 'the loveliest sound on earth, the noise of laughter and applause'. Yet Williams clearly displayed a lifelong attachment to his border experience on the banks of the river Dee which seemed almost a compulsion and took curious form. It is unfortunate that this same English biographer – unlike Williams's more judicious biographer the late John Russell Stephens – should use the term 'Welsh' as a catch-all adjective for every kind of easy stereotype. Welsh thrift, Welsh eloquence, Welsh stubbornness, Welsh backwoods (ten miles from Chester), 'proud Welshness', 'his native Wales' and such are all adduced. But it was clearly proximity to England, rather, that introduced Emlyn Williams to the sharp edge of cultural relativity early. When he was twelve the family moved to Connah's Quay. As he put it himself: 'fifteen miles only, but it was to the doorstep of England, and the fifteen might have been two hundred: we had left a Welsh peasant village for a working-class township where our language was a joke.' Williams then relates how his own parents virtually dropped Welsh within a year.

How this change was psychologically tied to the events that later made his career is clarified in Stephens's biography. The central element is the huge influence on Williams's life of one of his secondary school teachers, the legendary Miss S. G. Cooke. In Cooke's hands, Emlyn found intellectual confidence and won an open scholarship to Christ Church Oxford. This is the story told in his most-successful and most-remembered play (and later film) *The Corn is Green*. The play is surely still powerful today, both to read and to watch in production. But what actually lies behind this is the gut of Emlyn's relationship with his home country and his career too. His own autobiography's first volume *George* (the name he was usually known by) devotes nearly two hundred pages solely to his childhood and adolescence. By any biographical standards that is a vast amount.

For Williams wrote to Sarah Cooke twice a week for the rest of her life; that is to say, nearly half the century. Even more remarkably, he also sent her the manuscripts of all his plays for her comments. Sarah Cooke was not Welsh but Yorkshire, though she taught at Holywell for thirty years. But Emlyn, who never married, also retained unceasing contact with his own parents; the relationship with Cooke was hardly mother-substitution nor, it seems, a sexual one, open or covert. Many of the plays are set in Wales, although certainly Emlyn said of some of them that he was merely using what he knew best. More important, here, may turn out to be the repeated fascination with violent crime and evil. Emlyn wrote and published a book on the Moors murders, and a play on Crippen; he apparently relished – and excelled at acting – the grisly details in such parts. Little different from Ruth Rendell or even Patricia Cornwell, one might say, yet there is a complex narrative here between these compulsions, Emlyn's bisexuality, and this unique tie with an early schoolteacher all his life in not only personal but also professional context.

It is intriguing to have ended this border-country survey, fortuitously enough, with a poet from the southernmost tip and a dramatist from the northernmost one. The lives of both, furthermore, took them to worlds far removed from those pastoral scenes – bountiful or bleak – which the border embodies for so many readers. Davies's dirty jobs and doss-houses and Emlyn's dim world of fetish and greasepaint seem a long way from the verdant valleys of Wye and Usk or Gerard Manley Hopkins's lush picture of the Elvy near St Beuno's. But there is an anchorage in such limbo areas for both of them as for all these writers. Indeed, although they are not much performed now, one can easily overlook the many plays by Emlyn Williams set in Wales with Welsh characters. As well as *The Corn is Green* there are *The Druid's Rest*, *Trespass*, *The Light of Heart* and particularly *Pen*

Don, a theatrical failure but Emlyn's personal favourite, since he thought of it as his play for Wales. 'Anchorage' may be a fitting metaphor, usually where land meets water, just as borders are where one country meets another.

Idris Davies, T. H. Jones, Eiluned Lewis, Roland Mathias, Ernest Rhys and Hilda Vaughan have all had some border connection, although clearly they belong further into the homeland both geographically and by identification. R. S. Thomas's first curacy was at Chirk, where the line of the England–Wales border literally dissects the village, although one would hardly think of Thomas as either a borderer or someone of dual citizenship. Other recent and still-living writers, young and older, on the Welsh side and associated with this area include Gladys Mary Coles, Catherine Fisher, Russell Celyn Jones, Chris Meredith, Jan Morris and Alice Ellis Thomas.

But we end the century, or start the next, with a surprise. Iain Sinclair's novel *Landor's Tower* (2001) seems the genuine article. Sinclair was born in Maesteg, Glamorgan and lives in Hackney in London. In the novel – part-fiction part-fact it seems – a man named Norton is commissioned to write up Walter Savage Landor's tower-building project at Llanthony in the Black Mountains near Brecon. It never happens. Rather, Norton wanders about the border country, especially in and out of the Hay Literature Festival; further into Wales as far as Swansea (Landor's birthplace); and – improbably – to north Devon, chasing the Jeremy Thorpe scandal. Norton meets Thorpe himself.

But Sinclair is steeped in border literature, and sections long or short appear on Kilvert, Eric Gill and family (life as well as work), the Vaughan twins, David Jones and Bruce Chatwin. There are supporting cameos recalling the Hay-Festival/anti-Festival impresarios Peter Florence and Richard Booth, and the dubious nineteenth-century figure of Father Ignatius Lyne. Countering this, certainly, we find wider twentieth-century figures as diverse as Lady Penelope Betjeman, Terry Waite and the 'sculptors' Gilbert and George. But the border's imprint remains indelible, assured by repeated visits to the old Aust M4 Service Station at Chepstow, a comfort-point where Norton meets old buddies. The book is beautifully postmodern and its imagery continuously brilliant. Along with Sinclair's intense love–hate relationship with the area and his native Wales, this makes *Landor's Tower* a worthy candidate in the line of classic border novels like Raymond Williams's *Border Country* and Arthur Machen's *Hill of Dreams*. The ancient border, its mysterious provenance intact, is suddenly our very own.

FURTHER READING

Sam Adams, *Geraint Goodwin* (Cardiff, 1975).

Gladys Mary Coles, *Mary Webb* (Bridgend, 1990).

Moira Dearnley, *Margiad Evans* (Cardiff, 1982).

Ceridwen Lloyd-Morgan, *Margiad Evans* (Bridgend, 1998).

Jonathan Miles, *Eric Gill and David Jones at Capel-y-Ffin* (Bridgend, 1992).

Jonathan Miles and Derek Shiel, *David Jones: The Maker Unmade* (Bridgend, 1995).

Lawrence Normand, *W. H. Davies* (Bridgend, forthcoming 2003).

Tony Pinkney, *Raymond Williams* (Bridgend, 1991).

John Russell Stephens, *Emlyn Williams: The Making of a Dramatist* (Bridgend, 2000).

Mark Valentine, *Arthur Machen* (Bridgend, 1995).

Herbert Williams, *John Cowper Powys* (Cardiff, 1997).

Merryn Williams, *Wilfred Owen* (Bridgend, 1993).

CHAPTER 4

DYLAN THOMAS AND HIS WELSH CONTEMPORARIES

JAMES A. DAVIES

During 1931 Glyn Jones's first published poems appeared, under pseudonyms (M. G. J. Gower or M. G. Gower), in *The Dublin Magazine*. He published them in Eire because economically depressed Wales was, at that time, 'the dead centre of a vast poetic wilderness'. The only English-language magazine was *The Welsh Outlook*, conservative and dull, which published such poets as Huw Menai, A. G. Prys-Jones, and Wil Ifan, plus an early poem by Idris Davies. It folded in 1933.

As 1933 began Caradoc Evans, Richard Hughes, Rhys Davies and others were ensuring that Anglo-Welsh prose was in good shape. The state of poetry was very different. Apart from a detached and ageing W. H. Davies the spluttering torch was carried by *The Welsh Outlook* regulars plus Ernest Rhys and E. Howard Harris, all offering little more than facile romanticism and shrill patriotism, and writing as if poetry had not changed since the death of Tennyson. Vernon Watkins (1906–67) and Lynette Roberts (1909–95) had published nothing; Alun Lewis (1915–44) was still writing for his school magazine; Idris Davies (1905–53), apart from '*Respice Finem* (Look to the end)', his *Welsh Outlook* poem, was still publishing poems in Welsh and English in local newspapers and college magazines. The literary language and high-flown abstractions of '*Respice Finem*' demonstrated only too clearly and typically his enthusiasm for Romantic poetry; its glib rhyming, here and elsewhere, indicated the influence of *A Shropshire Lad*. But also during 1932 Glyn Jones (1905–95), still pseudonymous, published poems in John Middleton Murry's *The Adelphi* and Harriet Monroe's *Poetry (Chicago)*. These were, as Jones put it, 'practice poems', imitating various writers: 'Gold', for example, is in the style of aesthetic Yeats; 'Esyllt' is 'a sort of dramatic lyric in the manner of Robert Browning'. Though editors detected promise, at the beginning of 1933 Anglo-Welsh poetry was drearily reactionary, derivative and lacking in confidence.

Glyn Jones's small salient was reinforced by Idris Davies during 1933: 'March', a nature poem, was published in *Poetry Review*, 'Francis Drake', a squib attacking parliament, in *The Adelphi*. The decisive breakthrough, however, occurred on 18 May when *New English Weekly* published an early version of 'And death shall have no dominion', Dylan Thomas's first London publication.

Dylan Marlais Thomas (1914–53) was then eighteen and poised to conquer. In 1933 and 1934 his poems and stories commanded much attention: the appearance of 'Light breaks where no sun shines', for example, drew admiring letters from Geoffrey Grigson, Stephen Spender and T. S. Eliot. *18 Poems*, published on 18 December 1934, divided the critics but attracted great interest and influential supporters: the *Times Literary Supplement* wrote of its 'powerful as well as surprising imaginative audacities', and Edith Sitwell that it 'contained many beauties'. Dylan Thomas had arrived.

He had prepared assiduously with wide though unstructured reading, absorbing a British tradition. He had written precociously assured parodies, imitations and beginnings for his school magazine. He wrote collaboratively with his friend Daniel Jones. Above all, in his mid and late teens he filled the famous notebooks with experiments and explorations that often reflected the influence of modernism: automatic writing, surrealism, arcane vocabulary, half-rhymes, free verse, exotic subjects and experiments with syntax. His main thematic concerns were what has been called 'process', the body as a metaphor for external natural and social sequences; the related theme of the relationship between his adolescent self, particularly in its sexual manifestation, and a repressive suburban world; the activity of writing; relations with a father who embodied the tensions of upward social mobility; the Great War and modern memory. Understandably, many of the notebook drafts are slack or overwritten, but, as is well known, some are near-final versions of several of his best-known poems.

18 Poems is the true beginning of modern Welsh poetry in English. With *Twenty-five Poems* (1936), *The Map of Love* (1939) and the stories that became *Portrait of the Artist as a Young Dog* (1940), it forms a glittering path through 1930s literature. Thomas's writing is essentially middle-class and suburban; he has been linked by Tony Conran to John Betjeman. These are his strengths not his limitations and, in his poetry, often a matter of form, of strict patterning. For example, in the aptly titled poem 'I, in my intricate image', 75 of the poem's 108 lines end with variations of the letter 'l', the patterning (lines one, three, four and six in each stanza) being particularly strict in the first two sections. The accumulating images and conceits, and the thrusting energy of the narrative, are controlled, perhaps trapped, by such strictness. Here, as so often in Thomas's poetry, the relationship between form and content dramatizes the power of the bourgeois middle-class world over rebellious creative force.

We are constantly aware of that world: Thomas's work is pervaded by that suburban, middle-class upbringing – centring on home, garden, park, school and cinema – in Uplands Swansea between the wars, and by the sensibility it induced. Even his rural excursions, for example in 'After the funeral', in six of the seven short stories in *The Map of Love*, in 'The Peaches' and 'A Visit to Grandpa's', demonstrate the ingrained attitudes of the Uplands boy, whether expressed in the class-based hierarchy of children's games in 'The Peaches', or in the implicit superiority of the narrator to a strange and unattractive rural world in 'After the funeral'. The point is made most succinctly in the conclusion to 'The Orchards', the final pages of *The Map of Love*.

'The Orchards' is a story with powerful autobiographical elements: the central character is called 'Marlais the poet'. Frustrated as a writer and seeking sexual fulfilment he journeys west from Cwmdonkin until, finally, he

> slept till a handbell rang over the fields. It was a windless afternoon in the sisters' orchards, and the fair-headed sister was ringing the bell for tea. He had come very near to the end of the indescribable journey. The fair girl, in a field . . . laid out a white cloth on a flat stone. Into one of a number of cups she poured milk and tea, and cut the bread so thin she could see London through the white pieces. She stared hard at the stile and the pruned transparent hedge, and as Marlais climbed over, ragged and unshaven, his stripped breast burned by the sun, she rose from the grass and smiled and poured tea for him.

The rural picnic recalls Uplands gentility. In his journey's end is, inescapably, Marlais's beginning.

The Uplands still bore the scars of the Great War. This last haunted not only Thomas's school-magazine poems and the notebooks but also his first two volumes. War imagery is frequent. Two poems, in particular, demonstrate the extent to which the Great War seized Thomas's imagination. One, in *18 Poems*, is 'When once the twilight locks no longer', written on Armistice Day 1933. Its dream-sequence vividly evokes the horrors of the Western Front. In a draft of the poem, the line 'Some dead upon a slab of wind' effects a link with 'And death shall have no dominion' in *Twenty-five Poems*. This famous lyric, in which 'Dead men naked . . . shall be one/ With the man in the wind and the west moon', also uses the symbol of the dead body lying on open ground, its bones 'picked clean' by birds or rats, so suggestive of the Western Front.

Such references at first align themselves with those to the troubles of the 1930s, as, for example, in 'My world is pyramid', with its lines on the massacre of workers by fascists in Vienna in 1934, and in Thomas's most direct political statement, 'The hand that signed the paper', which attacks totalitarian power. Else-where, he exploits the salutes of the period: the communists' raised fist ('Why east wind chills') and the fascists' 'erected arm' ('Do you not father me'). The former, expressing the courageous defiance of the poor and oppressed, enters 'After the funeral' in Ann Jones's 'fist of a face'. However, by 1939 and *The Map of Love* the Great War was superseded by more recent crises, apparent in the volume's first poem, 'Because the pleasure bird whistles', where, in the reference to 'an old year/ Toppling and burning in the muddle of towers and/ galleries', is a world collapsing into conflagration. *The Map of Love* was written during the time of Italy's invasion of Abyssinia, the Spanish Civil War and German annexations in Europe. Such events penetrate the text so that it becomes a response to that troubled period.

Hence the recurring apocalyptic note. It is present in recurring violent imagery, such as the burned cathedral overwhelmed by a new deluge in 'It is the sinners' dust-tongued bell', and the fires that burn at the beginning and end of 'The Orchards'. Both the apocalyptic and violence as aspects of the Zeitgeist are central to 'A saint about to fall', the poem of late 1938 written for the birth of Thomas's son Llewelyn. First entitled 'In September', the month in 1938 when war had seemed imminent, the British navy mobilized and Chamberlain foolishly cried 'Peace in our Time', it then became 'Poem in the Ninth Month', linking birth and the historical moment.

The birth is described, Wordsworth-like, as a fall from a better place. But whereas, in the 'Immortality Ode', the child comes from a Heaven that remains a positive reference point, Thomas's heaven is devastated by the child's departure. That devastation is described in terms all too familiar in the late 1930s: 'The stained flats of heaven hit and razed', the 'chucked bells', 'spilled wine-wells' and 'flames and shells' point to a bombed city, a desecrated Eucharist and the Christian message overwhelmed by violence. Heaven is another Guernica.

'The violence of birth is a foretaste of violence on earth', suggests William York Tindall. Certainly the birth itself is described as courting disaster, as the foetus 'Lurched through [the] scuttled sea' of the womb. The baby enters a world faced with a new Deluge – 'the sour floods/ That bury the sweet street slowly' – and war's violent atrocities: 'earth is barbed with a war of burning brains and hair'. Thomas's imagery suggests the bayoneting of children, primitive survival, the physical stress of childbirth seen as an expression of general woe, birth as the entrance into the world of a bullet or a bomb, and that world as a 'thundering bullring', a troubling reminder of the Spanish Civil War and the Guernica bombing.

The invasive subject and the merging of private and public are profound comments on the historical moment. They are supported by the power struggle implicit in the poem's dialogism. Its dialogue with the 'Immortality Ode' forces the earlier poem to the margins of relevance, indicating the power of events in the late 1930s. Within the poem, the actual dialogue between the poet and his newly born son can be understood in terms of mood. The imperative weakened by the apostrophic in the son's interjection into stanza two – the five lines that begin with 'O wake in me in my house in the mud' – is set against the rest of the poem, in which the opening subjunctive modulates into the indicative, is changed utterly into an imperative that reacts to the new child's interjection and dominates a final stanza in which, briefly, the poet echoes the infant's apostrophic gesture ('O wake to see, after a noble fall').

That imperative, suggesting both bourgeois authority and the decade's authoritarian force, dominates but does not absorb, for example, the baby's plea to remember heaven as it was, and the tenderness of 'Cry joy' and 'you so gentle' in life's 'rough seas'. This modernist poem, truly dialogic, ultimately refuses the reader a sense of its unity, a refusal intensified by the abandoning of a regular rhyme-scheme. The poem increasingly suggests a disintegrative or fragmenting possibility, which also describes the 1930s.

The penetration of text by context is also evident in *The Map of Love*'s seven stories. As with a number of the poems, such as 'After the funeral' and 'Twenty-four years', the stories are all structured in terms of intrusion or invasive difference; we understand why the 'Prose' section opens with 'The Visitor'. Strangers enter unwelcoming and sometimes hostile new worlds, reflecting the decade's significant activities: the invasions, intrusions and penetrations by successful fascists, bewildered refugees and by the mobile and desperate unemployed.

The mobile, and immobile, unemployed were the casualties of the decade's economic depression, associated political extremism and social flux. In this regard the ruined 'boys of summer' may be suggestive, as are those sad lines in 'Before I knocked', in which the unfulfilled narrator is able only

> To drift or drown upon the seas
> Acquainted with the salt adventure
> Of tides that never touch the shores.

'All all and all', which closes *18 Poems*, hints at the need for a new social order. Further such political gestures occur in the next two volumes: we think, for example, of the final line of 'Why east wind chills' – 'And ghostly comets over the raised fists' – the communist salute, as has been noted, invoked in a poem rejecting compliance and complacency.

Economic distress is even more evident in *Portrait of the Artist as a Young Dog*. Its ten stories were written during 1938 and 1939 and, like all Thomas's work, reflect and explore the historical context. Thus, following *The Map of Love*, the *Portrait* stories are all structured in terms of intrusion. The main character, whether as narrator or protagonist, enters new worlds in which he is bewildered, uneasy or befriended. Those worlds are often economically depressed or close to those that are. 'The Peaches' in part describes the economic and cultural collapse of rural communities.

The urban equivalent is described emphatically in references to the
desperate unemployed, the homeless and the houseless dead in
'Just Like Little Dogs', 'Old Garbo' and 'One Warm Saturday'.
Such invasions of bourgeois spaces and class-based juxtapositions
also point to Thomas's use of the topography of pre-war Swansea
to dramatize (with sad prescience regarding his own life) swift
transitions from bourgeois order in a well-lit world into working-
class, drink-fuelled chaos, darkness and disorientation. Fragmentation is furthered primarily by the lack of chronology
between the first three stories, departures from first-person narration which introduce a second narrator, and the counterpointing
of realist narrative by inset stories, films and literary allusions
(especially to Tennyson). It is also furthered by the subverting of
community through private jokes, generally of a topographical
kind, and through misogyny: in the world of the *Portrait*, women
are either ridiculous or objects of sexual desire. Meanwhile, in the
wider world of the late 1930s monolithic Europe itself was
disintegrating.

Thomas's response to social change and to his own social
predicament is partly articulated through the relationship with his
father, David John Thomas. This is a response to the tensions
between his father's working-class upbringing and the professional
status he had achieved, between working-class habits never wholly
put aside and suburban gentility always savoured uneasily,
between Jack Thomas and D.J.. For example, associating 'Jack'
with Christ, in sonnet eight of the 'Altarwise by owl-light' sequence, is to present D.J. as a worthy man wronged and ultimately
destroyed by the world. Further, Thomas's sense of his own
predicament is partly grasped through his obsession, in such
poems as 'Before I knocked', 'I dreamed my genesis' and 'Do you
not father me', with the paternal role in his own conception. His
father destroys a seemingly superior pre-foetal state by effecting a
sequence of decline through birth into a hostile and frustrating
world. In 'I, in my intricate image', Thomas uses *Hamlet* references to stress fatherly authority and his own unhappy life. This
unhappiness was not simply his father's fault. His marriage to
Caitlin and the birth of their first child, in the context of a troubled
decade, were other contributing factors. Solipsistic obsession was
fundamental. It focused on the tensions of his upbringing, his
reaction against suburban repression and narrow-mindedness,

explicit in 'Ears in the turrets hear' and 'I have longed to move away'. 'I, in my intricate image' considers the need to reconcile his divided self, poet and person, described, with characteristic dark wit, as 'invalid rivals . . ./ On the consumptives' terrace'.

Writing, particularly writing poetry, was a fearsome necessity, dramatized as bodily draining: the shedding of 'syllabic blood' in 'Especially when the October wind', masturbation in 'My hero bares his nerves'. Poetry was a product of heart not head, it rejected 'the stony idiom of the brain', the aridity of concept and abstraction. (The assumption that Thomas's hostility towards the intellect means a lack of intellectual content in his poetry can lead to considerable misunderstanding.) Thomas sought to capture the dynamic essence of life, not simply to be, as he put it in a 1934 letter to Pamela Hansford Johnson, 'a freak user of words'. As he wrote, desperately, 'How shall my animal . . ./ Endure burial under the spelling wall?' He worried about losing early fluency, so that 'The lovely gift of the gab bangs back on a blind shaft'. In *The Map of Love*, two collapsing sonnets – 'When all my five and country senses' and, famously, 'Once it was the colour of saying' – dramatize his concern to change his style, to avoid what he considered to be his early aestheticism.

As for his relationship with Caitlin: one aspect is caught in 'We lying by seasand', the beautiful love poem much influenced by T. S. Eliot, in which a moment of loving calm is soon threatened by a hostile outside world. The dominant stormy side of his marriage is explored in 'I make this in a warring absence', a poem of 1937–8 which, in moving from aggression through reconsideration to reconciliation, seems apt for the time of appeasement. The arrival of Llewelyn was commemorated by 'A saint about to fall' and 'If my head hurt a hair's foot', both, as has been noted, linking that birth to the firing of a bullet or the dropping of a bomb. In 'After the funeral', influenced by Caradoc Evans, one of Thomas's literary heroes, his aunt Annie is mourned as a representative victim of grinding poverty, hard labour and narrow-minded Christianity. The poem's final gesture at Judgement Day tunes in to the apocalyptic Zeitgeist.

It is a cliché (partly true) that in *The Map of Love* Thomas began writing poems about other people, turning from inward contemplation to outward engagement. We also see his abiding ability to give general relevance to personal material: profound response to the 1930s is found in his poems about familial relations. Some inward contemplation continued, of course, in his work of the 1940s. *Adventures in the Skin Trade*, which he began in 1941, has a strong and, once again, all-too-prescient autobiographical element in its unfinished tale of the provincial young man moving to London and entering a chaotic life that becomes a series of metaphorical drownings.

Deaths and Entrances (1946) combines both public and private. This is most clearly and brilliantly seen in the group of poems about the London Blitz. These explore the feelings of those who sheltered from German planes, 'quivering through locks and caves', and seek to make sense of the deaths of children by attempting consolation through a pantheistic stress on the dead continuing as part of nature, or through an insistence on the survival of creative natural forces. But aspects of war are also used as metaphors for Thomas's personal life. Thus the enemy pilot, in the eponymous 'Deaths and Entrances', resembles the poet, both feared because both disturb or destroy existing worlds. 'A Refusal to Mourn' considers an appropriate response to the death of a young girl and so becomes another poem about the function of poetry. 'On a Wedding Anniversary' links the death through bombing of a married couple to his troubled relations with Caitlin.

Much the same can be said even of the apparently idyllic 'Fern Hill'. Written during the summer of 1945 by a Thomas troubled by personal problems aggravated by the end of the Second World War, and troubled further by Hiroshima and Nagasaki, it attempts an escape into memories of childhood. In the event, it demonstrates the problems of remembering and the impossibility of freeing memory from the effects of subsequent experience. The ending, with its bleakly secular notion of death as perpetual night and what can be read as a dislocating final apostrophe that prevents reassuring closure, emphasizes that at the heart even of 'Fern Hill' is rootlessness, uncertainty and despair.

Awareness of nuclear disaster is an important influence on the few poems that follow *Deaths and Entrances*, sometimes directly, as when, in 'Poem on his Birthday', he fears that

> . . . the rocketing wind will blow
> The bones out of the hills,
> And the scythed boulders bleed, and the last

> Rage shattered waters kick
> Masts and fishes to the still quick stars.

Thomas's note to 'In Country Heaven' describes the destruction of the world. His last completed poem, 'Prologue', links his own vulnerability – his disorderly existence in his 'seashaken house' – to the destruction of the world through a new deluge; his poems, he insists, perhaps too emphatically, will become arks, surviving the second flood, such optimism, as elsewhere in these final poems, straining against his writing's darker suggestiveness. Even in 'In the White Giant's Thigh', a poem mourning a lost past, there is the idea of complete annihilation.

Only in one respect is the later poetry consolatory. Three poems about his father demonstrate filial love. 'Lie still, sleep becalmed', in *Deaths and Entrances*, is at once a war poem and a poem about writing. It also presents his father as an Arthur floating to Avallon. Two later fatherly poems, 'Do not go gentle into that good night', advocating the setting aside of a genteel response to imminent death, and the unfinished 'Elegy', which, in contrast, praises his father for meeting death with dignity, together reconcile the 'Jack' and the 'D.J.' of the earlier work. Both poems incorporate literary echoes and allusions to pay tribute to Thomas's father as the man-of-letters he always wished to be.

Under Milk Wood, the unrevised 'play for voices' that now represents populist Thomas, owes something to the 'Nighttown' sequence of *Ulysses*, though without the politics or Joyce's darker sexual fantasies; to Edgar Lee Masters's *Spoon River Anthology*, though with the bitterness toned down; to Thomas's skill as a letter writer; and to his work, broadcasting and scripting films.

His best work for the BBC was the autobiographical or semi-autobiographical pieces in which he explored his upbringing, dramatized the social detail of ordinary life and asserted the power both of the imagination and of the past. Three of these are 'Reminiscences of Childhood', 'Memories of Christmas' and *Return Journey*. A fourth, 'Quite Early One Morning', is the most obvious antecedent of *Under Milk Wood* in that it draws an important contrast between the mundane world of a small Welsh seaside town and the riotous world of the imagination. Elsewhere are experiments with information conveyance and dual narration.

The film scripts are mainly hack-work. Thomas became a skilful writer of wartime propaganda, notably in Wales – *Green
Mountain, Black Mountain* (1942) and *Our Country* (1944), both of
which emphasize the values of work and community and the idea
of a new start when the war was over. He also worked on feature
films. Constantine Fitzgibbon estimated that Thomas 'probably
put more words on paper in this professional capacity than in any
other'. As a result he learned to write dialogue and to shape scenes.
His propaganda work was a matter of simplifying issues, creating
stereotypes and sustaining positive themes, all in the interests of
immediate effect. The strained optimism of some of his later
poems, such as 'Poem on his Birthday' and 'Prologue', may well
owe something to this.

Thomas's letters are often sharp, full of memorable phrases,
invariably entertaining and can be very funny. Certainly he raised
the begging letter to an art form. Elsewhere, he discussed his
poetics and the relationship between text and context. The letters,
particularly those to Pamela Hansford Johnson, offer revealing
self-examination. Other letters disturb: the love letters to Caitlin
chart desperate dependence; a late draft to Princess Caetani is a
despairing description of himself as a drowning Houdini struggling
to escape. Yet some letters of that period are humorous accounts
of day-to-day events in Laugharne, celebrating the comic
possibilities of small-town life. These, rather than the dark
psychological content of the 'Houdini' draft, fed directly into
Under Milk Wood.

Though, like all the best comedy, *Under Milk Wood* has a
serious purpose, Thomas was anxious to avoid over-darkening the
play. Written during post-war austerity and the age of the nuclear
deterrent, ostensibly it offered a kind of escapism, a lost Eden,
only to become yet another of Thomas's works to suggest the
impossibility of escaping. Like 'Quite Early One Morning', it
contrasts the world of private fantasies, the 'darkness behind the
eye', with seemingly controlled or repressed public behaviour.
Dreams and imaginings are always preferred to moralistic
actuality, as characters long for lost happiness. The play is popular
because of its abundant humour and warmth. It also touches on
serious ideas: that contrast between the imagined and the actual,
the idea of unjudging love, the power of the past, the disruptive
powers of love, the failures properly to communicate. Such ideas

remain undeveloped so that, given also that the play is not really complete, Thomas's literary career ends with unfinished business.

It was a spectacular career highlighting matters of central importance to any history of Anglo-Welsh writing. He achieved international standing and much popularity; indeed, we are still discovering the extent of interest and influence. His wide appeal raises questions about readership, and associated questions about his links with modernism. All are subsumed in the fundamental issue of Thomas as a Welsh writer.

Those first readers of 'I see the boys of summer', the first poem of his first book, would have been in no doubt that Thomas, though he prized neo-bardic vision, was rejecting the Welsh poet's traditional function of speaking to his own community. In that poem, as in much of his early work, he is a difficult writer, making few concessions to the general reader. He told a school friend that he wrote only for himself but this, of course, was not strictly true. Even in school-magazine poems about the Great War the sentimentalizing of death, for example, probably reflected an awareness of bereaved readers. When preparing *Twenty-five Poems*, following critical objections to obscurity in his poetry, he discussed with Vernon Watkins the need to provide alternative poems to what, in 1937, he called his 'exhausters'. He eagerly accepted the suggestion of Richard Church, his editor at Dent's, that he should turn from the neo-surrealistic early fiction to more approachable autobiographical stories. *Portrait of the Artist as a Young Dog* was the result. The general shift to writing that yielded more from a first reading also reflects critical feedback.

Thomas was a new kind of Welsh writer, the product of the bourgeois suburban upbringing only made possible in Wales by the late nineteenth-century appearance of an educated middle-class and urban expansion. Though occasionally we can recognize traditional functions – 'After the funeral' and 'Elegy', for example, are 'praise' poems – he restates the Welsh poet's role, replacing 'community' with 'readership' *and* reserving the post-Romantic right to be true to himself. In practice this last meant writing for an informed and sophisticated elite so that, paradoxically, he was also part of the growing gulf and antagonism between serious writers and the suburbs, let alone between the former and the masses.

Thomas was the first Welsh writer to be linked to modernism. He had read his Pound, Lawrence and T. S. Eliot, and it is not difficult to find modernist elements in his work. These include links with imagism, the use of myth, surrealism, apocalyptic tendencies, pervasive self-consciousness, rebellious individualism, let alone dislocated syntax and unusual language, plus, as Walford Davies has noted, 'the discontinuity of disparate images' and the 'irreducibility that comes from a relentless concreteness of presentation'. Further, an important aspect of modernism is its challenge to Anglocentric identity in its metropolitan form. As the Scottish poet and critic Robert Crawford had pointed out, it has a cultural-comparative quality, even a provinciality. Thomas, perhaps unconsciously, certainly offered that challenge: so much, perhaps all, of his work adopts, to say the least, that 'interstitial perspective' mentioned in Homi Bhabha's *The Location of Culture* (1994).

Yet, it is difficult not to share Thomas's own sense of his uneasy relationship with modernism, implicit, for example, in his insistence on 'form' and, hence, contempt for 'the sprawling formlessness of Ezra Pound's performing Yanks and others'. The connection, already noted, between form and his middle-class impulse towards order and authority, plus the value he placed on a strong narrative element in each poem, are further reasons for rethinking the relationship, even allowing for the authoritarian element in some modernist texts. Thomas's career began when the modernist movement had passed its peak. Poetry in Britain was dominated by 'MacSpaunday' social realism (Roy Campbell's celebrated conflation of MacNeice, Spender, Auden and Day-Lewis), against which, rather than against modernism, Thomas saw himself as reacting.

During the 1940s, though he dissociated himself from the extremes of the New Apocalypse movement, he was certainly part of the neo-Romantic strain in literature from 1930 to 1950. Influenced by modernism, if only in its use of the image as a structuring principle, neo-Romanticism flourished as interest in modernism declined.

Thomas is neither fully paid-up modernist nor out-and-out neo-Romanticist. Romantic elements in his work are always qualified. For example, the concern with 'process', with the 'cosmic significance of the human anatomy', which he mentioned in an early letter to Glyn Jones (March 1934), suggests an almost Wordsworthian sense of harmony between self and world. But in the important and representative 'process' poem, 'The force that through the green fuse', the relationship between body and world is subverted by the poet's existential isolation from nature, self and God. Modernist characteristics are, similarly, qualified by overt craftsmanship and a traditional sense of form that reflects an innate conservatism and a desire to conform, very different from the literary defiance of, say, Lawrence and Pound, which placed them at the heart of modernism.

The resultant combination in Thomas's work of Romanticism, modernism and the suburban sensibility, results in what might well be described as 'Welsh modernism'. Things fall apart, but not altogether. His originality and blazing literary personality forcibly unite that suburbanism with international dislocation. In so doing he forged a poetry for his (and our) time, in the process extending the possibilities of poetic language and syntax in work that often darts daringly into the violent, the sexual and the implicitly political.

With the partial exception of R. S. Thomas, a year older than Dylan but whose literary career began in the 1940s, Dylan Thomas almost completely overshadows his Welsh contemporaries. Despite his early death, he alone, of this chapter's writers, had a literary career in which achievement outweighs limitations or our sense of unfulfilled potential. Significantly, he was the only professional writer; the others wrote in their spare time.

Glyn Jones was a schoolteacher. Nevertheless, a steady stream of reviews, articles and letters on literary subjects, and other longer studies, made him, albeit part time, perhaps the only Welsh man-of-letters of the traditional kind. His 'non-creative' magnum opus is *The Dragon Has Two Tongues* (1968), a pioneering study of Anglo-Welsh literature. Like much of his occasional work it belongs more to belles-lettres than to modern literary criticism. Though beautifully written it is hardly rigorous; generosity invariably limited Jones's efficacy as a critic. Its value is in placing Anglo-Welsh writing as the product of a changing, predominantly English-speaking Welsh society, particularly in the south.

His first book was *The Blue Bed and Other Stories* (1937), well received both in London and in the USA. Like Dylan Thomas's early work, which influenced him strongly, it has strong modernist elements. Jones's interest in surrealism is evident, for example, in 'Eden Tree' – a story in which the protagonist digs up tears and excavates a cross – and, throughout the volume, in much imagery that effects startling defamiliarization: a small girl's wind-blown hair 'like the inverted claw of a honeysuckle flower'; a fading fire 'easing itself like an animal twisting for comfort'; a pit shaft 'like a huge inverted fool's-cap'; fields like 'sheets of green blotting-paper'. A second example is 'Porth-y-Rhyd', the volume's final story. This is a strange tale of a man, alone in a deserted and hostile landscape, who is ruined by grief for a dead lover and restored by an apparently divine encounter that also seems like an entry into death. Dylan Thomas's early fiction is a presence, but central to Glyn Jones's work is more familiar symbolism:

> In front of him was nothing except a laddered sea-sun on the sand, and the stones shagged black and green with weed, and stretching over him a thin white sky-skin with a crazy sun in it; when he turned to the shore, that too was empty in the distance and completely desolate . . . He stood in a warm pool and wept with his hands bloody over his face and the bleeding wounds of his feet sending out red growths into the water. It was bitter, knowing no man and being entirely alone on the earth. His life crumpled up and went dry and shrivelled, like a membrane. And then he felt the heat getting more than he could bear, and his tongue became like an earthy pebble in his mouth.

The Waste Land is a strong presence here. What is unique to Jones is the rendering of the natural scene, of the man's wounds, and of his life, in terms of the grotesque, the cancerous and the deformed. He offers, here, a dreadful affinity between man and nature, both ugly, drying, wasting away.

But Jones's first volume cannot be characterized only as late modernism. The volume is dominated by the novella, 'I Was Born in the Ystrad Valley', about an abortive attempt at a workers' revolution in which social superiors play a part. It may well reflect his experience of the General Strike of 1926 and, possibly, knowledge of the Merthyr Rising of 1831. The attitudes of the narrator, Wyn, the art-lecturer son of a collier, educated at an English university, are ruthlessly evaluated. They include his hubris regarding the poor and his fascist sympathies, the latter intensified by his, at times, homoerotic relationship with Alun, the ruthless fascist journalist who recruits Wyn into the revolutionary movement. The revolution having failed, Wyn returns to his home valley, whereupon realism is replaced by symbolism. Wyn falls upon the mountainside above his home, describing himself as 'huge carrion'; seemingly still conscious, he becomes part of the harsh natural setting until, finally, he is attacked with vicious cruelty by wild birds: 'Naked headed heavy birds snarl from their cruel slate-hooks, they beat with their raw wing-bones against my bitten face . . . And now at last the vultures lift their beaks out of my eaten eyes.' This sequence may draw on medieval accounts of fallen warriors preyed upon by birds, and on a bourgeois version of the Prometheus myth – the myth itself accessed through Jones's enthusiasm for Shelley – in which Wyn is punished for his radical presumption in trying to wrest from authority what he believes rightfully belongs to the people. In both readings the stress is on defeat; Wyn ends his life in suffering outside his home community. Both readings are complicit in the bourgeois text's absolute rejection of revolution even against an oppressive social order.

This story is very much of its time, the 1930s; the presence of an intruding narrator is a further reminder of Dylan Thomas's fiction. Such a narrator recurs throughout Jones's shorter fiction either as participant or as confidant, as occasionally patronizing observer, as anthropologist or, almost, as naturalist equipped with eager net and sketchbook, two classic middle-class roles. The world entered or observed is invariably working class, at best petit-bourgeois, inhabited by colliers, ironworkers and village shop-keepers, plus their slatternly wives. It is a site of constant, sometimes shocking, disruptive and violent intrusions: the dead into life, the living into death, God into a miner's cottage, a miner digging into the unknown, man into nature.

Jones's is a bleak vision, particularly of relations between men and women, most of which are strangely asexual. When they are not, the sexual is invariably linked to the deformed, struggles for power and helplessness. The title story is typical: the gardener beats an empty bed with a branch in a paroxysm of violent, sadistic sexual frustration. There is an obsession with the physically grotesque and repulsive. Two examples, both from 'Wil Thomas', can stand for many:

> His hair was white and cut short, and for a nose he had a hook like a large soft beak, big and fleshy, constellated all over with small equally spaced blue black-heads like pencil dots. His heavy jaw, wanting a shave, was like white velvet and his eyes were noticeable, being khaki –

his eye, more like, because he had only one. The place where the other
had been looked sore, the raw lids hanging loose, the flesh all round red
as though the eye-hole had been cut in his skin with a scissors.

Later, the returned dead minister forces one-eyed Wil to take into
his hand an offered eye: 'it was . . . slimy like a peeled plum, heavy
and moist as an egg-plum with the skin pulled off.' This is typical
of the constant emphasis on gross sensation or physical behaviour,
the latter including belching bakers, preachers with running noses,
dying miners with gangrenous legs. At its most extreme, as, for
example, in 'Wat Pantathro', human beings are reduced to a
number of ugly physical details, humanity slipping away from
grotesque stereotypes.

Jones's sheer love of language and his flair for visual strangeness
characterize all his shorter fiction. But accumulated descriptive
detail and, on occasion, overwrought poetical prose, too often
overwhelm an often slight narrative line. Because of this last it is
surprising that he turned to the novel.

He wrote three: *The Valley The City The Village* (1956), *The
Learning Lark* (1960) and *The Island of Apples* (1965). The first of
these is the story of a young man becoming an artist, reflecting the
author's own early ambition. The painterly – at times neo-
surrealistic – style is perhaps the book's main strength:

> I saw the dwarfed colliery like a ship with steaming funnels anchored in
> the valley. As we passed the rows of houses on the hills we were
> welcomed, house after house greeted us with the silver flashings of their
> sunlit windows, they were our salvo of silent guns. Far below, the grey
> tips folded their bat's-wings over their faces.

M. Wynn Thomas has commented that, in such passages, the
'familiar is deconstructed, as in modernist art, in order to be
reconstructed in all its wonderful, unpredictable and gratuitous
strangeness'. This is so, and there is, also, in such passages, a
savouring of experience that points to a fundamental humaneness.
Hence the author's endorsement of the progress of Trystan, the
novel's hero, who rejects conventional careers – as a teacher or a
preacher – in order to be true to his artistic self. Here, as so often
in Jones's work, the influence of D. H. Lawrence is very strong.
But though we can admire some vivid characterization – Trystan's

formidable landlady Miss Machen, his friend Gwydion – and the language's visual force, that same language can distract. Certainly the novel's final part collapses structurally, in part into neo-Joycean imitation. In this there may well be a failure of vision or, possibly, a failure to translate Romantic gestures into practicalities.

The Learning Lark is a dated and slackly written satire of corrupt educational practices in south Wales valleys. *The Island of Apples* is Jones's best novel. It is not without his usual faults, which include a wearisome and distasteful stress on the physically gross, at times linked to recurring references to maiming. The narrative line, slight at best, is again, at times, obscured by detailed description. The Arthurian connotations of the title suggest other Arthurian symbolism: the sudden appearance of the aptly initialled Karl Anthony; the dagger he gives to Dewi; the final voyage. Possibly the Arthurian legend is here subverted: a dagger seems less morally forceful than Arthur's sword; the final voyage ends not in Avallon but with Karl's death by drowning. A coherent symbolic framework is elusive.

The novel's achievement is also limited by its subject matter. There are no developed adult relationships, or young female characters. Apart from Karl Anthony, who seems about seventeen, the main characters are pre-pubertal boys aged twelve or thirteen. There is little sense of a wider social context: though the story is set in the first quarter of the twentieth century, the Great War, for example, hardly impinges; nor, in a time of economic hardship, does politics.

Yet, despite faults and limitations, *The Island of Apples* has great strengths. This story of young Dewi Davies and his friends in a drab Ystrad closely based on Merthyr, and the transformation effected by the arrival of the strangely exotic Karl Anthony, explores the relationship between the real world and the romantic, the factual and the imaginary. Though the power of the imagination is recognized and celebrated, the book's greater achievement is in the realization that the imagination can corrupt as well as inspire. Hence the insistence on the limitations of romantic imaginings dramatized through Karl's tawdrily glamorous boasting about his past that seems to owe much to pulp fiction, and how attractive fantasy can be inimical to community and appropriate responsibilities. Dewi, obsessed with glamorous Karl (further hints at the homoerotic), is drawn away from Ystrad and the adult world he is on the verge of entering and which Karl, as a seventeen-year-old mixing only with those much younger, seems to have rejected. The relationship inspires some of Jones's finest writing, in which, again, the ordinary is constantly defamiliarized. The sequences involving the gang of boys at their 'camp' on the hillside and, in particular, Karl's account of climbing the high pillar of a disused railway viaduct, for once show narrative drive dominating self-indulgent description.

Even the loose ends – the enigmatic Arthurianism, the un-explained discovery of Buddug in distress and with her dress ripped, the mysterious dagger in the murdered headmaster – and the improbabilities of the ending (the murder itself, together with the boys' attempted escape by boat) help blur the line between realism and the imaginary. The refusal to explain, the open-endedness of the novel, the subversion of apparent discourses (realism, fantasy), the links with magic realism, position this work between the modernism evident in *The Blue Bed* and the siren songs of postmodernism. This can be restated in terms of the limitations of realism or, a further reminder of Dylan Thomas, as a late example of Romantic modernism.

Jones's poetry, like his fiction, is a mixture of the achieved and the problematic. The definitive judgement has been made by Leslie Norris: too many of the poems are too descriptive, too lacking in central conflict. To this can be added the further objection that too many of his poems – 'Where all were good to me, God knows' is one example – are soft-centred explorations of valley life. That said, he has written a few poems that, if not truly premier league, are certainly in the first division of twentieth-century British poetry. One is 'The Common Path', the intensely moving poem about a schoolmistress who, so obviously troubled by what the observer later learns was fatal 'rectal cancer', is avoided by a younger, self-sufficient man who passes by 'on the other side', the Good Samaritan allusion deftly universalizing the particular. The poem is a triumph of tone, modulating from the patronizing to self-flagellating irony to bitter acceptance of fault. It sustains a narrative line, the 'moving column' that Dylan Thomas prized, through controlled lists of feelings and qualities, and carefully balances the colloquial and the lyrical. The keyword is 'control', such containment, particularly of Jones's tendency to dwell on physical detail, intensifying the effect of the poem's emotional cargo. This quality is found in most of his successful poems. In 'Easter' ('Morning in the honey-months'), for example, delicate descriptions of nature contain that of a dying woman portrayed unflinchingly but unsensationally:

> In death's stink now, with tears I watch her, old
> And hideous in her dying – bitterly
> She moans, her face death-dark, her tangled hair
> Tortured behind her little rolling head.

Closing Christian consolation is derived persuasively from felt suffering: 'Soon, soon, the doors of every grave shall open/ And the light of dawn shall shine upon the dead.' Jones's best poems are about loss. 'Bindweed', about a man's death in war, generates emotional complexity in that we do not know the sex of the narrator. If male, the poem has a powerful homoerotic charge. If female, this is not the only poem with a woman narrator, a further example of Lawrentian influence. 'Remembering Alcwyn', a memory of a cousin killed on the Western Front, is a recognition of war's tragic legacy; the intensity of the poet's feelings for Alcwyn as he returns to France and death drives the poem through realist detail. 'The Meaning of Fuchsias', which also remembers the dead, begins as another 'Fern Hill' – childhood recollected in fallen adulthood – controls lush description and modulates into a moving encounter with Jones's own past:

> So that I bear again the sudden burden
>   of my many dead,
>   And you, and all our darkened suns,
>   possess me through the doorways of my tears . . .

In 'Merthyr', lighter but no less serious, Jones, as in *The Island of Apples*, sets (and celebrates) community against romantic apartness. In a humorously self-deprecating style he describes his poetic inclinations: 'I fancy words', he admits, 'have a knack for telling bardic lies' and, critics tell him, 'a talent copious in metaphor.' Such gifts, we now see, brought their own problems: Glyn Jones was a considerable literary talent in need of the great editor he never managed to find.

Like his friend Dylan Thomas, he can seem another Welsh modernist, particularly in his early work. As such, despite warm feelings for community, he, like Thomas, was rejecting the Welsh writer's traditional role. In part this was because of his upbringing, middle-class in predominantly working-class Merthyr, and because of the solipsistic element in the post-Romantic English literary tradition in which he was raised. Further, though there is some force in the argument that Jones, out of his strong Christian faith, insists that, as Tony Brown has put it, humankind's 'physical reality . . . [has] a divine origin and a spiritual reality', readers surely remain uneasy at the constant stress on repulsive physical detail. In Jones's work it is difficult to avoid a misanthropic fastidiousness which allies him, for all his moments of compassion, not only with Swift but also with those writers and intellectuals who possessed little but distaste for the twentieth century's dirty, ugly, literate masses.

Idris Davies, however, wished to speak for and to his people. When Geoffrey Grigson patronized *Gwalia Deserta* as the product of 'a simple and superficial mind', Davies replied indignantly: 'I wish it was simpler than it is, for even now it is too "difficult" for . . . the folk whom I have tried to write about.' Yet, despite such community spirit and his upbringing and pit work in Rhymney, his life became a journey away from his roots. After studying in his spare time, playing 'the long and lonely/ Self-tuition game', he left Rhymney for Loughborough College and Nottingham University, before teaching in London. *Gwalia Deserta* was published by Dent, subsequent volumes by T. S. Eliot at Faber. The Second World War returned him for a while to a school in the Rhondda; in 1947 he secured a teaching appointment in Rhymney. Both returns were bitter disappointments: the valleys, he believed, had become vulgar and materialistic. He was then in the last years of his life, with all his important work behind him.

Davies had read Lawrence, Yeats and T. S. Eliot, but he much preferred Blake, Shelley, Tennyson and Housman. In his early poetry Romantics are filtered through Georgians to become Shropshire lads. One result, already noted, was the poem in *The Welsh Outlook*. Literary language apart, his penchant for 'strictly rhyming metrical verses' means that too many of his poems 'have an air of doggerel about them', as in 'The Valley Lights':

> O, some who used to love these hills,
> They died so that the free

> Should light again the lights of old
> Themselves no more shall see.

'Love poem' offers a similar glib combination of language, metre and rhyme. Tennyson's *Maud* is an obvious influence:

> And I murmured to the roses,
>   The purple and the cream:
> 'O warm and wild and lovely,
>   More wondrous than a dream.'

His occasional poetry, which includes poems on valley life, unexpected patriotic outbursts, such as 'An English Youth (Epitaph)' and 'Amy Johnson', some nature writing, and poems about visits to Cardiff, Ireland and London, establishes Idris Davies as a very minor Romantic misplaced in time and mistaken in aim. Very few of these lyrics escape the deadening effect of the second-hand. One that does is 'Marx and Heine and Dowlais', significantly a poem in free verse. It contrasts past London literary evenings with present experience of a depressed Dowlais that clearly illustrated Marx's 'rigid phrases' and where – since Dowlais was 'Naked and hard as flint,/ Romance in a rough chemise' – even Heine was not irrelevant. In this poem at least Davies demonstrates his ability to coin a memorable line and to handle colloquial rhythms; he shifts dialogically from realist description of London to a powerful imagistic evocation of Dowlais. Another success is 'The Black Tips of Rhondda', in which a surrealistic edge – the tips as grinning, gloating harlots – defamiliarizes a conventional valley subject. 'I was born in Rhymney', which has 112 four-line rhyming stanzas, holds the reader through an account of Davies's life, not only because of the intrinsic interest of the subject but because of the tension and sense of inevitablity generated by the ballad form.

Most of Davies's poems, however, including that product of sentimental memory, the late sequence *Tonypandy* (1945), are of little consequence beyond the documentary. His reputation depends almost wholly on *Gwalia Deserta* (1938) and *The Angry Summer* (1943). Yet these two sequences contain a number of poems that, if considered individually, appear to have all the faults of his occasional writing. Yet he had learned, possibly from Eliot, almost certainly from Housman, what could be achieved through juxtaposing different styles and forms within a sequence. As a consequence, that sequence becomes more than the sum of its parts and each part is enhanced by being part of a sequence. From Eliot and the 1930s 'pylon poets' he may also have learned a central modernist tenet, an eclectic sense of what might be suitable material for poetry.

Gwalia Deserta describes the effect on south Wales of the economic Depression of the 1930s. It is an exile's view, for by 1938 Davies had been away from Rhymney for eight years. He surely has himself in mind when he writes in one of the closing sections of the 'young man' who 'on the rain-washed platform . . . says goodbye'. The world he left behind, and the world before that, are the subjects of the sequence. The sections focus on a number of themes, one being how it all began, 'when greed was born', a history of suffering leading to the calamitous 1930s. Other sections point to the difficulty of sustaining basic human values. A number celebrate the persisting capacity for enjoyment sustained by despairing mining communities. Thus Davies writes in one of his most famous sections:

> Do you remember 1926? The slogans and the penny concerts,
> The jazz-bands and the moorland picnics.

Jaunts to Cardiff are described, with soccer matches at Ninian Park and pubs and tarts after the match when 'Tiger Bay *was* Tiger Bay'. Other sections celebrate the beauties not only of the mountains above drab valley towns but also of sudden urban moments, 'When the lights in the valley brag to the stars'. A desperately sad finale includes the memory of a group of young men on an evening walk to Merthyr:

> For we were boyish dreamers in a world we did not know
> When we walked to Merthyr Tydfil in the moonlight long ago.

The sequence ends with hope for the future and an insistence on the survival of humane values, so that, 'The things my boyhood cherished/ Stand firm, and shall remain'.

Gwalia Deserta, like some of his occasional poems, is distinguished by memorable lines and phrases. His description of the

1926 Great Strike – 'The great dream and the swift disaster' – is well known. Equally striking are his lines on 'our far Eldorados/ In invisible valleys of air' and, a further example, his description of unemployed miners busking in London, 'Begging with broken hands . . . / Out of the derelict lands'. Above all, the juxtaposing of sections in rhyming stanzas to those in blank verse, short lines to long, the colloquial to the poetic-rhetorical, one style often subverting another, creates an almost unbearable pathos close to tragedy.

Idris Davies's finest work is *The Angry Summer*, subtitled 'A Poem of 1926'. Written during the early 1940s, the darkest days of the Second World War, this is a far more complex and ambitious work than *Gwalia Deserta*. The single narrative voice of the earlier work now competes with others: Dan the grocer struggling to deal with penniless customers; an Anglican vicar trying to sympathize with the strikers; a Nonconformist minister, realist and ready supporter of those 'who dare/ To strike at the roots of their misery'; the tailor giving easy terms. Other characters and events recur: lovers on the mountainside, drunken Amos in the pub, busking excursions into Breconshire, calls to violent action, exhortations to fight the good political fight. The variety of styles, the various voices, create a sense of a community under pressure a world away from cosy memories of valley life. The whole is underpinned by the narrative of the Great Strike from the miners' decision to go it alone to the end of the action in the autumn of 1926. That ending is represented, in Section 48, as the sudden result of the treacherous complicity of union and government. This makes for a dramatic conclusion but is wholly unhistorical: in reality the strike collapsed slowly as men drifted back to work.

In such an ending Davies seems unable to accept or understand the comparative complexity of the disastrous defeat. In simplifying he confirms his status as a minor poet. A similar example, also from late in the sequence, is Section 45. It begins:

> Now on your quick allotment
> Plant your dream beyond disaster,
> Nourish roots to split the strata
> Of death.

Conran suggests that the garden scene in *Richard II* is a useful analogy; he points to the various connotations of 'quick' as evidence of Davies's suggestiveness. To this can be added the sense of 'allotment' as 'the strict portion that has been given', as well as the vegetable plot. But what follows these opening lines is simply confused. The 'scarlet rose' of line five is probably a symbol of left-wing political action but the next line – 'Keeping an eye on corn and flesh' is puzzling because seemingly far from the idealistic exhortations that follow. The line could mean being concerned lest 'corn and flesh' replace idealism, but this is not quite what is conveyed. Worse is to come: though cherishing, in Davies's Blakean phrase, 'the secret forest' of 'faith and fortitude and truth', the exhortee is then urged to 'wage an everlasting war/ On the swollen roots of vulgarity', which seems a trivial aim in comparison with support for the eternal verities.

As Valentine Cunningham has noted (see his interesting review 'Whistling in the Grime', *Times Literary Supplement*, 8 September 1995, 27), Idris Davies may be compared to Kipling in that both impinge powerfully and directly on readers' emotions. Both are adept at handling the cadences of everyday, working-class speech. The voices of *The Angry Summer* include miners as well as clergy-men and tradesmen; 'Let's go to Barry Island, Maggie fach', for example, captures those cadences and intensifies their emotional effect through being part of a multi-voiced sequence that is at times dramatic through contrasts, in which section often com-ments on section, and in which recurring images accumulate meaning. It is a considerable achievement.

It has been praised as a Welsh achievement: 'The essential thing about his English poems', writes Valentine Cunningham, 'is that they are not English, and that they are not written in English English.' This is only partly true, given the influence of the English Romantics, and the lessons Davies learned from Housman and T. S. Eliot. Further, the comment misses that achievement's para-doxical quality: the poet who wished to speak directly to a simple people not only plunges into the interstice between English literature and Anglo-Welsh writing but can be taken seriously only when purveying the fragmentation and dislocations of late modernism for a readership sufficiently sophisticated to grasp how his poem-sequences work.

Vernon Watkins, like Idris Davies, was a prestigious 'Faber poet'. When he died in 1967 he was among the favourites to succeed John Masefield as Poet Laureate. This eminence owed a

great deal to a technical virtuosity as dazzling as that of his friend,
Dylan Thomas, as can be seen in a stanza from 'Thames Forest':

> Dumb roots are whispering; light breaks in darkness;
> Frail fibres grasp there, clinging to the close clod.
> Under the warm green vellum of the meadow
> Trance-wise the seeds break.

The energy of the first two lines is derived from the dactyls; the
irregular third line is stressed to dramatize poised timelessness; the
hard-edged 'break' in line four brings the seeds to life. Such writing
seems effortless but is, of course, the product of almost every
evening of his life: after work in a Swansea bank he returned home
and wrote poetry.

Watkins was born in Maesteg, but from the age of seven he grew
up in Swansea, the same town as his close friend, Dylan Thomas.
After prep school and Repton, Watkins left Cambridge without a
degree and worked in a Cardiff branch of Lloyds Bank. A nervous
breakdown returned him to Swansea. That breakdown was the
first of three traumatic experiences, the other two being the
destruction of old Swansea in the Second World War and the
death of Dylan Thomas. We can recognize the poetry as a stay
against confusion – 'These fragments I have shored against my
ruins' – or, in Tony Conran's words, an attempt 'to assemble a
consistency of style that should assert eternal order against time's
fragmentation'. In practice this meant a shift away from concrete
reality.

Watkins wrote much but was slow to publish: he was thirty-five
when *Ballad of the Mari Lwyd and Other Poems* appeared in 1941.
During his formative years he was hardly in the mainstream of
British literary life, his only literary friendship of consequence
being that with Dylan Thomas. But while Watkins willingly acted
as Thomas's reader and private critic, Thomas rarely reciprocated,
even though Watkins claimed that his friend showed him 'what
was fresh in my work, and what was not'. In any case, Watkins
neither liked criticism nor seemed much affected by it.

The lack of a critical milieu was unfortunate. Much of his poetry
is not so much difficult as obscure. It repels because it 'is recondite
in its references and arcane in its idiom'. Too often it is an
exclusive and excluding poetry prone to soar into rarified rhetoric.

A comparison with Dylan Thomas is instructive. Many even of the grandest of Thomas's rhetorical gestures retain contact with the language really used by suburbanites: 'Heads of the characters hammer through daisies', he cries in 'And death shall have no dominion', the rhetoric made acceptable because it retains a link with the real world through the colloquial 'pushing up daisies'. On the other hand, reading Watkins's poems can at times seem like struggling away from life through rooms of cotton wool.

He does not help his cause by a style that can be bafflingly elliptical, nor by frequently retreating into arcane material, such as the Taliesin legends, and intensely private references. As an example of the latter: no outsider could guess, let alone know, that in 'The Broken Sea' the reference to 'the painter of limbo at the top of the fragrant stairs' is to Watkins's friend, the Swansea painter Alfred Janes, whose studio was above his parents' flower shop. Not quite so arcane is the Neoplatonism at the heart of much of Watkins's work. It has led Roland Mathias, his most perceptive critic, to cite the 'conquest of time' as his most dominant theme. This can be seen in the poem 'Foal', in Watkins's concern with 'the vessel of ages' that is, in Mathias's words, 'the Platonic replica, the original shape and spirit of the foal laid down in the beginning, of which the one living is merely the unknowing and accepting example'. It can also be seen in Watkins's treatment of nature. Though he can write of the natural world with a detailed precision reminiscent of Tennyson he is not a conventional 'nature poet'. Rather, natural creatures and objects are 'an evocation of an ultimate order'. As Watkins himself wrote: 'I marvel at the beauty of landscape, but I never think of it as a theme for poetry until I read metaphysical symbols behind what I see.' Poetry thus became a means of penetrating to and validating truths beyond the human. In time, these truths tended to shift from the Neoplatonic to the Christian.

The alliance of splendid technique and difficult material militates against reader-friendly poems; many are ornate and complex rhetorical structures where meaning can slip away in the face of pattering sound and exhibited skill. Thus, though there is a seer-like or visionary element in his work, evident in a plethora of extreme rhetorical devices, often exclamatory or apostrophic, such as 'I sing a placeless and a timeless heaven', or 'O, have you seen the leper healed . . .?' which might be described as Welsh in the popular 'bardic' sense of the term, Watkins, like Dylan Thomas, rejected traditional claims upon the poet. His work often demonstrates the solipsistic extreme of the post-Romantic British tradition. Another way of putting this might be to say that Watkins ignored his readers by retreating into poetry, showing comparatively little interest in ordinary, work-based, domesticated existence or in the urban setting in which he spent so much of his life.

His work is all too easily criticized. Like Glyn Jones he would have benefited from a strong editorial hand. It might at least have prevented him from choosing unsuitable forms – his excursions into the ballad and the long poem seem ill advised for a poet lacking in narrative drive – or countered a lack of poetic tact. This last can be illustrated from 'Returning to Goleufryn' in which much superb writing, particularly the first stanza describing revisiting his grandfather's house in Carmarthen which he had known as a child, exists alongside quaintly personifying apostrophe: 'Sing, little house, clap hands: shut, like a book of the Psalms', and by the determinedly poetic, 'O lead me that I may drown/ In those earlier cobbles'. To an extent, the poem recovers, particularly in its final stanza celebrating the dead and the past:

Yet now I am lost, lost in the water-wound looms
Where brief, square windows break on a garden's decay.
Gold butter is shining, the tablecloth speckled with crumbs.
The kettle throbs. In the calendar harvest is shown,
Standing in sheaves. Which way would I do you wrong?
Low, crumbling doorway of the infirm to the mansions of evening,
And poor, shrunken furrow where the potatoes are sown,
I shall not unnumber one soul I have stood with and known
To regain your stars struck by horses, your sons of God breaking in song.

This is exceptional writing. Significantly, it shifts from realist detail to luminous metaphor that warns against valuing sentimentalized recollection – childhood, in that final line, as a lost world of wonder and faith – more than the people who, then and since, have inhabited his life. The significance is in the shift: it points to Watkins's greatest strength and the need to read him selectively. For though there is no denying the strong lyrical impulse in much of his work, as in the 'Music of Colours' poems, and his constant ability to create lines of great beauty, it is necessary to return to the three traumata.

His nervous breakdown in 1927 helps explain why and to some extent how he wrote. It led to 'a revolution of sensibility', as he put it, through which he came to believe that poetry, and only poetry, would conquer time. This involved a rejection of linear time in favour of a Yeatsian cycle in which 'the present bulges with the enormous mass of the past' and finite life seems extended into infinity so that, to quote Watkins again, 'I was with them still when time was not'. Such thinking made him insufficiently concerned with sensual impressions.

The two later traumata, however, counter this. They emphasize what 'Return to Goleufryn' shows: Watkins is at his considerable best when the poems have a foundation of realist detail, when they begin and never wholly lose contact with the 'real' world, even though they may have an abstract or metaphysical theme. Three poems on different themes demonstrate this. 'Thames Forest', already quoted in part, is a superb descriptive poem that is also a moving statement about mutability and the relationship between natural and human death and resurrection; 'Sardine-fishers at Daybreak' and 'Bishopston Stream' are poems in which the fishing and the stream become metaphors for, respectively, the juxta-position of death and all that the dawn represents, and the idea of time passing. But occasional poems notwithstanding, those about the Second World War and Dylan Thomas's death, particularly the latter (some of which are also about the war), probably constitute his main (considerable) claim on contemporary readers.

Though 'Sea Music for My Sister Travelling' is a response to his sister's voyage to India by troopship, the poem has little to do with war. Watkins's main and aesthetically indulgent concern is to evoke the idea and movement of the sea on which his sister travelled. But 'The Broken Sea' shows Watkins at his best in the moving evocation of occupied Paris:

> Between two sirens shaking
> The immense, white, memory-crowded, sleeping capital:
> Villainous print at a lamp-post,
> A long shaft of moonlight,
> And the people that walked in darkness crossing the firth
> Of sleep and waking, moving in ghostly ritual[.]

The French predicament is made more poignant by the brilliantly used biblical echo that inserts Christian optimism into these lines. Equally effective is the section on bombed Swansea, in which

> The burnt-out clock of St Mary's has come to a stop,
> And the hand still points to the figure that beckons the
>   house-stoned dead.

Such desolation makes appropriate – for once – the romantic apostrophes that follow, and the firmly optimistic insistence on 'eternal Genesis'.

In 'The Spoils of War', echoes of Hopkins and of Dylan Thomas's war poetry are integrated into a poem on the death of a mother killed by a bomb as she looks after her child in a Swansea air-raid shelter:

> Pitched into light, under the wind and whine of bombs,
> When the pavings flew up to the stars in a volley of tombs.
> Night is burnt white in the dirt of a street in Manselton.

The great achievements of this poem include the sense of the loss of participation in the child's future – the 'skipping-rope world of to-morrow's names and games' – and piercing moments of grief amidst the dramatizing of violent bombing. The final line – 'Look on her face; mine eyes dazzle; she died young' – amends Webster's famous line from *The Duchess of Malfi*, a play in which a good woman is destroyed by evil, to universalize the wartime death. In that Watkins's intertextual procedure reminds us of T. S. Eliot, we here encounter a modernist flourish.

His greatest achievement is the sequence of lyrics written in response to the death of Dylan Thomas. The friendship began in 1935, Watkins's near obsession with Thomas as man and poet leading to numerous poems, the best known of which are 'Portrait of a Friend', which puzzles over the complex nature of Thomas's work and character, and 'Llewelyn's Chariot', one of several poems for Thomas's eldest child, Watkins's godson. Thirteen poems concern themselves directly with Thomas's death. They emerge as a sequence when read in order of volume publication and of printing within each volume.

The sequence can be compared to Tennyson's *In Memoriam A.H.H.*; it is, indeed, 'In Memoriam D.M.T.'. It begins with a three-poem introduction – 'The Sloe', 'The Return' and 'The Exacting Ghost' – in which the dead Thomas reappears vividly in dreams, before 'Birth and Morning', in which Watkins's son, who would have been Thomas's godson, lies under apple trees in a garden where Thomas maintains a presence as a 'magnanimous ghost'. 'The Curlew', 'Angel and Man', 'The Mask of Winter' and 'Buried Light' then comprise the sequence's bleakest section. Here the ideas are troubling: the contrast between the finality of Thomas's end and recurring nature, the inability to be consoled by the idea of a pantheistic life-after-death in nature, remembrance as a source only of grief, and the world as winter without hope of spring. The possibility of Christian consolation is noticeably absent.

The final lines of 'In the Protestant Cemetery, Rome', in which Watkins describes leaving the graves of 'paired friends', Shelley and Trelawny, Keats and Severn, is the sequence's fulcrum. Here, the cemetery's cypress and acacia represent death and life, both rooted in the same soil and symbolizing a new sense of harmonious relationship that includes acceptance of what has been lost. Gwen Watkins has noted that these lines suggest Laugharne churchyard; as such they mark a step away from grief, emotional progress that is sustained in 'A True Picture Restored'. That 'true picture' is now discovered not involuntarily through dreams but willingly through memories and Watkins's persisting sense of his dead friend's worth.

The conclusion, like the introduction, consists of three poems. 'The Present', responding to a Rollie McKenna photograph of Thomas that stood on Watkins's desk, insists that the poetry lives on by generating 'New meanings'. Despite an unexpected lurch into sentimentality in the last two lines – 'So calm the eyes beneath the brow,/ Held in a breath by angels there' (a revealing momentary lapse from the tight emotional control exerted elsewhere) – this poem and 'Exegesis' demonstrate both Watkins's acceptance of Thomas's death and his friend's continuing presence as an irreplaceable light in darkness that survives even the lurid distortions of legend that 'Only falsify/ Light broken into colours.'

The final poem, the intense and graceful 'The Snow Curlew', recalls 'The Sloe' in returning to winter but, at last, to a winter no longer divorced from the promise of spring. Watkins, in middle age, endeavours to begin the world again:

> It is good-bye
> To all things not beginning, and I must try,
> Making the driftwood catch,
> To coax, where the cry fades, fires which cannot fall.

Throughout the sequence Watkins increases the poignancy of remembrance by incorporating Thomas material, literary influences on him, and allusions to his work. The first includes the use of dreams, and references to the Second World War and to such Thomas places as Swansea, Laugharne and London. The second includes Henry Vaughan, Shelley, Keats, Tennyson, Hopkins, Hardy, Yeats and Wilfred Owen, a number of whom died young. Allusions to Thomas's own work include the air raids of *Deaths and Entrances* in 'The Return', and the apple-boughs of 'Fern Hill' in 'Birth and Morning'. 'The Curlew' points both to Thomas's numerous 'curlew' references, and to his general response to nature, especially coastal nature. In this poem, Watkins waits sadly on the shore for a Thomas already dead in New York, still hearing his 'cry' but knowing that, unlike the curlew, he will never return; the bird itself comes to symbolize the lost poet. 'Angel and Man', in representing existence as 'this sad field where the world tends her wounded/ And shrouds their limbs whose eyes are shut for ever', is a reminder of Thomas's poems on the Great War. Throughout the sequence the use of tight poetic forms, the stanza of four short rhyming lines as the norm, then skilful and dialogic variations, and the use of syllabics, can be seen as a tribute to Thomas's formal skills.

In Tennyson's *In Memoriam A.H.H.*, Arthur Hallam becomes more than merely Tennyson's friend. The particular, personal circumstances of Hallam's death enable an exploration of doubt and faith that, through wide-ranging imagery and reference, transcends the particular to become an ultimately consoling metaphor for those troubled by problems of belief in the mid-Victorian period. 'In Memoriam D.M.T.' is also grounded in the particular, in what have been described, in another context, as 'confidently deployed local allusions', such as those to a shared air-raid experience, to Thomas's would-be godson asleep in Watkins's garden, and to details of Thomas's life in Swansea, Laugharne and London. Patrick Kavanagh famously stated that the provincial imagination was always looking over its shoulder for metropolitan approval. To judge from his use of local and personal references Watkins never even moved his head. Like Tennyson, Watkins's imagery, mainly from dreams, nature and photography, together with Thomas's fame, enables him to construct a widely accessible 'living metaphor'. 'The Snow Curlew', the final poem that shows grief changed into hope and new beginnings, is typical: intimations of spring in winter, snow as a clean page waiting to be inscribed, the need to turn driftwood into a permanent source of flame, all universalize the personal sub-text. The replacement of the high rhetorical style with lyrical-conversational rhythms is a concluding, clinching version of the metaphorical mode.

Watkins rarely wrote such sharp, precise, accessible, and moving poems as in this sequence. In speaking for a world mourning the loss of an important writer he moves closer to the communal role he elsewhere seems to reject. But this is not very close. Here is a further example of an essentially Romantic poet occasionally gesturing at modernism, this last mainly through intertextual reference and the affinity with symbolist writing that Neoplatonism encouraged. The intertextuality is a potent reminder that Watkins is another poet of the interstice in which geographical Welshness meets English literature and where all the best Anglo-Welsh writing is to be found.

Watkins, undeservedly, has become a marginal figure within the Anglo-Welsh canon. Whether Lynette Roberts's work is part of that canon remains problematic. Though of Welsh parentage she was born and received her early education in Argentina before attending boarding school in England. In 1939 she married Keidrych Rhys, the editor of *Wales*; they set up home and raised a family in Llanybri, Carmarthenshire. She, too, became a Faber poet, with *Poems* (1944) and *Gods with Stainless Ears* (1951); a third volume, 'The Fifth Pillar of Song', was rejected by Faber in 1953, the few poems subsequently printed showing a sad decline, partly into sentimental cliché. Following her divorce in 1959 she stopped writing. After living in various places in England and Wales, old and in poor mental health, she entered a nursing home in Ferryside, Carmarthenshire, where she died in 1995.

Lynette Roberts lived permanently in Wales for only fifteen years, a period that coincides, almost exactly, with her literary

career. The only basis for considering her as an Anglo-Welsh
writer is that a number of her poems are set in Llanybri and
environs, even though the perspective is that of a foreigner. Her
life and work raise large and largely unanswered questions about
literary identity.

There are also nagging doubts about the quality of some of her
poems. This can be illustrated by two quotations. The first is from
'Rhode Island Red':

> In plate green meadows sheepdog and farmer brood,
> On galvanised can.
> Calling cattle from celandine and clover to mood,
> Song of joy I sing.

As the title suggests, the poem is about a chicken crowing or
clucking in a farmyard. Seemingly, part is from the chicken's
point-of-view. 'To mood' is puzzling. It could, of course, mean
'according to my mood', but the suspicion remains that the need to
rhyme overcame the requirements of coherent syntax. Further,
why should the sheepdog and farmer brood on a galvanised can?
They may be brooding whilst sitting on it; they may regard it as
disfiguring the natural scene. Yet, if a period replaces the comma
after 'brood', and a comma the period after 'can', all becomes
plainer, so that inaccurate punctuation seems possible. The
corrected final sentence states that the chicken sings its song whilst
perched on a diesel can left in the farmyard.

The second quotation is from 'Earthbound', about making and
taking a wreath for a dead villager: 'We walked the greaving room
alone,/ Saw him lying in his upholstered box'. 'Greaving' is a well-
known crux. 'Greave' means, of course, armour for the shin.
Roberts may want to suggest locals armoured against newcomers
(though, ludicrously, only with shin-guards) as well as the obvious
pun on 'grieving'. On the other hand, it may be a printing error. In
both examples we are never fully confident that we are reading
what the poet intended, because all too often there is a rough-hewn
quality – not to mention considerable obscurity – about Roberts's
work that suggests the draft rather than the finished product.

Yet, in *Gods With Stainless Ears* we can encounter such a line as
'The night sky is braille in a rock of frost', describing the clear
winter night over Llanybri. It is a piercing poetic thrust in which

'braille' is as richly suggestive as, say, 'curious stars' in R. S. Thomas's famous poem 'A Peasant'. 'Here are her contraries': apparent carelessness *and* the superb poetic moment. What is not in doubt is her originality and modernist spirit. Her best-known poem, much anthologized, is 'Poem from Llanybri', addressed to Alun Lewis when he intended to visit her. It is written in her strangely rugged, peasant-like language – 'primitive' poetry – evoking a world that seems more medieval than modern, into which Lewis is invited. Here is a defamiliarizing style, as with 'a breath you can swank', and 'children singing through the eyelet sheds'. Yet she tends to omit articles and conjunctions like a stereotypical Lancastrian.

Much of her best work is about the Second World War, viewed from a female-civilian point of view. A number of poems explore her own predicament, that of a highly intelligent, literary woman isolated in a small, damp and not particularly friendly Welsh village, bringing up children, short of money, her husband away at war, relations between them beginning to deteriorate. In 'Plasnewydd' the natural verities, represented by a cow in a field, are set, movingly if simplistically, against the idea of war. In 'Low Tide' she grieves for her departed husband gone to war, leaving her imprisoned:

> My eyes are raw and wide apart
> Stiffened by the salt bar
> That separates us.

'Raw Salt on Eye' is partly on the same theme and partly about her life as a superior stranger in a village of suspicious bumpkins possessing only 'full innate minds with loam'. In the poem as in the title she communicates an affecting emotional rawness, in part, once again, by stripping out articles:

> Hard people, I will wash up now, bake bread and hang
> Dishcloth over the weeping hedge. I can not raise
> My mind, for it has gone wandering away with him
> I shall not forget; and your ill-mannered praise.

'Crossed and Uncrossed', a poem about bomb-damage to London's Temple, has been described, overenthusiastically, as 'perhaps the finest poem on the blitz by any poet in English'. It yields its full meaning only when contextualized. Readers need to know the location of 'King's Bench/Walk', and that the poem is addressed to the mother of Roberts's friend, Celia Buckmaster, who lived in the Walk and helped to save what she could from the bomb-damaged building. Though the need for context should hardly trouble post-Eliot and post-Pound readers, more open to criticism is seemingly unnecessary obscurity, such as the two phrases 'and only wing grave' and 'Gather charred sticks to fight no gas', and the persistence of article-omission, as in 'Brings green peace and birds to top of Plane tree'. The poem has many felicities, which include the opening description of the ruined building and the firemen who 'Clung to buildings like swallows flat and exhausted/ under the storm', and a number of superb visual moments ('the lead roof dripping red tears', 'the catacomb of books', 'Still water silences death') that remind us that here is another poet able to create fine individual lines. The poem opposes a heroic female bourgeois spirit valuing restorative order to the bombers' legacy. Yet, once more, despite the affective power the rough obscurities suggest that more work needed to be done.

It is hard to be categorical about this apparent deficiency; her way with syntax and punctuation, her esoteric diction, even the unhewn quality of her work, might be an expression of her modernism. David Jones apart, Lynette Roberts is the most overtly modernist poet of those with Welsh connections, and never more so than in her long work, *Gods with Stainless Ears*, subtitled 'A Heroic Poem'. The poem has been summarized, by Nigel Wheale, as charting 'the progress of a wartime relationship between a young woman, isolated in a secluded area of south Wales, and her lover, a gunner on active service with a Welsh regiment. The girl conceives, but loses their child through the effects of poverty and distress, and is temporarily abandoned by the soldier.' In the final part of the poem the soldier and his girl are reunited. They rise above the earth into harmony, then return to a materialistic earth inimical to the imagination. The gunner enters a mental home, the girl re-enters the hard world.

Like *In Parenthesis*, with which it has much in common, Roberts's poem has the trappings of high modernism. Each part is preceded by an epigraph in Welsh and by a prose 'Argument'; the whole ends with translations of the epigraphs, and pages of notes explaining arcane references, some of which are to events in Welsh history. The eclectic diction includes military, medical and scientific language; at times it seeks to render musical effects, such as the impression of 'discordant fifths'; a visual element reminds us that the poem 'was written for filming'. As always in Roberts's work, there are superb moments, which include

> Soldier lonely whistling in full corridor train,
> Ishmaelites wailing through the windowpane.

and

> Men fall to arms. Men stemmed to die
> For the century. Then leap fast to the bone
>
> Take wailing bayonets from the ice of wound.

and the intertwining of military activities with basic human values and a longing for domesticity:

> Such battles of mule
> Stubbornness; or retreat from vast stone walls,
>
> Brought non-existence of past, present and
> Future 1,2,1,2,1,2, left, right, left, right,
> Accumulating into a monotonous pattern
> Of dereliction and gloom. When battles should be
> Fought at Home: as trencher-companions. *He at my side.*

and the vivid similes that describe the landing of sea-planes:

> Hydroplanes splash like
> Zinnias on inrushing tides; fussy as moorhens
>
> With tarnished back; whose legs of peeled elm
> Trail scarlet garters into the shaking tips
> Of reeds.

The first simile is brilliantly (and violently) visual: water splashes like the spread petals of the zinnia; the second wittily sets the creative and cheerful bustle of the amorous birds against all that the planes represent of war and destruction.

Yet, once again, alongside such vivid and original writing is eccentricity. Two examples can suffice: 'a wilderness of pavements blue crayoned/ With telegrams', impenetrable without Roberts's note and not wholly explained in that note. The description of the girl's loss of her baby includes the line: 'Razed for lack of/ Incomputable finance'. A note explains, but the line remains rhythmically dead.

Though work has barely begun on the detailed contextualizing of *Gods with Stainless Ears*, the poem has been related to MacDiarmid, T. S. Eliot and Robert Graves, to contemporary painting and, following Roberts's own suggestion, particularly as regards Part V, to contemporary film. The presence of Welsh people, places and history offers tenuous support for Roberts's claim to Anglo-Welsh status. The overall effect is to reveal the cultural richness of the poem. But though Tony Conran notes 'the fearless breaking down of barriers between private and public worlds' that places Roberts in the modernist/symbolist tradition, Nigel Wheale, one of Roberts's most perceptive commentators, is less sympathetic, regarding the poem as 'a curiously mixed achievement where it can be hard to separate what is rewardingly intransigent in the writing from what may be definitively obscure'. The same can be said of all her poetry.

Like Dylan Thomas and Vernon Watkins, Lynette Roberts is yet another bourgeois sensibility expressing itself in a high elitist style. That said, as a fully-paid-up modernist survivor she keeps her distance from the modernist *tendencies* of her Anglo-Welsh contemporaries. Like Watkins and Glyn Jones she would have benefited from ruthless editorial attention, though the problem of eccentric obscurity could have been mitigated by a more professional approach on her own part. Her Welshness is arguable. Her sad legacy is of potential unfulfilled.

This last is the even sadder fate of Alun Lewis who, of this chapter's writers, is the only one whose literary achievement might well have been comparable to that of Dylan Thomas. Lewis was not as precocious as Thomas. When he died, aged only twenty-nine, from a shot from his own revolver whilst on active service in India in 1944, he left much promising work but only a few achieved pieces of real consequence, primarily poems from his Indian period and, above all, his two short stories 'Ward "O" 3(b)' and 'The Orange Grove'.

Claims that he was 'arguably the finest poet of the age' and the vital link between 'Auden and the Thirties (and, beyond, Yeats and Eliot) to the Movement poets of the 1950s and Ted Hughes' are overstated and do him little service. His poems rarely disappoint wholly, but even the better known rarely satisfy. 'The Mountain over Aberdare', for example, combines precise and moving realist detail, with unabsorbed influence – 'Grey Hebron in a rigid cramp' echoes 'After the funeral', as yet another reminder of Dylan Thomas's ubiquity – and degenerates, via the contrived pun on 'rune', to a final line – 'This wet evening, in a lost age' – that reduces the poem to little more than neo-adolescent angst. The much-anthologized 'All Day It Has Rained', with its superb first section, is also damaged by its closing lines: 'the schoolyard's merry play' is too close for comfort to Georgian regression, and is followed by idealized Romantic excess in the closing callow reference to Edward Thomas. Similarly, 'The Sentry', in which Lewis transforms a conventional military subject into the notion of standing guard over 'this last/ Cold shore of thought', is a mixture of fine lines – 'The beautiful lanes of sleep', 'the guns' implacable silence/ Is my black interim' – and inappropriate imagery: to compare the waiting sentry to a bat – 'I hang/ Leathery-arid from the hidden roof/ of Night' – is to ignore how bats actually hang.

Within their limits, often those of the vignette or extended sketch, the short fiction collected in *The Last Inspection*, though at times derivative – 'They Came', for example, owes much to D. H. Lawrence – is always of interest. In the main it is low-key, carefully and sensitively observed exploration of army routine. Lewis wrote of these stories that 'the main motif is the rootless life of soldiers having no enemy, and, always, somehow, under a shadow'. Characters are often military stereotypes used by Lewis to explore issues of social class and personal identity amongst home-based soldiers. The slightly later 'Night Journey', however, in slipping from realism into melodrama highlights one of the main faults in Lewis's work, his failure, at times, to reconcile disparate styles. As one critic argues, a fine lyrical gift too often degenerates into 'poeticisms and generalities' in capital letters, citing 'Turbulence and Time' in 'The Soldier', 'Life' in 'Burma Casualty' and 'Time' in 'In Hospital: Poona (1)'.

Lewis's considerable but limited achievement can be clearly seen through a comparison with Edward Thomas, whose poetry he discovered in 1941, when undergoing basic training at Longmoor in Hampshire. Edward Thomas had lived nearby. Three details reveal how Lewis regarded his dead predecessor. He wrote in *Horizon*, in a review of Thomas's *The Trumpet and Other Poems*: 'I have been garrisoned for six months in Edward Thomas's country and walked his walks. I have sheltered from the rain in the beautiful house he built but did not inhabit.' The last is not true; it is hard to believe that Lewis did not know that. 'All Day It Has Rained' ends on the hill 'where Edward Thomas brooded long/ On death and beauty – till a bullet stopped his song'. The brooding, as has been noted, is Romantic idealization. The 'bullet' is an invention: Edward Thomas was killed when the blast from a shell induced a heart attack. His body was unmarked. Lewis changes Thomas into a poet of romantic reverie, abruptly severed from a home he never knew, and struck down in his prime by a German rifle. Such hero-worship intensified the influence on Lewis of Edward Thomas's poetry, evident in a comparison of Thomas's 'Rain' with 'All Day It Has Rained'. The former gains immeasurably when placed in its historical context. It is a disturbing poem; it is also puzzlingly overwrought if we do not know that it is a poem of 1916 when Thomas was a soldier, so that the poem's lines on the dead include the casualties of war.

In 'Rain', the poet is drawn into a purgatorial cleanness that is a necessary prelude to death. And death itself is welcomed: the only love he can feel is 'love of death'. Yet in a bleak conclusion that seems to place the limitations of life against the seeming perfection of death he begins to doubt the nature of what he feels. The poem ends with disorientation, fittingly because it is, centrally, about despair and helplessness in the midst of war: John Pikoulis observes that 'It is this terrible awakening, this sudden crystallisation of one's awareness of one's mortality, that the poem records.'

Edward Thomas's poem presses against the hypnotic lines in the first section of 'All Day It Has Rained', in which the soldiers share a sense of existence as dreamlike, disorientated, indifferent to what may once have mattered. But there is a crucial difference. Thomas finds himself alone, and in a high-romantic predicament beyond human love, eager for death. Alun Lewis and his comrades experience an interval in their lives, not a moment that is a prelude to death, even though death, the 'slaughter' of war, is a lurking possibility. The Lewis poem is an example of, perhaps paradoxically, controlled Romanticism, the control stemming from a bourgeois reluctance to move wholly out of the ordinary into the dark, tortured and death-welcoming states of mind explored by Thomas.

In the companion poem, 'To Edward Thomas', Lewis is drawn further into the dark desire at the heart of Edward Thomas's vision. The poem's final section and chilling final line – 'Till suddenly, at Arras, you possessed that hinted land' – with that too positive 'possessed', allows us to gauge the disturbing extent of Lewis's empathy; in the end the narrative stance, his decision to address the poem *to* Edward Thomas, allows him to refuse absolute involvement, and to indulge his bourgeois reluctance to abandon the known.

Until October 1942, when he left for India with his regiment, Lewis's writing is very much a matter of brilliant moments in flawed work. His reputation ultimately depends on his Indian work. Earlier flaws can still be found, of course, as previous reference to 'In Hospital: Poona (1)' demonstrates. Flaws notwithstanding, this poem dramatizes movingly the combination of distanced alienation and eroticism in thoughts about his wife Gweno in far-off Wales. The last line – 'But love survives the venom of the snake' – hints with strange prescience at his later love affair with Freda Ackroyd. Certainly the exotic immediacy of India and, of course, the imminence of active service, whilst not inhibiting persisting grand abstractions, give a harder edge to realist detail here and elsewhere. In addition, despite its ending, a poem such as 'Burma Casualty' shows a further advance in Lewis's skilful handling of conversational narrative.

'The Jungle', one of his last poems, and the two Indian short stories, are the true beginnings of great achievement. The first is an ambitious poem in which the jungle offers the poet a world of desired darkness and amoral natural violence, in contrast to the sordid troubled world of economic depression that has led to war. Though not immune to capitalized abstractions and occasional windy rhetoric, for perhaps the first time Lewis begins to exploit the potential of dialogic writing, juxtaposing, for example,

> The weekly bribe we paid the man in black,
> The day shift sinking from the sun,

> The blinding arc of rivets blown through steel,
> The patient queues, headlines and slogans flung
> Across a frightened continent, the town
> Sullen and out of work, the little home
> Semi-detached, suburban, transient
> As fever or the anger of the old,
> The best ones on some specious pretext gone.

with

> The banyan's branching clerestories close
> The noon's harsh splendour to a head of light.
> The black spot in the focus grows and grows.

and

> A trackless wilderness divides
> Joy from its cause, the motive from the act:
> The killing arm uncurls, strokes the soft moss;
> The distant world is an obituary,
> We do not hear the tappings of its dread.

Realism struggles against kinds of metaphor. Though the description of the valley town is linked to the wilderness through the idea of a point of light suggestive of the top of a mine shaft and through the mining disaster implicit in 'the tappings of its dread', what we are finally conscious of is the struggle between the different worlds these styles dramatize. Though occasionally the unabsorbed influence still suggests immaturity, this is, for the most part, complex and assured poetry in which a willingness to explore beyond the conventional reflects a new awareness.

'Ward "O" 3(b)' and 'The Orange Grove' both study soldiers helpless in crisis. The former is about a group of officers recovering from surgery in a military hospital and waiting for a medical board to decide their future. In its ability to sustain different storylines and to go beyond stereotypical characters, for example in exploring the thoughts of Dad Withers, the old soldier, who is discharged back to a home and family he hardly knows, together with a pervading but undefined eroticism and deftly handled and beautifully expressed nature symbolism, this story suggests the novelist Lewis would undoubtedly have become. In 'The Orange Grove', an officer, lost in India with the body of his dead driver, has to travel with and rely on a group of native Indians with whom he can hardly communicate. His journey is a struggle to retain contact with the world of duty and conventional responsibility.

Alun Lewis was born into a middle-class family in the predominantly working-class Cynon valley. His parents sent him to boarding school in Cowbridge and then to universities in Aberystwyth and Manchester. He was never at ease in his community and his brief literary career mirrors his life in being a struggle to establish a personal voice, a coherent literary identity. Modernism seemed to pass him by. Rather, he was a Romantic drawn to areas of experience beyond the ordinary but initially restrained by a bourgeois sensibility that does not, however, prevent the pervading eroticism already noted. As a purveyor of bourgeois Romanticism tinged with the erotic he can hold hands – or, at least, in Thomas's case touch hands – with Dylan Thomas and Glyn Jones as an archetypal Anglo-Welsh poet of the first flowering.

Each of this chapter's writers had a London publisher. They built reputations outside Wales. Though they supported and contributed to the first Welsh literary magazines in English, *Wales* in 1937 and *The Welsh Review* in 1939, such magazines hardly gave their literary careers a major boost. But in countering prejudice from Welsh-speaking Wales against English-language literary magazines, in fostering the idea of an Anglo-Welsh literature, and in providing publishing opportunities in Wales for Welsh writers in English, they helped lay the foundations for the 'second flowering' of Anglo-Welsh writing. The consequences, which include a wholly subsidized Welsh literary publishing industry, and the effect on Anglo-Welsh writers of being published in Wales, are not uncontroversial. It is noticeable that of the *present* generation of Anglo-Welsh writers the highest profiles have been achieved by those who publish regularly outside Wales. But there may not be an obvious link between this fact and literary quality.

Welsh magazines played little or no part in Dylan Thomas's rise to international stardom. And, of this chapter's writers, only Thomas, principally because of *Under Milk Wood* and such poems as 'Fern Hill' and 'Do not go gentle into that good night', is now widely read, especially outside Wales. *Wales* and *The Welsh*

Review were more valuable for younger or later-developing writers, such as R. S. Thomas, Emyr Humphreys and Leslie Norris. Yet, during the late 1930s and early 1940s, the relationship between the two magazines and the world of Wales can provide an apt paradigm for that between upbringing and writing on the part of each of our writers. That is, the uneasy relationship between magazines publishing work in English that was at times modernist and always elitist, and the respectable but rather narrow-minded Welsh society of the period, was similar to the tension between bourgeois writers and their innovative work, the latter, of course, informed by the former. Two final examples reveal such beginnings in ends. Alun Lewis's 'Dawn on the East Coast' is about a soldier on sentry duty who thinks of home and, the first part concludes, 'A girl laying his table with a white cloth'. Dylan Thomas's 'The Orchards', as has been seen, ends with a 'fair girl' spreading for Marlais 'a white cloth on a flat stone' on which she prepares her genteel picnic. At the heart of Anglo-Welsh writing's first flowering is a bourgeois, suburban, middle-class sensibility. Sometimes this may be a limitation. In the best work of the most gifted it is its great strength.

FURTHER READING

Sam Adams (ed.), *Seeing Wales Whole: Essays on the Literature of Wales* (Cardiff, 1998).

Tony Brown, 'Shock, strangeness, wonder: Glyn Jones and the art of fiction', *New Welsh Review*, 23 (Winter 1993–4), 43–53.

Anthony Conran, *The Cost of Strangeness* (Llandysul, 1982).

Tony Conran, *Frontiers in Anglo-Welsh Poetry* (Cardiff, 1997).

Patrick Crotty, 'The broken voice of Alun Lewis', *Welsh Writing in English*, 2 (1986), 170–4.

James A. Davies, *A Reference Companion to Dylan Thomas* (Westport, CT, 1998).

Walford Davies, *Dylan Thomas* (Milton Keynes, 1986).

Paul Ferris, *Dylan Thomas* (Harmondsworth, 1999).

Belinda Humfrey (ed.), *Fire Green as Grass* (Cardiff, 1995).

Glyn Jones, *The Dragon Has Two Tongues* (Cardiff, 2001).

Roland Mathias, *Vernon Watkins* (Cardiff, 1974).

Roland Mathias, *A Ride Through the Wood* (Bridgend, 1985).

Ralph Maud, *Entrances to Dylan Thomas's Poetry* (Pittsburgh, 1963).

Leslie Norris, *Glyn Jones* (Cardiff, 1973).

John Pikoulis, 'Alun Lewis and Edward Thomas', *Critical Quarterly*, 23, 4 (1981), 25–44.

John Pikoulis, 'The Watcher on the Mountain: the poetry of Idris Davies', *Poetry Wales*, 16:4 (1981), 85–91.

John Pikoulis, *Alun Lewis: A Life* (Bridgend, 1991).

M. Wynn Thomas, *Internal Difference: Writing in Twentieth-Century Wales* (Cardiff, 1992).

William York Tindall, *A Reader's Guide to Dylan Thomas* (New York, 1981).

Paul Volskik, 'Neo-Romanticism and the poetry of Dylan Thomas', *Études Anglaises*, 42:1 (Jan.–Mar. 1989), 39–54.

Gwen Watkins, *Portrait of a Friend* (Llandysul, 1983).

Nigel Wheale, 'Beyond the trauma status: Lynette Roberts' *Gods with Stainless Ears* and the post-war landscape', *Welsh Writing in English*, 3 (1997), 98–117.

CHAPTER 5

THE PROBLEMS OF BELONGING

TONY BROWN and M. WYNN THOMAS

It is towards the end of the First World War, and the place: the Wirral Peninsula, Cheshire. A little boy is playing on the beach. Over the sea towards the south-west there are tall grey-blue hills to be seen. His father points to them. 'That's Wales', he says, in English.

The distance and the parent's language are symptomatic, as R. S. Thomas was well aware when he used this memory to open his Welsh-language radio talk *Y Llwybrau Gynt* ('The Former Paths') in 1972. The talk itself is essentially his own account of how that English-speaking young boy became the *Cymro Cymraeg* (Welsh-speaking Welshman) he was by the time of the broadcast, living his life far to the west in Llŷn and largely in the Welsh language. And in its highlighting of the process of identifying with, and eventually imaginatively adopting, a culture into which one has not actually been born, and in which one has not been raised, this passage speaks to the condition of several of the writers with which this chapter is concerned.

In R. S. Thomas's case, determined reconstruction of identity began when, now married and in his late twenties, he again looked west, from Maelor Saesneg in Flintshire, where he was curate, to the hills of Wales:

I realised what I had done. That was not my place, on the plain amongst Welshmen with English accents and attitudes. I set about learning Welsh, in order to be able to return to the true Wales of my imagination.

That last phrase in this passage from *Y Llwybrau Gynt* is not only richly paradoxical but also a key one; the 'Wales' to which R. S. Thomas was to 'return' is manifestly constructed out of imaginative and emotional need. One can, however, only speculate on what caused Thomas to express this need and seek a new mode of self-realization at this point. There were practical factors – it was wartime and bombs intended for Merseyside were falling in the fields of the parish. But Thomas would not have had to learn Welsh if he merely wanted to avoid German bombs. To learn Welsh, to become a Welshman, was to reject not just the language but also the cultural attitudes in which he had been brought up and that had made him what he was: the conformist bourgeois values of his English-speaking home in Holyhead, largely it would seem inculcated by his Anglican mother ('Strange, and perhaps crucial [*allweddol*], is the relationship between a mother and her son'). As a young boy, he had been 'sent to some kind of school where the "nice" people of the town sent their children' and, growing up, before university, 'moved in refined circles'. The quest to become a Welshman is a search for another way of life, to lose what he had come to regard as his outsider status, to move *inside* Wales, into another cultural community. One might argue that it was the tensions created by that search, that remaking, that hurt R. S. Thomas into verse. One central tension, of course, he never overcame: his incapacity to write poetry in his second language: 'I can't speak my own/ Language – Iesu,/ All those good words;/ And I *outside* them' (emphasis added). One should not simplistic-ally identify the speaker as R. S. Thomas, but the frustrations in the poem are powerfully expressed and they continue to exist beneath the surface of his poetry. Of the invasion of Wales by English capitalists, he writes:

> . . . I was
> born into the squalor of
> their feeding and sucked their speech
> in with my mother's
> infected milk, so that whatever
> I throw up now is still theirs.

Again his identification of the original source of his stress is evident.

As Thomas learned Welsh in the early 1940s, it is clear that he was also beginning to read his way into the Welsh literary tradition, especially in poetry. His earliest prose writings in Welsh show a familiarity with a range of Welsh-language poets, as well as with the Bible in Welsh and, as Jason Walford Davies has shown, the range of allusion to Welsh-language literature in Thomas's poetry is extensive. Indeed for Thomas in the late 1940s and early 1950s the ultimate objective of the Anglo-Welsh 'movement' was the 're-cymrification of Wales': 'since there is in Wales a mother-tongue that continues to flourish, a proper Welshman can only look on English as a means of rekindling interest in the Welsh-language culture, and of leading people back to the mother-tongue.' In order to carry out this social role, Anglo-Welsh writers were to immerse themselves in the Welsh-language literary tradition. In an unpublished BBC radio broadcast in 1947, Thomas was at pains to point out that 'a growing realization of the plight of my country . . . together with the desire to live up to the reputation for difference implied by the terms Welsh and Anglo-Welsh, have been responsible for certain experiments of mine both in subject matter and in technique', and he pointed out how he had 'tried to introduce a certain amount of internal rhyme and assonance' into his poem 'Hill Farmer', which he then read:

> And he will go home from the fair
> To dream of the grey mare with the broad belly,
> And the bull and the prize tup
> That held its head so proudly up.
> He will go back to the bare acres
> Of caked earth, and the reality
> Of fields that yield such scant return
> Of parched clover and green corn.
> Yes, he will go home to the cow gone dry,
> And the lean fowls and the pig in the sty,
> And all the extravagance of a Welsh sky.

Having then read 'The Ancients of the World', which again shows 'internal assonances' as well as a knowledge of the *Mabinogion* (a number of the poems in his early volumes make explicit and rather self-conscious allusion to Welsh myth and history), Thomas commented that such experimentation and such expression of 'the needs of my country' are necessary:

For it seems to me that if we are unwilling to be called English poets, while at the same time we are averse from the title Anglo-Welsh, we have only the other to fall back on. But if we are to be known as Welsh poets then our work must be a true expression of the life of our country in all its forms.

It is interesting to note that, in this broadcast, Thomas sees his first, and most famous, expression of the harsh life of his hill-farming parishioners at Manafon, 'A Peasant', in the context of this specific concern to give expression to Welsh life. One might add that in its closing lines this poem shows signs of Thomas's reading of traditional Welsh-language praise poetry in the traditional metres. Medieval poets such as Iolo Goch had used that genre to celebrate the qualities of a great lord such as 'Hywel y Fwyall' (Hywel of the Axe) who was the military protector of his people: 'a brave war horse keeping the garrison . . ./ long will he keep the fort . . ./ he'll hold all lands and the bright tower'. But R. S. Thomas employed a similar register to affirm the qualities of a labouring man, thus underlining the fact of Iago's heroism:

> . . . Against siege of rain and the wind's attrition,
> Preserves his stock, an impregnable fortress
> Not to be stormed even in death's confusion.

Thomas's vision of Wales in these early years was an essentially communal one; he might be at present outside it, as the narrative stance of so many of his poems of the period demonstrates, but he longed to be able to identify more fully. In 'Welsh History', '*We* were a people' (emphasis added) and in 'Iago Prytherch' the hope is expressed that Iago will be 'the first man in the new community'. But, as he walked the hills of his parish, it was evident to the young vicar that the present was a very different place; everywhere he saw evidence of economic decline and cultural dereliction, epitomized for him by the ruins of the old *hafotai* (the shepherds' summer dwellings) in the emptiness of the high pastures:

When I am there, I hear the curlew mourning the people who have passed away and I dream of the days that were, the days of *Calan Mai* and the *hafoty*; days when the Welsh went to the high pastures to live for a season at least 'At the bright hem of God,/ In the heather, in the heather'.

Historically the practice of transhumance, the whole community moving with their flocks, traditionally on the first of May, from

the *hendre* (the 'old settlement') in the valley up to the high
pastures and the *hafoty*, probably died out in the nineteenth
century. But for Thomas it becomes a potent myth of a life utterly
different from the values of bourgeois England or from the Wales
that aped them; this communal life is Welsh speaking, simple,
close to nature, imaginatively alive and thus spiritually aware
(since the imagination is, for Thomas, 'the highest means known to
the human psyche of getting into contact with ultimate reality'). It
is a version of Saunders Lewis's vision of a Welsh-speaking, rural,
non-industrial, non-capitalist society, located in the specific setting
of Montgomeryshire. (Thomas had visited Saunders Lewis in 1945
to seek the great man's advice and blessing at the very outset of the
young poet's career.) The myth receives its fullest expression in
The Mountains (1968):

> [T]here is Eden's garden, its gate open, fresh as it has always been,
> unsmudged by the world. The larks sing high in the sky. No footprints
> have bruised the dew. The air is something to be sipped slowly . . . This
> is the world they went up into on May Day with their flocks from *yr
> hendre* . . . to *yr hafod* . . . They spent long days here swapping *englynion*
> [classic four-line poems in the strict metres] over the peat cutting.

It was a past Thomas could yearn for even as he describes its
dereliction: in 'The Depopulation of the Welsh Hill Country',
Thomas portrays (or imagines?) a local rural poet he had met on
the moorland: 'a strange emotion came over me. He was haloed
with the clear light and his face was alive, his eyes keen . . . And I
realised very clearly it was because he belonged there and was
happy there.' It is a remarkable Wordsworthian moment.

The discrepancy between the purity and intensity of this idealized
communal Wales of the past and the actuality of the present
inhabitants can only have contributed to the culture shock Thomas
experienced at Manafon; the actuality was a doggedly realistic
people more occupied with wrestling a living from the clinging soil
and the harsh weather than writing *englynion* in sun-filled pastures,
less concerned, as Thomas saw it, with the life of the spirit and the
imagination than the things of the body and the market:

> the loud unlovely rattle
> Of mucous in the throat, the shallow stream

Of neighbours' trivial talk . . .
          . . . herding pennies
Into a sock to serve you for a pillow
Through the long night that waits upon your span.
                                        ('Valediction')

At times the poems insist, almost obsessively, on the physicality of
the rural life in which the young vicar found himself. In John
Ormond's 1972 film on the poet for the BBC, Thomas recalls that
'coming from a bourgeois environment' which is 'cushioned from
some of the harder realities', he initially found the 'Muck and
blood . . . and the spittle and phlegm of farm life' to be something
of a shock. But, as J. P. Ward has pointed out, there is at the same
time, especially in the early poems collected in *Song at the Year's
Turning*, 'a libidinous relish for immersion in the liquid, glutinous
and messy'. The concern with the muck of the farmyard, the fluids
of bodily functions, is frequently expressed in a register – 'wades',
'pull', 'suck', 'cling', 'dabble' – surprisingly tactile for a poet more
usually noted for detached observation. In 'Song', published in
Stones of the Field, the overtly sexual images which express the
relations between the farmer and his land seem more akin to the
fields at the opening of Lawrence's *The Rainbow* than the hills of
Montgomeryshire; it is explicitly a relationship which is in contrast
to 'the times' prudery' which 'We' affect. Again, almost desperately
here, the poet seems determined to reject, to emancipate himself
from, the niceties of conventional bourgeois respectability, the
values in which he has been brought up. In his 1947 broadcast
Thomas speaks of this particular poem as showing 'something of
my feeling for the earth and my preoccupation with the problem of
the widening of the gap between man and the earth in the present
era'; it would seem to be a gap which for Thomas was not just a
social issue but a deeply felt personal one. In this sense Iago may be
shocking and 'other' but he is also a liberator (to use Jeremy
Hooker's term), a source of authenticity – although there may also
be, in the atavistic elements of the poem, what M. Wynn Thomas
has described as 'a desperation behind the affirmation', 'a will to
wholeness that is itself a symptom of sickness'.

    Despite the present-day actuality of the hill country, R. S.
Thomas still detects there the last remnants of the values of the old
pastoral community and celebrates them movingly in 'Those

Others' (a poem in which he sees this land as a place which 'At last took me in/ From the void of unbeing'):

> There are still those other
> Castaways on a sea
> Of grass, who call to me,
> Clinging to their doomed farms;
> Their hearts though rough are warm
> And firm, and their slow wake
> Through time bleeds for our sake.

But the tide is flowing inexorably against them, and the poem also registers the poet's 'hate':

> For men of the Welsh race
> Who brood with dark face
> Over their thin navel
> To learn what to sell.

It is a hate that is expressed over and over through the poetry of the 1960s, an invective aimed – in poems like, for example, 'Reservoirs', 'Expatriates', 'Traeth Maelgwn', 'Welcome to Wales', 'Sir Gelli Meurig' – not just at the modern consumerist world as represented by English tourists and capitalists flowing into Wales, but at the Welsh who are willing to accept the modern world's values and to collaborate with it. The power of the poet's invective on occasions can cause the poem to slide into the merely lurid – 'They have hard hands that money adheres/ to like the scales/ of some hideous disease, so that they grizzle/ as it is picked off'. But the scorn is a measure of the power of Thomas's disappointment: having reconstructed himself as a Welshman, committed himself to becoming part of a Wales which for him represents a life of imaginative vitality and fulfilment, he sees all around him the Welsh as having rejected those values and going determinedly in another direction. The terms in which he expresses the situation, even in the late 1940s, are, again, specifically those of his personal myth:

We have seen in Wales what does happen when we forget our land and our God and go a-whoring after false gods. Instead of the rich cultural life of *yr hendre*, we get whist-drives and dances the winter through;

instead of the satisfying life of *yr hafod*, we get the subsidy drawers in the lowlands, paying occasional visits in their cars to the hill flocks and herds. ('A Welsh View of the Scottish Renaissance', 1948)

In 'Border Blues', the narrator turns his back on the world of 'the ladies from the council houses' with their 'Birmingham yellow/ Hair, and the ritual murder of vowels', of pop songs and pantomimes in Shrewsbury:

> Excuse me, I said, I have an appointment
> On the high moors; it's the first of May
> And I must go the way of my fathers
> Despite the loneli – you might say rudeness.

But that loneliness haunts much of the later work; the moors when the speaker gets there are empty: 'What am I doing up here alone?'

If the original vision of 'the true Wales' of R. S. Thomas's imagination had been the communal life of the summer pastures, the later images are of the isolated individual and of lonely struggle. The men of imaginative vision are unheeded ('not silent, but stifled/ By vast noise'); intellectual vitality and imaginative resourcefulness are now embodied in images of exceptional individuals, often isolated or marginal to society. Dic Aberdaron reveals a

> . . . light
>
> generated by a
> mind charging
> itself at its own sources.

The 'Dead Worthies' include Williams Parry

> . . . quarrying
>
> his cynghanedd among
> Bethesda slate in
> the twilight of the language.

Welsh Airs (1987) ends not with a political poem but with 'Fugue for Ann Griffiths', a poem which reflects not only on the contrast between the 'calm' of her time compared to our own post-Holocaust, post-Hiroshima world, but also on her own isolated spiritual striving, 'the fathoms/ of anguish over which she had/ attained to the calmness of her harbours'. The poem, and thus the volume, ends on a note of dedication, prayer and even fragile hope:

> . . . at dawn the footprints
> of one who invisibly
> but so close passed
> discover a direction.

A motif which has its first expression in 'The Tree', expressing the sense of Welsh freedom and communality in the brief season of independence under Glyndŵr – 'we heard/ In the green shade Rhiannon's birds/ Singing tirelessly as the streams/ That pluck glad tunes from the grey stones of Powys'– recurs in the late poem 'Arrival' as a *private* moment of awareness of the timeless, the spiritual; there are no other people now. While the 'river dawdles' nearby,

> A bird chimes
> from a green tree
> the hour that is no hour
> you know.

The motif receives its fullest expression in the remarkable lecture 'Abercuawg' which R. S. Thomas gave at the National Eisteddfod in 1976. (It is noticeable that by now the poet who has remade himself as a Welshman lectures the Welsh themselves in their own language, from the very heart of the culture, about what he perceives to be the valuable essence of his 'Wales'.) 'Wherever Abercuawg might be, it is a place of trees and fields and flowers and bright, unpolluted streams, where the cuckoos continue to sing.' It is the direct opposite of the contemporary Wales, the consumer world, where most of us live: '[E]ndless streets of modern characterless houses, each with its garage and television aerial; a place from which the trees and the birds and the flowers have fled before the yearly extension of concrete and macadam.' For Thomas, such a world, such a way of life, in Wales or anywhere else, is literally soul-destroying. '[A]s a Welshman,' Thomas says, 'I see no meaning to my life if there is no such place as Abercuawg . . . For such a place I am ready to make sacrifices, maybe even to die.' But as Thomas's argument makes clear, Abercuawg is not an actual place, but a way of being; it is a transfigured 'Wales' which stands for a state of calmness, imaginative vitality and, thus, of spiritual perception, an awareness of Ultimate Reality, of God: 'through striving to see it, through longing for it, through refusing to accept that it belongs to the past . . . through refusing to accept some second-hand substitute, [man] will succeed in preserving it as an eternal possibility.' But it is clearly no longer a communal possibility. Modern society, it seems, may be beyond saving; the individual must seek his/her own salvation. There are parallels to be drawn with Eliot's vision in *The Waste Land*, particularly the last section.

And perhaps with *Gerontion*, for it is worth recollecting that in 'Claf Abercuawg' (The Sick Man of Abercuawg), which appears in the ninth-century sequence of *englynion*, *Canu Llywarch Hen* (The Song of Llywarch the Old), the speaker is old and lonely; his pleasure at hearing the song of the cuckoo, the song of summer, is mingled with sadness that those whom he has loved are dead and will not hear it, and with bitterness at his own situation. For the Welsh-speaking reader, then, the line 'Yn Aber Cuawc yt ganant gogeu' (At Aber Cuawc the cuckoos sing) evokes a poignant sense of elusive pleasure, of loss and of longing. And perhaps even more intensely than the early poetry, R. S. Thomas's remarkable later poetry is a poetry of longing. 'I thirst, I thirst/ for the spring water'; the speaker here, strikingly, is God, addressing the young Methodist mystic and ecstatic Ann Griffiths, but the words articulate the intensity of Thomas's own yearning. J. P. Ward perceptively sees Abercuawg as a state of 'personal unity'. In that sense, Thomas's search in the late work is of a piece with the sense of personal need which made him set out from Maelor Saesneg to find 'the true Wales of my imagination'. The journey, manifestly, ceases to be a geographical one and becomes an inner search; the striving for awareness of God's presence is not finally active and self-assertive, but quiet, patient, waiting for the moment of transcendence of human aloneness, the moment of community, now, not with others but with God. In 'Emerging', the poet realizes, having called out to God, 'Hear my prayer, Lord, hear my prayer', that

> . . . this is not what prayer is about.
> It is about the annihilation of difference,
> the consciousness of myself in you,
> of you in me.

And it is this poetry of spiritual search that comes over-
whelmingly to the fore in all of Thomas's late collections from *H'm*
(1972) to *No Truce with the Furies* (1995), his remarkable farewell
volume at the age of 82. Although other poems – to his wife, on
paintings, and on other subjects – also appeared during this thirty-
year period, the religious poetry overshadows them all, with the
possible exception of *The Echoes Return Slow* (1988), Thomas's
singular account (in poetry and prose) of the progress of his own
life, which is an astonishing spiritual autobiography. From the time
he moved to Aberdaron, that romantic sea-lashed spot on the
remote tip of the Llŷn peninsula, directly opposite the holy island
of Bardsey, Thomas seems to have largely abandoned political
poetry (but not political action) and dedicated himself, under the
influence of the ancient rocks of the region, to meditation on the
eternal. But the result was no poetry of retreat. On the contrary, his
attempts to reconcile belief in God with the cruelty and violence of
both the natural and the human world resulted in writing racked by
anguish, riddled with ironies, equivocating in syntax, daring in its
space-age vocabulary, challengingly heterodox in its theology, and
only occasionally lapsing into the calm of profound acceptance.
The same great irreducibly enigmatic themes are returned to again
and again, for thirty years, with Thomas's imagination haunted
and obsessed by them just as the aged Cézanne's imagination had
been haunted and obsessed by Mount Sainte Victoire. It may seem
a long way from his early obsession with Wales, and with Manafon,
and with Iago Prytherch. But in reality, it is, perhaps, only the
transposition to an entirely different key of Thomas's lifelong sense
of human beings as, in George Steiner's resonant phrase, 'transients
in a house of being whose foundations, whose future history, whose
rationale – if any – lie wholly outside our will' and of Thomas's
belief that poetry can (again in Steiner's words) 'make us, if not
at home, [then] at least alertly, answerably peregrine in the
unhousedness of our human circumstance'.

In addressing his poem 'Back?' from distant Australia to a
seemingly complacently entrenched R. S. Thomas, the peregrine

and culturally unhoused T. Harri Jones was implicitly acknowledging that the former had dealt differently from himself with the
harrowing problem of belonging:

> Back to the chapel, and a charade
> Of the word of God made by a preacher
> Without a tongue . . .
>
> Of course I'd go back if somebody'd pay me
> To live in my own country
> Like a bloody Englishman.

Two poems are revealingly printed directly before 'Back?' in
Jones's seminal volume *The Colour of Cockcrowing*: the title, with
its mixture of agricultural implication, religious reference and
sexual innuendo, complete with an ostentatious bow in passing to
Dylan Thomas, clearly signifies Jones's own conflicted psychology
and his uncertain cultural positioning. The first of these is a
nostalgic/satiric pastiche of hymn metre, 'Taffy was transported',
in which a Welsh convict dreams that 'the lost sheep find[s]
salvation/ Underneath a crooked star'. The second, 'My country,
my grief' (where the ambiguous title perfectly suggests the conflation of inner psychological state with homeland), opens with the
stark statement 'Anguish is my country'. Both are profoundly
expressive of Jones's own troubled state of being; of what might be
termed his psychological brokenness. No wonder that in 'P is for
Poetry' he saw poetry as challenged to express 'Predicaments of
landscape, old despairs' as well as to convey 'Paradox of language
or of love'. And indeed when, in further adding (of the woman
addressed) 'What speech had I before you gave me tongue?', he
resorts to an ancient and familiar poetic trope, he also alludes to
his own search for a speech alternative to that of Wales in the love
poetry at which he sporadically excelled.

Born in 1921 at Cwm Crogau, near Llanafan Fawr in upland
Breconshire, Harri Jones grew up known as 'Young Crogau'
because his dark, rugged looks made him the very image of his
grandfather 'Old Crogau', a dominant local figure, seemingly
hewn from local rock, whose first language was the Welsh of his
(and Jones's) native district. In being deprived of what he later
self-defensively scorned as 'the birded language', Jones was

effectively debarred from participating fully in his community in the way that had so strongly characterized his grandfather (for whom he was to write particularly moving elegies); and, as he also quickly began to grow disillusioned with the sternly puritanical chapel culture whose biblical values informed the life by which he was surrounded, Jones became doubly disabled from assuming the very role on which his nickname so mockingly insisted. He remained haunted by that second self throughout his life, indeed in important respects he lived a parodic inversion of it, as, fuelled by drink, he became a defiant, yet guilty, sexual adventurer. And this crippling, distorting sense of cultural displacement and of psychic dislocation found expression in his poetry, as he sought to build for himself a kind of alternative home in language.

The trajectory of Jones's life rapidly carried him away from his origins. First there was university education at Aberystwyth, then wartime naval service in the Mediterranean (and his war poetry remains to be properly explored), followed by marriage to a mildly bohemian English middle-class artist, and a career in education culminating in a university post at Newcastle, New South Wales, where, in 1965 when in his mid-forties, he was found drowned in a rock-pool. He had begun to make significant contributions to Australian literary culture – his Welshness probably helped him identify all the more readily with writers (including American writers) who continued to be ignored, or condescended to, by established English culture – but, in his poetry, he continued to gravitate compulsively back to the distant Wales he could not forgive or forget.

The poem 'Back?' acknowledges, then, that R. S. Thomas was Jones's alter ego, in that he had ostensibly been more successful than Jones himself in becoming integrated into the Welsh-language culture from which he had originally felt so definingly and definitively excluded. A lifelong physical and cultural migrant, Harri Jones never ceased to feel displaced, while also recognizing that there was no home to which he could fulfillingly return. His creative imagination was powered by the restless electrical play between those two poles of feeling. And, even in his turning to poetry, he was seemingly thwarted by the very times in which he was writing. Whereas in terms both of politics and of literary culture the 1930s and the 1960s in Wales have strong character-izing features that facilitate easy recall, the 1950s remain amorphous, associated in popular memory only with the sad final years of Dylan Thomas and his premature passing in 1953. And with his passing there faded the charisma of his style, a style that had so fatally captivated young emerging writers such as John Ormond, Dannie Abse, Leslie Norris and Jones himself. As the young poets of the Movement moved in – as literary undertakers anxious to be heirs and beneficiaries – and unceremoniously removed Thomas, so these Welsh writers were left orphaned, bereft of speech. Jones's response was to proliferate styles of writing, borrowing eclectically from models ranging from the seventeenth-century Metaphysicals to Wallace Stevens. Branded pastiche by mainstream critical opinion, this practice has recently been differently defined by Bernard Jones and Don Dale-Jones. In their view, Harri Jones's poetry was postmodernist *avant la lettre*, self-consciously ludic, featuring a virtuoso display of stylistic (and experiential) possibilities and thus perfectly conveying the multiplicity of his psychologically and culturally fragmented selfhood. It is a suggestive approach, that at least allows us to recuperate a body of work that has hitherto tended to be unjustifiably overlooked.

Harri Jones never did learn his grandfather's language, and thus never did enable himself to become 'Young Crogau' in anything but empty name. But like R. S. Thomas, numerous other Welsh writers have consciously chosen to move over to the other side of the linguistic border from that on which they were born and raised. In an unpublished paper on 'Anglo-Welsh criticism', Tony Conran sees the noted Welsh-language writers Saunders Lewis, Pennar Davies and Bobi Jones as, in linguistic terms, 'frontiersmen, not core members of Welsh-speaking Wales – so of course was Waldo Williams, so I'm not being derogatory'. The significant critics on the anglophone side of the frontier in his generation, Conran suggests, were Raymond Garlick, Roland Mathias, Harri Webb and himself. Conran's own occupation of the 'Anglo-Welsh' borderland has resulted in some of the most challenging criticism and, indeed, some of the most significant poetry to be written in Wales since the Second World War. Born in India in 1931, Conran suffered problems at his birth that caused cerebral palsy and he was taken home to be brought up by grandparents in north Wales. Though the Conrans had wandered the Empire in previous generations, the grandfather who brought him up was probably Welsh speaking, though Conran himself was not taught the language. As he noted in an autobiographical essay, 'I was separated from both my parents from 1939 to 1945, and from my father from my sixth to my fourteenth year. This had its effects on my growing up, as can be imagined.' On his growing up and also on his imaginative world, because, from Conran's various accounts of his childhood, what strikes one is a sense of separateness, of isolation. His physical infirmity presumably prevented participation in many schoolboy activities and his being 'moved from private school to private school (five in all) until I was fifteen' cannot have helped build friendships and security. After that he did, it seems, make friends, but 'neither school nor neighbourhood ever gave me a sense of belonging to a community. I had my own life, which was that of the mind and the imagination'. In an as-yet-unpublished autobiographical sequence, 'What Brings You Here So Late?' (2001–2), the narrator is, in 'A grown-up's vision, puny, pitiable', and takes on the persona, in the early part of the sequence, of 'poor love'.

Indeed, it is noteworthy how frequently, as a critic, Conran is a diagnostician of isolation and the need for community. In his reading of their cases, Edward Thomas and David Jones each find comradeship in the army. Conran describes Gerard [Manley] Hopkins as being an 'exile . . . from his own feelings' until he finds a 'rise of the heart' and 'a sense of being at home' (a key phrase for Conran, as we shall see) 'among his father's people, half-Welsh himself' at St Beuno's in north Wales and he begins to study Welsh poetry. Conran describes Glyn Jones, 'loneliness-haunted' in Cardiff in the early 1930s, turning back to the Welsh-speaking roots from which he had been dislocated by his English-language education, to study Welsh literature and, through that, to gain a sense of identity and self-realization. Conran adds: 'Welsh poetry is a very socially orientated art, it arises out of actual communities in place and time.' When Conran considers Roland Mathias (who figures later in this chapter), he refers to his 'long struggle against deracination, trying to recover and justify a Welshness he almost lost in his youth'; and he cites Mathias's remark that for David Jones 'Wales became, so to speak, the shibboleth with which he could put aside fear'. Such comments help us to understand the profound impact which Gwyn Williams's translations of medieval Welsh poetry had on Conran when he read them for the first time at university in Bangor in the 1950s:

[T]hey were a revelation to me . . . The bright, formal, exciting world of medieval Wales became my other home. Hywel ab Owain Gwynedd, Cynddelw, Dafydd ap Gwilym, Dafydd Nanmor and Tudur Aled became my brothers, flesh of my flesh, blood of my blood.

In 'What Brings You Here So Late?' the poet refers to his early college digs as a 'hermitage'; he was however already beginning to write poems ('oddity and poems') and what he found in the brilliant medieval world of Williams's translation was a culture in which the poet was not an isolated oddity but one in which, in a highly structured ('formal') society, the poet had a designated place, re-membering its past, giving voice to its identity and its ideals. It is a vision, clearly, which not only fulfilled Conran's personal imaginative needs – we notice that reference to 'home' and the imagery of familial bonds – but also gave him a conception of how a society might be organized and the role the creative artist might play in it, a conception which became central to Conran's writing career, and indeed to his political vision. The role of the Welsh poet was, and is, Conran emphasizes, essentially communal, whether that community is the formalized, courtly world of the *uchelwyr* (noblemen) which he found in Gwyn Williams's translations, or belongs to the *buchedd*, the way of life of ordinary folk in which the *bardd gwlad*, the folk poet, played an essential role: 'What excites me about Welsh poets is that they start with the community and the individual is always related to that community.' Moreover, the precise terms in which Conran recalls the impact of Gwyn Williams's translations are again worth noting:

Gwyn Williams imparted to me his basic *muthos* . . . According to this myth the old Wales had more or less collapsed with the Act of Union in 1536 . . . Like Eliot's myth of the 'dissociation of sensibility', it was a story of the Fall, of Paradise Lost.

The passage crucially connects Conran's discovery of and fascination with the Welsh medieval tradition with his own modern-ist poetic. Myth-making is, manifestly, a major aspect of mod-ernism: Eliot, Pound, Bunting and, closer to home, David Jones, as M. Wynn Thomas points out, all 'professed their undying love for "established" traditions that on closer inspection, proved conspicuously of their own making'. Whatever the actuality of the

world of the medieval Welsh *bardd* and the tradition which followed
– and few people know more about that tradition than Tony
Conran – it became for him a powerful enabling fiction. Indeed,
early in his career, it seems to have been a means of emotional and
creative survival; Conran has written on several occasions of his
lonely exile as a clerk in a Chelmsford factory, after graduating from
Bangor: 'I sat in the public library every evening translating Welsh
poetry, and I was received into the Church of Rome. These things at
least made me feel I belonged'. In his alienation, he found meaning
and belonging in the structure and formality that he identified both
in Welsh poetry and in the pre-Vatican II Roman Church.

Tony Conran's work as a translator has on occasion overshadowed his achievement as a poet. In fact, though, the two are
inextricably linked. His own poetic practice, his whole poetic
strategy, has been profoundly affected by what he found in the
Welsh-language poetic tradition. In other words, his career has in
a sense been a much more profound act of translation than the
actual translation of a body of poetry from the Welsh; what his
work does is to utilize what he discerns as the poetic procedures
and assumptions of the Welsh tradition in his own work, to
translate into the English language that poetry's very non-English
view of the world. In so doing he creates, perhaps uniquely, a
distinctively Welsh, or 'Anglo-Welsh' poetry (he has continued to
defend the term) – a poetry which he differentiates from the
English tradition: 'The English poet has to start with the idea that
he's alone in a strange world, he's lost his bearings towards the
people.' Thus, in Conran's view, English poetry, at least since the
Romantics, has been a poetry of self-expression, empirical, the
articulation of individual experience and point of view. 'Welsh
poetry', he writes 'impinged on me first as a way out of empiricism
– not that I would have put it like that, but English empiricism
(and all the other things about English culture that I hated, the
class-structure, the "there-there" attitude of superior sympathy)
was intensely claustrophobic to me.' Clearly there are implications
here that go beyond poetry into the political and national, and yet,
at the same time, are deeply personal. The poetry Conran himself
was writing in the 1950s and 1960s was

> not a poetry of experience but an attempt to create metaphorical para-
> digms of the recovery of innocence: that is something like allegories of

rebirth . . . [I]t was radically inter-personal, I and thou, not I and it,
because innocence and rebirth were not solitary things (though they
could be lonely) but a state of union . . . a couple in love, a field full of
folk.

'Innocence' here, it would seem, we must gloss as openness to
others; he goes on to describe his great labour of translating Welsh
poetry for *The Penguin Book of Welsh Verse* in the 1960s as
'another kind of paradigm of the recovery of innocence'. 'A field
full of folk' (deliberately echoing Langland) is, of course, itself a
translation, from the climax of Waldo Williams's 'Mewn Dau
Gae' ('In Two Fields'), where the poet sees the ordinary people
in the fields as an almost mystical vision of wholeness and
an intimation of a greater, transcendent Wholeness. The phrase
recurs in a number of places in Conran's recent writing, a
period in which he has also produced a substantial volume of
translations of Waldo's poetry. In that poetry, as Conran points
out, Waldo delineates his vision of a society of peace, based on
Welsh community-life, and offers this as an alternative to state
sovereignty, based on individualism, capitalism and, ultimately, on
military power.

   In his major sequence *Castles*, Conran has explored similar
tensions, albeit in his own distinctive, modernist way. Here power
– the power of the state, the power of the individual, even of the
assertive, self-expressive artist – is represented by individual castles
which have over the centuries imposed themselves on Wales: 'An
earl builds a castle, a viking inscribes a rune . . . The act is one of
assertion, of class-power or personal aggrandisement.' But this
theme is counterpointed by another: the way the castles, the power
they represent, are themselves ultimately brought to ruin, revert
back to nature. All our human structures, including the lives that
we painfully construct, are subject to the processes of time, the
poem suggests. The poem is divided into six sections (each in turn
divided into six 'variations') and each section is dedicated to, and
haunted by, a friend – or, in the case of the fifth section, the poet's
father – all of whom had died in the dozen years preceding the
poem's composition. But the poem is never merely personal or
even articulated from one point of view; reflecting on cubist
painting, Conran sees its rejection of the single point of view as
having been 'in the interests of truth: perspective and viewpoint

were telling lies about the nature of our experience in the twentieth century . . . Perspective trivialised our deepest feelings of duality' – a view which manifestly has particular resonance in the Welsh situation. Thus, even though the poem is at times one of the most personal that Tony Conran has published, the difficulties of dealing with such material, especially by a poet who has such negative views of poetry which expresses the 'suffering individual with his *angst* and his desperate subjectivity', are transcended by the ways biographical experience and personal feeling are filtered through the historical and the literary in a palimpsestic method reminiscent of, say, Geoffrey Hill's *Mercian Hymns* – or ultimately Eliot's *The Waste Land.* Issues of imperial power, for instance, appear in a section located at Caernarfon castle and are associated with the poet's father, who had been an engineer in India under the Raj; personal feelings arising from the strained relations between the previously absent father and his son are hedged with self-mockery, and controlled by biblical allusion, echoes of the litany to Elen (her supposed responsibility for the construction of Roman roads in Britain echoing the father's engineering) and by the formality of the verse:

> By all the rigmaroles of Egypt –
> Nine, seven, five, three and one,
> *Mary of the hosts* –
> I hated him with the spears of the wise
> *Have Mercy,*
> *Elen of the roads*!
> And wasn't I the sulking boy?

'Castles are instruments of social alienation, an alien power coming and breaking down the pattern of the people,' Conran comments in his interview with Ian Gregson; 'A castle is a wedge in the soul,' he notes in *Castles.* Castles, in other words, come in the poem to represent those forces which constrain and destroy community, indigenous communities at places like Tre'r Ceiri, the ancient hill settlement in the Llŷn peninsula: 'You go there and you are faced with an archaeological daydream of Eden . . . This is where we belong . . . what it means to have roots and to be at home.' The poem engages Wales's present and future, not just its past: in Variation XIV, set at Dolbadarn at the time of the

Enclosure Acts, the land is 'privatised' and when Llywelyn imprisons his brother Owain, also at Dolbadarn, the poet comments, 'All poor claimants/ To be suppressed'; in post-Thatcherite Wales ('There is no such thing as society') such terms have powerful political resonance.

   Given such hostility to capitalism and to 'market forces', Conran is profoundly uneasy with the notion of art as a commodity, to be sold in the impersonality of the market place. The theme receives its most anguished treatment in Conran's 'Elegy for Brenda Chamberlain', following the artist's suicide:

> Brenda, this death of yours,
> this acquiescence in the laws of the market
> – how could you do it?
>
> O little person, how is it you never saw
> that art's no art but as people take it
> – this boy, that woman, this old man –
>
> take it because it is given them,
> because it's useful to them,
> because it's good manners and a gift?

A significant number of Conran's poems have originally been written to friends, usually at milestones in their lives, at marriages or birthdays. Such poems, usually accompanying a gift or token, are, as Ian Gregson emphasizes in the 1995 volume of tributes to Conran edited by Nigel Jenkins, not *about* the act of giving, but are *enactments* of friendships, an art which is participatory, part of the communal celebration. In this sense there is a ritualistic element to such acts of giving; such occasions as marriages, are, as Conran writes of the celebration of the New Year in Waldo's 'Llandysilio-yn-Nyfed', 'ritual interruptions of the everyday . . . designed to release the imagination to make contact with what is important'; such comments underline the significance which Conran attributes to such ritual performance as morris dancing, folk song or the Mari Lwyd, which often feature in his work: 'Ritual is the art of community.' The gift poems are thus rituals of friendship and love, within the community; to John Wain Conran writes 'As poet, bringer of peace and friend./ Is there, humanly, a higher end?'

Rather like the traditional Welsh *llatai* poem, in which the poet sent an animal or bird with a message to his love, Conran's gift poems usually focus on the object which is the token of his friendship, an object of no value in itself: a piece of slate, a spirit level, bay leaves, lily bulbs. The object is often elaborately described; again the technique perhaps owes something to *dyfalu*, the elaborate layering of descriptive phrases, but to the contemporary English speaker the effect is essentially one of defamiliarization: bay leaves, for example, are

> Brittle, matt-surfaced,
> Lanceolate
> With the points tipped like spears,
> The edges undulate . . .

Indeed, the cumulative effect of these poems, as of much of Conran's late work, is to create a sense of the world around us as 'other', a place of strange or enigmatic presences. (A Conran landscape is rarely lush: more often it is a rugged north Wales world of rocks, flints and ferns.) Though one frequently senses a profound longing for the spiritual, for transcendent presence – evidence of the religious sensibility that Jeremy Hooker has perceptively attributed to Conran – the world we see in the gift poems and elsewhere is essentially one of material evolution and process (ferns have 'gathered/ Changed, held their ground, and evolved' through aeons of geological time); in the fourth section of *Castles*, the poet enters the Catholic church he has not visited for seventeen years and he experiences a vision of Christ on the Cross. Here is a place of 'oneness', it seems, an alternative to human loneliness and homelessness; but the 'precarious joy' seems to provide no abiding home. Elsewhere in the poem, towers reach 'Into white air', places have 'a high-pitched emptiness'; snowdrops grow 'in the blizzard of time'.

In an early poem, 'For the Marriage of Heulwen Evans', the poet wishes that 'of your children may be made whole/ All fragmentary generations'. But it is in this fragmented world, this Wales, empty of secure values, in which older communal traditions have long eroded, not the formal world of the *uchelwyr* or the organic community of the *buchedd*, that Conran must construct his poems. And for Conran, as we have seen, a poem is essentially a *constructed* thing, not merely mimetic, often overtly manifesting its constructedness; indeed, Conran seems to see all art in this way, writing of a painting by his friend Victor Neep, for example, that 'it was not just a visual object, but a dance. It had been built up layer by layer'. One is reminded both of the palimpsestic technique of poems like 'Elegy for the Welsh Dead, in the Falkland Islands, 1982' and *Castles*, and of the way Conran has seen *Castles*, *All Hallows* and *A Gwynedd Symphony* in terms of symphonic structures, in turn forming parts of a 'Welsh *Commoedia*'; 'What Brings You Here So Late?', subtitled 'Symphony Four', was originally structured around the cards of the Tarot. This is an aspect of his work that has been present from the beginning – witness his reference to the 'bright, formal . . . world' of medieval Wales revealed by Gwyn Williams. Conran responds, clearly, not just to a community that had structure and meaning but to the formal intricacies of its verse. It is this sense of poetry as structure that he repeatedly responds to in his critical writing. Of Dylan Thomas's *18 Poems* Conran asserts: 'Far from being inchoate, the best of them strike me as wonderfully ordered, formal pieces of work, intricate as a passacaglia or fugue.' Elsewhere, again in connection with Dylan Thomas, 'A poem is far more like a prehistoric standing stone in a field than it is like a photograph or a map', while a poem by Lynette Roberts is 'a made thing, not just a slice of life'. His reading of Idris Davies's lyrics in *The Angry Summer* as '*tesserae* in a dramatic mosaic' is a major factor in Conran's view that Davies is a central figure in the English-language writing of Wales; the 'mosaic' technique is, again, one which allows the 'multiple perspective' necessary to come to terms with our modern world, and particularly with our modern Wales.

Conran writes of David Jones as a constructor of 'edifices' through which he 'tried to further Welshness', constructing, from Wales's past, meanings for her future: communal, non-capitalist, uncoercive. In this sense, manifestly, and given the magnitude of his achievement, Tony Conran is by far the finest poet in the modernist tradition that Wales has produced since David Jones. 'It is time to make shapes of my country', he writes in 'Map into Heraldry', part of his sequence to the artist Paul Davies, published in *All Hallows*; in discussing this same sequence in his Gwyn Jones lecture (2002), Tony Conran writes: 'We are wassailers, soulers, little children in the night. We cry for a soul. That's our job, that's what artists do. And Wales as a nation is souling in us, crying for a soul.'

When Tony Conran wrote of Brenda Chamberlain that her 'great act of fiction was herself, steering her imagination between the real islands of a real outside', in a sense he was also speaking for himself and therefore of the imaginative bond between them. Equally talented as writer and as painter, Brenda Chamberlain (1912–1971), was born and raised ('I remember no restraints at all') in the bourgeois university town of Bangor, visited Copenhagen as a schoolgirl, and became a precocious student at the Royal Academy Schools in London. In 1936 she settled in Llanllechid, Snowdonia, with her husband and fellow artist John Petts and together they aimed to live a simple, sandal-shod life based on anarchist, pacifist and free-love ideals; like others who had gone 'back to nature', she searched for a more rooted, more authentic way of life in the Welsh countryside. They started the Caseg printing-press, to produce their own hand-coloured greeting cards (in the approved arts-and-crafts manner), and during the war collaborated with Alun Lewis in the producing of a remarkable collection of inexpensively produced broadsheets (see Chamberlain's *Alun Lewis and the Making of the Caseg Broadsheets*, 1970), featuring texts (by Lewis, Dylan Thomas and Lynette Roberts, and with some translations from the Welsh) accompanied by strong images. These were conceived as a cultural counterbalance to war, and thus intended to 'reach the People' and to 'capture the ears and eyes and pockets of the multitude'. The violence of war penetrated the pair's seclusion in many forms, most graphically when one of three Liverpool evacuee children, throwing a live mortar against a rock for fun, ended up 'twitching on the ground in the death agony, his brains spilling on the grass'. Later, when Petts and she separated, Chamberlain finished up living first for many years on Ynys Enlli (Bardsey Island), feeling she was returning to the ancient roots of her Manx family and thus to her own Celtic roots; a subsequent move took her away from Wales, though again to an island life that was both simple and apart from modern life (until the colonels extinguished democracy) on Ydra in the Greek islands, where she published a journal, *A Rope of Vines* (1965), and completed a play, *The Protagonists*. A complicated relationship with a young German, Karl von Laer, sustained over decades, resulted in several publications, including a neglected 'war-sequence', 'The Green Heart' (begun in 1941, but published in full only in 1958), and Chamberlain's only novel *The Water-Castle* (1964). And in her fascinating late work *Poems with Drawings*, an interleaving of texts and images, she poignantly wrote the epigraph, or perhaps the epitaph, of her own strange imagination:

> The dead whisper with the dead
> the living gossip with the dead
> the dead speak of loneliness
>
> The living tell the dead
> of how hard it is to be alive
> thereby destroying them a second time[.]

In *Tide-race* (1962) the remarkable record (dated 1946–60) of Chamberlain's stay on Bardsey Island, the legendary dwelling-place of 20,000 Celtic saints and site of medieval pilgrimage, she created, out of the hard facts of an elemental struggle to subsist and the raw materials of neo-Romanticism (there is something in common between her metamorphosing landscapes and seascapes and the polymorphic paintings of Ceri Richards), an intimate map of her own mythopoeic and cosmogenic imagination. 'The world he sees in the overdramatic light of an obsessed imagination', she writes of the ogre Cadwaladar, the island despot, 'big with grief and comedy like any ancient hero', whose epic feuds seem to have originated in the twilight of prehistory. The same could be said of her imagination, except that she is careful to ballast her saints' legends, seal stories and visions of ancient abbeys with mention of her neighbours' pettiness and reports of periodic visits (over the turbulent straits) to the mainland, just as her recounting of a vivid premonitory dream of death's claims upon her (*Tide-race* affords examples aplenty of Chamberlain's borderline mental states) ends with her explaining it in terms of mice nibbling around her in her sleep. Land and sea writhe with expressive (and often threatening) life in Chamberlain's work: 'they are immensely alive, these trunks that have thrust upwards from the soil and are in their highest boughs speaking with the air.' The ocean she finds almost irresistibly compelling, haunted in particular as she is by the many stories of magical exchange and intercourse between seals and humans, and by the legends of drownings. 'This rock-fragment which on a map is a drawing of a treasure island taking on an unreal fantasy in certain moods of summer weather, is set in an element too big for contemplation. The impact with reality is enough to unnerve a child' – and almost enough to unnerve Chamberlain, whose book is in a way written to 'contain' that uncontainable element, that unfathomable non-human reality.

'My reverie is of the known rock, overlaid by the weaving of imagination' writes Chamberlain. But that conveys only the fey 'Celtic' aspects of her writing. At its deepest, and most authentic, *Tide-race* derives from an entirely different order of imagination. It is in part her Gauguin-like Romantic dream of finding a 'primitive' place where 'I live like Andromeda bound to the rock rude; often writhing to free myself yet cherishing my bonds; at extremest tension, hoping for the wind to blow everything away, so that problems might be solved by elemental means beyond human control.' It is the dark underside of that vision, however, that appears in the most compelling parts of *Tide-race*, as in all Chamberlain's best writing and painting. Hers is the cosmos of a suffering, crucified consciousness, tortured by loneliness, sexual (and gender) confusion, unfocused need. And central to that cosmos is her plight as an outsider – to 'everyday' Wales, to her own family and background, and even to her gender (she was ever a questionable 'woman' in the limiting terms of her day). When, in her celebrated 'signature' poem 'Diving into the Wreck', Adrienne Rich writes of abandoning 'the book of myths/ in which/ our names [as women] do not appear', and of plunging into the water in search of a drowned identity, she could well have been speaking for the Chamberlain of *Tide-race*, a neglected minor classic of woman's search for selfhood that awaits the kind of illumination that may yet come from reading it in the light of *écriture féminine.*

In that her gender crisis is deeply implicated in her sense of being an outsider, Chamberlain resembles another highly significant writer, Rhys Davies. In fact, Davies (1901–78) was a multiple outsider – his shopkeeping family a modest class apart from the mining community it served, isolated from adolescence in his native Blaenclydach (up a tributary valley of the Rhondda Fawr) by his incipient gayness (what other 'industrial' writer venturing down a mine notices in coal only the delicate imprint of fossil fern?). Intrinsically uneasy with a 'Wales' he identified with the chapels' 'blight on the souls of [the] young', at the same time he was never at home in the London where for some fifty years he made his solitary home as a professional writer. And it was as a professional writer of growing renown (one of the first produced by Wales, 'a good bit of a pioneer', in Glyn Jones's phrase, when he began producing his Rhondda short stories in the early1920s) that he came fully into his own. He eventually became 'a bigshot' – Glyn Jones again – readily published, in his prime, by the *New Yorker*. That is not surprising, as he probably only ever felt at home in language and in the aesthetic form (which he sometimes fetishized) of the short story, refuge of the misfit and isolato. Moreover, his otherness is inscribed in his style, as well as being more manifest in his choice of characters and themes. He has with some justification been clinically classified as a narcissist; certainly his writing is highly burnished inside and out, to deflect both inner emotion (Davies as narrator is always impeccably cool) and outer curiosity (simple identification with the author is elegantly discouraged). But there are nevertheless shy, subtle filaments of sympathy in his fiction that reach out in particular to some of the outsiders, however grotesque, that he delights in creating, although tangled with those filaments are also strong impulses of distaste and visceral fear. This combination of emotions is most potently apparent when Davies deals – as so often he does – with the *danse macabre* of sexual relations and with the black comedy in the realpolitik of the power relations between men and women. A Welsh Strindberg, he sardonically relishes the inexhaustible human display of the full sophisticated repertoire of bizarre sexual relations. And like Lawrence – whose early admirer he was and whose friend he became – he was fascinated by a dream of a reversion to the more innocently primal, associating this in part with an imagined pre-industrial and pre-Nonconformist Wales, whose 'Celtic' heartland was the rural west but whose representative was Dr William Price, a figure that Davies, in his remarkable (and thoroughly unreliable) autobiography *The Print of a Hare's Foot*, treated as a hero, almost a father figure or alter ego, in the quest for psycho-sexual freedom in Nonconformist Wales.

Davies was what is patronizingly known as a prolific writer: in the 1930s alone he produced seven collections of short stories and six novels. His novels, always structurally flawed but fascinating in parts or aspects, have barely begun to be explored. His stories – and he produced some of the best there are in the canon of Welsh writing in English – are correctly treasured by some but remain too little known. A number – although perhaps 'clutch' would be a better word, given Rhys Davies's bleakly comical view of sexual relations – are undoubted classics. 'The Fashion Plate' is remarkable for its delicate distribution of sympathy between a woman in the ugly black mining communities, driven by emotional need to ruthless assertion of her craving for aesthetic style, and her poor husband, reduced by her excesses to pathetic butchery of himself. 'Nightgown' demonstrates subtle understanding of a downtrodden wife and mother's impulse to hug her comforting feminine secret – that she has hidden a treasure away from her brutally male family; a precious, expensive nightgown intended for her laying-out. A comic-sympathetic treatment of a social outcast is found in 'Catherine Fuchsias'; there are sobering hints of child sexual abuse in 'The Public House'; Davies's ambivalent feelings of his anthropologist's distance from his society are worked out to a complex conclusion in 'The Chosen One'. But the sheer volume of Davies's output means that such exquisite achievements of form and of psychological insight as these are forever in danger of being jostled to one side by the robust bulk of his shorter fiction – such readable but coarse-textured farces as 'King Canute' or 'Gents Only', or powerful but ultimately unsatisfying psychological studies such as 'Fear'.

Davies was fond of resonantly declaring that 'I do not exist for Wales, but Wales exists for me'. Only a half-truth in his case, one suspects, but nevertheless an important one, that highlights an outsider's strategy that, in its rejection of the temptation to 'belong' to contemporary Wales, is strikingly at odds with that adopted by Emyr Humphreys. His first novel, *The Little Kingdom* (1946), opens with farmer Richard Boyd gazing 'across the water' from the north-east corner of Wales and seeing 'the Wirral emerge from the early morning mist [to] become once more a solid and substantial rich-green sea-girt land, speckled with red-roofed houses'. The scene closely parallels Humphreys' boyhood experience of climbing to the summit of the Gop (the prehistoric burial mound in Trelawnyd, rumoured to be the grave of the Celtic warrior-queen Boadicea) and seeing the glinting spire of Liverpool cathedral in the near east, the craggy, mysterious profile of

Snowdonia to the distant west; the passage is also a mirror image of that view of Wales from the Wirral, mentioned at the beginning of this chapter, that entranced the young R. S. Thomas.

A product of the border county of Flintshire, Humphreys has remained all his life aware of the magnetic, hypnotic, insinuating and seemingly insolent power of England, having himself been so beguiled by it as a boy. Only in adolescence was the counter-attraction of Snowdonia irresistibly lit up for him when the bombing school on the distant Llŷn peninsula was set on fire in 1936 by the famous Plaid Cymru arsonists. It was, for him, a conversion experience, involving a realization, the implications of which have been worked out over a fifty-year writing career, through a remarkable number of plays, poems, essays, television documentaries, short stories and, above all, novels (twenty-one to date). The realization was the same as that of his friend, R. S. Thomas: 'I can't speak my own/ Language – Iesu,/ All those good words;/ And I outside them.' Emyr Humphreys the writer was born of the adolescent's sense of being an outsider, denied his birthright (his parents' language), condemned to find the script in which Welsh history, and even the Welsh landscape, was written to be totally illegible. It was, for him, a rude awakening to the colonial condition, and it made of him, as novelist, the Boadicea of modern Wales, a verbal guerilla fighter and resistance leader.

He came to style himself a 'dissident', and to align himself with the radical tradition of Welsh religious Nonconformity. But he also set out, by learning Welsh and steeping himself in the history and culture of the language, to see how far a born outsider could become an adoptive insider, while also exploring the opportunities offered by his cross-over experience to play (however guardedly, given his awareness of the disproportionate power of English) a mediating role in relation to the two linguistic cultures of Wales. In the process, he found that English proved resistant to becoming a Welsh language; that Englishness was, in his experience, part of the very genetic code of the language. These complex issues became subtly inscribed in the style and deep structure of Humphreys's work, even as it addressed them much more evidently at the level of content. He adopted a minimalist style, in an attempt to minimize the power of English to distort Welsh experience, and as a conscious corrective to the flamboyant wordiness that seemed to him to characterize some anglophone Welsh writing; he imported alienating narrative techniques from Brechtian theatre to manipulate readers into glimpsing and confronting their own historical condition, hoping to liberate them from the false consciousness of colonialism; and deep beneath his surface realist style he buried Welsh mythic matter (rather as Boadicea had reputedly lain buried under his beloved Gop), intending that readers should gradually come to share his own adolescent initiatory sense of coming to full identity, and thus mature self-understanding, only through the disinterring of the ancient life of 'native' Welsh history, everywhere buried beneath English colonial matter. He also constructed, like Tony Conran, his own enabling and would-be liberating myth of Welsh history in the important non-fiction work *The Taliesin Tradition*, an indispensable guide to the mental landscape of his writings.

Like R. S. Thomas, then, Humphreys can be most profitably understood with reference to Frantz Fanon's celebrated distinction between the three phases of colonial writing. In the first, a writer 'gives proof that he has assimilated the culture of the occupying power', and both Thomas and Humphreys believed that virtually the whole of Welsh anglophone literature remained stuck in that phase. In the second 'we find the native is disturbed; he decides to remember what he is', exactly as Humphreys did in his adolescence. And 'in the third phase [clearly exemplified by Humphreys's writings] . . . he turns himself into an awakener of the people; hence comes a fighting literature, a revolutionary literature, and a national literature'. A lifelong pacifist, Humphreys (appalled as a youngster by the ominous war-laden atmosphere of the 1930s) has (again like Thomas) supported direct non-violent action by the principled lawbreakers of Cymdeithas yr Iaith Gymraeg (the Welsh Language Society), while wrestling in his fiction with the torment of the brutal truth history teaches, that survival (of the highest values, let alone of peoples) has only ever been possible through violence. Throughout his career, he has also shown a sophisticated awareness (born in part of his experience of working, in the late 1950s and early 1960s, as a BBC radio and television producer) of modern media's power to shape mass consciousness, and of its subliminal promotion of the values of Anglo-American capitalism. Consequently, his writing has been consciously conceived of as resistant to such forces, just as he has always viewed his defence of Welsh culture as a 'local' instance of what Humphreys, a convinced Europhile and a committed intellectual on the best European model, believes to be a continent- and world-wide struggle against culturally levelling American consumerism.

Humphreys is further like R. S. Thomas in regarding his work as an extension of Welsh-language culture in another linguistic medium. Both writers have derived their own vocabulary of cultural and political understanding (and, indeed, the lexicon of their writing) from the anti-colonial rhetoric that has been a feature of that culture from the time of Emrys ap Iwan (in the late nineteenth century) to that of his great successor, Saunders Lewis, and onward to the present. Indubitably sons of Saunders (as anglophone writers of the previous generation had been contrast- ingly styled 'sons of Caradoc'), Thomas and Humphreys both believed that the cultural crisis of Wales could be solved only by political means, and acted accordingly; but, unlike the poet, the novelist is reluctant to make a clear distinction between his creative work and his political activity. The European orientation of his imagination also sets him apart from R. S. Thomas, while aligning him firmly with Saunders Lewis, who believed that the proper place of a Wales born of the collapse of the Roman Empire has always been within a European confederation of peoples. From the time that Humphreys worked with refugees in Italy at the end of the war as an organizer for the Save the Children Fund he has been infatuated with the country, and has returned to it repeatedly in his fiction; but his European allegiance is much wider and deeper than that, and has resulted in his feeling that his novels are best understood as European in preoccupation, style and structural character.

Set in Italy, *Voice of a Stranger* (1949) is one of the four novels of the first phase of Humphreys's career (the others being *The Little Kingdom* (1946), *A Change of Heart* (1951) and *Hear and Forgive* (1952)), that extended roughly from 1946 to 1952. In this early work, quickly recognized by English critics and mostly written when he was himself living outside Wales, he established several of the concerns that have lasted him a lifetime: the plight of conscience when an individual is confronted (even within the self) by the pathology of power; the totalitarian instincts in human nature and in human relationships, manifested in a myriad contexts and ways, including media control; the necessary but corrupting milieu of politics; the enticing individualistic impulse to lighten one's life by jettisoning responsibility to place and to people. These novels capture key aspects of their period through their depiction of the exciting, bewildering, potentially amoral chaos of a devastated post-war Europe; and the high hopes and proportionate disappointments of the brave new world of the Welfare State. Mostly located in places outside Wales – from London to Italy – they draw on Humphreys's experience first as aid worker, then as London teacher and habitué of the Chelsea bohemian arts scene (early friendships with artists such as Patrick Heron were later to have an impact on the novelist's modes of narrative representation) and they offer a fairly accurate graph of Humphreys's own existence as an exile. But the subjects addressed in the first of the set, *The Little Kingdom*, loosely but suggestively based on the Penyberth arson incident that had first introduced Humphreys to his Wales and thus to his creative theme, were those to which he returned to initiate the next phase of his writing, the product of his return to Wales, which roughly corresponded to his period in the BBC (1955–65).

The first of these novels, *A Man's Estate*, brought Humphreys's imagination home to Wales, and reconnected him to the fraught issue of inheritance (the theme of the work). But the double aspect of the novel's composition – simultaneously the product of the author's return to teach in Pwllheli and of his year abroad as writer in residence in Austria – neatly encapsulates the insider-outsider stance that is characteristic of Humphreys. In *A Man's Estate* can also be found that first substantial instance of his ambivalent treatment of one of his most important subjects: the cultural (and psychological) legacy of Welsh religious Non-conformity. While two of this period's output avoid Welsh subjects – *The Italian Wife* explores aspects of the Oresteia theme in the context of post-war England, while *The Gift* (1963) draws on Humphreys's BBC experience of working with actors, conveying the heady atmosphere of a brutally exploitative new entertainments industry – in the first of his major works, *Y Tri Llais/A Toy Epic* (1958), Humphreys went directly back to source, disinterring a manuscript he had discarded in his early twenties and reworking it to produce first a Welsh-language radio-play, then a Welsh-language novel, and finally the Hawthornden Prize-winning *A Toy Epic*. In many ways a highly personal portrait of the artist as a young Flintshire boy, this masterly short work shows him making, out of the configuration of localities and personal relationships that constituted Humphreys's formative experience of his native region in 'one of the four corners of Wales,' a template for his future mapping of the whole of his country's distinctive features. *A Toy Epic* is therefore the ur-novel of Humphreys's maturity, a fascinating exercise in cultural counterpoint. Through their respective stylized, lyrical monologues, the three main characters, Albie, Michael and Iorwerth, contrasted in character, social class and cultural positioning, weave an intricate, miniature image of early twentieth-century Wales. They also convey the increasingly doom-laden atmosphere of the 1920s and 1930s, as economic depression became the breeding ground of monstrous political ideologies, locked in mortal conflict. Himself consciously a product of these decades, Humphreys has repeatedly revisited the period in his work, usually tracing its malaise back, in the case of Wales, to the killing fields of the Great War (in which the novelist's father was gassed) and to the resultant death throes of the valuable 'civilization' of Welsh Nonconformist society.

This last was to become the dominant theme of another of the novels of the period – and probably Humphreys's single greatest achievement – *Outside the House of Baal* (1965). It employs a twin-track narrative that allows Humphreys stereoscopic historical vision, as he is able to hold present (the early 1960s) and past (the first sixty years of the twentieth century) in simultaneous focus throughout. And it pairs fascinatingly contrasting characters in the enigmatic figure of an aged idealist, the minister JT (alternatively a saint or a selfish, but deluded, exploiter of others) and his elderly sister-in-law Kate, forthright, practical, yet herself very possibly the equally self-deluded victim, in her crippling inhibitions, of the Nonconformist background they both share. By tracing their progress through the decades of the century Humphreys is able to reveal both the heroic and the suspect sides of Welsh Noncon-formity and to explore the social, political, economic and cultural factors that led to its disintegration. He is also able to dramatize his own politicized reading of modern Welsh history, touching on the change in the condition of women, the emergence of an anglophone industrial society, the anglocentric politics of Welsh socialism and the consequent politicization of a subaltern Welsh-language culture.

These are also the themes that dominate 'The Land of the Living', the great sequence of seven novels (1971–91) upon which he was able to embark at the beginning of his final phase, after he had retired to give all his time to his writing (supplementing his income by producing documentaries for HTV and, subsequently, plays for S4C, the Welsh-language channel for which he had long campaigned). Such was the scale of this achievement that it unfortunately tended to eclipse the two fascinating shorter works he published in the eighties, *The Anchor Tree* (1980; a novel about Welsh America) and *Jones* (1984; an anatomy of Welsh post-colonial mentality in the form of an intimate portrait of a Welsh academic who has opted to spend a hedonistic lifetime in London). Both are slim works compared with the sequence, which deliberately adopts the formula of romance fiction to develop a kind of saga-history of modern Wales by following the opportunistic Amy Parry's triumphal progress from rags to riches down the decades of the twentieth century, restlessly acquiring values, friends and lovers as she goes, and as restlessly abandoning them one after another in her ruthless quest for power and for money. For most of the sequence, Humphreys refrains from overt authorial comment, as he had done in *Outside the House of Baal*, and as with that novel he maintains this illusion of disinterestedness by building the work out of a historically linked series of dramatic *tableaux vivants* that give the impression of unmediated experience of the action yet deny the reader direct access to the psychological and social mainsprings of those actions. Only in *Bonds of Attachment* (1991), the last novel to be completed, did Humphreys adopt more conventional third-person and first-person techniques to chart the attempt made by Peredur, one of the dying Amy's sons, to establish redeeming psychological contact with his dead father (one of Amy's many victims) and to solve the enigma of his mother's past.

Peredur therefore retraces in reverse the steps by which a whole world has, over the seven novels, emerged in Amy's wake – as if, as narrative device, she were the equivalent of that legendary Olwen in whose footsteps clover so magically sprang. As it extends over the sequence, this world builds Humphreys's world of twentieth-century Wales, like the images that used slowly, magically, to unfold in old pop-up books. The symbolic geography of 'Humphreys country' (the Welsh equivalent of Faulkner's Yoknapatawpha County) is revealed, from the border-country hillsides of Amy's upbringing to the anglicized enclaves of the bourgeois coastal towns, and from the long stretch of the Llŷn peninsula to the cramped valleys of the south Wales coalfield; the main features of the ideological landscape are also clearly marked, from nationalism to socialism to communism; and the myriad characters that people this landscape – several of them endowed with a power to command the reader's attention that almost, yet never quite, rivals that of Amy herself – are often representatives of the contending political and cultural philosophies of modern Wales as much as they are individuals of complex personal psychology.

Those novels, short stories and novellas that Humphreys has published since the completion of the 'Land of the Living' sequence run the risk of seeming like an afterthought, whereas, in fact, they have a powerful presence of their own, as do the poems and plays he has produced over his career. *Unconditional Surrender* (1996) broods on the implications for Wales of its involvement in the Second World War and on the fateful terms on which it settled with itself and with the modern world at the war's conclusion; *The Gift of a Daughter* (1998) hints at parallels between the fate of an ancient Welsh-language culture and that of the even more ancient Etruscans; while in *Ghosts and Strangers* (2001), a collection originally conceived as four linked stories exploring the ambivalent power of love, he has continued the European theme, adopting a form (the novella) he associates more with the Continent than with England, and repeatedly meditating on the European dimensions of the contemporary Welsh situation.

One of the earliest, and shrewdest, of commentators on Emyr Humphreys's work was his contemporary Roland Mathias. Like Humphreys (and unlike most Welsh writers in English), he is a committed heir of Welsh Nonconformity and also resembles the novelist in the outsider's relationship to Wales that has been the mainspring of his work (in the essay 'The Border' he imagines himself as being denied passage westward beyond Offa's Dyke as 'one who has counted himself out and in so many times'). Born in Talybont-on-Usk, Mathias, son of an army chaplain, was raised in and around army camps in various parts of England, although the family's return visits to Wales were frequent. Thirty-three years old before he settled his own family in Wales, following his appointment as headmaster of Pembroke Dock Grammar School, Mathias, who had been a conscientious objector on pacifist grounds during the war, left the country again some years later, only returning permanently to live in the Brecon area upon his early retirement in 1969. Throughout his career, however, it is his intense concern with the anglophone literature of Wales, interwoven with his detailed and learned interest (as an Oxford-trained historian) in the country's history, that has informed all his monumental work as 'poet, short-story writer, critic, editor, scholar, historian, preacher, lecturer and educationalist' (as his biographer Sam Adams has described him). Almost single-handedly he succeeded – partly through the co-founding (in 1949) and the longterm editing (1961–76) of the literary journal *The Anglo-Welsh Review* (originally *Dock Leaves*) – in establishing the study of Welsh writing in English on a sound scholarly, historical and critical footing. His efforts in this respect were immense, and he persisted in them, with typical moral tenacity, in the face of widespread institutional, educational and cultural opposition from within Wales itself. Lurking somewhere at source of all this effort was undoubtedly that sense of personal need to access his own past and to place himself in relation to it that manifests itself not only in his creative work but in Mathias's detailed critical treatment of a wide range of writers – he thereby virtually constructed (at much the same time as Tony Conran) a literary tradition, traceable back to the Middle Ages, to which he could relate. But the outsider in him may have benefited him (as well as tormenting him) in other ways as well; there is in Mathias's whole bearing towards the anglophone culture of Wales a confidence in its evident worth and consequence that is frequently absent from those brought up in a Wales still largely overshadowed and cowed by English example.

Mathias's short stories vary considerably in kind and in quality, but are always readable. Some draw on his experiences as a teacher, others are little more than brief portraits or oral tales and reminiscences, yet these allow him to experiment with the monologue form and to taste the tang of local idiom and inflection in a way that corresponds to some of his poems. The best, however, are those that are rooted in the deep personal concerns that are also manifested in his poems. Thus 'Cassie Thomas' is a subtle, sympathetic study of a woman of modest background who painfully constructs a false, brittle self of competence and control that allows her to 'pass' as a teacher; it is a psychological portrait of divided selfhood that interestingly echoes Mathias's own cultural experience, except that his Nonconformist morality would allow him to cope with such a psychic crisis only by striving always to achieve integration in the name of moral integrity. (That said, his need to adopt historical personae is very evident in his poetry.) A Welshman's return from Australia to visit the family's ruined Welsh farm is strikingly evocative of Mathias's own tortured feelings about 'roots', and includes a revealing mention of the man's (forbidden) wish to 'cut from himself the part that could not forget'. Mathias's brief experience of living in Germany as a small boy, combined with his later brave pacifist stand during the war, is the basis of 'The Rhine Tugs', the most complex and suggestive of his stories. It is in part about 'history', the contrasting ways in which the past is remembered and constructed by nations and individuals (latterly the theme of Penelope Lively's celebrated Booker-winning novel *Moon Tiger*). It is also in part about magic and enticement – towards the past, towards freedom and (most significantly) towards a mysterious (and dangerous) voyage 'aboard' language. It is therefore about the making of a poet, as, unexpectedly, is another excellent and moving story 'Block System', about an old Welsh farmer, belatedly become London milkman, who is lost for words when faced with a Milk Marketing Board tribunal. Even his streetwise daughter is impatient with Ben, giving no credit to 'those who were slow of speech, least of all when they revealed a dumb sense of exactitude. And slow of speech Ben certainly was. He would have stuttered a little if he had got the words out quicker. But until recently they had come up out of him with dignity.' Mathias, himself a stutterer when young, and deemed 'slow' at school, cared passionately, as man and writer, for exactitude and dignity of utterance. And like Ben, his use of words suggests one who knew how some could be 'odd and pointed at one end . . . like pears', knew their power to evoke (and indeed to *be*) sensation ('he held [the word 'horse'] to his cheek, rough and satisfying', and could turn them over and over and feel their 'strength go through him').

Mathias is an extraordinary poet – so learned in his discourse and reference, so tortuous in his syntax, so forbidding in his recondite vocabulary as to seem at times a parody of a schoolmaster pedant, yet capable of producing (on these same uncompromising terms) a handful of the best post-war poems to come from Wales, and always quite unmistakably a poet of remarkable (and demanding) moral, intellectual and aesthetic probity.

The strong, bony, moral backbone of his religious convictions can be seen running through four of his best poems, and can be felt in the knobby, gnarled texture of the language itself. (Like Geoffrey Hill, Mathias stands forever aghast at 'the tongue's atrocities' and consequently cross-examines his every word before, during and after utterance to make sure it is, in every sense, 'answerable' for itself.) In 'Testament', the closest anyone of Mathias's unyielding persuasion could possibly come to the vulgarity of confession, he acknowledges himself to be a 'child of belief' and knows himself to lack the moral stature of his 'puritan' ancestors. This is a tormenting contrast worked out on a much bigger scale, and in terms of landscape, in the marvellous 'Brechfa Chapel', a magnificent jeremiad against the shoddiness of modern society. The pilgrimage to the chapel itself climaxes in an emblematic contrast between the building and the 'black half-world' that 'bleaks by its very doors'. Most striking of all is the cacophony produced by the chaos of birds clammering all around, 'harrying the conversation of faith', so that Mathias is brought to resolve that 'Each on his own must stand and conjure/ The strong remembered words, the unanswerable/ Texts against chaos'. It is, of course, his very credo as a poet, and it illuminates his practice in 'Burning Brambles', a poem in which all of Mathias's distaste at the ineradicable corruption that is abroad and (most harrowingly) within is worked out in his attempt to uproot and burn the brambles that so shamelessly tangle and entangle. And in 'Porth Cwyfan' he produces another 'landscape' poem which this time brings him to a discomfiting encounter with the issue of his own questionable 'place' in Wales, the feeling that he, too, is an invader. It is a remarkable meditation on the fate of being an outsider, a fate that haunts, in different but related ways, all the writers considered in this chapter.

FURTHER READING

Sam Adams, *Roland Mathias* (Cardiff, 1995).
Sandra Anstey (ed.), *Critical Writings on R. S. Thomas* (Bridgend, rev.ed., 1992).

Damian Walford Davies (ed.), *'Echoes to the Amen': The Achievement of R. S. Thomas* (Cardiff, 2003).

Jason Walford Davies, 'Allusions to Welsh literature in the writing of R. S. Thomas', *Welsh Writing in English*, 1 (1995), 75–127.

Kate Holman, *Brenda Chamberlain* (Cardiff, 1997).

Jeremy Hooker, *Imagining Wales: A View of Modern Welsh Writing in English* (Cardiff, 2001).

Nigel Jenkins (ed.), *Thirteen Ways of Looking at Tony Conran* (Cardiff, 1995).

P. Bernard Jones and Don Dale-Jones, *T. H. Jones: Poet of Exile* (Cardiff, 2001).

Meic Stephens (ed.), *Decoding the Hare* (Cardiff, 2000).

M. Wynn Thomas, *Internal Difference: Writing in Twentieth-Century Wales* (Cardiff, 1992).

M. Wynn Thomas (ed.), *The Page's Drift: R. S. Thomas at Eighty* (Bridgend, 1993).

M. Wynn Thomas, *'Outside the House of Baal*: the evolution of a major novel', in Sam Adams (ed.), *Seeing Wales Whole* (Cardiff, 1998).

M. Wynn Thomas, 'Emyr Humphreys: regional novelist?', in K. D. M. Snell (ed.), *The Regional Novel in Britain and Ireland, 1800–1900* (Cambridge, 1998).

M. Wynn Thomas (ed.), *Emyr Humphreys: Conversations and Reflections* (Cardiff, 2002).

John Powell Ward, *The Poetry of R. S. Thomas* (Bridgend, rev. ed., 2001).

Justin Wintle, *Furious Interiors: Wales, R. S. Thomas and God* (London, 1996).

Ioan Williams, *Emyr Humphreys* (Cardiff, 1980).

CHAPTER 6

POPULAR IMAGES

JOHN HARRIS

Wales has seemed obsessed by self-image; by how writing about the country might register in the world beyond. This self-consciousness produces a sensitivity to all shades of adverse comment, an angry defensiveness the more readily displayed when such comment is delivered, as it were, from within the fold, by native writers capable through their use of English of reaching an international audience. It leads to demands of a national literature perhaps the reverse of what one might expect: that it serve as the handmaid of nationality and be in spirit celebratory; non-transgressive, non-adversarial. Writers are praised as cultural bridge-builders, not as demolitionists. Internal divisions must be dampened down, for a literature which parades Welsh differences over supposed national defects gives ammunition to those with low opinions of Wales – especially the English, stuffed with prejudice enough.

It was in this fashion that the *Western Mail* applauded Anne Adaliza Puddicombe, the novelist Allen Raine, who had accepted the writer's patriotic duty and herself massively contributed to what a leader in the *Western Mail* on her death described as 'the tardy realisation of the national character of the Welsh by the people across the border'. The term 'best-seller' lacks precision. To the publisher Michael Joseph it came to represent a sale of 50,000 in the original edition. Thanks to the commercial libraries, novels in the 1930s might achieve 100,000 in hardback while by the 1970s hardback sales of 20,000 could place a book in the British best-seller lists. Raine, by any yardstick, could be counted a 'best-seller' (the term was then establishing itself) and Hutchinson's totals for her novels match known figures for Ouida (Louis de la Ramée), another best-selling novelist of the period. Beginning with *A Welsh Singer* (1897), most of her eleven novels topped a quarter of a million copies, not counting sales in America (by far the largest

overseas market for British books). In terms of popularity she
rivalled Marie Corelli, Hall Caine and Silas Hocking, or so
thought the *Bookman*, the influential literary monthly that
welcomed this wholesome new voice from Wales much as it had
greeted the Scottish idyllists. *Punch*, too, saw the beginnings of
another Celtic Kailyard, with Raine promising to do for Wales
what James Barrie and Ian Maclaren had done for Scotland. It is,
perhaps, no wonder therefore that the Scottish pen-name
recommended itself, though, in a letter on 10 October 1906, she
recorded that it came mysteriously in a morning dream: 'just as I
awoke I heard the words "Allen Raine" and saw it written in white
letters before my eyes.'

Raine happily embraced her task. Writing on 23 April 1898 to
H. D. Trail, editor of *Literature*, she emphasized that 'it has been
the great desire of my life to shew the poetry and interest of Welsh
life to the nation with which we are linked'. Hers was a literature
of community, not of divisive class ('the middle & lower classes
being so much more immediately connected in Wales than in
England'). Adjudicating at an eisteddfod in her home town of
Newcastle Emlyn, she praised the 'quaint truthfulness of some
sketches of Welsh village life'. Satire was less acceptable,
particularly when directed at habits of rural worship: 'Humour is a
delightful tool for an author's use, but, to be perfectly pleasing, it
must be kindly as well as keen, and must never be used as a
weapon.' That Wales had its stains she admitted – they were not
totally expunged from her work – but she preferred 'the poetry of
Welsh life', the flowers of the Cardiganshire river-bank to wading
through the mud beneath.

This preference she shared with the bulk of fiction readers,
whose taste for Celtic pastoral nostalgia took sales of Maclaren's
Beside the Bonnie Brier Bush (1894) to some three-quarters of a
million. The house of Hutchinson, its list heavy with middlebrow
fiction, pushed Raine to similar effect and in a variety of physical
formats (most innovatively in sixpenny paperback). Meanwhile
Appleton's, the New York publishers of Hall Caine, presented
Raine to the American market in their Town and Country
Library, an outstanding fiction series that included Conrad and
Gissing. At the time of her final illness, the *Bookman* (April 1908)
reported how 'tributes to her work flow in from all quarters of the
world – from the Yukon territory to Jamaica – and from readers

of every class and profession'. And, writing in 1906, Constance A. Barnicoat placed Allen Raine in the top ten favourite novelists of girls, aged 15 to 18, in British high schools ('among them some of the best standing'). Raine, we surmise, was read not out of rocketing interest in Wales – the south Cardiganshire coast and its hinterland is no more than a backdrop for her celebrations of romantic love – though, as George Hutchinson observed, she was bringing to English fiction a new geographical terrain: at least his own firm had received no stories about this part of the country before.

Wales shared the general enthusiasm, as the City Librarian of Cardiff confirmed. Raine was serialized in the *Cardiff Times* and saluted by *Young Wales* as a bastion against 'the decadence and unhealthiness' of contemporary British fiction (her books became Sunday school prizes). On the accuracy of her portraiture the *Western Mail* had no doubts: 'No fiction writer of her own or of any other time showed such a delicate appreciation of the lights and shades of Welsh character, or knew better how to reproduce them on a canvass full of movement and life' (23 June 1908). Others were less sure. 'If the novel is to be judged as an intimate chronicle of the state of society, or of actual men and women reported with a corresponding reality in art, Allen Raine's books hardly count as Welsh documents at all.' Ernest Rhys's verdict, delivered in the *Manchester Guardian* (27 June 1908), befits a critic convinced of literature's social mission and one who had organized a discussion group for Durham miners. Yet Rhys acknowledged Raine's qualities as storyteller, 'her positive enjoyment in her own narrative'; hers was work sincerely offered, not written to empty formula. Emlyn Williams went further, confessing that as a child he had known *A Welsh Singer* by heart, 'but whose characters I never dreamt of connecting with the Welsh world around me'. Caradoc Evans, a writer born to oppose Allen Raine, spoke of 'nice false' novels about Wales; he admired her stellar success but her country heaven was not the Wales he knew.

For Keidrych Rhys and Gwyn Jones, facilitators of the new Anglo-Welsh literature, Evans became a founding father who (as Jones graphically put it) had destroyed the sandcastle dynasty of Allen Raine. Evans had power and originality – those who hated his work admitted it – while Raine, coming to fiction in her sixties, seemed old-fashioned even on publication. To the *Welsh Outlook*

in 1918 her popularity was a thing of the past, and a correspond-
ent in *Labour Voice/Llais Llafur* writes (18 December 1915): 'Her
works are ephemeral; they have no permanent value and are not
now in demand . . . We never took any stock of her, and do not do
so today.' Nevertheless, Raine remained well represented in
miners' libraries during this period but, although the book-trade
evidence is ambiguous (she was reissued in the 1930s and has
found a much later market in Wales), her appeal was essentially
transitory – as is the case with most best-sellers.

One has to jump forty years for another mass-circulating novel
of Wales, a period of regular breast-beating over Welsh fiction's
failure to achieve substantial markets – or any markets at all.
Owen Rhoscomyl at the turn of the century had congratulated
Allen Raine on breaking down the antipathy to stories dealing
with Wales; and later writers sensed a continuing prejudice against
Welsh fiction, whether in the minds of paying readers or the
London publishers who served them. For Rhys Davies, one of the
few Welsh authors dependent on sales of his books for survival, it
was Wales's unglamorous image that proved the obstacle: in
particular, the woes of the workers and 'the gloom associated with
Welsh mining life'. Perhaps 'a novel of Welsh middle-class life
written in low Trollopian key' would stand more chance, he mused
before a radio audience (17 January 1950), knowing how anti-
pathetical was such a notion to the Welsh writing spirit. You could
not expect a Welsh novel along classic English lines, agreed
Geraint Goodwin in *Welsh Outlook*, alluding to the national
predilection for the short story:

> No Welshman ever sees life steadily and sees it whole though he may
> see it the more clearly during the length of his vision. His genius is a
> bright, unyielding spike of light . . . What we call the English attitude is
> something different – a greater range but a lesser depth.

For Goodwin in 1930, at the outset of his writing career, it seemed
a case of pouring one's material into pre-existing moulds. The
English demanded distortion – diverting bits and pieces, never the
complex whole. Just how rigid were London publishers' requirements, and how readily authors complied with them, are questions
not readily answered, but the image persisted of Anglo-Welsh
authors dancing to alien tunes. As did the notion, amongst

no-nonsense Welsh critics and reviewers, of a 'real Wales' out
there, beyond sentimental idyll and malevolent satire, patiently
awaiting its chronicler. Creative writers better understood the
processes of imaginative literature. 'What *is* the real Wales?'
questioned Rhys Davies;

> I don't ask people to accept my picture of Wales as the real one; it is
> inevitable that as people differ in temperament, in views, in beliefs,
> many should reject my picture of their country, should find certain
> elements exaggerated, others omitted. A piece of writing is mainly a
> sort of flowering, a fulfilment of oneself.

In this light he viewed the mid-1930s blossoming of valleys fiction
– first books by Jack, Gwyn, Glyn and Lewis Jones joining his
own regular output. Only Jack Jones achieved any substantial
visibility and even he did not travel well: the *Saturday Review of
Literature* complained in 1936 of an absence in America of any
contemporary fiction from Wales. Three years later its prayers
were answered by a novel that stormed the world.

Published at the outbreak of war, *How Green Was My Valley*
proved an instant triumph, to the delight of Michael Joseph, the
fledgling publisher who, on the strength of a draft opening
chapter, had commissioned this first novel from a totally unknown
author (the only time he would ever do so). Years later, in June
1968, Richard Llewellyn (the pen-name of Richard Lloyd) recalled
his preparatory work for the book: how he had researched coal-
mining in Wales and Welsh religion, and the rise of the unions.
Then he tore up his research, 'simply because a novel is people and
fact is a nuisance; but it has to be known. Error is always in a grin
at your elbow.' The candour is refreshing, though Llewellyn is
simply confirming the approach of fiction writers, who take as
much or as little from the everyday world as suits their purposes.
Predictably, he cast his social history as family chronicle – the fate
of one rural Welsh family drawn to the prosperity of the south
Wales coalfield, the break-up of that family reflecting wider social
tensions. It was an approach urged by publishers. 'You are apt
to philosophize a bit too much, and to make an essay of what
should be a vivid and passionate "self-story",' explained Hamish
Hamilton when rejecting Idris Davies's 'Collier Boy' (9 September
1936). Family saga was the best way to bring industrial history to

life, as Jack Jones had recently shown to considerable commercial effect, and Llewellyn now settled on a vivid and passionate self-story for his own collier boy, Huw Morgan.

Why this novel of a Welsh mining village in the years before 1910 should so resonate across an international readership remains something of a mystery. Surely not out of any deep-seated fascination with Wales, though the Welshness of the book is pervasive. *How Green Was My Valley* portrays the Welsh as they (and indeed all peoples) like to see themselves, particularizing the feeling that values are locally derived, in a rural landscape deemed the true home of the nation. *Heimat* permeates the novel, the valley in the first phase of mining imagined as a pastoral paradise. The belief that relationships are sounder in a sacred rural setting is a universal one, but particularly rooted in Wales, with it idealization of country communities as God-fearing, clean-living, democratic and neighbourly. It is a transposed peasant society that *How Green Was My Valley* celebrates: the Morgans as once they were – self-reliant craftsmen, philosophers and musicians, at ease with doctors, solicitors and benign local coal-owners in a cultural world that fuses the popular and the highbrow (Plato, choral singing, rugby football), all centred around the chapel. Theirs is a united community, in politics as in religion, though threatened by atheistical socialism in the shape of alien militants importing class confrontation. For Llewellyn this was the Fall; and crucial to the novel's appeal is its assertion of more primary loyalties, to family and place, to community and nation. We are made aware how through the emotional life a patriot is formed. (The glorification of nation troubled one or two critics in 1939, but readers at large ignored, or simply did not receive, the sinister political messages within Huw's blinding epiphanies.) 'My Valley, O my Valley, within me, I will live in you, eternally.' As Llewellyn made clear, the Green Valley is 'not only a place in Wales; it is that which lay around us', 'an essence of good living, that you shall taste only once or twice while you live, and then go on living with the taste in your mouth' – as Huw must continue to live, in the post-lapsarian world beyond childhood and Wales.

Reviewers caught the tone of the novel, its distance from realism. For Richard Church it had 'the freshness of folksong and the old Celtic tales', while even the *New Statesman*, sceptical of its politics, confessed that the book made good reading: 'he writes as

fluently as Dylan Thomas, if with a more controlled imagination.'
Llewellyn sought a poetic language distanced by time and place, a
biblical-bardic prose purposefully antique. His publisher furthered
this sense of remoteness by removing from the book all place
names surrounding the valley, a process of de-localization which
heightened the mythic dimension. Here was no gloomy tract on
unemployed miners; 'it covers a period', the publicity ran, 'when
South Wales prospered, and coal dust had not blackened the
greenness of the valley. It is not an industrial or "proletarian"
novel.' Such was Joseph's confidence that he set a run of 25,000
(staggering at a time when first novels did well to sell 2,000 in
hardback), and in addition to the trade edition (priced 8s 6d) he
offered a signed limited edition costing three times as much –
another extraordinary gesture in the case of an unknown author.
But Joseph's judgement was vindicated. Launched in unpropitious
circumstances, *How Green Was My Valley* achieved home sales of
a 1,000 a week over the next two years, and 60,000 copies in 1942,
following John Ford's film. The sales pattern denotes an archetypal best-seller; that is, a fast seller whose initial heady rush
moderates into a continuous appreciable demand. Colonial sales
almost matched British ones, while in 1940 Llewellyn topped the
American best-seller charts.

Many have seen *How Green Was My Valley*'s success as related
to its perfect timing, to its acceptable wartime messages on miners
and unionism, on the wholeness and wholesomeness of communities, and the need for national unity at a time of crisis. But
success so universal and enduring calls for other explanations.
Habent sua fata libelli: books have their own destinies, quotes
Goronwy Rees. There are books that from the moment of publication assume a life of their own; the world takes possession of them,
independent of the circumstances of publication or the author's
original intention. Such books, argues Rees, can be read in a
variety of ways, as social commentary, as polemic, or as myths and
fables of the human condition in its most universal form.
Commonly, 'they concentrate on the life and adventures of a single
person, for whom other characters are in the nature of foils,
challenges, sometimes simply arguments. These are the hero's
other possible selves, and his problem is to come to terms with
them, which is in fact a way of coming to terms with himself.'
Since this situation is of universal application, these books make a

very direct and personal appeal. Michael Joseph offered another, insider's observation: that best-sellers were often novels built on the grand scale, with endings felt to be satisfying rather than happy. The preponderant motif might well be religious in character, 'but whatever form it may take, it invariably appeals to a deep-rooted human instinct. There is . . . inevitably something primitive in anything that appeals to people in the mass.' Llewellyn taps into the elemental – childhood as Eden; a lost Golden Age; the bonding with family, community and nation; the differing powers of men and women; the active presence of the past.

By good fortune we can learn how the novel struck a sample of readers, through a portion of fan mail, accessible in the National Library of Wales, that was written to Llewellyn between 1971 and 1983 (the year of his death). It comes from all over the world and provides a rare insight into the mysteries of mass appeal. Plainly, the fans reach a level of bliss denied to academic critics. Repeated readings increase the pleasure, up to a dozen quite commonly, though there are higher claims: 'I must have read it a hundred times'; 'you can read me a line from *How Green Was My Valley* and I will tell you the rest of the page' (this from a Californian admirer). The impact of the novel is manifest ('I have never read anything in literature which has touched me so deeply and powerfully'); it confirms deep instincts – 'all parts of my mind were at one time or another personified by your characters. I lived in your book, literally' – and in an intimate, personal way: 'I have thought all these years that you wrote that story for me alone' (the words of one Scotswoman). Interestingly, the qualities picked out by these readers are the ones Llewellyn prized: a genius for story-telling, a beauty of language ('You are the impossible: a mixture of Dylan Thomas . . . and Margaret Mitchell'), and characters that step off the page – Huw especially, though not exclusively ('I feel I know Huw personally' is a common reaction). The novel's public and political dimensions for the most part fail to register, even the blatant Anglophobia. 'An author has power in his choice of words so I think it very sad that you emphasize so much in your characters their hatred of the English!' writes one Gloucestershire reader, but hers is an isolated viewpoint. The English are avid fans and, along with the rest, see the book as a 'stunning portrayal of life, love and death' within the context of one Welsh family – which is every reader's family, as remembered ('it never fails to recapture the atmosphere and texture of my own home and upbringing') or yearned for ('as families are meant to be, and as I wish mine had been'). Llewellyn's country, like his family, effortlessly transports itself, to France ('in reading your book I felt it was also my country') and around the world. Yet the novel is also accepted as quintessentially Welsh (autobiographical? correspondents enquired – to which Llewellyn answered, 'No') and it burnished the national image. 'I have developed a fascination for Wales that drives me to search out and learn all I can about the country,' writes an American enthusiast; and with national virtues so manifest – 'such honesty, courage and integrity' – little wonder that another signs off, 'I love the Welsh, I love your books, and I love you.'

One particular letter affectingly reminds us of another point concerning classics of this magnitude; that their appeal is to children as well:

> I am a 17 years old Norwegian girl. I don't know how many times I have read your book *How Green Was My Valley*. My mother gave it to me when I was about ten years old, just as I discovered that life was not only happiness and fun . . . Your book made me open my eyes, look at the world as it is, accept it, and still avoid getting raving mad.
>
> If I was to live quite alone on a very faraway place and was allowed to bring with [me] only three books, I think I would choose the Bible, my diary and your book. I think those three would help keep my sense clean.

There is a notion that only in Wales was the novel's reception muted. This is true in part. Sales in Wales were high and Welsh reviewers enthusiastic, but from the outset there were strong dissenting voices. Glyn Jones's phrase, 'literary hokum', sums up intellectual reaction: a distaste for the book's inauthenticities and blatant melodrama. There was surely envy also, of a maverick who had invaded home territory to such devastating effect. Llewellyn was worlds away from the Anglo-Welsh literary experience, with its precarious little magazines, a possible niche in some anthology and the hoped-for call from a decent publisher. Here was the province of Letters, untarnished by commercial success, whereas Llewellyn with just one leap had become that most enviable of creatures, a writer who could live by his fiction. *How Green Was My Valley* dwarfed all other novels of Wales. 'Is there a great efflorescence of Welsh literature?' asked George Lyttelton of Rupert Hart-Davis as late as 1958. 'It hasn't reached East Anglia. But if the idiom is that of that *delicious* book *How Green Was My Valley* I hope it soon will. I don't think I have ever heard your opinion of that masterpiece.' Hart-Davis was anxious to promote the poet R. S. Thomas (together with T. Harri Jones) and had recently taken on another Welsh novelist with an appreciable popular following.

Richard Vaughan (the pseudonym of Ernest Lewis Thomas, a Muswell Hill teacher of English) had leapt to prominence with his own first novel, written during wartime Army service though not published (by John Murray) until St David's Day 1951. *Moulded in Earth*, the story of young lovers who overcome a bitter family feud concerning ancient grazing rights, is set in a landscape which Vaughan considered his own (although he came from the Pontypool area), the Black Mountain region of Carmarthenshire. It was, he wrote in reply to an enquiry, 'a wild, romantic part of Wales . . . a place of deep, dark valleys, surrounded on all sides by rolling tracts of mountain, and dominated by the grim, precipitous Van Rock'. Better recreated in exile (as Richard Llewellyn had found), this boyhood province was inspirational, and widely representative. As Vaughan explained, his novels

> could just as naturally be set in parts of France, Germany, Yugoslavia, or any place in the world where men live close to the earth, whose concepts of birth, death, love, hatred, and the will to wrest a living from the soil are the same the world over.

Vaughan's characters supplied the dynamic, 'so alive and real to me that all I have to do is to confront them with a situation and leave them to resolve that situation according to their lights'. Plotting concerned him little, since his plots were of the utmost simplicity. 'I never plan a novel in detail. I know my characters through and through before I start writing. I also know the direction and trend of my story.' Vaughan sought a popular audience through the revivification of elemental tales and his publishers helped him achieve it, initially by an effective serialization on *Woman's Hour*, one of a number of radio programmes creating new readers for fiction. A Book Society recommendation, *Moulded in Earth* justified the additional 10,000 copies that John

Murray had printed to meet the anticipated demand. The novel passed into translation (with a Welsh version in 1991) and, according to the best-seller pattern, was adapted for television ('he draws his characters and events in harsh vivid colours, delving deep into the emotional paradoxes which characterize country folk', ran the puff of 1964).

For the most part, reviewers applauded the individual note that Vaughan brought to a well-tried plot. He had caught the Welsh mountain spirit in the lyrical pulse of his prose; and through the beauty of nature imagined rather than by means of a cold naturalism ('and impressionism means more to me than mere photographic accuracy', Vaughan confirmed). James Hilton, author of *Goodbye, Mr Chips*, thought the novel had true poetic realism, the 'flavourful exaggeration of childhood tales'. But the archetypal free-standing story was not to everyone's taste. The *New York Times* saw in Vaughan's reworking 'the poesy of simple-mindedness' in the tradition of 'the lyric lout' (doubtless a reference to *How Green Was My Valley*); Vaughan's style jarred, his spicing of literary English with strong Welsh idioms producing 'a kind of piebald rapture'. Concerning the Welshness of his writing, Vaughan proffered some distinguishing qualities:

I have a natural love of words; I have to guard against extravagant rhetoric. I am deeply religious, but not church-going. I tend to make my characters larger than life; there is a constant preoccupation with the thought and idea of death – this is all very Welsh and must, I suppose, be reflected in my work.

Well before Richard Vaughan, Welsh fiction had begun to seem predictable, both in content and style, and its rhetorical extravagances in particular (what Dylan Thomas described as 'shouting a little louder than life') could be seen as intrinsically falsifying. Even Rhys Davies had wearied of Welsh fiction, with its adherence to coal pit, kitchen and chapel ('I have written so much of that kind of thing myself'), while for Denis Bottrall, reviewing R. S. Thomas's *The Stones of the Field* for *Life and Letters Today* (1948), the disenchantment was with 'those endless fictions of feuds, lusts, soils and souls which for some reason or other (probably length) were foisted on us as works of Welsh genius in the nineteen thirties'. The barb against length is pointed, Jack Jones being famously advised by Hamish Hamilton to curb his sprawling narratives. The requirement for shorter novels produced a string of later books whose failure Jones attributed to a drastically curbed afflatus: 'Yes, I should have let it rip, let it all come out in the washing as it did in my first half-dozen novels.' Gwyn Thomas ran into similar difficulties when Michael Joseph, a publisher not averse to big books (witness the 650 pages of *How Green Was My Valley*), demanded extensive cuts in *All Things Betray Thee* (1948). Thomas's authorial stance is classically Anglo-Welsh: he explained in a 1950 radio broadcast how he was writing out of memories, for 'those groups I loved as a boy, a circle of fruity, excitable characters sitting around me on the hillside at dusk'. (A far cry from Emyr Humphreys, as anxious as Gwyn Thomas for popular recognition, though through Welsh middle-class novels in low-pitched Trollopian key. He scorned the over-intense lyricism in so much Anglo-Welsh novel-writing, as also its heavy reliance on 'characters'.)

Vaughan enjoyed a brief period of popularity while *How Green Was My Valley* marched steadily on, becoming as Michael Joseph had prophesied, a 'Twentieth Century Classic', under the Penguin imprint. By 1954, however, its position as the premier Welsh literary icon was under serious challenge, surprisingly not from a novel but from 'a lyrical – sometimes slapstick – picture of a small Welsh town-that-never-was, from just before dawn to just before midnight', as Dylan Thomas, prefacing a solo reading from *Under Milk Wood* at Tenby Arts Club (2 October 1953), described his 'play for voices'.

Raine, Llewellyn and Vaughan all burst unknown upon the public with triumphant first novels, whereas Dylan Thomas prior to *Under Milk Wood* was the most popular poet in Britain: even before his death (in 1953), his *Collected Poems* managed sales of 10,000 at a time, so the publisher declared, when poetry was a drug on the market. Book-trade wisdom insists that talk sells books; we buy books that are in (and on) the air. Thomas's radio broadcasts had enormously extended his reputation, while the drama of his life and death fired the public imagination. The promise of fresh work from the poet, an ambitious new departure which had occupied him for years, provoked wide general interest and *Under Milk Wood*, first broadcast on the Third Programme on Monday evening, 25 January 1954, did not disappoint. 'One had heard nothing like it before, and we may never hear anything like it again,' declared Gwyn Jones. It was a desired change of direction for Thomas, as he explained in *Saturday Review* (6 June 1953) to an American reviewer: 'The kind of poetry I was writing was not fluid enough to represent lived-around subjects, and I wanted to find a form that would be.' *Under Milk Wood* desegregated literature, blending fantasy and realism, Kailyard warm-heartedness and unflattering satire, in a style embracing vanguard poetics, surrealist excursion, unabashed lyricism, a salty vernacular and wild passages of humour that (as the *Times Literary Supplement* pointed out) owed something to radio comedy. Yet Dylan's mark was everywhere ('It is gay & sad and sentimental and a bit barmy. So am I') and his much expressed enjoyment in the piece – this no 'sullen art' – communicated itself immediately. Within a fortnight, the *Observer* was publishing an abbreviated text of the play and, before its full appearance in book form, the magical radio broadcast had been repeated several times. As Gwyn Jones said when facing the hard-back edition, it seemed curiously late in the day to be encountering *Under Milk Wood*. Dent's drab little piece of bookmaking, so failing to live up to its contents, sold out before publication (5 March 1954) and by 1955 had reached a seventh impression, with almost 54,000 copies behind it.

Under Milk Wood now seeded itself promiscuously, two Sunday night stagings at the Old Vic foreshadowing the 1956 theatre production, unveiled at the Edinburgh Festival before transfer to the West End and Broadway. The work gained unstoppable momentum, with continuous press exposure both in Britain and the United States. The theatre critic Kenneth Tynan touched the heart of the play in a brilliant *Observer* review:

> We are gripped, as in comedy we have immemorially been gripped, by a bunch of characters with one-track minds who, though they incessantly collide with one another, never make real contact. Not less than *Bartholomew Fair*, *Under Milk Wood* is a true comedy of humours.

We each make sense of the world and take our pleasure within it in our own eccentric way. (As for the imperfections of the world, they are part of the world: 'Oh, isn't life a terrible thing, thank God?') On *Under Milk Wood*'s language, Tynan rivals his author:

> He conscripts metaphors, rapes the dictionary, and builds a verbal bawdy-house where words mate and couple on the wing like swifts.

Nouns dress up, quite unselfconsciously as verbs, some balancing three-tiered epithets on their heads and often alliterating to boot. Hopkins with a skinful? Tap-room baroque? However we sum up the play's style, it lightens up the sky as nothing has since *Juno*.

Besides the intoxicated language, there seemed something additionally Welsh in the pattern of Thomas's life, in his early attachment to poetry and the romantic agonies that ensued. Dylan Thomas, Tynan suggested, had come to stand as representative of his nation as opposed to the English ('a manner of life on whom respectability has been thrust'). We incorporate authorial persona in our response to most texts. How could we not with Dylan Thomas?

Whatever the acclaim of outsiders, Welsh ambivalence towards the poet intensified as rumours of his lifestyle were confirmed. 'Strangely enough, everyone who talks to me about him, almost without exception, is either most hesitant and faltering in praising him or else quite ready to dismiss him,' claimed Wil Ifan, Congregationalist minister, crowned bard and archdruid (*Western Mail*, 23 February 1954). Indeed, the 1957 television production of *Under Milk Wood*, watched by an audience estimated at nine million, saw a dusting down in Wales of epithets last used against Caradoc Evans, 'charlatan' the mildest of them. Thomas was 'the apostle of dirt' with 'a mind like a sewer' and his book 'a farrago of nonsense', 'sordid and obscene'. The Evans parallel was directly invoked, as quite extraordinarily it had been in a Dent reader's report inveighing against 'pornographic fantasies . . . the product of a sick mind'. *Under Milk Wood*, judged a senior BBC official, was unfitted for the Welsh Home Service or for any kind of family listening, while Cardiff's Empire Games committee banned a performance of a play deemed 'not truly representative of Welsh life'. Nor was such hostility confined to 'the boot-wearing fuddy-duddies . . . who elect each other regularly to cultural committees and panels' (as Keidrych Rhys described a British Council Welsh committee seeking to delete Dylan Thomas from a list of Welsh writers recommended to overseas readers); in the pages of the *Sunday Times*, Augustus John dismissed *Milk Wood* as 'a humourless travesty of popular life' much inferior to Caradoc Evans, that 'far more conscientious historian'.

As it happens, Thomas had salvaged his play from the plan of another work having some degree of social criticism and a Welsh political dimension. The idea was to make his characters even more eccentric.

> Then I'd have a new nationalist Government taking over Wales. One of the new Government's inspectors comes to Llareggub and says to the mayor, 'We're taking charge of affairs here now, and we've decided to declare this disgraceful town an open-air lunatic asylum.' The townspeople scream with rage and each person defends himself, and his seemingly insane actions. In the end they accept, preferring to remain 'mad', because their insanity appears to them healthier than the sanity of the Government.

Vestiges of this earlier scheme can perhaps be traced in *Under Milk Wood*'s opposing sets of characters, the eccentrics who celebrate their individuality and the sour puritans who condemn them. But the plot was too restricting. 'You know, if you feel you're hacking it out, you're either incompetent or doing something wrong.' The original plan abandoned, 'I guess I just got boozed up on the language. I also did another unpardonable thing, I fell in love with one of my characters, so that Polly Garter gets too much attention at the expense of others.' Happily, Thomas followed his instincts, finding his mythic Wales in Mary Ann Sailors' town that is the Chosen Land ('she is not at all mad: she merely believes in heaven on earth'). In his worksheet jottings he makes plain his partial picture: 'What have I missed out? Incest/ Greed/ Hate/ Envy/ Spite/ Malice.'

As ever, it is the artist's selective portrait that agitates the critics. One imagines that for the majority of readers the strength of *Under Milk Wood*'s humour bespeaks a mature self-confidence and ease of national identity, but there are those who detect in the play a stagy, demeaning note symptomatic of this author's refusal ever to take Wales seriously.

> [Thomas] is a pernicious figure, one who has helped get Wales and Welsh poetry a bad name and generally done lasting harm to both. The general picture he draws of the place and the people in *Under Milk Wood* and elsewhere is false, sentimentalising, melodramatising, sensationalising, ingratiating.

Not a few Welsh heads will nod in surprising agreement with Kingsley Amis's judgement, expressed in his *Memoirs*, their hostility fuelled by Thomas's obliterating power, by the deep shadow his international eminence casts over other writing from Wales. Here one can only sketch the dimensions of *Under Milk Wood*'s success: how it ranks as Dent's best-selling title (some 15,000 copies a year in the mid-1990s); how it is continuously recycled in other formats, on stage, film (recently as an animated cartoon), television, record and radio. Its worldwide impact was immediate: by the end of 1954, for example, it had gained a half-dozen repeats on the BBC Overseas Service and within six weeks of the initial British airing was being broadcast in German translation.

As Auden said, we do not read books, books read us. The world looked at Llareggub and saw Our Town, its characters instantly recognizable and absurdly real, living out their illusions and obsessions under the imperatives of love and death. 'It would be hard', thought Randall Jarrell in *Harper's Magazine* (October 1955), 'for any work of art to communicate more directly and funnily and lovingly what it is like to be alive.'

> And just to make sure that this last work of his would be able to mesmerize anybody at all, Thomas puts most of the poetry into prose: whether you can read poetry or not, read modern poetry or not, you can read *Under Milk Wood*.

The Rape of the Fair Country (1959) returns us to the more traditional type of best-seller, a romantic family chronicle freighted with social history. Coming to Wales in 1950, the War Office quantity surveyor George Alexander Graber, an ex-army officer with one Welsh-speaking grandparent, lived quietly near (and later in) Abergavenny where, as Alexander Cordell, he produced his hugely successful novel, the first of a Welsh trilogy. The book is set in the troubled valleys of Gwent during the years before 1839, at a time when the furnace workers were attempting, in the face of ruthless ironmasters, to organize their union and fight for the People's Charter. The story had clear dramatic potential and Cordell took great pains to get his detail right, regarding himself as a committed historian passionate about Wales and its past. When Gwyn Williams dubbed him 'the people's remembrancer' he disliked the phrase, insisting he was a historian whose facts could be proved. In this respect, his greatest coup was the uncovering of a bundle of Home Office documents relating to the Merthyr Rising while researching *The Fire People* (they were printed as an appendix to his novel of 1972). He took much from local historians, about a way of life still alive in the communal memory. But it was Cordell's invented situations, not his Chartist history, that troubled some of the critics. Goronwy Rees, sympathetic to the political drift of the novel, saw a straightforward historical romance,

> full of tempestuous passions, lusty adventurers, beautiful and promiscuous ladies, and the naked opposition of virtue and vice; the only difference is that the glamour and kitsch which are usually devoted to the service of wealth are here lavished upon the poor. It is as if the Deep South of *Gone With the Wind* had undergone a transformation scene, as on a pantomime stage, and reappeared in the South Wales valleys.

Other Welsh writers were more enthusiastic, and eager to appear so. A Gollancz publicity leaflet had Jack Jones, Gwyn Thomas and Emlyn Williams applauding 'an incredibly good novel', 'a most remarkable bit of compassionate evocation', 'a real find'; and above them, Aneurin Bevan acclaimed 'a tremendous book'. The public clearly agreed. Within two years, *The Rape of the Fair Country* sold over half a million copies, prior to its paperback issue by Pan (the initial printing set at 80,000). Overseas sales were buoyant, in America and Europe, with translations into eight languages quickly following.

Cordell's was an accessible story, told with vigour and conviction. 'I intend a compliment when I say that his history reads like fiction,' ran V. S. Naipaul's review in the *New Statesman* (17 January 1959). As for the prose, this Englishman had all the eloquence of his adopted country – though Naipaul saw an economy in the writing that was rare in sagas of this kind ('though not long, *The Rape of the Fair Country* gives an impression of size'). Inevitably the book brought to mind the other Welsh bestsellers: *Under Milk Wood* was still in the air, discernible to some in the novel's bubbling sub-Llarregub style and the brisk shifts of mood. The *How Green Was My Valley* parallel came more naturally and, if lacking the poetic unity of that book, *The Rape of the Fair Country* scored on the grounds of truthfulness. Cordell had brought to life a brutalized yet vital community, its resilience and its humour, its warmth and solidarity. 'An authentic document', thought Elizabeth Bowen in the *New York Herald Tribune Book Review* (26 April 1959), and an addition to Welsh industrial history.

Cordell became embittered by a lack of recognition in Wales, both from professional historians and a Welsh literary establishment uncomfortable with commercial success. That indeed is the way with best-sellers, routinely dismissed as lacking in ideas, psychological depth and an implied view of the world. Yet, if predictable in certain respects, these books are never the outcome of an impersonalized mixing of ingredients according to some recognized formula. Novelists write out of compulsion about what they can make believable. Cordell was an active socialist ('the great people are the little people who have achieved everything in spite of everything', he remarked in a late television interview, 2 July 1992), Llewellyn a Welsh nationalist unashamedly of the Right, while Richard Vaughan's native parish remained 'my whole life . . . its people cast in the very same mould as myself'. And for Dylan Thomas it was the secret self that mattered, our private worlds more real than the public one outside.

In Iris Gower (the pen-name of Iris Davies), Wales has a present-day major selling author thriving in the field of 'sagas, romance and historical fiction' (to use the broad classification of the book trade). Her publishing profile is revealing. Almost her entire output – some thirty novels so far – remains in print, in Britain, the United States, Canada and Australia, with a significant portion available in hardback and in large-print editions. This bespeaks a favourite of library patrons, and it is among the most-borrowed authors, rather than in the lists of top sellers, that Gower's name is to be found. In fact, according to the Public Lending Rights statistics issued in January 2002, she currently ranks thirty-fourth in the top one hundred library authors: mostly those established writers of fiction whose books are on the shelves in bulk (Catherine Cookson heads the list, with J. K. Rowling, by some margin the top best-seller, languishing in fifty-seventh place). Gower found a natural champion in Alexander Cordell, who saw her as having 'brought another dimension to story-telling – that of the informative backcloth' (early industrial Swansea is her favoured fictional terrain). 'Other novelists will have to take heed or be outpaced,' Cordell warned. And here it is worth reflecting

that Iris Gower's kind of writing needs no heavy publishers'
promotion, or even the benefit of reviews, since it answers a
genuine popular taste. Meanwhile English-language literary
culture in Wales keeps afloat on subsidy and canonizes writers
who are no longer names to the reading public.

FURTHER READING

Ian Bell, 'How green *was* my valley?', *Planet*, 73 (1989), 3–9.
Tony Bianchi, *Richard Vaughan* (Cardiff, 1984).
Mike Buckingham and Richard Frame, *Alexander Cordell* (Cardiff, 1999).
John Harris, 'Queen of the Rushes: Allen Raine and her public', *Planet*,
    97 (1993), 64–72.
John Harris, '"A hallelujah of a book": *How Green Was My Valley* as best
    seller', *Welsh Writing in English*, 3 (1997), 42–62.
Derrick Price, '*How Green Was My Valley*: a romance of Wales', in Jean
    Radford (ed.), *The Progress of Romance: The Politics of Popular Fiction*
    (London, 1986), 73–94.
Peter Stead, 'How green is my valley now?', *New Welsh Review*, 15
    (1991/2), 4–9.
Dylan Thomas, *Under Milk Wood: A Play for Voices*, ed. Walford Davies
    and Ralph Maud (London, 1995).
Chris Williams, 'Master of a lost past: the novels of Alexander Cordell',
    Planet, 121 (1997), 12–18.

CHAPTER 7

POETRY WALES AND THE SECOND FLOWERING

TONY CONRAN

The earlier Anglo-Welsh renaissance, the so-called 'First Flowering', had taken place in a tragic world, and, what is more, a theatrical one. Whatever else Hitler and Churchill were, they were certainly good theatre! And in the arts, after the great triumphs of the English novel in the first third of the twentieth century, the play had come into its own again. The stage was probably closer to the centre of literary sensibility than at any time since the Restoration. Even verse drama and poetic tragedy were being written and performed – though one can exaggerate this: commercial theatre was still dominated by the 'well-made play.' But radio, which is closer to theatre than either television or film, proved a fertile medium of new drama, one which poets like Louis MacNeice and Dylan Thomas were to exploit. We need not be surprised that many of the larger works of the poets of the Anglo-Welsh First Flowering were quasi-dramatic – *The Angry Summer*, *The Ballad of the Mari Lwyd*, large stretches of *In Parenthesis*, *The Anathémata* and the 'fragments' of *The Sleeping Lord*; and of course, *Under Milk Wood* itself. But the influence went even closer to the bone than that, for T. S. Eliot's modernism had crossed the tragic soliloquy of the Jacobean dramatists with the schizoid derangement of the French symbolists ('JE est un autre,' Rimbaud had said, 'I is someone else') to create a new lyric form, the soliloquy of a man who suffers yet is without a biography, the poetry of *Geronion*, *The Waste Land* and *Ash Wednesday*. Dylan Thomas – and particularly in the marvellously precocious soliloquies of his first book, *18 Poems* – is Eliot's greatest follower, a writer of tragic force and mighty line.

But by the late sixties much of the dramatic power had gone. True, the tragi-comic symbolist theatre of the absurd kept something of the grand modernist tradition alive. *Waiting for Godot* is probably the last full-length masterpiece of theatrical modernism. Beckett, however, became more and more minimalist. The theatre turned to 'kitchen-sink', which is as close to prose fiction as original drama can well go. The natural inheritor of kitchen-sink in the more continuous medium of television has been soap opera. In literary terms, the novel was king. Picaresque, comic, undercutting the pomp of tragedy with irony and burlesque, novels like *Lucky Jim, Hurry on Down* and *Room at the Top* seemed to be at the cutting edge of new post-war, post-modernist sensibility. Actually, they were profoundly conservative and insular, not at all what we would call postmodernist, but harking back for the most part to a kind of eighteenth-century Englishness that had very little appeal to Wales.

It is strange, though, that our consciousness of Anglo-Welsh writing of the sixties should be so dominated by poets. Up to the Second World War the Anglo-Welsh novel had been more in evidence than the poetry, with Jack Jones and Rhys Davies professional and prolific writers, and Gwyn Jones, Lewis Jones, Margiad Evans and Geraint Goodwin each with at least two or three novels to their credit, and of course Richard Llewellyn with *How Green Was My Valley.* Indeed, even as late as 1965, it must have seemed as though the novel, along with its poor relation the short story, had re-established its hegemony in the Anglo-Welsh literary scene. Gwyn Thomas published his last novel in 1958, but there was no reason to think he would not write more. Glyn Jones had turned to novel-writing in the mid-fifties. His third was published in 1965, and again there was no reason to suspect it would in fact be his last. Emyr Humphreys had made a very convincing reputation for himself in the post-war period. His nine novels up to *Outside the House of Baal* (1965) had treated the 'Matter of Wales' with a new seriousness and power. The *New Companion to the Literature of Wales* (1998) links him with R. S. Thomas and David Jones as inaugurating a new attitude, more patriotic and scholarly, and more concerned with the continuity of Welsh experience down the centuries. But *Outside the House of Baal* was the only major novel he published in the sixties; there was a fairly sizeable gap in his output until *National Winner* (1971) began the sequence collectively called 'The Land of the Living' which has dominated his later maturity. Three other novelists were just establishing themselves in the early sixties: Ron Berry published five novels during the decade, Alun Richards published six through the sixties and seventies, and

Raymond Williams, critic turned fiction-writer, had the first two parts of his trilogy, *Border Country* and *Second Generation*, out by 1964. Again, however, there was a gap. The third novel *Fight for Manod* did not appear until 1979.

Poetry meanwhile had languished. Apart from the growing reputation of R. S. Thomas and the uneven achievement of T. H. Jones very little seemed to be happening in the fifties and early sixties. True, Vernon Watkins was still publishing: his death in 1967 marked the final end of the period dominated by Dylan Thomas and Keidrych Rhys's magazine *Wales*. David Jones's *Anathémata* (1952) also seemed to have little to do with modern Wales. It was not until the late sixties with the 'fragments' that were to be collected in *The Sleeping Lord* (1974) that his work re-entered our bloodstream and began to seem a significant part of the Anglo-Welsh renaissance.

The old Wales was in tatters after the long years of Depression and war, though the coal industry had revived and the Labour government at last nationalized the mines. Aneurin Bevan's National Health Service, on the model of the colliers' own medical scheme, aimed to be genuinely classless with free medicine for all. The same was broadly true for education. The paradox of socialism was that it needed a large professional class to service it. Doctors, teachers, administrators, social workers and so on, had to be trained. There was a period of ill-adjusted growth, when a new middle class was in being, students were coming out of university looking for jobs, but Wales was not yet able to absorb them.

Exile, therefore, was central to the experience of those who became the poets of the sixties, who had started their working lives when the necessity to emigrate was clear. Harri Jones ended up in Australia, Dannie Abse in Golders Green. But even poets who were to return to Wales – John Ormond, John Tripp, Gillian Clarke, Sally Roberts Jones and myself – had long or short spells working in or near London. It hardly occurred to any of us that we should make a career in Wales – the job-market, though better than before the war, was still depressed, the general mood of bewilderment and lack of centre survived from the thirties. What was left in Wales seemed narrow, petty-bourgeois and hypocritical.

Then, like everywhere else, Wales started to be affluent. It was possible to envisage going back. Even for poets who did not return, the changed conditions of the mid-sixties led to a profound nostalgia for Wales, a centripetal and lyrical re-affirmation of Welsh distinctiveness. This is what Meic Stephens called the 'Second Flowering', as we find it in poets such as T. Harri Jones (who died before it was properly under way), Leslie Norris, John Ormond, John Tripp, Bryn Griffiths, Sally Roberts (Roberts Jones as she became) and Meic Stephens himself.

At the core of all this activity there was a struggle between two ideologies, two capital cities, two ways of perceiving Wales. Were we to continue to be part of the London scene, a group of colourful immigrants gradually assimilating to the 'British' (that is, English) norm? Or were we to regroup round the new capital of Cardiff and create a cultural market in Wales itself, on the backs of a language we could not speak but which justified our separatism – even, to an extent, in English eyes? For a writer, it resembled the century-old struggle between free trade and protectionism: either you let cultural goods – poems, novels, plays – find their own level as exotic accessories to the English-speaking world (free trade), or you had to protect your nascent market in Cardiff with 'trade-barriers' and bureaucratic distinctiveness.

The key figures of this struggle are Bryn Griffiths and Meic Stephens. Bryn Griffiths (among other things) has been a merchant seaman, who has based himself in London and Australia, where his wife came from, as much as his native south-west Wales. In the mid-sixties the signs of a new renaissance in Anglo-Welsh poetry were palpable in London. Poets like John Tripp and Robert Morgan felt alienated from contemporary English poetry, and in 1964 Bryn Griffiths founded the *Guild of Welsh Writers* as a mutual support and pressure group. London publishers – Dent, Faber, Chatto, Hart-Davis – were still interested in publishing Anglo-Welsh material, even though their expectations of finding another Dylan Thomas were beginning to fade. Dent published Bryn Griffiths, and in 1967 his anthology *Welsh Voices* appeared under their imprint. It was the most lively and exciting selection of contemporary Anglo-Welsh poetry ever to have appeared, and still holds its own more than thirty years later. As John Tripp says, the dawning of the Anglo-Welsh renaissance, 'the Second Flowering', was due in no small measure to the enthusiasm and unselfishness of Bryn Griffiths himself.

As a poet, Bryn Griffiths was often criticized for a too easy Dylanesque charm. He shared with Dylan Thomas, also, a

passionate interest in making poetry out of physical sex, though
his poems are much more outward-going, less visceral than
Dylan's and often express considerable tenderness and awareness
of the women he loves:

Stoning Fruit

She swings soft on a stalk of strange thought.
Buried in her, the hard kernel of her years,
the stone waits under the stressed skin
to be bitten free from white flesh —

where I plunge now,
biting, knifing, driving like a shark
through the swollen dark waters of her thighs –

where my life now
knows of her grief's sediment
settled here into a stone worn with tears.

I bite to the core
where she, swaying, hangs above me –
my tongue spearing, savaging, for fallow seeds
till she breaks into the long forgotten throes
of strange fruit stoned of the moment's needs.

In this fine poem about making love to a woman whose sexuality
has grown difficult through long disuse, the literary echoes are
certainly a factor in our appreciation: Lawrence's 'Figs', Yeats's
'Too long a sacrifice/ Can make a stone of the heart', and the final
surprising reference to Billie Holiday's song about lynching –
'black bodies swaying in the southern breeze,/ strange fruit
hanging on the poplar trees'. But they are used, in a very complex
and humane way, so that the 'long forgotten throes/ of strange
fruit stoned' really does flood us with insight, the strange
proximity of orgasm to death which presumably lay behind the
Elizabethan slang use of 'death' to mean sexual coitus.

This type of sex-centred poetry did not endear him to the rather
stuffy teacher-dominated Cardiff scene in the late sixties and
seventies. Bryn Griffiths's 'Love Poem' perhaps illustrates the
confrontation:

> I wrote a love poem once.
> It was simple, straightforward,
> erotic I thought.
> Another poet I knew
> was embarassed by it.
> I think it must have been
> the honesty that disturbed him.
> Not that he *said* anything,
> mind you, it was just
> the cant of his tall head
> and the way he held thought
> in parenthesis . . .
>
> We were never such friends again.

Bryn Griffiths is an uneven poet – I remember with shame a review reprinted in *The Cost of Strangeness*, in which I slated one of his pamphlets – and the fact that he more or less abandoned Wales for Australia probably has not helped; but his poetry has never been properly assessed. Talk of 'Dylanism' seems largely beside the point. In his best Anglo-Welsh book, *Scars*, the sensibility is far more like the later Idris Davies than it is Dylan. Certainly nowhere else in the early Second Flowering (and hardly in R. S. Thomas) is there such a willingness to engage with the social nitty-gritty of contemporary Wales:

> 'But I *love* Wales and the Welsh,'
> said the Englishman, said the Englishman,
> said the Englishman – buying up
> cottage after cottage, farm after farm,
> until the entire countryside
> smacked of flat English shires . . .
>
> So each year the Englishman came
> to spend a few summer days in Wales.
> And each year he wondered
> why the natives – strange,
> but lovable people – seemed less.
> ('All Men Kill')

When we turn to the other impresario, Meic Stephens, though his influence was everywhere, it is not so easy to distinguish what we are dealing with. Stephens was teaching in Ebbw Vale and sharing a huge house with (amongst others) Harri Webb, the Dowlais librarian, poet and editor of *The Welsh Nation*. Stephens started the Triskel Press in 1963 to publish *Triad*, a collection of poems by Webb, Peter Gruffydd and himself; and followed this in 1965 with the first issue of *Poetry Wales*. In 1967 he became Literature Director of the newly established Welsh Arts Council. Since the Arts Council's Literature Committee, whose public servant he was, had responsibility for subsidizing literary magazines, he resigned his editorship, only to be reinstated a year later when it became clear that without him *Poetry Wales* would not survive.

In the issue of *Poetry Wales* after his temporary resignation as editor, Stephens allowed himself a valedictory article, 'The Second Flowering,' which summed up his position more explicitly than bureaucratic discretion later allowed. After a brief survey of his magazine's history and the rush of talent it had uncovered, he takes Bryn Griffiths to task for queering the pitch with *Welsh Voices*. Griffiths had not researched the job properly, he'd not read enough of the poets he'd tried to represent. *Welsh Voices* was not the sort of anthology Stephens thought was required: it was an interim report designed to publicize an interesting poetic movement for a London-based market, not an official survey of a 'literature' to justify a separatism new-rooted in Cardiff. The quarrel may have been conducted in purely literary terms but the hidden political agenda is never far away.

It was an ideological struggle, but this is not to imply that Stephens and Griffiths were in overt and conscious opposition from the start, one supporting a change to a Cardiff-based culture, the other hankering for London success. On the contrary, the two men were in broad agreement about the need to create a Welsh base for Anglo-Welsh literature. However, one is entitled to wonder what in practice such an agreement in principle meant. As far as Stephens was concerned, there is no doubt that he took the Cardiff road, and thought through the tactical and bureaucratic implications of what he was doing. But with Bryn Griffiths the case is very different. He wanted to give Wales and its anglophone literature a better place in the sun, but like most artists who live by their wits he saw no reason to close doors. He had a London market, of a sort, and, like Keidrych Rhys before him, he felt no contradiction between exploiting it and his nationalist aspirations. He thought of *Welsh Voices* as a blow for Wales, much as Keidrych Rhys had with his 1940s anthology, *Modern Welsh Poetry*, published by Faber. The ideological struggle in Griffiths ran underground and only surfaced with his reaction to Stephens's criticism. By their fruits ye shall know them: in this case, by the two anthologies, Griffiths's *Welsh Voices* and Stephens's *The Lilting House*.

In his *Poetry Wales* essay on 'The Second Flowering', Stephens goes on to describe what he sees as the new national consciousness manifested in his poets. Most of them support nationalism, he says, so he could not help making *Poetry Wales* a nationalist publication. He dissociates himself from R. S. Thomas 'brooding on rural decay' as an emotional dead end:

> The new poets, it seems to me, are not so much concerned with 'things as they are', although the occasional poem is still in their repertoire, as with seeking a creative way out of the present impasse.

(As we have seen, one of the strengths of Bryn Griffiths's poetry is its concern with 'things as they are'.) Stephens then talks of his fear that Anglo-Welsh poetry will end up, like Wales itself, merely peripheral to England; and he issues a rallying call to poets to return from exile, live in Wales, and engage in a rapprochement with Welsh-language culture.

And, of course, a lot of the poets did, or had already done so. John Ormond, John Tripp, Sally Roberts (Jones), Raymond Garlick and Roland Mathias all came back, late or soon. Of those who did not – Dannie Abse, Leslie Norris, Bryn Griffiths – Dannie Abse was by then embedded in the London scene, a 'Maverick' opposed to the 'Movement' school of English poets; so that when he appeared in the early issues of *Poetry Wales* he did so almost as a guest poet from England. He was certainly no nationalist, though he kept a weather eye open to what was happening in his native land. He came into his own in Wales during the late seventies and eighties, when Welsh poets in English again started to write about 'things as they are' and saw in his work something of a role model. Leslie Norris, also of an elder generation to Stephens, was adopted by *Poetry Wales* as we shall see, and *Triskel* published a pamphlet of his poems; but Bryn Griffiths, young enough to rank as a contemporary, never returned to the fold.

When I was rereading those early issues of *Poetry Wales* it surprised me how much they were dominated by two bodies of work: first, my translations of Welsh poetry, particularly of the twentieth century – Saunders Lewis, Gwenallt Jones and Waldo Williams for example – which were soon to be collected in *The Penguin Book of Welsh Verse* (1967); and second, the poems of Harri Webb. It is mainly these two that give the magazine its sense of centring down on Wales, of seeking 'a creative' – that is, nationalist – 'way out of the present impasse', and its rapprochement with Welsh-language culture.

As Raymond Garlick remarked in an early letter to the editor, Harri Webb was the most distinctive new talent that the young *Poetry Wales* had to show. He must also have seemed to Stephens at this stage nearly the ideal Anglo-Welsh poet – political, witty, determinedly middlebrow, rooted in the valleys yet also committed to Wales as a whole; a writer who objected to Dylan Thomas both for his 'unWelsh' smuttiness and for mocking Wales to amuse English readers. That Webb could sometimes be embarrassingly sentimental and simplistic probably didn't worry Stephens – both men shared a populist devotion to doggerel, 'poems and pints' and the like.

The dominant mode of the new *Poetry Wales* school was to be the elegy, which may sound paradoxical in view of Stephens's contention that the new poets were concerned with seeking 'a creative way out of the present impasse' – that is, with the future. Surely, elegy is mainly about the past? But, if we look at the work of Harri Webb, the emotional dialectic which gave rise to Anglo-Welsh elegiacs is presented in quite undisplaced terms, and we can see how the whole process was indeed future-directed.

Firstly, then, we have an idealization of Wales herself, similar to Padraig Pearse's of Ireland, and of Wales's defenders, such as the two Llywelyns and Owain Glyndŵr, or a modern *prifardd* (chief poet) like Gwenallt. The poems which explore this aspect, in general, have not worn well: even such a popular anthology piece as 'The Stone Face', about discovering at Deganwy a sculptured head supposedly of Llywelyn the Great, seems over-rhetorical and unreal:

Seven hundred and fifty years of darkness.
Now in a cold and stormy Spring we stand
At the unearthing of the sovereign head,
The human face under the chipped crown.
Belatedly, but not too late, the rendez-vous is made.
The dream and the inheritors of the dream,
The founder and father, and those who must rebuild
The broken fortress, re-establish the throne
Of eagles, here exchange the gaze of eagles
In the time of the cleansing of the eyes.

This is not the place to do it, but it would be a useful exercise to compare these lines with the superficially similar, although slightly earlier, imagery of Waldo Williams in Welsh, in such deeply felt poems as 'Preseli' and 'Yr Heniaith' (The Old Language).

Secondly, there is satire or invective (in Webb's case) against those who betray the 'real' Wales; or guilt (in poets like Harri Jones, Leslie Norris or Sam Adams) at having betrayed it oneself, through becoming middle class or imitation English or not being able to speak Welsh. And thirdly, very intimately connected with this sense of betrayal and guilt, the impulse to remember, to elegize this or that part of one's own Welsh past, as if to cauterize the pain by bringing it out into the human light of day – even to laugh at it. Like the short stories of Gwyn Thomas, many of the best Anglo-Welsh elegies (and Webb's in particular) are sardonic and even comic in spirit. Webb, indeed, mocks the whole process in 'Synopsis of the Great Welsh Novel':

It is all seen, naturally,
Through the eyes of a sensitive boy who never grows up.
The men emigrate to America, Cardiff and the moon. The girls
Find rich and foolish English husbands. Only daft Ianto
Is left to recite the Complete Works of Sir Lewis Morris
To puzzled sheep, before throwing himself over
The edge of the abandoned quarry. One is not quite sure
Whether it is fiction or not.

Webb's sentimental nationalism and (perhaps) his prowess as a journalist and popular entertainer have distracted critics from paying proper attention to his elegies. Poems such as 'The Boomerang in the Parlour' (about his father's wish to emigrate),

'The Old Parish Churchyard', 'Not to be Used for Babies' (about a drunken, old-fashioned milkman he knew as a child) or 'That Summer' (about his childhood memories of the 1926 General Strike) are varied and lively examples of the genre and surely close to being his central achievement as a serious poet.

But, fourthly, the elegiac mode does not simply mourn what is lost. It asserts the continuity of the mourner with what has gone before. The king is dead, long live the king! In Webb's case, this inheritance is seen in political terms – the poet dedicates himself to giving Wales new life as a nation again. In 'A Loyal Address', for example, he imagines the country rising to 'the voice that rallies' as a kind of latter-day Boadicea:

> When the night of the grey Iscariots
> Lies dead in the red of our dawn,
> Queen of the scythe-wheeled chariots,
> Rise up, ride out, reborn!

Again, much of this seems empty rhetoric and unreal. But fervent nationalism of this kind in fact only makes explicit what (in class terms) is always implied by the elegists. Anglo-Welsh elegy was so compulsive a form for the new, largely anglicized middle class because it said that the old Wales of the *gwerin* – the common people – was dead; because it mitigated the guilt of poets who had 'betrayed' *gwerin* values in becoming middle class; but also because it claimed for the poet (and therefore for the new middle class as a whole) the legacy of a Wales that the *gwerin* had vacated. Anglo-Welsh elegy is like the song of a thrush: it defines and defends a territory for its singer. It claims an inheritance, both against the ghosts of the old Wales which it praises but certifies as dead, and against the English who saw Wales merely as part of Britain.

Harri Webb's pre-eminence as a significant poet of the Second Flowering more or less began and ended with the first, heroic age of *Poetry Wales*, before Meic Stephens got his Arts Council post. Partly it was generated by his growing optimism about the eventual success of Welsh nationalism, evidenced by Plaid Cymru's winning its first parliamentary seat at Carmarthen in 1966; but surely also by his friendship with Stephens, a fellow poet, editor and nationalist, who published his poems and brought him out of his literary isolation. It must have been disconcerting – it was to me – when Stephens became Literature Director of the Welsh Arts Council, the very body that distributed the English government's cultural largesse. Webb's hilarious parody of a 'Cywydd o Fawl' ('praise poem' in the manner of the ancient bards) couched in the weird, artificial Welsh-English of Caradoc Evans's *My People*, is his sardonic greeting to the new order:

> Flap we our lips, praise Big Man,
> Bards religious shire Cardigan.
> Not frogs croaking are we
> Nor vain crows are bards tidy.
> Wise is our speak, like Shadrach,
> Hearken you now, people bach.
> Mouth some, Cardiff ach y fi,
> Not holy like Aberteifi.
> Twp it is to speech so,
> In Cardiff is gold yellow,
> Truth it is and no fable,
> All for bards respectable.
> White Jesus bach, let no ill
> Befall Big Heads Arts Council.
> Pounds they have, many thousand,
> Like full till shop draper grand.
> Good is the work they are at,
> Soaped they shall be in Seiat,
> Reserved shall be for them
> A place in Big Seat Salem.
> Praised they shall be for this thing,
> Money they are distributing
> Like Beibl Moses his manna,
> Tongue we all, bards Welsh, Ta!

('Big Man' in *My People* signifies God. 'Ach y fi' expresses disgust. 'Twp' means foolish. 'White Jesus bach' – white (Welsh *gwyn*) can mean 'holy' and 'bach' means 'little' but is used as a familiar term of endearment. A *Seiat* is a religious meeting. 'Big seat [of] Salem' is where the deacons or elders of Salem chapel sit.)

The Second Flowering's age of innocence seems to have ended with Stephens's appointment, though that was certainly not the only factor involved. The struggles of the Welsh Language Society (Cymdeithas yr Iaith Gymraeg) to improve the status of Welsh

were increasingly militant and successful after the passing of the
Welsh Language Act in 1967, and rather sidelined the older
fashion of nationalism (wanting dominion status for Wales as
a bilingual country) that Anglo-Welsh poets tended to aspire to.
We might, more or less, wish the language movement well but by
definition, as English-language writers, it was not really our
business. The growing point in Wales had moved beyond us, to
a purely Welsh-language base in such things as the magazine
Barn and the songs of Dafydd Iwan. We were, almost as much as
the English themselves, puzzled outsiders to what was going
on. The way Plaid Cymru in 1969 allowed itself to be wrong-
footed by the immensely popular Investiture of the Prince of Wales
at Caernarfon also played a part in this first Anglo-Welsh crisis of
confidence.

All the same, it stands to reason that if one of the more
articulate and active members of a cultural minority movement in
opposition suddenly ups and joins the government as an enlightened patron of minority culture, it will tend to spread
uncertainty and disaffection among the brethren and defuse any
lingering current of revolutionary protest. From the early seventies
onward, the Anglo-Welsh elders were not noted for the fervent
expression of nationalism. There were two exceptions: one was
R. S. Thomas, who owed very little to *Poetry Wales* or the Welsh
Arts Council – he continued to publish in London and simultaneously to give allegiance only to Welsh-language culture in Wales;
the other was Raymond Garlick, as we shall see.

This is in no way to devalue the work of Meic Stephens either as
editor or cultural commissar. He opened doors, he was an enabler.
His work at the Arts Council gave Anglo-Welsh literature the
official apparatus it needed – the Welsh Academy, Arts Council
prizes and bursaries for writers, *The Oxford Companion to the
Literature of Wales* (1986), and a series of monographs on the
Writers of Wales – even a new highbrow bookshop in Cardiff to
sell the books the Welsh Arts Council was subsidizing. Writers
were, of course, well represented on the Literature Committee, but
as literary worthies, a part of the patronage system, rather than as
artists affecting the culture by what they wrote. And so, because
all this protection and patronage was applied from above and did
not arise from any real pressure of writers or their readers, it
tended to make Anglo-Welsh poetry seem like a Red Indian

reservation, nothing to do with what ordinary anglophone Welsh people saw as their culture. This impression of being worthy but irrelevant was not helped by the fact that so many of the poets were teachers (as was Stephens himself of course) who saw the function of their art in largely educational terms. The cause that most preoccupied them was the attempt to include Anglo-Welsh material on A-level syllabuses in Welsh secondary schools.

Welsh Arts Council patronage was custom-built for part-time writers. That was one reason it tended to encourage poets – 'bards respectable' in Harri Webb's phrase – rather than novelists or prose-writers who had to live by writing. For a part-time Red Indian a reservation is quite a pleasant place; but if you live there and for one reason or another cannot escape, the experience is likely to be bitter and frustrating. The quintessential poet of the Anglo-Welsh reservation was therefore none of the teachers, nor even the television film director John Ormond, but that 'son of desolation', John Tripp. Tripp was working as a press officer at the Indonesian embassy in London but an Arts Council grant tempted him back to Cardiff in 1969 to try his luck as a freelance writer; he remained there till his death in 1986, scraping a precarious living from poetry and journalism.

To hear John Tripp read in congenial company, such as the annual get-together of the Welsh Union of Writers, was a very different experience from reading his poetry on the page. He would use some jokey reference – often to the Arts Council or its minions – as a kind of motto or theme-song, and whip us into frenzy with it. His poems became hysterically comic war-dances, punctuated by gales of savage laughter. The ironic war-dance is the ground-bass of much of Tripp's poetry and explains its tendency to emotional monotony when it is read in bulk. Despite its wide range of subject matter, it always exhibits the same victim status, the same mock-heroic defeatism before the English, or the tawdry, or the latter-day Welsh who are selling their country down the river. It generally makes for better poetry when it is his own personal inadequacy or fear that is the enemy oppressing him, as in the well-known 'Diesel to Yesterday', about his mixedfeelings at coming back to a Wales dominated by tourists with their bank-notes 'and a petrol-stenched lust for scenery/ to shut in their kodaks':

I catch myself out in error, feel
    ignoble in disdain.
The bad smell at my nostril
    is some odour from myself –
a modern who reeks of the museum,
    not wanting his own closed yesterday
but the day before that,
    the lost day before dignity went,
when all our borders were sealed.

Tripp started to write poetry very late. He had been living in London as a journalist for many years, and did not actually know much of Wales at first hand before he came back to Cardiff in 1969. Wales was indeed 'an imagined country' for him, and many of his first poems are rather crude attempts to rewrite Welsh history (often in terms of military defeat or English treachery) as a kind of compensation for his sense of exile. He sees Henry VIII, for example, as a gloating monster, deflowering Wales betwixt wives:

'In the wick of my heart,' he dribbled,
    'I have all love and zeal and honour
for these people.' Then he picked up a quill
    and signed the lethal bond,
stitching Wales into the cloth
    of his realm, before retiring to bed
with his queen of the year.

Neither in these historical pieces nor in the later Audenesque 'potted biographies' of his culture heroes is Tripp at his best. He is more convincing when he can dramatize his situation in a fictional or semi-fictional context, like the visit from the stocktaker in 'On my Fortieth Birthday' or in 'Notes on the way to the block':

Well, now to get down
off this bloody cart.
A few in the crowd
give me a helping hand,
eager to speed my departure.
Nice of them. I never knew
I had so many friends . . .

> I mount the steps, alone,
> see from the corner of my eye
> the executioner approach
> wearing a jester's cap and bells.
> Good. We don't want black
> or melancholy at a time like this.

The fear of death and the sense of his own futility and that of society as a whole was offset until the 1979 referendum by his idealization of Wales: it is arguable that the failure to achieve even the limited devolution on offer made Tripp a better writer because a more honest one. Tripp's sensibility was essentially modern, urban, streetwise – and desperate. There is a sense in which Wales was a daydream for him, an escape from the alienated existence he knew most about, with its fancy-dress executioners, its bus-shelters in Bridgend, and its stocktaker dressed in black 'like that old advertisement for Sandeman's port'. As with some of the great comedians he could at times give the trivial and futile the status of myth.

The three poets we have looked at so far are heirs of Idris Davies. Like him, their main concern is Wales: Gwalia deserta or Gwalia renovata, Wales a desert or Wales renewed – the 'green desert' of Harri Webb's title: and their own problematic status as poets and spokesmen for their country. Like him, they stand outside the middle-class suburban world of English versifying. In English terms Bryn Griffiths was clearly the most acceptable of the three, for he found a London publisher; but, without Meic Stephens and *Poetry Wales*, I doubt if either Webb or Tripp would ever have made much headway.

Like Idris Davies, too, they paid for their isolation with an occasional uncertainty of technique and sometimes of tone. On the whole, however, they do not need to affect the *faux naïf* of Davies's usual stance – perhaps Webb's deliberate crassness comes nearest to it. They share with Davies a highly ambivalent relation to modernism – on the surface they seem very unmodernist indeed, yet none of them, not even Webb, could have written as they did without the challenge of modernist ideas, even if they seem sometimes to have misunderstood them. John Tripp, for example, that least impersonal of poets, quotes with complacent approval T. S. Eliot's insistence on the impersonality of poetry. The very

different modernisms found in Welsh poetry, in Saunders Lewis or
Gwenallt for example, and in the early R. S. Thomas may also
have been factors influencing their work.

There is not much left in these poets of the quasi-epic vision of
Idris Davies's two great sequences, *Gwalia Deserta* and *The Angry
Summer*. The poetic strength that derived from the class struggle
of the miners in the twenties and thirties had been lost by the time
Davies wrote his third published sequence *Tonypandy*. After that,
as his editor Dafydd Johnston says, his poetic persona 'seems to
have split into two quite distinct roles, the popular entertainer and
the bitter satirist' – a bifurcation that is not unreflected in the work
of Harri Webb, John Tripp or even Bryn Griffiths. But certainly
with the two last poets, as with Davies himself, the sequence,
almost more than the individual lyric, continued to seem a natural
unit. If there is anything approaching *Gwalia Deserta* in post-war
Anglo-Welsh poetry it is surely John Tripp's sequence 'Life under
Thatcher'.

The Idrisiaid, children of Idris, as I'm tempted to call them,
seem to me the most interesting and noteworthy writers in the
young *Poetry Wales*, even though the greatest single poem in the
magazine was not by them but by a teacher, Leslie Norris's 'An
Old House'; while the sheer accomplishment and character of the
television director John Ormond certainly stand out.

Turning now to the teacher-poets who appeared in the early
issues, we shall ignore here two of the finest among them, Glyn
Jones and Roland Mathias: they belonged to an earlier generation,
though both were indeed achieving a new strength and maturity.
Glyn Jones was a contemporary of Idris Davies and nine years
older than Dylan Thomas and, like them, a contributor to
Keidrych Rhys's pre-war magazine *Wales*. Mathias, also a contemporary of Dylan Thomas, though a late developer, was one
of the founders in 1949 of *Dock Leaves*, later *The Anglo-Welsh
Review*, and when Raymond Garlick, its first editor, moved to a
post in the Netherlands in 1960, he took over the editorship. Both
Glyn Jones and Mathias were sympathetic to *Poetry Wales*, and
published poems in it; but neither really shared its ethos.

The case of Raymond Garlick is more complex. An Englishman
born and bred in London, since his student days (apart from seven
years in Holland) he has lived and taught in Wales all his life. As a
critic and editor he has consistently championed Anglo-Welsh

writing as a literature on a par with American or Australian, in English but not of England.

Garlick's early poetry was that of a convert – to Wales, to Roman Catholicism and to what one can call 'educationalism' – innocent and enthusiastic, and mostly in romantic-sounding pentameters. But when he left Wales to teach in Holland in 1960, his poetry changed with him. Short lines now predominate, and there is a much greater emphasis on moral and political point-making. His poetry begins to argue, to sound opinionated. It finds a mission in finding a European context for Wales. Even in the sympathetic notation of the Dutch landscape it becomes inescapably political:

> I have lived where blood
> Had flooded down men's hands.
> Though I look for a Wales
> Free as the Netherlands,
> A freedom hacked out here
> Is a freedom without worth,
> A terror without beauty.
> Here it must come to birth
> Not as a pterodactyl
> Flailing archaic wings,
> But the dove that broods on chaos –
> Wise as a thousand springs.
>   ('Matters Arising')

When he returned to Wales in 1967, he found that Welsh resistance to anglicization had stiffened. Cymdeithas yr Iaith Gymraeg was mobilizing Welsh youth into passive resistance and there were clashes with the police. His son was arrested, man-handled and beaten, and imprisoned twice. His wife and sister-in-law also stood trial. His poems contributed a sense of outrage, but also an ideology of martyrdom – the pope was at this time declaring several Welsh Elizabethan martyrs to be saints of the Church, a process to which Garlick gave his enthusiastic support. The passion of the saints, and indeed of Christ before Pilate, was reflected for him in the confrontation between the Gandhi-like civil disobedience of the patriots, on the one hand, and, on the other, police violence and the crassness of the judiciary.

The seventies, then, were a time of struggle, even of bewilder-ment for the poet; and they ended in disaster. His Welsh nationalism was hopelessly defeated in the 1979 referendum on whether Wales should have a parliament; his marriage broke up; and his Catholicism was strained by the Vatican Council's new reforms and the abandonment of Latin, and he slowly came to realize that he did not believe in the existence of a deity and never had, and that 'the whole thing had been make-believe'.

Garlick was crippled as a young boy and suffered a series of painful operations. Don Dale-Jones in his monograph on the poet quotes him as saying that 'those who survive [such trauma] are liable to be assertive and having been all their lives inevitably self-preoccupied, may find it difficult to form close relationships'. This condition of partial impotence – not sexual, of course, but a failure of feeling and emotional spontaneity – is grounded in what his later poems call 'survival' and 'identity', which seem to me merely names for his ego, locked in its self-preoccupation and assertion; and to be the opposite of the negative capability (as Keats called it) of the artist or poet.

Now, in Garlick, there has always been a lovingness, openness, joy, struggling to escape the ego. And in his best work, in *A Sense of Time*, circumstances, disasters, faith, love of his family, and Wales itself, conspired to blow his egotism apart. (I am not speaking morally now, but of Garlick as a creator, an artist.) Among these 'allies' was his Catholic feeling for the saints, for Christ, for something tender 'out there' beyond the ego's assertiveness and chatter. Catholicism made him a finer poet than he would otherwise have been. It opened in him ways where he could love without fear.

I think that the triple catastrophe around the time of the referendum was a real initiation. It led him into a wilderness of doubt, betrayal, lack of meaning, loneliness. He was experiencing again the wound of his lameness, only this time as a crisis in his world-view, not simply in his physical being. The remarkable poems which he wrote some years after he thought his poetry had stopped for good seem to me a real breakthrough into the true voice of feeling. At the end of *Collected Poems* (beginning with 'The Wreck') there are seven of them, and maybe there are three or four others in the body of the book; I have about seven or eight more that he sent me. He was going to call the book 'A New Beginning':

Like that lame man, after forty
Years he threw away the crutches
Of his verse and now at last walked
Freely, easily, round the bazaar
Of words. Step upon step, counting
Them like syllables, he wandered
Through enjambed and dappled alleys.
Still tentative but gradually
Achieving confidence, he sketched
The warm reality . . .

('Life Drawing')

Instead of that, he decided to publish a *Collected Poems*, and survival and identity got the better of him. First, he censored out nearly every reference to his Catholic beliefs; and second, he rearranged his poetry in what he calls a 'thematic' order. Together, these decisions amounted to a very strong and insistent filter on his literary career. With some poets you can ignore chronology. With Garlick – as with Wordsworth – the strategy of 'thematic' arrangement is suspect, because both of them have been involved in history, and both of them have changed their minds.

Garlick opted for an identity and a survival that is basically timeless. He repaired his defences. He censored his imagination. He cut his poetry to shape. But the crucial question is one he had already asked himself in 'Beginning Again' – 'Can a man be born again?' –

Certainly
Not at his age, he concluded.
The only hope was to retrace
His steps past the defaced signposts,
Trying to puzzle out just where
He took wrong turnings, and to plod
Back up the rutted lanes to some
Remote and solid patch of ground
From which he might begin again.
The muddied tracks of memory
Wound back, and just before they petered
Out he found himself in the park
Of early childhood, climbing on
A swing, limbs agile and unflawed.

In my poem, *All Hallows*, Imagination says of him,

> 'What of my creature Raymond?
> Does he ride the storm like Pity,
> Like a naked new-born babe?'

Does he? Perhaps he does, for his last, rather humble little collection, *Travel Notes*, shows his grandchildren giving him opportunities of love he probably never thought to have again.

Garlick is by no means typical of the Anglo-Welsh teacher-
poets. First, because he is English, without any of the bitter-
sweet experience of growing up in a depressed Welsh community
that fuelled so many of their elegies; he talks a great deal about
Wales but very little about ordinary Welsh people. Second,
because, unlike other teacher-poets, he is not very interested in
demonstrating or exploring his own sensibility. He is almost
eighteenth century in his attempt to make poetry out of his
opinions. (He is Augustan in other ways too: in his common-sense
persona, his emphasis on communication, his distrust of too much
intellect.) And third, Garlick seems to me a tragic figure, a
protagonist even in spite of himself, and the only Anglo-Welsh
poet of his generation to come anywhere near the brink of tragic
freedom. That he seems to have baulked at it is unfortunate in one
sense, in that he did not become the great poet that his 'new
beginning' presaged; but one cannot blame a man for refusing to
be Lear.

Perhaps to talk of 'typical' teacher-poets is misleading. John
Stuart Williams (b.1920) does not have much in common with
Peter Gruffydd (b.1935), for example. Williams seems by comparison rather dry and academic, writing in a style of lyric epigram
as often as not about the heroes of Greek antiquity, though he
does sometimes deal with Welsh themes; whereas Gruffydd is at
his best notating sensory and emotional experience, often of family
life, in a freewheeling 'lovely gift of the gab'. Robert Morgan
(1921–94) was a collier as a young man and most of his rough-cast
poetry is about memories of mining life. He is very different again
from Sam Adams (b.1934), an HMI and intellectual threatened by
the guilt of deracination. In his best-known poem, 'Hill Fort,
Caerleon', Adams imagines himself meeting a genuine Welsh Celt:

The path is blocked. A swarthy
Sentry bars my way, his spear-
Tip sparks with sunlight.
He challenges in accents I know well;
The words I recognise but the sense eludes.
I am ashamed and silent. He runs me through.

Perhaps the work of Sally Roberts Jones (b.1935) – a public librarian not a teacher – also belongs with this group, though her quiet feminism makes her more committed than most.

There is no space even to mention most of these poets. With many of them one is in doubt whether they are poets who happen to teach for a living or teachers who write poetry as a spare-time accomplishment, almost like a hobby. One has to remember that the teaching of English literature in secondary schools, with its 'creative writing' and 'practical criticism', was probably the single most devastating intellectual attack on Welsh values in our time, substituting an English-style empiricism and a view of poetry 'that makes nothing happen' for the rationalism and socially motivated art of the Welsh tradition. English teachers were willy-nilly caught up in this cultural revolution and a proportion were from time to time tempted by it into writing poetry themselves.

The most immediately impressive of the teacher-poets is Leslie Norris. There is no doubt of his professional status as an artist. He was the son of a milkman from Merthyr Tydfil and was invalided out of the RAF in 1941 and, after the war, trained as a teacher in Coventry. He has taught at various schools and colleges in the south of England and in America. Though a frequent visitor, he has not worked or lived in Wales since 1948. As a young man, Norris published two books of verse and then, for twenty years, almost nothing. In the mid sixties, however, he began writing again and since then his volumes of poetry and short stories have built up into quite a substantial œuvre.

The first of these was actually published by Meic Stephens as one of the first *Triskel* pamphlets, *The Loud Winter* (1967); later the same year, seven of its ten poems appeared in *Finding Gold*, his first major collection. This group contains some of Norris's finest achievements. 'The Ballad of Billy Rose' is deservedly popular, as an evocation of south Wales boxing and guilty compassion for a fighter physically blinded by the sport:

> I had forgotten that day
> As if it were dead for ever, yet now I saw
> The flowers of punched blood on the ring floor,
> As bright as his name, I do not know
>
> How long I stood with ghosts of the wild fists
> And the cries of shaken boys long dead around me,
> For struck to act at last, in terror and pity
> I threw some frantic money, three treacherous pence –
>
> And I cry at the memory – into his tray, and ran,
> Entering the waves of the stadium like a drowning man.
> Poor Billy Rose. God, he could fight
> Before my three sharp coins knocked out his sight.

The last line depends on the fact, mentioned earlier in the poem, that the boy Norris had also paid 'three treacherous pence' to watch the fight in the first place.

However, the poem is not simply a rather extreme emotional reaction to Billy Rose's fate, nor is it simply propaganda against professional boxing. The crucial lines are surely: 'How long I stood with ghosts of the wild fists/ And the cries of shaken boys long dead around me'. Poem after poem in *The Loud Winter* remembers the dead young men of the 1939–45 war, whom Norris knew as boys. In 'Autumn Elegy' he gazes unmoved at the rich and alien autumn colours of southern England where he is working. 'Live wood', he says, 'was scarce and bony where I lived as a boy.' It is not that he cannot appreciate 'such opulent/ Panoply of dying',

> But that I remember again what
>
> Young men of my own time died
> In the Spring of their living and could not turn
> To this. They died in their flames, hard
> War destroyed them.

In 'The Old Age of Llywarch Hen', Norris as Llywarch says:

> Crutch there, do you hear the loud winter?
> . . . But here in my room is the world's lonely centre

> Where the voices of the young are the voices
> Of ghosts.

In 'Early Frost' he writes of his schooldays in Merthyr,

> these are my
> Ghosts, they do not need to ask
> For housing when the early frost comes down.
> I take them in, all, to the settled warmth.

'The Ballad of Billy Rose' fits into this pattern. The pathos of the blind boxer destabilizes Norris with grief and guilt as 'ghosts of the wild fists/ And the cries of shaken boys long dead' return to haunt him. Billy Rose is both a trigger for the poet's memories and a symbol of the human courage and cruelty which turned his schoolfriends into ghosts. The consequent weight of emotion is, for my taste, almost too much for the poem to bear.

We do not know why, twenty years after the war had finished, these ghosts demanded so much of him. The experience made him into a poet, but it was not easy to focus. Only once, in 'An Old House', does Norris squarely confront what it meant. As with 'Billy Rose' the technique is close to short-story writing. The style is probably more literary than he would later allow, and the debt to Edward Thomas is clear, both in style and subject – old houses were one of Thomas's main themes – but the influence was in no way disabling. Rather, it allowed Norris to write a masterpiece, one of the great elegies for the dead of the Second World War, and perhaps the greatest single achievement of the Second Flowering.

It is a poem where memories and experiences overlay and change one another, a bitter learning process that we can oppose to innocence. In 'An Old House', the present derelict and treacherous site is explored by Norris and his dog; it was played in when he and his friends were children; and before that it was the scene of a girl's murder. The three times react on one another, in the context of a whole life. The children have some kind of horrid experience in the house while Norris is left sceptical and angry:

> What they had seen I could not make them say.
> In the harsh sun I found my freckled courage,
> Jeered, was angry, went home a different way.

And walk a different way for a whole life.
Five simple years soon took them to the war
That burned their vision on all Europe's houses.
In the old house it was their death they saw.

The girl's murder and its supposed traces, like the blindness of
Billy Rose but more convincingly, trigger a confused but horrified
vision of human suffering and cruelty. Norris, as a boy, finds his
'freckled courage' enough angrily to disbelieve in it as incredible:
he will 'walk a different way for a whole life'. Now, though, he
acknowledges the horror. Their own violent deaths in the war five
years later was the vision they saw then, burned on all Europe's
houses as by the blitz.

After such roads I stand in the rind of the day
With my poor ghosts. Headlights stain the snow,
Light leaves the monotonous sky. Heavy with night,
Down the steep hill the wary motorists go,

Stiff on the packed ice. I whistle to my dog;
His eyes rejoice. The fall I call him from.
Now winter bellows through the travellers' air
And with a sigh I tell the dead go home.

It is clearly a poem that deserves closer analysis than we have
space for: the dog, for instance, with its suggestion (as often in
Norris) that it is a symbol of the poet's social persona and savoir-
faire, delighted to be called back from such a static transaction
with ghosts. At the beginning of the poem,

Seeing him near the wall, I call my dog.
He lifts his head and its unholy eye.
An old dog knows the form and will not fall.

Surely the fall the dog is called from is more than physical.
   It does not seem to me that Norris has ever recovered the power
of *The Loud Winter*. As M. Wynn Thomas remarks, the danger
was that he would grow 'too comfortable with recollection, too
wryly practised a producer of gentle plangencies, and too consciously rapt a story-teller' – to which I would add, too concerned

with elaborating his own poetic persona, an image of himself as a charming, cultured man, a motorist full of regrets but nowhere at home. Nevertheless Norris remains a very readable and accomplished poet, if not quite the vibrant and exciting writer who appeared so briefly in 'An Old House'.

Of the remaining poets – that is, those who are not teachers – the work of Herbert Williams deserves mention though he soon fell out of the limelight, probably because of the pressure of the journalism he lived by. We must hurry on, however: the achievement of Ormond Thomas, or John Ormond as he later called himself, demands our attention.

The two names might almost belong to two separate writers, so different is his early poetry from that of his maturity. Ormond is the one poet born in the 1920s to belong both to the tragic, numinous, modernist-schizoid world of the First Flowering and to the comic-depressive, secular, single-focus representationalism of the Second. He came from Swansea and knew both Dylan Thomas and Vernon Watkins. He was included in Keidrych Rhys's 1944 Faber anthology, *Modern Welsh Poetry*. As the culmination of his early poetry, in 1948–52 Ormond wrote a long sequence *City in Fire and Snow*, in memory of Swansea destroyed in the Blitz. It is the last major attempt by one of the younger Anglo-Welsh poets to respond to his or her time in the tragic mode of Dylan Thomas. Randall Jenkins calls its stance 'elaborately literary', but I would see it as high tragedy;

> She stood with the wings of the cold
> Spread over her, the air antlered
> And hung with the lights of his long
> Love stars, each nailed in its own north.
> She moved as he approached, knelt down
>
> And then in silence
> Lay to lie for me and his love,
> Postured and praising in the white
> Roses of winter's enormous bridals
> Of the children of the ghost
> And the frost of spent stars.

It is beautiful, but as Jenkins implies, it doesn't work. John Ormond was not really a tragedian. He had to find himself as a

ed enough confidence in his vision to become his own man, the writer
that he really was.

The poets we have touched on so far (in Auden's phrase) 'sing of
human unsuccess'. They have been in their various ways artificers
in the aesthetic of failure. So are most twentieth-century poets,
because in our time poets are rarely on the winning side. But as far
as one can make out, John Ormond was a successful man, as the
world counts success. His work as a journalist on *Picture Post* and
particularly as a director of documentary films for television was
acclaimed and satisfying. He was happily married and rich enough
to live part-time in Tuscany. He was respected as a poet, with
collections published by Oxford University Press and Penguin
Modern Poets. As his films about poets and artists show, he was
more interested in the aesthetics of achievement than the pathos of
failure. When I first met him, 'Hello, maestro,' he said. I have
always felt that that greeting told me a great deal about John.

The real Ormond emerged, then, in 'Cathedral Builders', a poem
about a medieval stonemason looking up at the great cathedral he
has made, now full of the pomp of bishops who are ignoring him;
and about how he cocks his eye at it and says with defiant pride: 'I
bloody did that.'

It is this concern with achievement, couched in verse whose
polish and urbanity echo the success, that causes the heart to lift
when one reads Ormond after other Anglo-Welsh poets such as
John Tripp or Leslie Norris. For example, in his poem 'first for,
and now in memory of Ceri Richards' the painter, he praises the
salmon for its long journey from the deep sea to the upland
streams where it mates, achieves vicarious immortality, and dies:

> At last her lust
> Gapes in a gush on her stone nest
> And his held, squanderous peak
>   Shudders his final hunger
> On her milk; seed laid on seed
> In spunk of liquid silk
> So in exhausted saraband their slack
> Convulsions wind and wend galactic
>   Seed in seed, a found
>   World without end.

> The circle's set, proportion
> Stands complete, and,
>> Ready for death,
> Haggard they hang in aftermath
> Abundance, ripe for the world's
>> Rich night, the spear.

So (is it not implied in the dedication?) the artist gives his life to achieve an artistic 'world without end' and then dies, haggard, successful and emptied of purpose.

These long, rapt, meditative lyrics, 'Salmon', 'Monuments', 'Tuscan Cypresses', are probably at the centre of Ormond's work, but to concentrate only on them would be to ignore his wit, his delight in the seemingly trivial, his manipulation of surfaces. These qualities make his love poems some of the most successful to have been composed in Wales since Dafydd ap Gwilym.

> Be bread upon my table still
> And red wine in my glass; be fire
> Upon my hearth. Continue,
> My true storm door, continue
> To be sweet lock to my key;
> Be wife to me, remain
> The soft silk on my bed.
>
> Be morning to my pillow,
> Multiply my joy. Be my rare coin
> For counting, my luck, my
> Granary, my promising fair
> Sky, my star, the meaning
> Of my journey. Be, this year too,
> My twelve months long desire.
>> ('In September')

Indeed, the use here of *dyfalu*, or piling up of comparisons, and, in 'Cat's Cradles', the serious play of mixed fascination with the string's intricate pattern and impatient desire to finish it and make love could almost come from Dafydd:

> What can I say
> (again that touch, your fingertips at mine)
> except 'Be quick, be careless.

Forget these fine
adjustments to the thread.
        Why not mislay one strand
        and let all ravel and slackly run?'
So that elsewhere, nearby,
        I shall not sigh impatience
        but breathe the air you exhale
When softly you design
        (your calm undone)
        how next you move,
when, with an even lighter touch,
        your fingertips and lips
        silence me, and consent,
        in meeting mine.

But more typically Ormond is the weaving of flowers into what is a
most delicate allegory of phallic fidelity in 'Captive Unicorn':

He day-dreams of jack-by-the-hedge, lances
Of goldenrod to crunch on, tangled
Heart's ease, salads of nipple-wort.

His nightmares are acres of fool's parsley.
He wakes hungry for self-heal
And the clingings of traveller's joy.

Released in winter, he does not stray.
The tip of his horn a blind periscope,
He trembles in sweet dung under deep snow.

Like Dafydd also, for all his comic bravura, Ormond conveys a
sense of sadness and loss in the face of mortality. He certainly does
not lack cognisance of the darker side of experience.

    And yet, ultimately, one registers disappointment that John
Ormond, easily the most sophisticated writer of the Second
Flowering, was not a greater poet than he was. There is no
inherent reason why the aesthetics of achievement should lead to
lesser poetry than the aesthetics of failure: otherwise the whole
medieval tradition of Welsh poetry, not to speak of the *Aeneid* and
The Faerie Queene, would have to be considered minor. Indeed it is
arguable that great tragedy arises more as a critique of heroic
success than as a consequence of failure. In our own century, one

could point to Wallace Stevens as sharing many of John Ormond's presuppositions. The American poet was also successful in the world and also concerned with the nature of artistic achievement ('the supreme fiction') and its relationship to human existence. His intense stylization is considerably less user-friendly than Ormond's customary air of involving the reader in a rather special kind of conversation; yet there is no question which poet cuts deeper. Wallace Stevens takes us into a rigorous solitude where we can know our humanity afresh. By comparison Ormond's world seems cosy.

One can speculate why this should be so. The audience-conscious kid-gloved culture of middlebrow television may be part of the answer; another may be the recourse to talk over a drink as the customary emollient of the world's ills. But certainly the lack of intellectual challenge in the literary environment of Arts Council Anglo-Wales must take its share of the blame. Poetry all too easily became an accomplishment, not a risk-taking cutting edge.

The attempt to build Cardiff into a cultural capital, first unofficially through *Poetry Wales* and then through the official patronage of the Welsh Arts Council, I have likened to economic protectionism as opposed to the more or less free trade of the London market. Protectionism, like patronage itself, is an essentially feudal strategy, only adopted by capitalist economies either as an offensive weapon in a trade war or as a temporary defence for young or underdeveloped industries not yet capable of standing on their own two feet. Of the latter policy the classical example is the Ireland of the twenty-six counties, from the inception of the Free State in the 1920s to the Republic's conversion to free trade in 1965.

Cultural protectionism is designed to allow a different kind of talent to flower than that favoured in the big world. Harri Webb and John Tripp, who would probably not have gained recognition in London, were enabled to became significant writers. This is more or less true of many other poets. *Poetry Wales* and then Arts Council patronage allowed them to be published and to develop as artists.

The dangers of protectionism are equally well known. Though it can give a kick-start to a culture, the lack of real competition quickly begins to undermine it by encouraging the acceptance of mediocrity and intellectual stagnation. Artistic values are confused with moral convention, exemplified by the notorious Irish censorship of the 1940s and 50s. There was nothing so clear-cut in Arts Council Anglo-Wales, of course. Overt censorship would have been too repugnant to have been tolerated. Nevertheless one can look a long way either in *Poetry Wales* or in the poetry books subsidized by the Welsh Arts Council for any intellectual excitement or significant experiments in form. The two most intelligent poets of the period, Harri Webb and John Ormond, both failed to reach their potential stature though for very different reasons – Webb being diverted into political balladry, Ormond through his very accomplishment. Modernism is conspicuous by its absence. Lip-service was paid to David Jones of course, but woe betide a poet who followed in his footsteps: Gerard Casey's *South Wales Echo* (Enitharmon, 1973) was virtually ignored. The charming, vaguely e. e. cummings-like work of Terry Hawkes was allowed to wilt into obscurity. Peter Finch was kept on the books as a token modernist, but his knockabout Cardiff-based little mag, *Second Aeon*, was allowed to subside, leaving no issue. Presumably it did not fit into the Arts Council image of what Anglo-Welsh culture should be.

Secondly, and possibly as a concomitant to this lack of intellectual challenge, there was an altogether excessive emphasis on subject matter, and indeed on the Welshness of the subject matter. Here we can quote chapter and verse for, in Stephens's valediction to *Poetry Wales* already referred to, he says:

> I am convinced that before a poet writing in English can fully justify his position as Anglo-Welsh, he needs either to write about Welsh scenes, Welsh people, the Welsh past, life in contemporary Wales, or his own analysis of all these, or else attempt to demonstrate in his own verse those more elusive characteristics of style and feeling which are generally regarded as belonging to Welsh poetry.

There is no question which of these two conditions was the more concrete or easily fulfilled, especially by poets largely illiterate in Welsh. Hence the overproduction of elegies for every aspect of valleys culture that were such a cliché of the time. The second condition was so difficult, indeed, that Stephens was always rooting round for a 'good critic' who would define to his readers' satisfaction 'the Welshness of Anglo-Welsh verse'. But until he found one, a Welsh subject matter was an obvious advantage.

Thirdly, although the appearance of *Poetry Wales* certainly acted as a catalyst – 'Anglo-Welsh poets at last seemed to be as numerous as blackberries in the woods,' as Stephens put it – still there is a sense that the Cardiff revolution was imposed from above, by bureaucratic fiat, rather than growing naturally from the soil. Edinburgh had always been a cultural capital in Scotland, but Cardiff in 1967 was the nearest thing Wales had to a provincial English city, like Nottingham or Bristol. As such, it had (and still has) its own mix of cultures and cultural artefacts, partly indigenous, partly immigrant, but mostly a reflection of what was happening in other urban centres of the Anglo-American world. The new 'metropolitan' status of their city bemused rather than enlightened its inhabitants. As far as Cardiff was concerned the Second Flowering was a bit like a poorer version of BBC Wales – a lot of second-class 'Welshies' on the make. And the feeling was mutual: John Tripp gave up expecting hope from the capital, the new Wales would have to come from the villages. Meanwhile Cardiff's own creativity tended to go unsupported.

What was true of Cardiff was to a possibly lesser extent true of Wales as a whole. The Second Flowering played its part in establishing anglophone Wales as a cultural centre of gravity again, after the Depression and two world wars. No one had to move to London now! But the writers of the Second Flowering were almost all exiles, incomers or *revenants*, and to the younger poets who succeeded them, who had mostly lived there all their lives, they seemed out of touch with contemporary Wales and the way Welsh people felt and lived.

FURTHER READING

Tony Conran, *Frontiers in Anglo-Welsh Poetry* (Cardiff, 1997).

Tony Curtis, 'Grafting the sour to sweetness: Anglo-Welsh poetry in the last twenty-five years', in idem (ed.), *Wales the Imagined Nation* (Bridgend, 1986).

James A. Davies, *Leslie Norris* (Cardiff, 1991).

Jeremy Hooker, *The Presence of the Past: Essays on Modern British and American Poetry* (Bridgend, 1987).

Nigel Jenkins, *John Tripp* (Cardiff, 1989).

Dafydd Johnston (ed.), *The Complete Works of Idris Davies* (Cardiff, 1994).

Brian Morris, *Harri Webb* (Cardiff, 1993).

Meic Stephens, 'The Second Flowering', *Poetry Wales*, 3:3 (Winter, 1967), 2–9.

M. Wynn Thomas, *John Ormond* (Cardiff, 1997).

CHAPTER 8

BOTH IN AND OUT OF THE GAME: WELSH WRITERS AND THE BRITISH DIMENSION

KATIE GRAMICH

Just as, in the halcyon days before the professionalization of rugby, talented Welsh players of the national game were occasionally enticed to go to England to play the more lucrative rugby league, so Welsh authors writing in English have done so in the knowledge that, both east and west of them, there was an English-speaking league which they might – if they adapted their game – one day join. Clearly, many Welsh writers have never felt the temptation, or indeed the desire, to join that league. To many, it might seem like an insult or a compromise of their Welshness. One remembers Glyn Jones's proud declaration that, although he wrote in English, he never wrote a word in that language except about Wales and the Welsh. That assertion of national allegiance and commitment can be taken as representative of many of the so-called 'Anglo-Welsh' authors of that generation and even later ones. (One thinks of figures such as Harri Webb and John Tripp, but the specifically Welsh focus and subject is there, also, in less notably patriotic writers, such as Caradoc Evans and Dylan Thomas.) Yet there has also existed another group of Welsh writers in English whom one might describe as being more catholic in their choice of subject and/or more ambivalent in their relationship with their homeland. Indeed, for many writers in the latter category, it does not seem to have been the literary equivalent of a choice between rugby union and rugby league but rather a decision to play both games simultaneously.

Arguably, the 'Anglo-Welsh' writers of the First Flowering had to be more assertive in affirming their Welsh identity in order to prove their existence at all, against the assertion in 1938 by such an influential critic as Saunders Lewis that they did not exist. On the other hand, from the outset, certain writers were willing to play the other game. Gwyn Jones, for example, one of the key members of the First Flowering, both as creative writer and critic, published

some works which had no apparent connection with Wales. A year
before the appearance of his well-known south Wales industrial
novel, *Times Like These*, in 1936, Jones had brought out not only
Four Icelandic Sagas but also *Richard Savage*, a novel set in
eighteenth-century England. Similarly, in later years, even a writer
such as Gwyn Thomas, who not only wrote about his native
Rhondda but invented himself as an ebullient Welsh wit on
national television, also wrote novels which had nothing at all to
do with Wales, such as *The Love Man* (1958), based on the Spanish
story of Don Juan. Raymond Williams may be regarded as
another academic/creative writer and critic in the same mould as
Gwyn Jones, while Siân James is a markedly Welsh (and Welsh-
speaking) writer who is also capable on occasion, like Gwyn
Thomas, of turning her hand to writing about non-Welsh subjects.

No writer consents readily to being pigeon-holed. Indeed, many
writers assert very vocally their freedom to write about whatever
subject they choose, without being constricted by issues of
nationality or political allegiance. One can see in the decision of
some writers to focus on non-Welsh subjects an inspiration deriving from an academic or scholarly interest (such as Professor
Gwyn Jones's interest in English Augustanism and the Icelandic
sagas and Gwyn Thomas's interest in Hispanic literature). Others
may make that choice as a gesture of rebellion against what Joyce
called 'the triple net', and I think this rebellion is particularly
noticeable in some writers of the Second Flowering who may be
seen as reacting against the overt cultural and political nationalism
which began to flourish in Wales in the 1960s, as evidenced in
Meic Stephens's *Poetry Wales*, for example. Still other writers may
be regarded as using Wales as a conveniently exotic landscape
against which to set their works, in much the same way as some of
the female Gothic writers of the late eighteenth century chose
'Wild Wales' as a backdrop for their romantic romps. However,
though the above reasons may be used to explain many writers'
works, I think it is also true to say that there can be a more general
diagnosis of the phenomenon of the dual-game player which is
connected to the particular historical and cultural circumstances of
Wales: it is that 'divided sensibility' which Dai Smith and other
Welsh historians have documented.

Welsh writers who use the English language can, like the rest of
us from this country, choose to write either 'Welsh' or 'British' in

their passports. Some might see nothing problematic about this choice, viewing 'British' as a designation which embraces and includes that 'other', 'Welsh'. At the other end of the scale, some might, like R. S. Thomas, see 'Britishness [as] a mask, beneath [which] there is only one nation, England'. Recent commentators on nationalism and national identity have chosen to emphasize their 'invented' nature. This is not to say that they are false or fabricated but they are shifting, ideological entities, rather than eternal essences. In a sense, writers such as those discussed in this chapter exemplify this post-structuralist view of identity. They take on different identities or at least adopt varieties of their authorial selves in publishing different works. This might be seen not as deviant but as characteristic writerly behaviour – as Keats said: 'What shocks the virtuous philosopher, delights the chameleon poet.'

Dannie Abse is not a Keatsian poet but he is certainly chameleon-like. His work as both poet and prose-writer is marked by duality. Foremost among the many dualities which energize his work is that between his Jewish identity and his Welsh identity; close behind this primary tension is that between his dual role as doctor and poet, reflected in the binary title of his *Collected Poems: White Coat, Purple Coat 1948–1988* (1989). Unlike his contemporary, Bernice Rubens, also from a Jewish background in Cardiff, Abse tends not to compartmentalize his work into that which is about Jewishness and that which is about Welshness. Indeed, both identities coalesce in a complex and fruitful way in his work. An early poem of his is actually entitled 'Duality':

> Twice upon a time,
> there was a man who had two faces,
> two faces but one profile:
> not Jekyll and Hyde, not good and bad,
> and if one were cut, the other would bleed –
> two faces different as hot and cold . . .
>
> . . . I am that man twice upon this time:
> my two voices sing to make one rhyme.
> Death I love and Death I hate,
> (I'll be with you soon and late).
> Love I love and Love I loathe,
> God I mock and God I prove,
> yes, myself I kill, myself I save.

> Now, now, I hang these masks on the wall.
> Oh Christ, take one and leave me all
> lest four tears from two eyes fall.

Indeed it is not Keats but Yeats who is invoked here, recalling the
Irish poet's dictum that the poet is inevitably 'a self and an anti-
self in creative conflict' and an individual who must don the masks
of poetry. Yet Abse's Jewish identity is also signalled in the veiled
allusion to Shylock's speech, 'If you prick us do we not bleed?', in
the fourth line of the poem. A more elegant and assured expression
of duality, this time between past and present selves, is found in
the well-known later poem, 'Return to Cardiff':

> 'Hometown'; well, most admit an affection for a city:
> grey, tangled streets I cycled on to school, my first cigarette
> in the back lane, and, fool, my first botched love affair.
> First everything. Faded torments; self-indulgent pity . . .
>
> . . . No sooner than I'd arrived the other Cardiff had gone,
> smoke in the memory, these but tinned resemblances,
> where the boy I was not and the man I am not
> met, hesitated, left double footsteps, then walked on.

Abse is a versatile and complex writer, erudite at one moment,
broadly comic the next. He is also one of the rare authors who has
excelled in more than one genre; although he is primarily known as
a poet, his autobiographical prose is almost as well known and, most
recently, his novel *The Strange Case of Dr Simmonds and Dr Glas*
(2002). He has also experimented with dramatic form, as evidenced
in the publication of his *The View from Row G: Three Plays* (1990).

The tonal and thematic range of Abse's voice and the complexity of his projected identity are well expressed in Abse's first
volume of autobiographical fiction, *Ash on a Young Man's Sleeve*
(1954). Interestingly, Welshness and Jewishness are not seen here
as opposing allegiances but as compatible and ordinary for the
ten-year-old child living in Cardiff in 1934:

> I used to take two pebbles and throw them at each other. They were
> boxers fighting or two armies locked in a stony embrace. One was
> Wales, the other was England or France or Siam, or red-haired, freckle-

faced Keith Thomas. My mother was born at Ystalyfera one rainy
Tuesday, my father on Guy Fawkes night in Bridgend, so Wales always
won . . . It was Friday night and we were Jewish. The two candles
burning symbolised for me holiness and family unity. My mother could
speak Welsh and Yiddish and English, and Dad knew swear words as
well . . . It was July 1934 [and] . . . the noise fell over the world. Oswald
Mosley posing on a lonely platform in London behind an immense red,
white and blue Union Jack. 'We are English' – shouted Mosley – 'we
the English are being throttled and strangled by the greasy fingers of
alien financiers.' And he was talking about Dad and Mam, Wilfred and
Leo, me and Uncle Isidore.

This foreshadowing of the Holocaust is indicative of a continuing
and understandable preoccupation in Abse's work. It leads to a
continual probing and questioning of the basic morality of human
nature, as in the plays *House of Cowards* and, especially, *The Dogs
of Pavlov*. The latter is based on an actual experiment conducted
by an American professor, Stanley Milgram, to find out how far
ordinary people are prepared to go in obeying orders which inflict
pain on others. As in the real experiment, in Abse's play volunteers
are instructed to administer electric shocks of increasing intensity
to another person when she answers questions incorrectly; the
volunteers believe that the experiment is to investigate how punish-
ment aids learning. The 'victim' is actually an actor and the electric
shocks are faked. Disturbingly, Milgram found that most
volunteers obeyed orders to administer the electric shocks, even
when the effect they could see on their fellow human beings was
(apparently) extreme pain. The parallels with what happened
under Nazi rule during the Second World War are clear and are
made explicit in Abse's play. Sally Parsons, the actor who plays
the victim in the experiment within the play, becomes increasingly
angry with the volunteers, who all consent so readily to inflict
apparent pain upon her:

SALLY: . . . They don't know I'm acting. They think I'm a real victim.
And afterwards I feel like a victim and I hate their guts.
DR OLWEN JONES: You shouldn't allow yourself to get that involved.
SALLY: What gets me is how they depreciate my worth afterwards. They
say I'm stupid – that I deserve to be shocked.
DR DALY: The victim always has to be thought inferior. That was but
one finding in other scientific experiments.
DR JONES: Anyway, one knows that from history.

Nevertheless, Abse derives some comfort and optimism from the fact that a small minority of the volunteers refused to pull the levers or simply pretended to be administering higher doses of the shock treatment. As he says in an introductory essay: 'We must find our consolations where we can.'

It must be conceded that Abse is much more consummate a poet than he is a playwright. Considerably less rhapsodic than his contemporary, Leslie Norris, he is nevertheless capable of lyrical intensity, though his more habitual mode is crisply ironic. His verse often takes traditional forms, such as quatrains and rhyming couplets, but he uses colloquial language and natural rhythms to endow these forms with a distinctively modern sensibility. There is a strong element of the bizarre and the grotesque in his work, as in his 'Funland' sequence which is set in an asylum. As Abse himself said of the poem 'the earth . . . is a lunatic asylum whose inmates live out suffering lives of black comedy'. Death and suffering are, indeed, constant preoccupations, perhaps not surprising for a poet-doctor who faced these issues every day of his professional life. The poems are striking for their complete lack of sentimentality, as in the memorable poem entitled 'Carnal Knowledge' in which the doctor-speaker addresses the corpse which he is dissecting. Yet these themes often have a poignant personal dimension, too, in moving poems about the death of his parents and in those trying to grapple with memories of the Holocaust.

Intense self-questioning is apparent time and time again in the poems, often conducted in a disarmingly intimate, colloquial tone. At the same time, that first-person speaker can often turn outwards towards us as readers, addressing us directly as 'you', catching us out, implicating us in this continual interrogation of subjectivity. The division perceptible between doctor-persona and poet-persona is often quite stark, both in the poetry and prose; as the narrator self-consciously admits in *Ash on a Young Man's Sleeve*: 'Between fragments of conversation I saw myself, self looking upon another self – and that other, a white-gowned, white-masked surgeon.' More succinctly and lyrically, he expresses the division in 'Song for Pythagoras':

> White coat and purple coat
>   a sleeve from both he sews.
> That white is always stained with blood,
>   that purple by the rose.

And phantom rose and blood most real
  compose a hybrid style;
white coat and purple coat
  few men can reconcile.

White coat and purple coat
  can each be worn in turn
but in the white a man will freeze
  and in the purple burn.

Like Abse, Menna Gallie may be regarded as a writer
characterized by a duality, not of identity, but of allegiance. There
is a clear feminist vision underlying virtually all of Gallie's
writings, together with a socialist commitment which is particularly evident in her industrial novels, such as *Strike for a Kingdom*
(1959) and *The Small Mine* (1962). She is a writer who does not
restrict her settings to Wales, focusing on Northern Ireland in her
novel *You're Welcome to Ulster!* (1970) and taking her protagonist
on a European journey (and a sexual adventure) in *Travels with a
Duchess* (1968). Gallie was also a Welsh speaker who translated
Caradog Prichard's *Un Nos Ola Leuad* into English but who felt
frustrated with what she saw as the restrictions and prudery of
much of the literary production in her first language. Nevertheless,
Gallie was identified very precisely as a Welsh writer by the
English press. 'Fresh and beguiling from the land of her fathers
comes Menna Gallie,' enthused the *Times Literary Supplement*
over her first novel, *Strike for a Kingdom*. Other English critics
compared her work with that of 'the Thomases', Gwyn and Dylan,
regarding her 'racy' language and sometimes outrageous humour
as characteristics of a distinctively Welsh prose style.

When one examines her novels in some detail, one can see that
there is some justification for the English critics' comments. *The
Small Mine* opens with a scene underground, in which Joe Jenkins
is about to clock off for the day. The claustrophobic atmosphere
of the mine is vividly imagined, from the point of view of the tired
worker himself, with not a scrap of sentiment or euphemism.
When Joe rejoins his fellows, we realize that these characters are
talkers, lively, witty, impassioned, like Gwyn Thomas's characters
but with more individualism and less eccentricity. The village
community is brilliantly evoked, with all its petty rivalries, its

allegiances, its familial closeness. The prose is tumbling with
energy; Gallie has a wit's knack for the telling phrase, such as: 'her
teeth were bad copies – in the Welsh have-them-all-out-and-save-
trouble tradition.' Yet the novel is more than capable of turning
from comedy to tragedy within a few pages: Joe is later killed in
the mine, blown to bits in an explosion:

> They didn't find all the pieces when eventually they got the way clear
> and the roof off, and they could only assemble the shape of a man on to
> the stretcher and after the post-mortem the coffin was kept in the
> mortuary until the last possible minute in case the mother should be
> tempted to remove the lid.

Gallie goes further than either of the Thomases in delineating
the wholeness of a community, in that she highlights women's
experiences and characters, rejecting the simple Welsh Mam
stereotype, though the novel is, significantly, dedicated 'To Mam'.
Gallie is particularly acute in depicting male–female relationships
and in doing this her prose style becomes more experimental,
lapsing into internal monologue which alternates between male
and female characters. The villainous character, nicknamed Link,
is also given extended passages of interior monologue which give
the reader an insight into the self-torturing workings of his mind.
Children, too, are important characters in their own right in this
novel, with their own intense concerns and anxieties. It is entirely
appropriate that the 'hero', Joe, dies midway through the text; this
indicates quite clearly that this is a novel which has no hero or
heroine – it is a portrait of a community, and the narrative
technique is suitably democratic. Although it is clearly a novel
with a socialist ideology, it manages to avoid both the naked
propaganda which mars Lewis Jones's *Cwmardy* (1937) and the
serious intellectualism which tends to make Raymond Williams's
novels somewhat forbidding.

The novels Gallie published which do not have Welsh settings
nevertheless have a distinctive Galli(e)c voice. *Man's Desiring*
(1960), for instance, is primarily an acutely observed satire of
academia, focusing on the adventures of an innocent Welshman
newly arrived in the snobbish fastnesses of Oxbridge. It has echoes
of Kingsley Amis's *Lucky Jim* (1954) but is, on the whole, funnier.
At Griffydd Rowland's first University drinks party, everyone

keeps introducing him as 'Dr Rowlands' and though Griff conscientiously denies his doctorate at every turn, no one will strip him of his false status. As one of his interlocutors explains: 'it's usually safer in the academic world, don't you think? Those who are like to be acknowledged, and those who aren't enjoy the flattery.' Part of Griff's unease at the English university is his perception of his own otherness in such a setting; as he explains to Mrs Webster the cleaner, who recognizes his *hiraeth*: 'I live down in the south where the coal mines are. We live in a small village and everybody knows as soon as you're constipated there and everybody cares about you . . . Up here nobody much seems to care about anybody.' Similarly, the main protagonist in *You're Welcome to Ulster!* is a Welsh woman, Sarah, who goes to Northern Ireland for a week's escape when she finds that she has a lump in her breast. Both Griff in *Man's Desiring* and Sarah in *You're Welcome to Ulster!* are not only Welsh but Welsh speakers, and snippets of the language are used in the texts, though the settings in both are outside Wales. It seems to me that these are unmistakably Welsh novels. Gallie remains a neglected and underrated novelist, whose works richly deserve republication, a process already begun by Honno, the Welsh Women's Press.

Like Menna Gallie, Alice Thomas Ellis is a writer whose forte is satirical comedy. Sometimes the milieu of her novels is emphatically English but she makes occasional forays into Wales in novels such as *Unexplained Laughter* (1985), as well as in her autobiographical *A Welsh Childhood* (1990) which deals with her upbringing in north Wales. She is a writer interested in moral issues, such as loyalty and betrayal, and in matters religious, particularly questions of mortality, sin and redemption. In the context of the latter, the author's Catholicism is an important influence on her work, occasionally suggesting hints of Graham Greene. Thomas Ellis's autobiographical writings display a clear affection for north Wales but they also reveal the detachment evident in her novelistic depiction of her native land. In *Unexplained Laughter*, for example, the centre of consciousness is the sophisticated English visitor to Wales, Lydia, who regards the native Welsh as decidedly strange, ranging from the pleasantly odd to the downright deranged. Although she herself, particularly with regard to her scepticism and her wavering feminism, does not remain unscathed by authorial irony, the Welsh characters are

presented as exotic others. They may collectively teach her a moral
lesson or two but their own behaviour is often questionable. There
is a saint-like Welshman apparently immune to temptation,
tellingly named Beuno. But there is also a mad girl, Angharad,
endowed with an irritatingly mystical sense of unity with the earth,
and some minor characters who display Welsh xenophobia and
narrow-mindedness. The novelist seems to be addressing a sophisticated and urbane English audience and suggesting that the
Welsh are a fascinating lot when you venture out to witness their
antics from your holiday cottage. Interestingly, feminism is presented as an English import and something of an indulgence, while
the native Welsh women display no such perilous leanings. There
is no doubt that Alice Thomas Ellis is a skilful novelist with an ear
for comic dialogue and an aptitude for creating atmospheric
settings, but the representations of Wales she offers in her fiction
tend to strike the Welsh reader as limited by their Anglocentricity.

The autobiographical *A Welsh Childhood* is, sadly, no corrective. Thomas Ellis, with cheerful obliviousness to Welsh readers'
sensibilities, entertains us with the information that the inhabitants
of Penmaenmawr in her childhood were extremely suspicious of
baths and, indeed, she 'still know[s] people in the district who
regard bathing as a risky business'. Usefully, she informs us that
she has 'never yet met a Celt who could scramble an egg'. We are
treated to gems of wisdom such as 'Taliesin wouldn't half be
surprised if he visited Deganwy now'. The narrator's supercilious-
ness is hard to stomach:

> Last time I went there (Anglesey) the day started fine, and then,
> perhaps symbolically, there descended a great Celtic mist. I peered
> through it looking for the pink-washed cottages of my memory, but
> they'd gone. All over Wales hundreds and hundreds of the old stone
> cottages have fallen down and in their place have appeared
> 'Dunroamin' – suburban bungalows with geraniums and lobelias in
> flower baskets, pointless balconies of meanly-wrought iron, two-tone
> cladding and picture windows, and little lawns so that middle-aged
> people can mow them and feel close to the earth, claiming their
> territory with pokerwork signs announcing 'Dunroamin'. And, of
> course, there are always the housing estates – living graveyards.

There are flashes of what appears to be patriotism: 'The Welsh . . .
who have a genuine and ancient culture, have been perceived as

savage and backward by the insular English, who have lost theirs. It is very annoying.' The 'ancient culture' is a highly Arnoldian giveaway: what interests Thomas Ellis about Wales is its 'Celtic' mist and magic, stories and legends about saints, witches, ghosts, murderers and eccentrics in the 'ancient' Welsh past. The present is dead. We live in our housing estates or suburban villas, it would seem, and she has nothing to say to or about us. The author's flair for comedy is much less assured here than in the novels. She suggests, for example, that the Welsh and the Egyptians are descended from a common stock, adducing as evidence 'similarities between Welsh and Egyptian . . . family structures, the most marked being the vast preponderance of aunties common to both peoples'. The narrator's strenuous attempts at eccentric charm become increasingly tedious: 'Now with "improved communications", i.e. roads everywhere, there is no telling what riff-raff may be abroad on the hillsides.' No telling, indeed. Unsurprisingly, the *Daily Mail* approves of Alice Thomas Ellis, clearly identifying her as one of its own: 'Her dry ironic style is as English as Jane Austen and as fortifying as a glass of vintage brandy.' Personally, I'd prefer a glass of Felinfoel, but then I'm probably one of the riff-raff.

There is nothing Anglocentric about the work of Bernice Rubens but, on the other hand, her fictional renderings of Wales and the Welsh are frequently more bizarre than realistic. Like Dannie Abse, she is a Jewish writer from Cardiff but unlike the poet, she does tend to compartmentalize her works into those dealing with Jewish characters and relationships and those which are set in Wales. The former is by far the *larger* compartment. *I Sent a Letter To My Love* (1975) and *Yesterday in the Back Lane* (1995) are examples of novels which focus exclusively on Welsh characters with no Jewish connections, while novels such as *The Elected Member* (1969) and *Kingdom Come* (1990) focus on the Jewish inheritance.

I Sent a Letter to My Love and *Yesterday in the Back Lane* have explicit Welsh settings: Porthcawl and Splott, respectively. Characters are given distinctively Welsh names, such as Dai, Blodwen and Gwyneth, and often speak fluent 'Caradoc Evansish'. Rubens noticeably steers clear of the chapel, though her characters often go there, off-stage as it were. Her Welsh characters are sexually frustrated or maimed, narrow-minded, obsessive; admittedly, the same could be said of many of her Jewish characters in other novels. Rubens is clearly a gifted writer but it is not to her novels that we turn for an intimate and subtle portrait of Wales and Welsh people. Dialogue, particularly, tends to edge toward the indeed-to-goodness variety: ' "Good god mun, would you believe." . . . "What's the matter, Evans bach?" the manager said. "White as a sheet you are." "Mr Jones," the clerk squeaked, "there's a letter for Mrs Thomas . . ." "Give it to her mun," Mr Jones said . . .' Rubens is much more interested in, and adept at portraying, extreme psychological states, familial tensions and anxieties, phobias, eccentricities. One reads *I Sent a Letter to My Love* with pleasure because it offers a poignant picture of loneliness and frustration, exploring in intimate and unsettling detail what it feels like to be an ugly, unloved girl trapped in an unfulfilling role. Porthcawl is an appropriate backdrop to Amy Evans's anguish. Splott, in *Yesterday in the Back Lane*, is even more of a theatrical backdrop, one which the reader cannot help but suspect was chosen for the comic effect of the name. Again, the novel's interest lies in the psychological study of the main character, who irresistibly declares in the novel's first sentence: 'My name is Bronwen Davies, and yesterday I killed a man.' Rubens's themes, then, are often bleak but her mode is almost always grotesquely comic. In this, she certainly displays her Welsh credentials, for her humour is often reminiscent of writers like Glyn Jones or Gwyn Thomas.

Broad comedy is also a forte of Alun Richards, who excels at depicting characters of cringe-worthy vulgarity, such as the eponymous protagonist of his story, 'The Former Miss Merthyr Tydfil'. Indeed, Richards is highly skilled at creating thoroughly unpleasant characters, especially females; he seems to do so with an almost missionary zeal. Nevertheless, there is no doubt that Richards's evocation of Welsh speech, places, characters and social relations is invariably accurate, often uncomfortably so. Not unlike V. S. Naipaul, Richards is an unforgiving satirist, lampooning Welsh obsessions and pretensions with no mercy. Moreover, he has an acute ear for dialogue and he makes nice distinctions between kinds of Welshness. Although Ivy once had the chance of being 'Miss Merthyr Tydfil', she makes the point of telling us that she is not from that town 'but had her visitor's qualification through her aunt who worked in Hoover's'. She herself is from Ruby Street, Aberdarren, 'as common as dirt' according to her husband Melville's parents, who were 'very chapel and self-contained'. Melville's Mam had not even allowed her son to tie his own shoelaces before the age of eleven: 'The Welsh Mams in Ivy's book should have been turned over to the S.S. and given to the Gestapo for training . . . She herself was not that kind of Welsh.' In depicting Ivy's husband Melville, Richards mocks the Welsh exile's sudden rediscovery of his roots and his sentimentalization of a working-class, valleys background. Ivy may be crass ('Art be buggered!' she thinks) but at least she is not hypocritical. Despite the cruelty of the humour in this and other stories, Richards leaves scope for the reader to feel compassion for even the most unsympathetic of characters. He may excel at satirizing Wales but there's no doubt that there is an intensity of attachment underlying that satire. With Caradoc Evans, Richards might say that he wishes to expose the running sores of his country in order that they may be healed, though it is only fair to add that Richards's characters never stoop to speaking Caradoc Evansish. He is an author who scrupulously differentiates between different areas of Wales and allows debates about definitions of Welshness to bubble underneath the comic surface of his texts. Clearly the south Wales valleys provide him with his central point of reference: an English-speaking community with a distinct consciousness of their Welshness. Welsh speakers tend to be depicted in worryingly negative terms in some of Richards's stories, though the hostility displayed toward the language is attributed to crass characters such as Moira in the story 'Cherry Trees', whose idea of witty repartee is 'What's the Welsh for "Piss off!"' and who invariably describes people speaking Welsh as 'jabbering'.

Richards is an extremely prolific and successful writer who has written not only unmistakably Welsh short stories such as the one discussed above but also novels, plays, television series, biography, autobiography and history. Two of his works focus on Welsh rugby, still a recognizably national obsession, and these exceptionally well-written books (a biography of Carwyn James and a history of Welsh rugby) show that he is very much 'in the game'. However, his work for television shows that Richards is quite capable of playing the other game, too. Like the defecting rugby players of old, his motivation for doing so may well be commercial. Many of his non-Welsh works are concerned with his other obsession, namely the sea, as evidenced in his authorship of episodes of the popular television series *The Onedin Line* and in his editorship of the *Penguin Book of Sea Stories*. (He is also well known as the editor of the two volumes of *Penguin Welsh Short Stories*.) Sometimes, he manages to combine both Welsh and maritime themes in the same work, as in his novels *Ennal's Point* and *Barque Whisper* and in the short story 'The Widow-Maker', but more often, like several of our other dualists, he keeps them apart.

Leslie Norris is a writer who would probably have agreed with Rhys Davies's slogan 'Down with Passports in Literature!' At a time when political and cultural nationalism was experiencing a resurgence in Wales during the 1960s, Norris was resistant to the calls for overt Welshness. He is a writer who has spent much of his adult life in exile from Wales and I think that this fact has coloured his literary production considerably. There is no doubt that he is, fundamentally, a Merthyr writer, emerging from a similar milieu to that of Glyn Jones but his experience of living in England and in the United States has shaped his work in significant ways. Norris is a writer who proves how fruitful exile and distance can be for the writer. The state of outsider, someone who doesn't quite belong even in his homeland, is a state which may be deeply discomfiting on a personal level, but for a writer it has enormous potential. Exile and loss are the dominant themes of Norris's work as a poet and a short-story writer but there are also epiphanic moments of celebration and sheer joy in the natural world and in poignant human relationships. Being 'out of the game' in Orem, Utah, while teaching at Brigham Young University in Provo, has meant that Norris has profited from an American influence on his poetry, which has distanced it from the strongly Romantic strain which had earlier threatened to make his poetic voice sound anachronistic.

Speaking of his childhood in an interview with Meic Stephens, Norris has said: 'I was always seemingly at the edge of things, a condition I think that has always remained with me.' Being 'at the edge' implies both distance and proximity, an observant intimacy. Norris is one of those exiled writers acclaimed outside his native land but not as well known as he should be within it. Partly, this self-exile has been a deliberate distancing, a cultivation of the independence and detachment which keeps the writer's sharpness honed. The exile has been a physical one for many years: until his retirement, Norris was Professor of Poetry and Creative Writing at Brigham Young University, Provo. Before his self-imposed exile to the United States, he was wont to make contradictory statements about Wales and Welshness, claiming allegiance at one moment and at the next distancing himself from what he saw as Welsh parochialism. In this slipperiness of attitude, Norris is unlike his fellow Merthyr writer, Glyn Jones, whose commitment to Wales was always unquestioned and absolute. And yet Glyn Jones himself gave generous praise to Norris's work from the start, recognizing a distinctively Merthyr voice, as well as a splendid poetic talent.

Anyone who has lived in North America will recognize the temptation to accept the label of Britishness. 'British' in that continent has a very different and usually more benign connotation than it does in Wales. And, after all, Norris lived for many years in England before emigrating to America. As he says in 'The Green Bridge':

> I live in England, seem English,
> Until my voice and wider
>
> Eloquence betray me: then
> I am a discovered alien.

A number of his stories have English settings, affectionately evoked. And yet Norris, like Glyn Jones, has translated Welsh poetry into English, notably the *cywyddau* by Dafydd ap Gwilym included in the *New Poems* of 1986. Norris's maternal relatives were Welsh speaking and he moved among them as a child, understanding but not speaking the language. Again, Norris conjures up a situation where he is just on the edge of belonging.

Primarily regarded as a lyric poet, Norris is nevertheless an accomplished short-story writer. His two main prose collections, *Sliding* (1978) and *The Girl from Cardigan* (1988), contain the kind of stories which leave the reader profoundly moved. As the title suggests, 'Sing it Again, Wordsworth' is a Romantic story which expresses 'thoughts that do often lie/ Too deep for tears'. Similarly, stories such as 'Shaving' or 'The Kingfisher' focus on intense human

emotions common to us all, expressed in a language of simplicity
and poetic power. Given the subject matter of his stories, it would
be easy for Norris to plummet into sentimentality, yet this very
rarely happens. As a short-story writer, he has the poet's knack
of discovering exactly the right image to place, reverberating and
epiphanic, at the centre of his narrative. The flight of geese in the
story of the same name is an instance of this, as are the eponymous
waxwings and the holm oak in their respective stories.

Norris is not a particularly wide-ranging author. He returns
again and again to the same themes, similar settings and emotions,
both in the poems and the stories. And yet the precise command of
language, the sheer brilliance of the imagery, the rightness of the
characterization, are such that the limited range is not perceived as
a deficiency. He does have his personal obsessions, such as the
idolization of the craftsman and the celebration of vigorously
masculine pursuits and bonds.

Although Norris's first volume of verse appeared in the 1940s,
critics tend to agree that he finds his true voice in the 1967
collections, *Finding Gold* and *The Loud Winter*. The poems from
these volumes certainly display a distinctive, mature style and
introduce Norris's characteristic images and themes as well as
some of his obsessions. The tone is elegiac and autumnal, while
the craft of the poet is concealed in a deceptively casual manner.
Images are taken from the world of nature and the recurring
concern is with time passing, the loss of childhood and the
recuperative but painful force of memory. The voice in the poems,
as in the stories, is almost always in the first person. These are
Wordsworthian poems full of emotional intensity. Indeed, a poem
such as 'A February Morning' seems to be a kind of translation of
Wordsworth's 'Solitary Reaper' into a different context. At the
same time, the poems are deeply rooted in a Merthyr boyhood,
with its masculine obsessions, like boxing and football. Traditional
definitions of masculinity seem, however, to be called into question in poems like 'The Ballad of Billy Rose', 'The Strong Man'
and, supremely, in 'Elegy for Lyn James' The latter is full of tonal
ambiguity, managing to be both a poem in praise of an ideal of
manhood and one bewailing the squalor and poverty which make
this particular ideal necessary.

The idea of patrimony is central in Norris's work. Father–son
relationships are poignantly evoked, while Norris also identifies

and pays homage to his literary fathers: Wordsworth, Edward Thomas, Vernon Watkins, Dafydd ap Gwilym. Perhaps the recurring theme of war as a cruel watershed may be connected to this concern with the bond between father and son, for the 'dead boys' who are elegized in his work represent a discontinued, curtailed patrimony. The emphasis on boyhood, both in the poems and the stories, may be read as an artist's attempt to revivify the 'dead boys' who had perished in the war and to re-establish a lost continuity.

Norris's characteristic form as a poet is the contemplative lyric but he also writes successful narrative poems, such as the moving 'Ballad of Billy Rose' and 'A Small War'. Latterly, he has moved to the poem sequence, such as 'Stones Trees Water'. The development which the *Collected Poems* demonstrate is one away from the intricate, dense patterning which one inevitably associates with the Welsh poetic tradition and towards a much more open-textured verse, more prosaic but perhaps more limpid, which one tends to identify as typically American. But Norris's poetic patrimony is unmistakable: certainly there is an American influence in the later work, but Norris remains a Merthyr boy, who significantly places a poem to his father at the end of the *Collected Poems*. Where he himself stands, though, is as uncertain as ever. The poem 'Bridges', placing the speaker in the middle of a bridge, perpetually between two places, sums up his position:

> I have a bridge over a stream. Four
> Wooden sleepers, simple, direct. After rain,
> Very slippery. I rarely cross right over,
> Preferring to stand, watching the grain
> On running water. I like such bridges best,
> River bridges on which men always stand,
> In quiet places. Unless I could have that other,
> A bridge launched, hovering, wondering where to land.

Like a number of the 'dualist' writers, Leslie Norris has had an academic career as well as a life as a creative artist. Similarly, though to an even greater degree, Raymond Williams had two authorial personae. Rather like Professor Gwyn Jones before him, Williams had a dual career as a formidable scholar and cultural critic on the one hand, and in that guise he initially veiled his

Welshness, while in his other guise as novelist, he focused unblushingly on specifically Welsh settings and characters. However, this personal separation in his work became less apparent as his career progressed, and he became more willing to acknowledge a Welsh identity in his academic writings, often using autobiography as a starting point for historical and cultural exploration.

Border Country (1960), *Second Generation* (1964) and *The Fight for Manod* (1979) constitute his first trilogy of novels, all of which contain Welsh settings and characters. They are, centrally, explorations of identity and belonging, not only in terms of geography and topography but also in terms of family and community relationships, political allegiances and historical consciousness. Welshness is a constant concern in Williams's work; true to his probing and questioning turn of mind, Williams interrogated the whole notion of personal identity, and he did so at a time of growing nationalist consciousness in Wales during the 1960s which of course coincided with more general shifts in the cultural climate of Britain during the same period.

In the opening pages of *Border Country*, Williams's protagonist, Matthew Price, is cheered up by a West Indian bus conductress who smiles at him in a warm, personal way amid the alienating anonymity of London. A number of critics have alluded to the aptness of this scene, suggesting as it does the continuity of the process of migration, which is the subject of Matthew's academic research. Matthew himself, as a Welsh immigrant, is personally involved in the subject of his research; like much of Raymond Williams's own work of historical and cultural criticism, the starting point of Matthew's enquiries seems to be autobiographical. On one level, then, *Border Country* is very much a novel of the new 'personal' type which Williams takes pains to decry in *The Long Revolution*, condemning Virginia Woolf and James Joyce for what he sees as the 'luxury' of their focus on the 'personal'. He regards Joyce's *Portrait of the Artist as a Young Man* as 'powerful and in its own terms valid [but] taking only one person seriously', and he goes on to say: 'As it is now developing the personal novel ends by denying the majority of persons.' Unsurprisingly, then, on another level, Williams's *Border Country* is, in its historical span and detailed social description, a realist text conforming to Engels's definition of the term, as 'typical characters in typical situations'.

At the close of his chapter on realism and the contemporary novel in *The Long Revolution* (1965), Williams asserts that 'a new realism is necessary, if we are to remain creative.' Significantly, though, Williams does in his later work move away from realism to a more fantastic mode of writing, just as he came to re-evaluate modernist experimentation more positively in his later critical texts. Tony Pinkney has indeed argued that the unfinished *People of the Black Mountains* trilogy is postmodern in its techniques and narrative strategies. Even within this more experimental form, though, it seems that Williams displays a renewed commitment to the ideas of continuity and community, that 'balance' which he sees as the crowning achievement of the nineteenth-century realist text.

Unlike that of Alice Thomas Ellis, for example, Raymond Williams's Welsh background and upbringing coloured his entire novelistic output and, arguably, the majority of his academic texts as well. That this has not been sufficiently acknowledged is, I think, partly a result of the fact that many commentators on Williams's work hitherto have been ignorant of, or uninterested in, Wales and Welsh identity. His perennial concern is with the relationship of the individual and society, and this concern may be traced ultimately to his own experience of the Welsh community of Pandy in the 1920s and 1930s. George Eliot, whose work Williams greatly admired, was concerned in the 1860s with what she perceived as a breakdown of the traditional close-knit *community* of English rural life into the alienating society of the urban centres. Williams, a hundred years later, can be said to share this concern but with his focus firmly on Wales, where community was still a reality. Welsh society as it is depicted in *Border Country* is a network, an integrated whole which might be described in terms of George Eliot's famous 'web' of relationships. Yet Raymond Williams does not idealize. He chronicles very accurately the dilemma of the individual like Matthew Price or Kate Owen (the rebellious Welsh Mam in the novel *Second Generation*) caught and sometimes frustrated by that web and yet upheld by it also.

Williams sees communal structures as characteristic of Welsh cultural and political life: in *Border Country*, the local eisteddfod is the locus of communal experience in which even the most sceptical outsiders – like Matthew Price and his father – are caught up: 'It was time now for the choirs and Will knew, looking up, that it was no use at all even trying to stay separate . . . the border had been crossed.' Will (otherwise known as Matthew) nevertheless has rebellious tendencies, often directed against the communal structures/strictures of society. When he returns to Glynmawr as an adult, there is a continuing tension between 'Matthew' as individual and 'Will' as part of this communal network of society. Matthew, then, is living uncomfortably in two worlds, or rather, as the title and dominant trope of the novel suggests, in that discomfiting border country between them.

There is often a comparison between English and Welsh society in Williams's novels; his Welsh characters are usually repulsed by the restrictions of class they encounter in English society and which they find alien to their own experience. In *Border Country*, for example, Matthew Price memorably describes England as:

> a great house with every room partitioned by lath and plaster. Behind every screen, in every cupboard, sat all the great men, everybody . . . If you went out of your own cupboard, to see a man in another cupboard, still you must wait for the cupboard door to be opened, with proper ceremony, and by a proper attendant. If you didn't respect another man's cupboard, what right had you, really, to expect him to respect yours? Since proper men lived in cupboards, you could hardly insult your host by implying that he did not.

This extract also illustrates how deftly Williams uses ironic humour in his novels. Too often, Williams has been caricatured as a ponderously clumsy theorist trying, and failing, to write good novels. This is very far from the case: Williams readily admitted 'a problem with form', but his novels are always intensely imagined, often humorous and invariably engaged with those issues which continue to perplex any thoughtful Welsh reader.

Oliver Reynolds is another Cardiff-born poet who, like Dannie Abse, has earned a place for himself in the mainstream of con-temporary English writing. His work has often been labelled postmodernist, perhaps less because of his experimentation with defamiliarizing typographical techniques than because of his char-acteristic detachment. Yet Reynolds is not simply a poet who has gone over to play the other game completely, for in some of his collections to date one finds unsettling references to Wales and the Welsh. Most notably in the pamphlet entitled *Rhondda*

Tenpenn'orth (1986) Reynolds provides a bleak vision of a derelict landscape, ravaged by Thatcherism and a kind of collective amnesia. The ten poems are littered with place names, from Pontygwaith and Llwynypia to Ponty and Tylorstown: it's almost as if the poet is deliberately documenting the continued, tenacious existence of these places, despite all the odds. Reynolds focuses on dispossession and a sense of pointlessness, as in the poem entitled 'Penrhys':

> Through the estate (daubed
> With hammer-and-sickles
> And 'Socialism in our time'),
>
> An ice-cream van
> With Sisyphus at the wheel
> Loops the tinny notes
>
> Of 'The Teddy Bears' Picnic'
> Over and over,
> Wheezing at the altitude.
>
> In the cemetery,
> bilingual death
> Has been at work
> chiselling graffiti
> in neat sun-catching gold:
> *Bu farw . . . bu farw . . . bu farw.*

'To whom it may concern' begins with an epigraph taken from a Welsh Office Report: 'In strictly economic terms it could be said the valleys no longer have a reason for existing.' The savage poem which follows takes the form of an imaginary letter from the Secretary of State for Wales to 'Jones/Jenkins/Rees/Roberts (delete whichever is inapplicable)' informing them that they have no future and offering an ideal solution – wholesale emigration:

> Sufferers from *hiraeth* (I trust that's right)
> Needn't fret: Patagonia's just hours away
> And there are echoes of home in your Islands'
> New name: Falkland Fawr and Falkland Fach.

Nevertheless, the unmistakable political message of these poems, together with their references to Welsh popular culture (such as Gren, the cartoonist, Terry Holmes and the Arms Park) and their relatively straightforward expression, distinguish them quite strongly from the rest of the poet's output. *The Player Queen's Wife* (1987) does contain two poems from *Rhondda Tenpenn'orth* but is otherwise unconcerned with Wales, while 'DTs on Oliver's Island', with its playful references to Brains SA and Dylan Thomas, is the only poem in *The Oslo Tram* (1991) which betrays its author's origins. A more recent collection, *Almost* (1999), is largely a volume of love poems, except for the final 'Disclaimer' which appears to be a found poem and includes an apparently random set of Welsh words, namely *cig* (meat), *hiraeth* (homesickness), *diolch* (thanks), *mochyn* (pig), *Duw* (god), *twp* (foolish), which are cited as words which 'may offend certain sensibilities . . . Redress, however, is unlikely.' Reynolds is certainly a poet capable of impassioned expression, be that political or amorous, but his more characteristic position is one of wry, ironic detachment, which may, after all, be more representative of the Zeitgeist of the period in which he lives. Indeed, in an age when the whole notion of a stable identity has been called into question, the post-structuralist notion of an individual occupying shifting subject positions, rather than possessing a monolithic identity, may be more pertinent to writers such as Oliver Reynolds.

What, finally, is the significance of these writers who are 'both in and out of the game'? Could they be seen as representatives of what Ned Thomas has called 'contributionism', that is the notion that Wales has a small contribution to make to the great tradition which is English literature? Or is it no longer possible to be straightforwardly Welsh in the sense embraced by Kate Roberts when she refused to escape the 'triple net'? Could it be that we have all – at least partially – escaped the 'triple net' now? In a recent conference on Cultural Criticism, the Cambridge academic Stephen Heath, in attempting to define 'literature', suggested that the role of literature was precisely to refuse to play the same game. He likened literature to the extremely talented African soccer teams in the World Cup: these teams did not eventually win in the tournament because they were unwilling to play strategically, to instrumentalize, but rather continued to play their own, 'other' game, for pure pleasure and joy in the game itself. If the writers whose work I have been discussing do indeed play their own game, then they may also be serving literature itself better than most.

FURTHER READING

Tony Bianchi, 'Aztecs in Troedrhiwgwair', in Ian A. Bell (ed.), *Peripheral Visions* (Cardiff, 1995).

Joseph Cohen (ed.), *The Poetry of Dannie Abse* (London, 1983).

Tony Curtis, *Dannie Abse* (Bridgend, 1985).

James A. Davies, *Leslie Norris* (Bridgend, 1991).

James A. Davies, 'Dannie Abse's autobiographical fiction', *New Welsh Review*, 56 (Summer, 2002), 14–20.

Angela Fish, '"Flight Decks of Experience": the life and writings of Menna Gallie', *New Welsh Review*, 18 (Autumn, 1992), 60–4.

Katie Gramich, 'Cymru or Wales?: Explorations in a divided sensibility', in Susan Bassnett (ed.), *Studying British Culture* (London, 1997), 97–112.

Nicholas LeMesurier, 'Surviving the earthquake: the novels of Bernice Reubens', *New Welsh Review*, 18 (Autumn, 1992), 26–9.

Shaun McCarthy, 'Home from the sea: tradition and innovation in the novels of Alun Richards', *Anglo-Welsh Review*, 78 (1985), 59–71.

Tony Pinkney, *Raymond Williams* (Bridgend, 1991).

Dai Smith, 'A novel history', in Tony Curtis (ed.), *Wales: The Imagined Nation* (Bridgend, 1986).

R. S. Thomas, *Cymru or Wales?* (Llandysul, 1992).

CHAPTER 9

'PULLING YOU THROUGH CHANGES': WELSH WRITING IN ENGLISH BEFORE, BETWEEN AND AFTER TWO REFERENDA

JANE AARON and M. WYNN THOMAS

I

The decade of the sixties was a period of considerable political and cultural upheaval in Wales. Protests against the drowning of Capel Celyn, Cwm Tryweryn, to provide Liverpool with water; Saunders Lewis's warning of the imminent death of the Welsh language and the consequent formation of Cymdeithas yr Iaith Gymraeg (the Welsh Language Society); the first Plaid Cymru MP and the triumphant Labour counter-attack culminating in the literally crowning glory of the Investiture of the Prince of Wales, these were some of the landmark events of a period that partly in consequence saw the establishment of key political and cultural institutions – Secretary of State for Wales, the Welsh Office in Cardiff and the Welsh Arts Council – and these in their turn transformed the scene. Under its remarkable founding Director, Meic Stephens, the Literature Department of the Welsh Arts Council funded and indirectly managed a series of initiatives that profoundly altered the institutional base of Welsh publishing and, by thus altering the conditions of production, in turn significantly influenced output.

One of the most significant new ventures was the founding of what was, in effect, the first English-language publishing house committed to producing the work of Welsh authors, an initiative stemming in part from the success of *Poetry Wales*, a poetry magazine begun by Stephens in the mid-1960s to provide Welsh poets with a 'home base'. And Poetry Wales Press (later Seren Books, who came to produce an increasingly diversified portfolio) facilitated the emergence of a new generation of poets, including Duncan Bush, Tony Curtis, John Davies, Robert Minhinnick and Sheenagh Pugh, all of whom (excluding Minhinnick) went on throughout their rapidly developing careers to use the press as their publishing outlet and were duly rewarded, after several decades of successful production, by having the press publish substantial selections from their work. One hallmark of these poets was the relative conservativeness of their choice of idiom and form, contrasted with the experimental work of Peter Finch that appeared contemporaneously. The roots of this work lay in the array of 'language' poetries (concrete, cut-ups, sound and so on). Flourishing in the British counter-culture of the 1960s and presided over by the likes of Bob Cobbing, this 'alternative' poetry dated right back to the Dadaist period but had been enthusiastically taken up by the European and American post-war avant-garde that featured in Finch's influential *Second Aeon*, a poetry magazine that contrasted dramatically with the *Poetry Wales* of the same period.

The work of the 'Seren poets', as they may conveniently be called, not infrequently had something in common with what, by then, could reasonably be termed a modern 'tradition' of Welsh writing in English. This sense of continuity was sometimes acknowledged by them, as when Tony Curtis published a study of Dannie Abse (a poet whose mature work, quietly cadenced and moderate in idiom – a reaction against Abse's early infatuation with Dylan Thomas – helped set the tone for much of the new poetry) or when Robert Minhinnick paid fond tribute to Glyn Jones, the electrifying verbal and nervous energy of whose early poetry anticipated that of Minhinnick's. But many of the continuities instanced were probably unconscious, and perhaps all the more telling for that. Portrait poems are an obvious recurring feature, another is a poetry of local patriotism – primarily identifying attachment to *bro* (locality) rather than nation. It can take the form of Minhinnick's early 'Eeels at night', where, fishing in the Ffornwg, he watches the 'strange night turbulence of eels' and feels their slipper texture 'like a wound opened in myself' – the wound from which Minhinnick's own powerfully eruptive poetry comes, its inner turbulence narrowly channelled through a constantly pressurized vocabulary and rhythm. But it also appears in Bush's 'Bardot in Grangetown', where the sympathetic identification with a mentally 'simple' trainee mechanic is, in part, Bush's expression of imaginative solidarity with the whole underclass of workers whose silenced history is so memorably recorded in 'Navvies' and other poems from *Salt* (1985). For many of these writers, in keeping with their predecessors in the 'tradition', a place is also a people, and a people is the working class of an industrial south Wales the desolating decline of which in the post-war period of savage deindustrialization is repeatedly elegized in some of their best poetry – indirectly through the fairground scenes of Minhinnick's sequences 'The Resort' ('our culture has its midden on the sands') and 'Fairground Music' (where the dizzying speed of modern changes is conveyed through the Big Wheel ride, 'the whole town's like a film reeled back/ As we rush towards the ground'), and directly in his portraits of a society of drifters ('YOPS' and 'Looters'). A sense of dislocation is not only conveyed, but scrupulously explored, in all its psychological subtleties, right back to its social roots in John Davies's important early sequence 'The Visitor's Book', and many years later the same experience is ambitiously, and revealingly, worked out in his excellent volume *Flight Patterns* (1991), at the centre of which is the image of transit between Wales and the USA.

The USA has, in fact, been a very important presence in the work of several of the Seren writers, its complex appeal appropriately examined at the very pivotal centre of Bush's *Midway* (1998), the violence at its core powerfully anatomized in Curtis's 'The Deerslayers' (1978), where the obvious debt to American idiom and poetics (of all the Seren poets, Curtis is the one who has profited most from the cunningly measured and nuanced outspokenness of some modes of American writing) is a silent admission of the fascination of a society that is nevertheless also repellent in its brash, vulgar, unheeding power. The essence of violently metamorphosing modernity worldwide can almost be smelt in the States, the heady aroma of burning rubber and singeing flesh that Curtis's imagination inhales in 'The Death of Richard Beattie-Seaman in the Belgian Grand Prix, 1939' and that wafts through so much of his poetry whenever his awareness is particularly heightened. This excitation by points of violent physical, sensuous and psychological collision partly explains his almost obsessive attraction to the events of the Second World War which he is too young actually to remember, and it appears even in the fine poem 'Lines at Barry', where he traces his own personal history of family migration:

> Three lifetimes, two wars running to this moment –
> and none of this is unique, this telling,

this drawing from memory of lines
where, steely-silver, what we are now
touches everything that made us,
and is dangerous, and shines.

The America of Curtis and of Bush is very different from that of
Nigel Jenkins, published not by Seren but by Gomer, whose study
of Nixon's post-Vietnam USA, *Circus* (1979), is an early, typically
satirizing, example of Jenkins's misgivings about the country's
cultural imperialism viewed from the vantage point of a poet who,
unlike most of the Seren group, is openly committed to writing a
re-educative poetry that will instill pride in a 'colonized', culturally
amnesiac Welsh people. Jenkins shares with several of the Seren
poets, however, a radical left-wing sense of international responsibilities (again in a strong 'Anglo-Welsh' tradition) ranging from
nuclear disarmament through women's rights to environmental
issues. One of the most valuable features of his work, as it has
developed over three decades, has been its manner of successfully
blending some of the rhetorical practices of such politically
committed American poets as Gary Snyder and Denise Levertov
with indigenous Welsh modes of writing, deriving in part from the
bardd gwlad tradition of serving a community by producing
topical, occasional pieces that are entertaining, historical, caustic,
reflective or panoramic in vision by turns, somewhat in the manner
of two of Jenkins's favourite models, John Tripp and Harri Webb.
It is the kind of exhilarating variety of approach that makes his
multifaceted collection *Ambush* (1998) distinctive and noteworthy.
    Whereas Jenkins writes out of a total commitment to the culture
of Wales, Sheenagh Pugh prefers to place herself at deliberately
awkward angles to any collective concerns. Hers is a terse, tart
style of dissenting witness, as she carefully polices her own lyrical
impulses. Her work is characterized by a wryness that conveys
the awryness of her vision – she sees not the absurdity of
McGonagall's verse, but the pathos of his failed attempts to
communicate his humane vision; not only the cruelty of torturers
but the way it can disconcertingly coexist with tenderness. She is a
confirmed disturber of the peace of a world that conceals its own
casual, ubiquitous violence under verbal and conceptual clichés. It
seems appropriate that some of her best poems come in the form
of translations from the German of poetry written during the

devastations of the Thirty Years War, as it is that she shows sympathy for the callously discarded – even for the discarded words that litter our dictionaries. Her poetry is like the art of the studiously remote cameraman:

> You are the itch
> in others; you can make them
> see clear, if only you watch
>
> exactly; if you record
> just what happened. Do not be tempted
> to turn the camera inward:
> your stricken looks are no concern
> of the public's. They need the word
>
> on what you saw, not how
> you felt.

Hers is the principled awkwardness she ascribes to her wished-for alter ego, Christopher Marlowe: 'Just wish I'd been half as dangerous,/ as quick, as insufferable to all/ who didn't like to be pricked into thinking.'

Pugh's misgivings about her own lyricism contrasts with the trust shown in such an impulse by Gillian Clarke, perhaps the most accomplished 'new' poet of the period since the early 1970s. A relatively late beginner, owing to her failure, as a young woman and then as a young mother, to find sufficient models in her own culture to reinforce her secret wish to be a poet, Clarke emerged in the 1970s as seemingly already quite a mature talent, her turning to poetry more or less coinciding with her removal from the Cardiff of her birth to the west Wales countryside to which her Welsh-speaking father's people belonged. From the beginning she was producing a beautifully intuitive, sensuously exploratory poetry in what she herself came to regard as a 'female' mode of writing, feeling her way forward through language towards forms of meaning inseparable from the shapes, colours, forms and textures of her verse. It is therefore no wonder that she is a passionate lover of the visual arts, of painters such as Georgia O'Keefe, who 'walks out of the rectangles/ of hard, crowded America/ and floods the skies over southern plains/ with carmine, scarlet,/ with the swirl of poppy-silk'. That is exactly how Clarke's own feminine and feminizing imagination works: her writing is a kind of magnificat for a world whose sumptuous strangeness is brilliantly reclaimed and proclaimed in the measured intemperateness of her poetry.

Clarke's lyricism has if anything grown more assured, her expression of it more economical, with the passage of time. Although her rapt affirmations may, on occasion, be less darkly nuanced in their phrasing, more unguardedly blithe, and correspondingly less compelling in some of her work, at her best she is the most intensely and radiantly sensuous of writers. Clarke discovers, in the very act of registering sense experiences, a means of sharply defining the way in which they nourish the mind and amplify intelligence, and such is the radiance of some of her writing that it makes her a notable laureate of light, accepting alike of its benign lucidity, its burning ferocity and its chill pallors. 'The imagination's caverns cry for symbols,/ shout to the hot sun in the present tense', she writes, and out of the passionate immediacy of intercourse between her mind's dark caverns and the blaze of universal being come poems about animals and birds and wind-mills, about childhood and childbirth and children, about Port Talbot and Tadzekistan, about the rural landscapes of Llŷn and Ceredigion and about the urbanized landscape of south-east Wales. She is also one of the few contemporary poets to have devised convincing ways of sustaining the lyrical impulse over a longer distance. In this respect, 'Letter from a Far Country', 'Cofiant', and 'The King of Britain's Daughter' remain three of her most commanding achievements.

For then young poets such as Clarke and Jenkins, committed to safeguarding Wales's cultural distinctiveness, the cultural and political rhythm of the 1970s must have seemed depressingly similar to that of the 1960s. In that previous decade, an exciting period, when the culture seemed to be mobilizing itself for significant advance, ended with the dead end of the Investiture; and in the 1970s, years of confident anticipation of political progress came to a sickening conclusion with the anti-devolution vote in the 1979 referendum, an event that so disheartened some senior writers that they were silenced for a period, and a historical watershed memorably recorded in a striking elegy for a people, Jim Jones and Jon Dressel's co-authored bilingual text *Cerddi Ianws* (1979).

II

'It's a tragedy, what happened on March 1st . . . and you can't expect your poets to be the same again,' said John Tripp of the 1979 referendum on Welsh devolution, in which the 'Yes' voters failed to gain more than 20 per cent of the vote. While some rallied defiantly around the concept of self-government for Wales, despair at this catastrophic close to their hopes for Welsh independence is clearly reflected after 1979 in the work of other Welsh writers in English – novelists as well as poets – who had espoused the nationalist cause. Emyr Humphreys, for example, incorporates the trauma into the plot of *Salt of the Earth* (1985), the first post-1979 novel he published in the 'Land of the Living' sequence. In this novel, the two characters who had previously most strongly represented Welsh nationalist hopes both come to sorry ends; Val Gwyn, incarcerated in an isolation hospital with tuberculosis, has his disease confirmed as terminal, and Enid More dies in child-birth. Although her child survives, thus representing some symbolic hope of revival, Enid's death remains a devastating shock for her friend Amy, who declares: 'I've lost the best part of me and I can't believe it.' *Salt of the Earth* is set in the Wales of the 1930s but its characters refer to their unhappy nation in language highly reminiscent of the metaphors of despair adopted by 1980s writers. Early in the novel, Professor Gwilym, for example, pronounces judgement on the Welsh:

> A people who have lost their sense of independence have lost the capacity to stand on their own feet. They will let anything happen. They have abrogated the right of decision to a Higher Authority. The serf mentality fears freedom more than death itself.

His references to the fatal 'serf mentality' of the Welsh parallel those of Welsh-language novelists and poets of the 1980s, like Angharad Tomos or Gerallt Lloyd Owen, who also felt that the results of the 1979 referendum had given them good reason to fear that contemporary Wales was more afraid of freedom than of death itself.

'This country/ of failure' is similarly mourned in R. S. Thomas's post-1979 poems. In some of his 1970s poems, such as 'The Small Country', Thomas, ameliorating his earlier harsh pronouncements on a sick nation, had allowed himself to feel some hope for a Wales animated by the language movement but, after the referendum vote, the Welsh in his poems are once again 'the lost people'. In 'Perspectives', he sees modern Wales as a nation fallen into autumnal decline, whose only promise of spring relies on borrowing artificial – and, to Wales, destructive – energies from England:

> such the autumn

> of a people! Whose spring
> is it sleeps in a glass
> bulb, ready to astonish us
> with its brilliance? Bring
> on the dancing girls
> of the future, the swaying
> pylons with their metal
> hair bickering towards England.

For Thomas, the English-language speakers of Wales constituted in particular 'the lost'. While Welsh-language speakers still had the ancient tongue to fight for, their monoglot brethren had become 'exiles within/ our own country', eating 'our bread/ at a pre-empted table'; 'We have our signposts/ but they are in another tongue.' As a nation, the Welsh had voted themselves out of existence, and were left with no centre apart from the language around which resistant forces could regroup. The concept of a distinct Welsh identity was so shadowy that there seemed to be little of substance left to which aspiring artists might anchor themselves. It was feared that Welsh writers in English, after 1979, would give up the struggle of upholding and defending an amorphous identity which dared not stake its claim to independent life, and turn towards England for their subject matter. Indeed, in 1985 Harri Webb, with his characteristic directness, described Welsh writers in English as lost to their country to such a degree that their work had become of little account. 'I don't believe that writing in English about Wales matters very much any more,' he said: 'Anglo-Welsh literature is, more or less, a load of rubbish. It has only marginal relevance to Wales now.' As is shown in his *Collected Poems*, it was a remark made in the context of having realized he was himself finished as a writer.

But if Webb's remark also had more general application, then we have a puzzle, if not a mystery, on our hands. For, looking back at this period today, with the hindsight of a post-1997 perspective, it is evident that the majority English-speaking communities of Wales cannot have been as 'lost' to their country during the inter-referendum years as these devastated campaigners of the 1979 referendum would have us believe. The 30 per cent swing which, by a narrow margin, won the second, 1997, Welsh devolution referendum for the 'Yes' voters was more marked in English-speaking south Wales than it was in the majority Welsh-speaking communities of the north and west. Neath Port Talbot's percentage of 'Yes' voters (66.3 per cent) was the highest in Wales, greater than that of Gwynedd (63.9 per cent) or Carmarthen (65.3 per cent). The numbers of pro-devolutionary voters in the south Wales valleys generally, with Rhondda Cynon Taf at 58.5 per cent and Merthyr Tydfil at 57.9 per cent, were commensurate with Ceredigion's at 58.5 per cent. And those of Caerphilly (54.7 per cent), Bridgend (54.1 per cent) and even Blaenau Gwent (55.8 per cent) were higher than Anglesey's at 50.7 per cent. Compared to South, West and Mid Glamorgan's average of 17.3 per cent 'Yes' voters in 1979, these figures stand as evidence that a change of attitude of major political significance took place in the pre-dominantly English-speaking communities of Wales during the 1980s and 1990s.

That such a fundamental shift should not in any way be reflected in English-language culture of Wales during those same years would be strange indeed. It would, for example, contradict the Marxist categorization of literature as part of the social and political superstructure which reflects changes in the economic base and records the emergence of new alignments. Rather, we would expect to be able to trace in the literature of the inter-referendum years the progressive, if embattled, rise of a new sense of Welsh identity, and a resurgence of belief in the nation and its capacity to govern its own affairs. And yet it is true that no single author or recognizable new movement did emerge, in terms of critical recognition at least, to revolutionize the mindset of Welsh writers in English between the two referendums, and challenge the viewpoint of the post-1979 jeremiads. All the same, under a cover of desolation and seeming disarray, it may be that something resembling a new spring was in process, and it is our purpose, in the next part of this chapter, to explore that possibility. In the final part, we turn to the English-language writing of contemporary, post-devolution Wales, to consider in what ways, if any, the establishment of a National Assembly of Wales is affecting current cultural developments.

III

When R. S. Thomas, in 'Perspectives', spoke of 'the dancing girls of the future . . . bickering towards England', he did not, of course, mean to refer to the new generation of women writers who came to the fore in Welsh writing in English during the 1980s. Yet, at the time when Gillian Clarke, Hilary Llewellyn-Williams and others, first started to publish their work, many did see them as but the mouthpieces of an internationalist women's movement, with little to offer Wales except an indictment of the patriarchal element in its traditions. By today, however, a number of critics have recognized that the work of these writers functioned so as to make room for women within a male-dominated Welsh culture which had previously seemed reluctant to include the feminine. While Clarke's seminal 'Letter from a Far Country', for example, did indeed put on record the manner in which women in Wales had historically been subordinated, it also stressed the fact that Wales had always been the land of our mothers as well as fathers:

> First see a landscape. Hill country,
> essentially feminine,
> the sea not far off. Its blues
> widen the sky. Bryn Isaf
> down there in the crook of the hill
> under Calfaria's single eye.
> My grandmother might have lived there.
> Any farm. Any chapel.
> Father and minister, on guard,
> close the white gates to hold her.

The very landscape of Wales is here presented as feminine, with its hilly curves and crevasses, and the sea – traditionally associated with the feminine – not far off. Bryn Isaf, the representative homestead, under the eye of the chapel in the same way that the grandmothers were guarded by their menfolk, is also by implication personified as female. The suggestion is that Wales, as a country and as a social construct, has always been shaped by female as well as male forces. When these women poets of the 1980s rewrote Welsh myth from the point of view of its female characters, as in Hilary Llewellyn-Williams's 'The song of Blodeuwedd on a May morning'; or gave voice to Dafydd ap Gwilym's hitherto silent lovers, as in Clarke's 'Dyddgu replies to Dafydd'; or re-created the enthusiasms of those numerous female converts who helped to bring about the Welsh Nonconformist revivals, as in Ruth Bidgood's 'Banquet', they were making Welshness a concept with which more women could identify. The death throes of the sexual double-standard in Wales was also celebrated in such texts as Penny Windsor's two collections *Dangerous Women* (1987) and *Like Oranges* (1989), both published by the Welsh feminist publishers Honno Press which, since its establishment in 1987, has done much to further women's writing in Wales. Women novelists also undertook the task of reclaiming Welsh culture for women: Mary Jones's *Resistance* (1985) sympathetically interpolates the Welsh-language movement from the point of view of an initially alienated English-speaking female in-comer; and Siân James's *Storm at Arberth* (1994) resurrects the power of the Celtic mother-goddesses in a modern comedy. By inserting women's perspectives into Welsh writing in English, such texts helped to create a Wales for which, in 1997, women could vote without feeling alienated; they were no longer required to choose between loyalty to their gender or to their nation. Far from distracting attention from the needs of Wales, therefore, or attacking the already fragile concept of Welshness from an alien perspective, these writers were rather expanding the idea of Wales to make it more inclusive of the female 50 per cent of the populace.

Another omnipresent concern of women writers in 1980s Wales, and one not unconnected with the emphasis on women's experi-ence and the construction of Welsh female identity, was eco-politics: the importance of safeguarding the fragile balance of natural life was a theme central to such collections as Sheenagh Pugh's *Earth Studies and Other Voyages* (1982), and Christine Evans's *Cometary Phases* (1989). In the works of Evans, Llewellyn-Williams, Bidgood and Clarke, this concern was evoked primarily in reflective poems on the rural Welsh landscape in which all four poets chose to make their homes, though none of them had been reared there. The 'new nature' poetry (as Gillian Clarke termed it) which they produced was imbued with a scientific respect for, and fascination with, the interconnected patterning of living cycles. Traditional Welsh ways of life which had hitherto worked in close connection with such patterns were respected in these poems as having a wisdom of their own, more pertinent than ever in the modern 1980s context of accumulating warheads and nuclear threat. When Jean Earle, for example, describes the act of cleaning her step, 'rubbing with bluestone in the old way', as

> My scour against the world's indifference
> To important symbols – the common roof,
> Likeness of patterns,

the mundane and stereotypically female domestic task becomes imbued with a spirit of resistance in the face of contemporary negligence which has the effect of endearing readers to that 'common roof' under which the bluestone was traditionally employed – that is, working- or peasant-class Wales, with its old values now treasured in a new light. Similarly, when Ruth Bidgood, in such poems as 'Heol y Mwyn (Mine Road)' and 'Slate-quarry, Penceulan', reminds us (with an intensity which no doubt came from the fact that she, like Earle, was reared in the coal-mining villages of south Wales) of the threatening hollows carved out by defunct industries under the sunny surface of the Welsh landscape, she too is evoking a particularly Welsh historical resistance to the exploitative forces which undermine the security of both human life and nature. In fiction too, Glenda Beagan in such short stories as 'Shining Stones' from her collection *The Medlar Tree* (1992) or Catherine Merriman in her novel *State of Desire* (1996), in which the chief protagonist plays a central role in her community's fight against a local open-cast mine, show women calling upon traditional Welsh values of community and respect for nature to resist contemporary threats to the environment.

The association of green values with the peace movement, and in particular the Greenham Common campaign – started as it was in September 1981 by Anne Pettit from her smallholding in south Wales – is also strongly present in the work of these writers.

Throughout the 1980s the peace camp at Greenham served as a potent symbol for many Welsh women, English- and Welsh-speaking alike; there is barely a Welsh woman poet of this era who does not have a Greenham poem in her œuvre. Not only women writers but many male artists too, gave their primary political allegiance to peace and ecological movements in 1980s Wales. Tony Curtis, in his poem series 'The Deerslayers' and poetry collection *War Voices* (1995), explores the dehumanizing consequences of purposeless destructions of natural life and the defilements of war. Robert Minhinnick, founder of Friends of the Earth Cymru, incorporated that movement's politics into such literary works as his poetry collection *Life Sentences* (1983) and his volume of essays *Badlands* (1996). The success of CND (Campaign for Nuclear Disarmament) Cymru in making Wales the first nuclear-free zone in Europe in 1982 was commemorated in the work of various poets. Nigel Jenkins, for example, has a poem describing a CND rally at Brawdy, a military base in rural Pembrokeshire, where attempts were made to establish a Greenham Common-style peace camp. His lines demonstrate the way in which the politics of the peace movement, combined with eco-politics, was during the 1980s given a specifically Welsh twist:

> Though today we're a thousand
> there's none living or dead who doesn't stand
>   at this fence,
> head-on some, backs turned most, suiciding softly
>   in booze and t.v. . . .
> There are birds here I still can't name,
> flowers in hedgewall the world has forgotten.
> Time, before we go . . .
> to stand & hold, *yn llygad haul*,
> to vision through sunmist out & beyond of
> – come, gone, come again – a
>   ship riding.

The protesters here are seen as standing in the breach and upholding the green heritage of Wales, in the name of ancient Welsh traditions suggested by the quotation from the eisteddfod prayer in which the archdruid pleads for peace *yn llygad haul*, that is, 'in the eye of the sun'. This prayer, devised by Iolo Morganwg in the late eighteenth century, fuses Christianity with elements of the old Druidic religion and is used here to suggest that their peculiar and distinctive heritage has marked the Welsh out as a green and peace-loving nation, with a history of living close to the earth and attentive to its needs. This image of Wales was markedly successful in the important task of drawing many of the numerous immigrants who settled in rural Wales during the 1980s into political sympathy with the indigenous people of the area. Having come to Wales for its greenness, they identified with the political concept of a green Wales, demonstrating the truth of the maxim 'small is beautiful', at that time propagated by Plaid Cymru. The official support which the Green Party in Cardiganshire and North Pembrokeshire gave Plaid Cymru candidate Cynog Dafis helped to win him a parliamentary seat in the 1992 general election, and set the pattern for an integration of political interests which did much to encourage green-minded incomers to vote 'Yes' for Wales in 1997. Once again, therefore, the preoccupation of the representative Welsh writer in English with issues not apparently directly related to Wales – in this case, with green and peace politics – worked ultimately not to divert attention from Welsh needs but to expand the concept of Welshness so that a new and numerically significant group of voters could experience their concerns as incorporated within it.

This new coalition of interests was, of course, unintentionally much fortified by the impact on Wales of Margaret Thatcher, and her monetary and neo-imperialist politics. The 1982 Falklands war, in which a number of Welsh soldiers were killed, was a grim reminder of British imperialism, and of Wales's ambivalent relation to it. The ironies of that war – that Welsh soldiers should die fighting a people within whom were numbered the descendants of Patagonians who had gone to Argentina in the first place in order to escape the pressures of English cultural colonialism in nineteenth-century Wales – exacerbated anti-imperialist feelings in Wales. In his 'Elegy for the Welsh Dead, in the Falkland Islands, 1982', Tony Conran drew attention to these ironies by evoking the sixth-century Welsh poem, *Y Gododdin*, in which Aneirin mourned those who died fighting the Anglo-Saxon invaders at Catraeth. Conran's elegy begins with a translation of Aneirin's lines, then elides the present-day Falkland dead with the *Gododdin*'s lost warriors:

> Men went to Catraeth . . .

> . . . from the streets and byways of Wales,
> Dragons of Aberdare, Denbigh and Neath –
> Figment of empire, whore's honour, held them.
> Forty-three at Catraeth died for our dregs.

The poem served as a reminder of the manner in which Wales's history had been one of resistance to invasion, of defeat and subsequent colonization, rather than of imperialism, and functioned to unite those antagonized by the neo-imperialism of the Thatcher regime more strongly with Wales as a more sinned against than sinning alternative. In a series of works produced in the early 1990s, *Castles: Variations on an Original Theme* (1993), *All Hallows: Symphony in 3 Movements* (1995) and *A Gwynedd Symphony*, first performed in 1996, Conran strove to create in his readers a sense of Welsh citizenship, through reminding them of the intricate politics of their past, not least the 1979 referendum vote which he describes as 'a green force aborted'. But the more successful resistance movements of Welsh history also feature in his poems; Rebecca and her daughters, for example, are remembered in a poem from the 'All Hallows' sequence, dedicated to the memory of the artist Paul Davies. When the old blind crone – Rebecca in disguise – taps at the obstructive toll-gate with her stick and cries, 'there's something put up here/ Across the road, I cannot go on', her 'daughters' reply:

> Nothing should bar your path, old Mother –
> Not a great gate, nor bolted custom,
> Nor opportunities taken away,
> The theft that is wealth, or dumb respect.

In fact, of course, during the 1980s a great many opportunities were taken away from the 'old Mother' – Wales – as Thatcherism exerted its grip on the heavy industries and on the trade union movement. Support for the 1984–5 miners' strike, and the anger generated by the pit closures that preceded and followed it, eroded 'dumb respect' for the status quo, and lessened any sense of fellow-feeling with an English populace which bafflingly kept voting back into power a Tory government which seemed intent on bringing

Wales to its knees. This anger found expression in the pamphlets of the Red Poets' Society, with their stated aims of 'turning the world on its head with Welsh socialist poetry', and giving voice to an industrial community once again, as in the 1920s and 1930s, bereft of its occupation and plunged into unemployment. In his dialect poems, Mike Jenkins, the editor of the Red Poets' Society, literally adopted the south Wales voice to express the region's plight:

> we're staggerin down'n alley
> lookin f' coins in-a dark
> an the ground's all manky
> with-a spew of industry
> slippin us, limbs wheelin.
> The las pit in Wales,
> las red kite in-a country.
> Slike a fault-line runnin
> right through ower omes:
> this int no vandalism
> it's an act of atrocity.

In experimenting with dialect in such a manner, Mike Jenkins emphasizes the difference between the people of the south Wales valleys and their Whitehall rulers. They may ostensibly be speaking the same language – English – but the valleys people do so with such a difference that they are marked as 'other' as soon as they open their mouths. That otherness becomes in Jenkins's work a voice which has just as much of a legitimate right to be translated into poetry as any other form of verbal communication, and a difference in which one can take pride, for its resilience and its refusal easily to accept humiliations.

The resilience of the south Wales industrial communities also found expression in fiction during the 1980s. While two earlier exponents of the social realist traditions of Welsh working-class fiction, Alun Richards and Ron Berry, may not have published many novels during the post 1979 period, the publication of their autobiographies and collected short stories helped keep alive a tradition of committed writing – for and of a community by a member of that community – which now was passed on to a new generation of novelists. The 1984–5 strike was fictionalized, from the miners' point of view, in such novels as Roger Granelli's *Dark*

Edge (1997), while Christopher Meredith's 1988 novel *Shifts*, on the 1977 closures at the steelworks in Ebbw Vale, fleshed out in fiction the manifold social consequences of the demise of the heavy industries of Wales. For all their primary concern with portraying the impact of industrial closures and the miners' strike on the predominantly male workforce, both of these novels also reflected the manner in which economic change affected female as well as male experience. *Shifts'* central female character, Jude, goes through changes which finally persuade her that she has to define herself, without tying her identity to that of either her husband or her lover. Accordingly, she serves as representative of that generation of valleys women whom Gwyn Alf Williams described as experiencing 'shifts' in their lives of revolutionary proportions, as the collapse of the heavy industries affected the gendered patterns of employment, and as the second wave of the feminist movement made its impact felt. Similarly, Susan, the heroine of *Dark Edge*, represents the 1980s generation of valleys women who won more than they had initially bargained for as a consequence of their activity in support of the miners' strike. Defying her policeman husband, Susan joins the women's support groups, and this move out of the confinement of her increasingly violent marriage eventually gives her the strength to leave her husband. Her politicization as a result of the strike becomes a feminist as well as a socialist awakening.

Commenting on the emergence of feminist attitudes amongst women involved in the 1984–5 miners' strike, the post-colonial theorist Homi K. Bhabha, in *The Location of Culture* (1994), cites their characteristic movement, from traditional, trade-union and male-focused socialism to a socialism now including feminism, as a definitive example of 'the hybrid moment of political change'. 'The transformational value of change,' Bhabha suggests, 'lies in the rearticulation, or translation, of elements that are *neither the One* (unitary working class) *nor the Other* (the politics of gender) *but something else besides*, which contests the terms and territories of both.' 'What does a working woman put first?' he asks. 'Which of her identities is the one that determines her political choices?' In Wales, women's recorded responses to their involvement in the strike's support groups indicate that yet another term must be added to their ongoing negotiation of values and identities during this period: nationalist, as well as feminist and socialist, allegiances were reanimated by the strike. A number of the women interviewed by Jill Miller in her book *You Can't Kill the Spirit: Women in a Welsh Mining Valley* (1986) suggest, in their testimonies, that they were consciously fighting for the future of their nation, as well as their class and their gender. Gwyneth, for example, says:

> The [women's group] gave me a lot more confidence to express my feelings, thoughts and ideals. My ideas became much clearer, and as a result I was more determined than ever that we shouldn't and wouldn't give in to this government which was trying to destroy a community that took generations to build . . . I'm proud to be a miner's wife, I'm proud to be part of that community. I'm proud to be Welsh too.

Dark Edge suggests that Welsh working-class males, as well as their female counterparts, were similarly made more aware of their nationalist allegiances through their involvement in the strike. At the close of the novel, the striking miner Edwin, walking the hills above his valley town, feels himself to be 'stepping over the backbone of his land. All its tortured history lay under his feet . . . And it *was* Wales, not just "the valley". It had always lain close to the surface, chipping away at his consciousness.' Energized by this nationalist consciousness-raising, Edwin determines 'to make another attempt to learn the language that should have been his by right', as a 'sign-post' of the 'hybrid moment of political change' that he is undergoing.

Christopher Meredith's *Shifts* closes similarly, with its central male character, the soon-to-be-made-redundant steelworker, Keith, determining to learn Welsh in the attempt to hold on to a sense of identity in the face of the incipient collapse of his known community. 'How we knew ourselves/ Was how we laboured' says Robert Minhinnick of the south Wales identity in his 1983 poem 'Smith's Garage'; but these post 1984–5 fictions show Welsh men and women attempting to get to know themselves through their national rather than work identities. Their decision to learn Welsh make both Keith and Edwin representative of a popular movement within the valleys communities of their generation. The 1970s and 1980s saw the establishment, by grass-roots demand, of Welsh-language primary and secondary schools, and adult learning classes, throughout the valleys: between the 1981 and

1991 censuses, the numbers of Welsh speakers in South and Mid
Glamorgan, and in Islwyn in Gwent, went up for the first time in
the twentieth century. In one scene from *Shifts*, Keith explores a
condemned old house in his neighbourhood, and finds in it a card
dating from the early years of the twentieth century, the back of
which is covered with pencilled notes. Looking 'urgently' at these
notes,

> Keith felt in the smashed building the presence of the dead people who
> had moved through it, treated it as their own briefly. This could be
> something like contact. He smiled as he held the card at the darkening
> window. This Jonah, trawled from the wet darkness was being brought
> into a fading light, and though he had words, he said nothing. The
> notes Keith held were in a language that was his own, but that he could
> not understand.

The Welsh language is not being presented here as some essential
transmitter of ethnic values; Keith doesn't yet understand it, so his
satisfaction at finding the card could hardly come from that.
Rather it serves as a marker of a difference and a marker of a
refusal to give up on difference and accept the loss of a distinctive
representative voice. To this marker of difference Keith knows
enough to attach the label 'Welsh', and hence 'his own'.

These fictions illustrate the manner in which, pre-1997, 'hybrid
moments of political change' led – in the south Wales valleys in
particular – to a shift in popular attitudes towards the Welsh-
language issue, making it a force which could now serve to unite,
rather than as hitherto to divide, the south and north of west
Wales. By the close of the 1980s, the sharpest concerns were not
the Welsh linguistic division, but the repeated humiliations that
Wales had undergone during the Thatcher years, humiliations that
also served as a reminder of the exploitative manner in which the
Welsh workforce had also been abused during earlier epochs of the
twentieth century. A new breed of dramatists, as well as poets and
novelists, began to flesh out the ills of contemporary Wales, and
stage the cultural effects of the attrition of those heavy industries
on which so much of the Welsh identity, as well as the Welsh
economy, had for a century and a half been based. Ed Thomas,
from Abercraf in the Tawe valley, illustrated in his play *House of
America* (1988) the disastrous effects on his generation of

unemployment, and the loss of past identity patterns based on work. The only chance for employment for the two brothers, Sid and Boyo, comes from the open-cast mine newly established in their neighbourhood, and when they fail to get a job in that they are left with little hope for the future:

> SID: They used to say I was too young, now we're too bastard old. That was the last chance I'm giving them to give me, Sid Lewis, a job. They've wrecked my plans and I've got to do something about it.
> BOYO: They were Mickey Mouse jobs anyway, a dog could have done them.
> SID: Anything with no brain and a coat could have done them, that's the problem, Boyo, everything round here is Mickey Mouse, wus. Division four, small time, second class toys.
> BOYO: The only way to look at it is to forget about it . . .
> SID: I tell you, I've been born in the wrong country, I have . . . I wish I'd been born someone else, somewhere else.

In his alienation, Sid elaborates an escapist fantasy world for himself and his gullible sister Gwenny, in which they inhabit the Beat America of Jack Kerouac and his lover, with what Thomas shows to be disastrous effects for their sense of reality. Looking elsewhere to other alien cultures for solace can only lead ultimately to an increased despair with the realities of the here and now in Wales. The intended effect of such a play as *House of America* is to heighten and make more overt the felt need for a specifically Welsh cultural and political solution to Welsh problems.

This process of accumulative resentment of perceived humiliations is interestingly dramatized in another of the works of Wales's new generation of playwrights, Ian Rowlands's one-act monologue *Marriage of Convenience*, first performed in 1996. In this play, set on the day of the royal wedding between Prince Charles and Lady Diana, a lad from the south Wales valleys turns his back on the street festivities going on in his neighbourhood and spends the day on the hills, with friends from his Welsh-language school. But when he returns home, his stepfather who has always disparaged his mother's decision to send him to the Welsh school, attacks him for absenting himself. The stepfather says,

> 'Graham and Barbara, Alan and Doreen, the whole bloody street kept asking, "Where is he?" What the hell were we supposed to say eh? That

you were on a fascist picnic? His nibs were lording it up on top of an hill with all his Welshie friends 'cause his family are not good enough for him? . . .' My mother grabbed his arm, 'Let me go woman, it's about time someone taught your fucking son a lesson.' The lesson began when his fist landed in my face . . . I made no effort to free myself from his grip, I allowed him to stamp his impotence upon my face, realising that each blow hurt my mother much more than it could ever hurt me. I conceded the battle for the sake of overall victory.

The next day the stepfather is forced to leave, the beating he administered to her son having finally turned the mother against him. The son has won his freedom through accepting blows, sufficient to gain for him the sympathy of his mother and alienate her from her spouse, just as it could be said that Wales, that 'old Mother', won her modicum of freedom in 1997 through the fact that enough of her people were sufficiently antagonized by the blows Wales received during the Thatcher years to vote for her greater independence. The losses of the Falklands War, the threat represented by Britain's nuclear armaments policy, the humiliations of the miners' strike and, above all, the closure of the heavy industries were all blows to Welsh pride as well as to the Welsh economy, and served as bitter reminders of similar past assaults. In 1997 it was clear to just sufficient of the Welsh voters that such a stepfather as the English administration had proved itself to be could no longer be trusted to rule the roost at home for the best. The 30 per cent swing towards the 'Yes' campaign during the second Welsh devolution referendum cannot but have been fuelled by resentment at these repeated blows, a resentment which may not have led to open hostilities, except during the year of the miners' strike, but which nevertheless succeeded in uniting the Welsh against the status quo in just sufficient numbers to vote in devolution.

By their consciousness-raising activities of imaging and analysing the political and cultural changes which took place during the inter-referendum years, Welsh writers in English contributed to the 1997 result. They may have appeared to work deviously, often pursuing concerns and goals which seemed unrelated to Welsh needs, but those concerns succeeded in drawing in new adherents to an expanded and more inclusive image of Wales, in which a more varied and heterogeneous percentage of the Welsh

population could feel they had a stake. The devious route they
took is suggested in a poem by an incomer to Wales, Chris
Torrance, who did much in the 1980s and 1990s to further the
development of Welsh writing in English by his teaching as well as
his example. In his as yet uncompleted magnum opus *The Magic
Door*, by marrying ancient Welsh symbols with snapshots of contemporary Wales, he too, like Tony Conran, succeeds in pulling
off associations between the old Wales and the new which serve to
affiliate mixed loyalties. His poem 'The Fox' in *The Book of Heat*
(1996) describes a peculiarly Welsh type of recalcitrant resistance:

> I am
> Brychan,
> the Red-Haired
> of Garth Madryn
>
> I am a fox
> I retire
> to a lair . . .
> I like
> to have cover
>
> I
> am Brychan, foxy
> light of foot,
> maybe a little
> short of stature . . .
>
> pulling on the rope
> over the wall
> I am the fox
> pulling you through changes

'Pulling on the rope/ over the wall', the red-haired Celtic fox
escapes from the prison of his past, while still managing to avoid
any more damagingly direct confrontation with his former
captors. Through devious means, not always at the times
recognized as such, Welsh writers in English also, like the fox,
helped to pull the Welsh people 'through changes' during the
period 1979 to 1997. As well as recording the various experiences
of Wales between the two referenda on Welsh devolution, their
work contributed to the construction of that more expansive and

heterogeneous image of Wales which finally persuaded sufficient of the Welsh to vote it 'over the wall' and into a more autonomous existence in 1997.

IV

In 2001, the London-based and London-identified writer Iain Sinclair dedicated his latest publication, the novel *Landor's Tower*, to 'the poet of *The Magic Door*'. A collage of the heterogeneous past and present cultural influences which go to make up the character of the Welsh border, linked together in this fiction by a detective, or quest, plot, *Landor's Tower* is the first of Sinclair's many novels to be set in Wales, and also the first in which he has announced himself, on the book's jacket, as 'born in Wales'. With its references to the two-faced 'cussedness of the fore-lock tugging, piss-in-your-boots Welsh', the book can hardly be said to cast lustre on the Welsh character, yet its publication is exemplary of a number of new developments within the field of Welsh writing in English. Firstly, it serves as an example of the recent increase of interest amongst mainstream and highbrow English presses in publishing books located in Wales, a change which has occurred alongside a rise in productivity within the publishing scene in Wales itself. Secondly, that Sinclair, born in Maesteg, Glamorgan, of Scottish/Welsh parentage, should in 2001 for the first time bill himself as Welsh-born can be seen as representative of a currently greater readiness amongst cultural practitioners on the UK stage to acknowledge their Welshness, or indeed in some cases to choose and forge for themselves, through their cultural practice, a Welsh connection not straightforwardly given to them in terms of their ethnicity or location. And thirdly, *Landor's Tower*'s focus on the past and present heterogeneity of Welsh border culture is illustrative of an increased authorial interest in exploring the hybridity and multifacetedness of Wales, rather than searching for a unitary and homogeneous Welsh identity. The prime catalyst for these current cultural changes would appear to be the establishment of the National Assembly for Wales.

For all the marginal nature of the 'Yes'-voters' win in September 1997, the official transmission of authority to the Assembly in May 1999 was popularly celebrated as if it marked the coming into being of a liberated nation. Images associated with that evening's concert – of the red dragon in flames over Cardiff Bay, for example, or draped over Shirley Bassey as she sang in her birthplace – appeared to many as symbols of a regenerated Wales, embarked on a new mode of existence promising greater national self-determination in spheres not restricted to the political. The sudden breakthrough to mainstream recognition of Welsh popular music, with four Welsh bands (the Manic Street Preachers, Catatonia, Super Furry Animals and the Stereophonics) topping the UK charts in 1998–9, as well as a swathe of new Welsh actors and actresses claiming the limelight in London and Hollywood film studios, all contributed to the 'Cool Cymru' phenomenon. In this context, it is not surprising that the UK's presses should show a greater readiness to publish books located in Wales than they have evinced since the years of the 1920s and 1930s Depression, when publishers like Victor Gollancz and Faber were publishing Welsh working-class fiction and poetry. To proclaim oneself as both 'other' and new (let alone cool) is to create interest, particularly perhaps amongst the highbrow fiction-reading public, attuned to expecting novels to open up to them worlds other than their own.

During most of the second half of the twentieth century, however, Welshness was certainly not fashionable in England. As late as 1995, publishing agents for English presses were still warning novelists not to set their fictions in Wales because a Welsh location 'did not sell abroad', or so at least Catherine Merriman was told when she tried to market her novel *State of Desire*. But, by the beginning of the twenty-first century, certain London presses had changed their minds sufficiently about the appeal of Welsh locations to allow some novels to make their Welshness boldly apparent in their titles: Bloomsbury Press for example, published both Martin Pryce's very successful *Aberystwyth Mon Amour* (2001) and John Williams's *Cardiff Dead* (2000). Other fictions emerging from London publishers make their Welsh locations manifest in their back-cover blurbs. Jonathan Cape has recently published Niall Griffiths's first two novels – *Grits* (2000), another Aberystwyth fiction, which is advertised on its back cover as a novel about 'a small town on the west coast of Wales', and *Sheepshagger* (2001), the story of Ianto, 'a feral ignoble savage from a near-derelict hovel in the mountains of west Wales', according to its blurb – and Desmond Barry's *A Bloody Good Friday* (2002), with the words 'Merthyr Tydfil' in very bold print loudly announcing its location on the back cover. Heinemann publishes Alison Taylor's series of detective novels located in Bangor; Anna Davis's *Melting* (2000), located in Cardiff, has appeared from Hodder & Stoughton; Macmillan has had success with Trezza Azzopardi's *The Hiding Place* (2000), a Tiger Bay novel; Viking, of the Penguin group of publishers, won an Arts Council of Wales Book of the Year award with Stephen Knight's *Mr Schnitzel* (2000), partly located in Swansea; and Stevie Davies's novel *The Element of Water* (2001), published by the Women's Press, is also in part located in Swansea. And so on: this list is by no means inclusive.

Some of the writers mentioned above have only the barest of ethnic connections with Wales but have chosen to make Wales their base and the location of their fictions, such as the Liverpudlian born and half-Irish Niall Griffiths. Others, like Stevie Davies, at the same time as they turn back to Wales for a fictional location, are themselves in person returning to live and work in Wales. Others again, like Trezza Azzopardi, have made it clear that they do not see themselves as Welsh writers, yet their choice of a Welsh location for their fictions means that their work, too, inevitably contributes to the new range of images available of Wales. And when one adds to these London-press authors, the products of the recent growth in the publication of English-language creative writing within Wales itself, then the impression of a newly vitalized Welsh literary culture is marked. The Bridgend press Seren Books, formerly Poetry Wales Press, remains the most active and well-established publisher of Welsh writing in English, and is currently successfully promoting the careers of a new young generation of writers, such as poets Owen Sheers and Samantha Rhydderch, and novelist Richard John Evans. Gomer Press, a largely Welsh-language publisher, appears to be producing more English-language material than hitherto, and the magazine *Planet* has set up its own publishing imprint and is producing volumes of poetry and prose marked by a strong political dimension, like Mike Jenkins's Merthyr dialect poems or Charlotte Williams's autobiographical account of growing up half Afro-Caribbean in rural north Wales. The cooperatively run feminist press, Honno, has, in the last few years, seen its profits rise, at a time when women's presses in the UK generally are fast folding or being swallowed up by larger conglomerates, and the newly established Parthian Press, headed by an editor who is himself a successful new writer, Lewis Davies, is very energetically filling the gap between the small, experimental presses and more mainstream publishing, with its range of characteristically abrasive, in-your-face, drama, fiction and poetry.

Indeed, an abrasive grittiness seems generally to characterize much of the new Welsh writing in English which has emerged since 1997, in a way which could be said accurately to represent a nation which, for all its sense of new beginnings, includes some of the most deprived and underprivileged communities in western Europe. At times, when reading Rachel Tresize's account in *In and Out of the Goldfish Bowl* (2000) of growing up abused and neglected in the council house estates of the Rhondda, for example, or hearing the Blackwood characters of Patrick Jones's plays rant against 'this fucking war we call living today' (*Fuse*, 2001), it is difficult to imagine the Wales their words portray as doing anything but staggering into a very uncertain future. The paraplegic and Down's Syndrome adults who inhabit Lewis Davies's *My Piece of Happiness* (2000), Jason, the wheelchair-bound hero of Richard John Evans's *Entertainment* (2000), and Davey Daunt with his heavy leg-brace, the narrator of Desmond Barry's *A Bloody Good Friday* (2002), all seem ominously representative of a disabled nation. Yet each and every one of these characters are shown to be energetically struggling towards self-realization and fulfilment within – not without – their communities. And in the act of so doing, all of them also actively resist any attempt to define Welsh identity in terms of a narrow and prescriptive 'normality'.

Hybridity, in fact, appears to be of the essence of this newly vitalized Welsh publishing scene. In *A Bloody Good Friday*, many of whose characters belong to the long-established Irish contingent of the Merthyr population, Davey Daunt castigates those old-fashioned readers who might have expected his 'Welsh mam' to be of a more orthodox Welshness. 'What, you may ask, is Welsh about this mam with her Virgins and Val Doonicans?' he says:

> Should she not be chapel? And speak Cymraeg? Well, where else does she belong? Born and bred in Merthyr. Father, Irish miner, devout Catholic, born in Cork; her mother, Catholic convert, born in Aberdare

. . . never been out of Merthyr until she was twenty-four and went on
her honeymoon to London. Who defines Welsh? Richard Llewellyn?
How green was my fucking valley? Gimme a break. Spend a bit of time
in the Gurnos, or on the Ely Estate in Cardiff, or in Tiger Bay.

The hybrid population to which Daunt refers finds itself
represented in many of the Wales-located texts currently issuing
from the Welsh and English presses. The poet Catherine Fisher,
for example, includes in her latest poetry collection, *Altered States*
(1999), a moving series of sonnets on the landing on the mudbanks
off Newport of her Irish forebears, in flight from the famine, and
the slow integration of their offspring, 'home receding into legend,
and all the while/ unnoticed, this is home'. Leonora Brito's short-
story collection *dat's love* (1995), one of the very few literary works
to issue from the Cardiff docklands' long-established ethnically
mixed communities before 1997, has recently been followed by
Afshan Malik's dramatization of the negotiation of Asian and
Welsh identities, and Trezza Azzopardi's novel *The Hiding Place*,
on the Maltese community of Tiger Bay in the 1950s. Charlotte
Williams's *Sugar and Slate* (2002) is perhaps the fullest exploration
to date of such conflicting ethnic identities in Wales, intertwining
as it does the histories of Williams's Afro-Caribbean father's
people and those of her Welsh mother from the slate-quarrying
communities of north Wales. In 'Rice and peas', one of the poems
which embellish the prose narrative of *Sugar and Slate*, Williams
expresses her fear for her future well-being, when old age will have
curtailed her capacity assertively to insist that her difference be
recognized in Wales:

> Am I to be culturally marooned
> and in white space cocooned
> in my old-girl days in Wales?
>
> . . .
>
> Damn place
> got me heart but don't
> recognise me face.

Through spelling out both her difference from, and her connections with, the traditional concept of Welshness in *Sugar and Slate*,
and inserting her viewpoint into contemporary Welsh culture,

Charlotte Williams makes it easier for such faces as hers to be recognized as Welsh, and for Welshness itself to be recognized as hybrid.

Since 1997, another minority culture previously cocooned in 'white' or rather heterosexual space has also been presenting its difference more confidently in Welsh writing. Roger Williams's dramas of gay lifestyles in Cardiff were followed by John Sam Jones's tellingly entitled short-story collection, *Welsh Boys Too* (2000); and Gillian Brightmore's 'blue' vignettes of Welsh lesbian lives by the more assertive lesbian fictions of Pembrokeshire-born Sarah Waters – though, significantly perhaps, none of Sarah Waters's novels is located in Wales or features Welsh characters. However, Stevie Davies's temporally multi-layered novel *Impassioned Clay* (2000) very positively portrays as one of its central protagonists a seventeenth-century Welsh lesbian, and the fact that this novel was short-listed for an Arts Council of Wales Book of the Year award is indicative, perhaps, of a current desire to see differences in sexual as well as ethnic orientation more openly acknowledged in a more heterogeneous Welsh culture.

These developments suggest that with a greater degree of independence, and the strengthening of the sense of identity that it gives, has come a greater capacity to recognize and accept the diverse elements within Welsh culture. At the same time, however, achieved devolution has led, at least temporarily, to a renewed intensification of the political divisions between the two linguistic cultures of Wales, as a new wave of in-migration threatens the survival of the Welsh-language in its north-western heartlands, and pro-Welsh-language activists test out the National Assembly's professed readiness to promote the native tongue. Language politics seems once again to be splitting Wales into tribal divisions, in a manner predicted by the Algerian freedom-fighter Frantz Fanon in his analysis of likely developments in the politics of newly enfranchised nations. A new nation previously dominated by another will have internalized a distorted and disfigured sense of its own past, Fanon argues, with the result that its 'national consciousness . . . will be only an empty shell, a crude and fragile travesty of what it might have been'. Consequently, in 'young and independent nations, the nation is passed over for the race, and the tribe is preferred to the state'. Within the context of Welsh writing in English, increased tension around the language issue has led to some writers claiming, provocatively, that they cannot be Welsh, because within English-language culture there is nothing they can identify with Welshness. 'I don't believe in *Wales*,' says the playwright Dic Edwards, for example:

> A culture reflects a unity. Without a unity there is no culture. Wales is not a unity and so there is nothing that can be called Welsh culture. It may even be the case that the thing *Wales* does not exist in any really meaningful sense. *Cymru* exists while *Wales*, as the word suggests, describes a strangeness. Those who live in this strangeness are like people without a true home. People on the street. Evictees. People who live in this strangeness don't have the cultural experiences of a people who belong (to a nation, say), they have the experiences of the evicted.

Edwards's 'evicted' appear to represent the non-Welsh-speaking Welsh, whom he sees as refugees with no country or culture they can call their own. The two linguistic cultures cannot, according to this analysis, exist side by side: one of them has to annul the other, and Edwards here chooses to represent the English-language culture as the most vulnerable, though the statistical evidence would appear to suggest that, if no rapprochement ensues, it is the minority Welsh culture which is far more likely to be terminally 'evicted' and silenced.

Yet where is the evidence that 'without a unity there is no culture'? It could more convincingly be claimed that no truly unified or strictly homogeneous culture has ever existed. Certainly, Welsh-language culture, for one, has never been anything but hybrid, created and re-created as it has been through the centuries in response to a plethora of warring folk, bardic, Latin, Roman Catholic, Norman, English, Puritan, Methodist, socialist and American influences (to name but the most obvious). One aspect of the hybrid nature of Welsh-language culture today is humorously portrayed in Peter Finch's poem 'St David's Hall', in which an older generation issues complacently out of a concert performance, 'their souls . . . enlivened/ by po-faced Elijah & enormous cymrectitude', only to be faced by

> the ones who didn't bother to go in,
> unworried about identity, sitting in the bar worse than Cerys,
> Welsher than R. S., louder than Iwan Bala.

New Wales unselfishly immersed in the national pastime
alcohol alcohol antipathy antidote,
not mentioned anywhere in the Assembly agenda.
Dim pwynt see bachgen, it's like breathing
you don't think, you do it, pwy yw Saunders anyway?
Over the speakers gloriously come the Furrys.

In this macaronic poem, as in Peter Finch's more characteristic experimental word-play productions, Welsh words and phrases feature, without translation, alongside the English; it is assumed that English-speaking audiences in Wales will have sufficient knowledge of Welsh to make some sense of them, just as it is also assumed that they will have sufficient knowledge to appreciate the significance of the poem's references to figures from the two linguistic cultures of Wales, as well as to its visual arts and popular music cultures. Such work helps to create the audience that it expects, that is, an audience which, while not necessarily bilingual, would still be well-enough informed to appreciate the gist of the poem, and would be as much at ease with the way in which the two languages and cultures exist side by side within it as the laid-back youth the poem portrays.

Nor can it be assumed in Wales today that this imagined audience is necessarily middle class; statistically, given the current popularity of Welsh-language schooling in the industrial heartlands, a Rhymney valley audience is more likely to appreciate this type of macaronic verse than a Vale of Glamorgan one. A new trend in performance poetry in which Welsh- and English-language poets share a platform has been proving popular in the clubs and miners' institutes of south Wales as well as in the arts and community centres of the north and west. In 2000, for example, Ivor Thomas toured Wales performing poems from his new collection *Unsafe Sex* alongside Ifor ap Glyn presenting his similarly provocative Welsh-language poems; and, in 2002, Lloyd Robson and Grahame Davies went on a cross-Wales trip giving joint readings of their respective English- and Welsh-language portrayals of present-day Cardiff. On the page as well as on the stage, literatures in the Welsh and English languages have also more frequently been seen side by side of late, with new anthologies like *Oxygen* including both English- and Welsh-language poetry, and some Welsh-language poets, like Menna

Elfyn, making a point of publishing editions of their work in which English-language translations appear alongside the Welsh originals. Bilingual poets too have emerged, like Gwyneth Lewis, whose work in both languages often evokes the pains but also the energizing pleasures of standing on an edge, between two cultures. 'I admire the edge,' she says;

> the sides of roads where the ragwort blooms
> low but exotic in the traffic fumes . . .
> It's offered me freedom, so I choose to stay.

Edgy, but all the more vital for it, Welsh writing in English, by and large, is today contributing to the bringing together of the Welsh tribes, not to form some kind of bland conformity, in which the various cultures would have but a contributionist relation to one another, but to encounter, record and negotiate that diversity which is modern Wales. In its very diversity lies its richness and appeal. At the close of *Sugar and Slate*, Charlotte Williams finally opts for Welshness out of the array of possible ethnicities available to her precisely because Wales is so diverse – 'as mixed up as I was', she says: 'I like it because it is fragmented, because there is a loud bawling row raging, because its inner pain is coming to terms with its differences and its divisions, because it realises it can't hold on to the myth of sameness, past or present.' To quote Ron Davies AM, one of the progenitors of the new Wales, who may himself be said to have suffered more than most from the propensity of too homogeneous a culture to evict its minorities or compel them to closet away their apparently less acceptable difference, the hope is to create a 'vibrant, diverse and tolerant Wales,' and 'a Welsh national identity based on civic values and not ethnic criteria'. To what extent the inhabitants of Wales can achieve this aim, and whether or not they can do so without losing in the process any of the facets of Welsh difference, only future years can tell.

FURTHER READING

Tony Bianchi, 'Aztecs at Troedrhiwgwair', in Ian A. Bell (ed.), *Peripheral Visions* (Cardiff, 1995), 44–76.

Hazel Walford Davies (ed.), *State of Play: Four Playwrights of Wales* (Llandysul, 1998).

Menna Elfyn (ed.), *Trying the Line: A Tribute to Gillian Clarke* (Llandysul, 1997).

Katie Gramich and Andrew Hiscock (eds), *Dangerous Diversities: The Changing Faces of Wales* (Cardiff, 1998).

Jeremy Hooker, 'Ceridwen's daughter: Welsh women poets and the uses of tradition', *Welsh Writing in English*, 1 (1995), 128–44.

Jeremy Hooker, *Imagining Wales: A View of Modern Welsh Writing in English* (Cardiff, 2001).

Nigel Jenkins (ed.), *Thirteen Ways of Looking at Tony Conran* (Cardiff, 1995).

Dafydd Johnston, 'Making history in two languages: *Y Pla* and *Griffri*', *Welsh Writing in English*, 3 (1997), 118–33.

Claire Powell, 'The art of noise: Peter Finch sounds off', *Welsh Writing in English*, 2 (1996), 138–61.

Harri Roberts, 'A Tower of Babel: heteroglossia, the grotesque and the (de)construction of meaning in Glyn Jones's *The Valley, the City, the Village* and Nial Griffiths's *Grits*', *Welsh Writing in English*, 7 (2001–2), 106–29.

M. Wynn Thomas, 'Prints of Wales: contemporary Welsh poetry in English', in Hans-Werner Ludwig and Lothar Fietz (eds.), *Poetry in the British Isles: Non-Metropolitan Perspectives* (Cardiff, 1995), 97–114.

Daniel Williams, 'Harry Secombe in the junkshop: nation, myth and invention in Edward Thomas's *House of America* and David Mamet's *American Buffalo*', *Welsh Writing in English*, 4 (1998), 131–56.

CHAPTER 10

PARALLELS AND PARADIGMS

NED THOMAS

I

This chapter comes at the end of a volume which is itself the culmination of a series of *Guides to Welsh Literature*. In respect of this volume none of the three main words in the title is unproblematic. Six volumes deal with literature in the Welsh language from the earliest texts to the present day and the word 'Welsh' there refers before all else to the language in which the literature is written. One could argue, without difficulty, for the inclusion, as exotic branches, of the literature written in Welsh in Patagonia or the United States, though someone might wish to stake a claim that these were separate literatures, however embryonic. This seventh volume deals largely with twentieth-century writing in the English language, but here the claim made is that the literature can be distinguished from mainstream English literature and defined as Welsh in the sense of 'belonging to Wales' – though that phrase can be taken in a variety of senses: in relation to authors it can mean, variously, Welsh by descent or birth, by residence, commitment or affiliation; in relation to works it can mean Welsh in authorship, theme or subject matter or in some vaguer quality of spirit or, just occasionally, it might relate to form.

On the same basis of 'belonging to Wales' one might make the case for a comparative treatment of the literatures of Wales in Welsh and English (and at the Renaissance, of work by Welsh authors writing in Latin). At least one of the contributors to this volume has taken that approach. Indeed, if the common historical experience of a given territory has been expressed in more than one language and given different linguistic formulations, then it may be that only comparative study will give the fullest understanding of that experience. Thus one could argue that Caribbean literature is best studied in its Spanish, French, English and Dutch (both creole and standard-language) expressions. We know there are practical (and often departmental) obstacles to such cross-language studies; but if the time comes when every child brought up in Wales is equipped to read both Welsh and English, then perhaps a 'Guide' based on those principles will be required. In the mean time, one can say that the present organization of these volumes reflects a linguistic discontinuity but also presupposes some social continuity or, at the very least, an aspiration towards such continuity. That decision on the organization of the series was a publishing decision, and, Reader, let me confess – dropping the last pretence at objectivity – that, in an earlier capacity as publisher, I commissioned this volume. The same publishing decision that added one volume on writing in English to the series on Welsh-language literature, also defined it as a relatively recent literature and effectively ruled out an alternative perspective on Anglo-Welsh literature (associated most particularly with Raymond Garlick and Roland Mathias) which sees it, too, as having a centuries-long tradition in Wales.

The image of the 'Guide' is also problematic, though once it did not seem so. Dent's Everyman series confidently carried on its endpapers the words: 'Everyman I will go with thee and be thy guide . . .' The idea of the Guide was that the reader would be conducted by a knowledgeable insider around an agreed literary territory and shown and taught to appreciate the chief glories but also, perhaps, some of the hidden and interesting byways of that place. Today most of the assumptions behind such an image are questioned in academic circles. From what partial point of view and with what set of values does the guide speak? Can we agree on the canon of 'chief glories', who's in, who's out, who is central, who is on the margin of the discussion? This volume has several guide-voices, not all of whom make the same assumptions or have the same priorities.

And as for 'Literature' where do we draw the line between 'literary' writing and other kinds of writing? What is the cultural and literary status of best-sellers? Are we concerned with cultural or aesthetic judgements? And then, there is not only 'literature' but 'a literature'. Should we today continue to create the kind of boundary implied by the concept of 'a literature' or prefer to study certain types of writing across geographical boundaries as in the discussion of 'working-class writing' or 'women's writing' or 'travel writing', and particularly when the various texts are in the same language and thus lend themselves relatively easily to textual and stylistic as well as thematic comparison?

In theory there is room for every kind of categorization to yield its own insights. However, in the world of publishing, reviewing, school syllabuses, examinations and departmental structures, funds for research and for appointments in higher education, choices are constantly being made about the allocation of resources, and these in turn reflect pressures and priorities which are ultimately political in the broadest sense. So there will be movements and counter-movements in respect of the way literature is categorized and studied.

The rise – slow though it has been – of Welsh writing in English as a field of study over the last quarter of the twentieth century, has gone hand in hand with a growth of Welsh institutions and a certain limited increase in Welsh consciousness. With a devolved National Assembly taking an interest in the school curriculum in Wales and in the arts generally, one may expect further growth. The particularist agenda is quite clear in this case. However, one should not take the alternative 'universalist' categories at their face value as being uncoloured by particular cultures and political situations. 'Women's writing' or 'working-class writing' or even, perversely, 'literature of place' courses may sometimes privilege writers from larger and more powerful cultures and advance as universal some values that nevertheless have a particular cultural colouring.

These general critical issues arise everywhere and perplex discussion, but often as a reaction against, and as a sophisticated critique of, well-established literary canons which, though modified, are never wholly overthrown. Jean Rhys's *Wide Sargasso Sea* (1966) may modify and enrich the response to *Jane Eyre* but it relies and indeed feeds on the reader's familiarity with the latter. And, whatever authors from the past are exhumed from obscurity in the seminar room, for the wider public, films and television series go on underlining the classic stature of Shakespeare's histories or Jane Austen's novels.

But in the case of 'Anglo-Welsh literature' (used in this chapter for convenience not with ideological intent) or 'Welsh writing in English', where there is no really settled canon or even a single set of agreed criteria which might establish such a canon, the issues arise at the very start, at the very moment when this literature is beginning to have a small institutional presence in schools and universities. Where others have a map of their literature which they may wish to modify, we are just beginning to construct a map but in a critical atmosphere in which we cannot fail but be reflexively aware of the forces that shape our drawing of it – which does not make a map less necessary.

I take the idea of a map from Margaret Atwood, writing in the context of Canadian literature:

'Who am I' is a question appropriate in countries where the environment, the 'here' is already well-defined, so well-defined in fact that it may threaten to overwhelm the individual. In societies where everyone and everything has its place a person may have to struggle to separate himself from his social background, in order to keep from just being a function of the structure.

'Where is here?' is a different kind of question. It is what a man [*sic*] asks when he finds himself in unknown territory, and it implies several other questions. What is this place in relation to other places? How do I find my way around it? . . .

What a lost person needs is a map of the territory, with his own position marked so he can see where he is in relation to everything else. Literature is not only a mirror; it is also a map, a geography of the mind. Our literature is one such map, if we can learn to read it as our literature, as the product of who and where we have been. We need such a map desperately, we need to know about here, because here is where we live. For the members of a country or a culture, shared knowledge of their place, their here, is not a luxury but a necessity. Without that knowledge we will not survive.

II

A number of definitions or maps of English-language writing from Wales were formulated by critics as the twentieth century progressed. It is not my aim here to list them all or even to give an exhaustive account or evaluation of those which I do mention, for this would involve setting each against its own time and against the then-existing body of Anglo-Welsh literature. Instead, in what follows I have drawn on some of these texts as quarries of ideas which we can test for their usefulness today. Believing that one can also understand one's situation by analogy, I also cite some texts from other places or other disciplines.

In 1937, Saunders Lewis gave a lecture entitled 'Is there an Anglo-Welsh Literature?', to which Raymond Garlick published a riposte in 1971. The former is generally agreed to be the first attempt at setting out a consistent theoretical position, even if it was one that provoked disagreement among those who later addressed the same questions. While Saunders Lewis allowed that there was 'a group of Welshmen writing in English whose background and themes are consistently Welsh', he did not allow the existence of a body of compositions that might be called a separate literature, having its own peculiar traditions and character. Behind his position stands a whole philosophy of organic community:

> A writer of literature belongs to a community. Normally, he writes for that community. His instrument of expression – the speech he uses, – has been shaped for him and given to him by that society. Moreover, there belong to that society traditions and experiences and a secular mode of life as well as a literary heritage which have impressed themselves not only on the language but on all those who so use it that their use of it is seen to be literature. Every literature implies the existence of a separate moral person, an organic community. Such a community, possessing its own common traditions and its own literature, we generally call a nation.

Today, in the critical climate of the English-speaking world, this seems a rather hermetically sealed account of literature. Are we not all on some cultural border, in some historical interstice, exiles, marginals, members of diasporas, living at some interface, and more so in Wales perhaps than in many places? But interfaces and borders imply something to be on the border *of*, and certainly in much of the European continent, the *language* in which a work is written is still very widely taken as a rough-and-ready definer of which literature a given work belongs to, while still allowing all kinds of tangential and problematic relationships with the community whose language that literature is written in.

Perhaps we have to allow that there are many literatures which do indeed roughly correspond to the Saunders Lewis model, though they too will be more subject to outside influence today than they were in 1937; and that there are others, written in languages of wide extension such as English, Spanish or Arabic, in which internal differences between regions of the same language-area are perceived from inside those regions as having crucial significance, though from outside they may still be assimilated to the literature of the language in which they are written. How many of the readers of this chapter are careful to distinguish the famous Latin-American writers by their countries of origin, let alone by the regions of those states with which they may be associated?

The discussion should perhaps be situated within the broader political discussion of a dialectic between globalization and localization. The same broad civilizational influences which carry across linguistic boundaries are felt even more powerfully within the same language-area, and furthermore within that area there are influences that make themselves felt at the level of genre and style and of the language itself – as American usage, for example, affects British English. Nor can one say with certainty for which community writers in English write. The local community is no longer something given with the language. Readership may be decided by a convergence of the writer's and the reader's personal ideological commitments, as when one writer chooses to write about Wales and gains a certain constituency, while another chooses not to but still finds readers, including some in Wales; or it may be decided by the strength or weakness of local publishers as against metropolitan publishers. So, on the one hand we can note processes which work towards a single market, a mixture of traditions and of varieties of English; but, on the other hand, within that larger space, there is a tendency for the region to position itself by an emphasis on unique characteristics, a tendency to be observed in the cultural as in the economic sphere. Indeed, a strong cultural profile is considered an economic asset in a world of liberalized trade in which regions within the same nation-state as well as in different nation-states compete against each other for inward investment.

The argument so far can perhaps be restated thus: the concept of Anglo-Welsh literature is a critical site in process of construction. It cannot be understood in terms of the classic European model where a literature is coterminous with a language and a territory but it can be understood within the wide spectrum of literatures in English where difference is constructed within the same language by a whole array of factors. Here it occupies a still precarious position compared with literatures such as American or Australian literature in English, where different natural environments, political independence, separate education systems, the power of large publishers and an evolving body of native criticism have defined what is written there as a separate literature both in the minds of Australians and Americans and for the rest of the world. But we should remember that these were not always regarded as separate literatures and that we are concerned not with fixed states but with processes which have political and institutional but, also, literary-critical dimensions. The growth of institutions in Wales has already been noted, but we should not underestimate the strength of those other factors which integrate us very closely with British life. In this situation, how is a Welsh criticism to draw the map, to differentiate Anglo-Welsh literature from others, and make it meaningful as a body of work in the first place to the people of Wales?

A 'regional' British literature, an English expression of Celtic, Cymric values, a proletarian literature, a colonial, or even a post-colonial literature (a possibility canvassed in a recent issue of *SPAN*), or a unique amalgam of influences – all these have been advanced as descriptions of Anglo-Welsh literature and, implicitly, of what it is to be Welsh. Each description finds credible points of reference in the spread of writing that exists, but excludes or marginalizes other work, and we have a protean capacity to adapt and plead our case in the terminology of the times. The dear old Celtic imagination for which we were praised by Matthew Arnold in *On the Study of Celtic Literature* (1867) still refuses to lie down and die as a claimed Welsh literary characteristic. The earlier Gwyn Jones was happy in 1957 to argue the case for Anglo-Welsh as a lively regional literature within Britain, though he later modified his stance to allow for a more national claim. The 1960s and 1970s saw the growth of the colonial analysis, fed by the struggles of national liberation movements in other parts of the world, while the 1980s – the Thatcher years and the miners' strike of 1984–5 – revivified the proletarian emphasis. Meanwhile, Welsh cultural institutions such as the Arts Council chose mechanically applicable criteria such as place of birth or place of residence as defining the Welsh writer – a kind of 'neutral' construction that may be democratically necessary and institutionally inevitable but, given the mobility of population in Britain, not one that is likely to yield a very meaningful map. This is perhaps the place to note that over a quarter of today's Welsh population was born outside Wales.

III

Anglo-Irish was the prototype against which Saunders Lewis in
1937 measured emergent Anglo-Welsh writing, and we can find an
astute early discussion of the questions with which we are concerned in the first chapter of Daniel Corkery's *Synge and Anglo-
Irish Literature: A Study* (1931), a work that Saunders Lewis is
very likely to have read. Corkery, like Lewis, would have preferred
his country to have had one literature which was not in an imposed
language, but both have to admit, in the case of Ireland, a large
and long-established body of work in English which yet claims to
be Irish.

For Corkery, it is not a simple matter of differentiating English
from Irish literature but of distinguishing the authentically Irish
from false versions of Irishness. This is a very characteristic feature
of colonial situations, that the colonized feel their 'reality' has been
falsely constructed not only by perceptions from outside but by
locals brainwashed by, or pandering to, the fashions of the
imperial centre. Where writers do not inevitably 'belong' by virtue
of the language they write in, their Irishness or Welshness is
necessarily constructed according to one set of criteria or another.
The debate over what those criteria should be can become an
ideological battleground.

Corkery's account of Anglo-Irish literature distinguishes an
early period when this literature's 'moulds' (an interesting concept)
cannot be distinguished from those of contemporary English
literature. He notes the long tradition of expatriate writers who
may or may not exploit their Irish background but who write for
an audience that is not Irish. Some of these writers may, in times
of national mobilization, veer towards identification with their
country but, when the national movement subsides, they are not
inevitably joined to their community, as a writer in Irish would be,
and become part of the greater market for English-language
writing. Corkery, borrowing a phrase from Walt Whitman, describes this literature as 'something escaped from the anchorage
and driving free'. How much greater the scope for this kind of
writing must be in English in the days of Internet novels and
international publishing corporations.

Corkery's next phase is the development of a colonial literature
'written to explain the quaintness of the humankind of this land,

especially the native humankind, to another humankind that was not quaint, that was standard, normal'. Often written by the Anglo-Irish 'Ascendancy', this literature took as its leading theme the decline and fall of a 'Big House' and was out of touch with the three great forces which, according to Corkery, differentiated Irish from English national consciousness, namely the religious consciousness of the people, Irish nationalism and the fact that Ireland was a largely peasant country. These are the themes that he finds present in true Anglo-Irish literature. This authentic literature belonged to a 'submerged underworld' – it was often popular poetry which would be judged of dubious merit by established aesthetic literary standards but found its audience at home. It lived in Corkery's phrase 'by native suffrage' where the colonial and expatriate literature lived 'by foreign suffrage'. But it did not find its way into the schools, where aesthetic standards forged elsewhere prevailed, so that Irish children were taught a literature which offered no mirror to their own lives.

Margaret Atwood's *Survival* (1972), which seeks to define Canadian literature in English, recalls the same school-taught English classics that did not speak to the Canadian child, alongside the American commercial popular culture spread by television and advertising, but then also a kind of semi-literary undergrowth of not very highly prized work which has to be *discovered* to be true Canadian literature. And what defines it as Canadian for Atwood? A number of related themes clustered around the concept of survival in a hostile environment which she claims is typical of both English- and French-Canadian literature.

In both Atwood and Corkery one can note the idea of discovering an authentic reflection of the people's life below levels of false consciousness induced by a colonial situation. Authenticity in each case is defined by themes that are presented as truly relevant in the sense that they explain us to ourselves. Criteria of social relevance are pitted against purely aesthetic criteria – or perhaps it would be truer to say that the neutrality of purely aesthetic criteria is questioned. An undergrowth of literature that remained undervalued by aesthetic criteria is discovered to be more relevant, and in both cases there is a preoccupation with the education system and the social transmission of values.

In the 1970s and 1980s all these elements can be found within Anglo-Welsh criticism, though rarely together in the same critic.

Both Raymond Garlick and Roland Mathias were concerned professionally with the education system and sensible of the need for elements in the English syllabus which connected with the immediate environment of children growing up in Wales outside the Welsh language. Gerald Morgan's anthology *This World of Wales* (1968) aimed to supply that very need.

Tony Conran is a prime example of a critic who explored an undergrowth of authors considered at best 'second-rate' by metropolitan standards – Huw Menai, Idris Davies, W. H. Davies – and found them crucial to understanding who we are, important features of our map. He marks their position in a Welsh social and cultural history and, in so doing, defines a space for them between the Welsh-language tradition of folk-poetry and complete *embourgeoisement* and assimilation into what he perceives as English values. In order to include W. H. Davies (who had no Welsh in his background as did the other two mentioned), Conran develops the notion of 'seepage' or cultural influence across the division of language. 'What I have called seepage', writes Conran in *The Cost of Strangeness* (1982), 'is one of the reasons why Anglo-Welsh poetry belongs to us, the people of Wales, and is not to be hived off as interesting but minor English verse.'

But although these features mentioned by Anglo-Welsh critics have much in common with colonial situations, the sharper discourse which actually *called* the Welsh situation colonial, and Anglo-Welsh a colonial literature, came only from critics strongly identified with the Welsh language, such as Bobi Jones and myself. Parallels with Third World situations and indeed with European minorities were striking in relation to the mechanisms of language suppression and the psychology of induced inferiority-feelings related to language, while the Marxist concept of false consciousness allowed one to interpret as victims of colonialism even those writers who did not see themselves as victims. The truth is that there was little identification with the colonial hypothesis among late twentieth-century Anglo-Welsh writers themselves, except for R. S. Thomas, Emyr Humphreys, Harri Webb and, in one period, John Tripp, and then always in the context of language. The theory of internal colonialism developed by Michael Hechter (1975) but powerfully challenged by John Lovering (1978) was not proven in classic Marxist economic terms and, in retrospect, one can see that the colonial analysis of Welsh society was always strongest in relation to language. Complicity with the imperial project, whether at the level of Welsh Liberal politicians preaching free trade or of south Wales miners fuelling the gunships of empire, was extensive, and Wales, when the coal economy was booming, could hardly be compared with an expropriated colony.

A class analysis, on the other hand, spoke to many Welsh people, and to many Welsh writers who came from working-class backgrounds. Our traditions of militancy and unionism, and Labour leaders such as Aneurin Bevan, gave Wales an honourable place in the history and iconography of movements dedicated to the reform of the British state – but always as contributors to the larger unit. These traditions were reflected in literature too – in Idris Davies's poetry and in the industrial novels of south Wales – although as creative works they are, of course, open to a variety of readings. All this reinforced a British-Welsh identity that was incompatible with the colonial analysis. If, by the beginning of the twenty-first century, the decline of heavy industry, the liberalization of the world economy and the decline of the nation-state as a regulator of markets and wages, have all undermined the classic class-analysis and the fixation of the left with control of the state apparatus, it has also to be said that the experience of ex-colonial countries, with their revealed internal ethnic tensions and divisions and their corrupt *comprador* elites in the pay of multinational companies, has undermined the decolonizing rhetoric of earlier years. When a South Korean multinational company can invest in south Wales because of the low level of wages or a Dutch-based multinational close a steelworks in the same area with impunity, neither the rhetoric of a British working-class struggling to capture and control the dominant heights of the British economy, nor the alternative rhetoric of an internal colony struggling for freedom from a metropolitan centre, has quite the mobilizing force of earlier days.

IV

The idea of Anglo-Welsh literature as a unique amalgam is one that, with the disappearance of more severely ideological interpretations, has perhaps the greatest credibility today, though there is plenty of room for discussion of what the elements in that amalgam are and what weight the respective elements should carry. In *Frontiers in Anglo-Welsh Poetry* (1997), Tony Conran offers a good starting-point for this discussion:

> Anglo-Welsh poetry differs from other poetry in the English language in three main respects. First, it has in its background, a different civilization – it is like English poetry written by Irishmen or Indians. Secondly it shares its territory with another linguistic community which regards its tongue as the right and natural language of the country – a claim which Anglo-Welsh writers often accept, and which even if they dispute, they cannot ignore. In this respect, Anglo-Welsh poetry is like English poetry written by Nigerians or Maoris. Thirdly, it derives from a special sort of society, which I shall call 'the buchedd' from a Welsh word meaning 'a way of life' or 'ethos'. In this third aspect, it is more like poetry in English written by Americans. American society, like Welsh, was consciously without an upper-class, deliberately egalitarian, puritanical in morals, a product of cultural revolution following the break-up of accepted social patterns.

Historically, and in the context of poetry only, there is much to be said for Conran's first point. In the social role of the poet in Wales, and the social significance of form, Conran sees a carry-over from Welsh and Celtic civilization. The communal, the celebratory – these are the backbone of the Welsh tradition for Conran, whether they are found in medieval Welsh poetry or in Idris Davies or Dylan Thomas. The corollary of this view, of course, is that poets in Wales or from Wales who write another kind of poetry stand outside the Welsh tradition or have betrayed it, and are indistinguishable from English poetry. It is possible that two things are being overlooked here: first, that Welsh-language tradition is also evolving and may not for ever be set in the praise-poetry mould; and secondly, that there may be alternative non-metropolitan English traditions that do not offer the absolute contrast that Conran's thesis requires. It is, perhaps, as well to recognize that what is a useful analytic concept in retrospective cultural criticism turns into a literary manifesto and becomes politically prescriptive when applied to living writers.

Conran's third point concerns the existence of an egalitarian, Nonconformist culture, embracing Welsh-speaking and non-Welsh-speaking Welsh people, that was dominant up to the First World War and exerted an influence on literature long after that, often by producing a reaction against Nonconformity. He uses the Welsh word *buchedd* to describe this ethos or way of life. Against this background Conran reads Idris Davies's *Gwalia Deserta* and *The Angry Summer* in a specifically Welsh way: 'His greatest work incarnates and mourns *buchedd* values, far more than it does socialism or simply working-class bitterness or hope.' Conran has a great empathy for this period, and the invocation of a time when Wales was united by a culture (crossing differences of language) that differentiated it from England has a persisting symbolic appeal. But he recognizes that this culture was breaking up even in the second quarter of the twentieth century, and the implication of this is that Anglo-Welsh literature, defined by relation to that culture, is a period phenomenon. Can we today speak with any confidence of a single 'Welsh way of life' differentiated from England? If that case can be made, it will certainly not be in terms of Conran's *buchedd.*

Conran's remaining point concerns language – that Anglo-Welsh literature is written on a territory shared with another language and influenced by this fact. While the number of mainly Welsh-speaking communities continues to decline and Welsh speakers continue to be a small minority, the status of Welsh has greatly improved in the last quarter century; its public and media presence, and the number of domains in which it is used has grown, so that the awareness of this other language is probably greater today among non-Welsh-speakers across the whole territory of Wales than it has been for a long time. However the old class-correlations with language have changed and the particular circumstances in which first-language Welsh-speakers became Anglo-Welsh writers through the pressures and opportunities of an English education system are unlikely to be repeated. In other words, the Welsh language is still a living factor in the contemporary environment of Anglo-Welsh writers, but it is an evolving factor. So one might, for example, expect references to the Welsh language to be more present in a realist novel set in Wales, but one would not expect Welsh to be present as it once was as a hidden shaping influence on imagery or syntax.

Quite apart from the actual *content* of Conran's analysis, which is historically very enlightening, his method reveals the difficulties which beset what I have called the unique amalgam view of Anglo-Welsh literature. It will, almost inevitably, involve establishing some relation to Welsh literature on the one hand and to English literature on the other, and the danger is always that one reifies these other literatures, attributing to them essential qualities, when they are in fact complex and evolving phenomena, like Anglo-Welsh literature itself. It is very hard to keep one's eye on three evolving literatures and a changing social history all at once, as I have argued in *Thirteen Ways of Looking at Tony Conran* (1995; ed. Nigel Jenkins). In this context, the image of the map also has to be interpreted with a sense of its limitations. Margaret Atwood's emphasis is on looking retrospectively at a body of work and learning to read it in a certain way that will tell us where we have come from. But maps are also used to show where one is going or might want to go, and that is not something one can predict by a reading of past literature, although one may prefer certain directions and commend certain themes and preoccupations.

V

Analysts of the voting in the Welsh devolution referendum of 1997 concur in seeing it as largely identity-based. People did not simply vote as their party allegiances dictated but according to their feelings of Welshness or lack of them. The most strongly 'Yes'-voting areas were either in the more strongly Welsh-speaking western half of the country or else in the former industrial valleys of south Wales. In the sociologist Denis Balsom's 'three-Wales model', the first area is *y fro Gymraeg* (the Welsh-speaking heart-land) and the second 'Welsh Wales'; the third area, which he calls 'British Wales', is the rest of the territory where identification with Wales was weaker and where a majority voted No in 1997.

To explain the vote in the more strongly Welsh-speaking areas one must posit a mixed linguistic and ethnic identity. For 'Welsh Wales' one has to posit a strong ethnic identity, though of relatively recent creation. On the one hand, this is the area with the highest percentage of people born in Wales. On the other hand, we know that it was an area of massive in-migration not much more than a century ago. The two areas, taken together, also correspond very roughly with the region which has been given Objective One status by the European Commission – a measure of the highest level of regional deprivation within the European Union. It was the convergence of the two senses of Welshness within this region which made possible – by a hair's breadth – the vote in favour of devolution, nevertheless leaving a majority of the population of Wales either voting against or not voting at all.

This is not the place to go into all the possible factors involved in the rapprochement that undoubtedly occurred in the last quarter of the twentieth century between the two affirming versions of Welshness – they would include, no doubt, the experience of the Thatcher years, and the growth of the Welsh schools movement – but the definition of an area of discussion called Anglo-Welsh literature or Welsh writing in English may, as suggested in chapter 9, also have been significant for the small numbers of the Welsh intelligentsia involved in that discussion. The participants included those who, while writing in English, identified strongly with *y fro Gymraeg* (typified by R. S. Thomas or Emyr Humphreys), others who identified strongly with the English-speaking tradition of the south Wales valleys (typified by Dai Smith), with contributions from time to time from those newly arrived from England or otherwise representing 'British Wales'. The discussion, which can be followed in the literary magazines and in a number of single volumes, was not always an amicable one, but it did expose everyone to views other than their own.

M. Wynn Thomas has carried the discussion further not only by arguing for this very pluralism as a way of defining Wales, but by studying the interaction of the two literatures of Wales in some detail and thus deepening the terms of the discussion. The very titles of his books, *Internal Difference* (1992) and *Corresponding Cultures* (1999), proclaim a commitment to relationship as well as to diversity, though he never pretends that the relationship is an easy one. What was a personal undertaking in his case has become an institutional necessity with the coming of the National Assembly, which faces the task of devising a cultural policy that might at one and the same time satisfy very different cultural constituencies and be consistent with its democratic mandate. The report 'A Culture in Common' commissioned by the Assembly and debated in 2001 approaches many of these same questions with great goodwill but perhaps insufficient sense of the difficulties involved. It deals of course with arts besides literature, and one is bound to wonder whether non-verbal arts may not, at least in the short term, have a better chance of creating a sense of common ownership.

There is every reason, in Wales as elsewhere, to prefer a view of culture which allows for plurality, fluidity, dialogue, interaction and even conflict, over a definition that is totalizing and static and essentialist. That is a view to be striven for within every culture and every language, for language is the vehicle of that dialogue between the various elements. But every language is totalizing in a quite different sense in that it strives to imagine and comprehend and name its own universe, its own pluralism. Bearing this in mind we have to ask what is the meaning of 'multiculturalism' within a particular discourse, and within a given language and culture.

What is often meant within English-language discourse in Britain is tolerance and even encouragement of a number of background cultures and languages within a society which has English as the foreground language – or to be plain, the dominant language. Many speakers of immigrant languages are happy to accept such a place for themselves, always providing that sufficient resources are made available to support their background culture and that it is respected. Welsh speakers on the other hand, like other European territorial minorities, claim a historic space in which their culture too can be a foreground culture, allowing people of different backgrounds to participate. This yields a more European view of Britain, like continental Europe, as a mosaic rather than a melting pot, and requires a rather different account of multiculturalism.

In Welsh terms, the future alternatives suggested by the two discourses I have described might on the one hand be something like the Irish model, where English assumes the mantle of the Welsh national literature, where translation from Welsh becomes a means of assimilating it to the English culture of Wales, where Welsh literature in the original becomes the preserve of a few and for the rest a background feature distinguishing us from the English. This is a prospect which a lot of Welsh speakers fear, but neither is it so easy for English-speaking Wales to achieve, given the uncertainty of self-definition and the mobility of population. The alternative would be a Basque or Catalan model where the resources of the regional government were put wholeheartedly behind the reclaiming of the national language and to support literature and other arts in that language. Plenty of individuals in those regions write and work in the state language, Spanish, but their work is then considered to belong to Spanish literature and to be supported by the Spanish literary market. This alternative would leave no place for a discrete Anglo-Welsh literature but, given the mixed nature of the Welsh population and the very mild surge of national feeling which led to devolution, it is a future which is unlikely to come about.

A humane third way would promote the comparative discussion of the two literatures within each language-group, studying the texts in the original language (something that could be in reach of new generations in Wales). Perhaps we need, instead of departments of Welsh and English, departments of *literature* and syllabuses in *literature*, rather as the African novelist Ngugi suggested, in his essay 'On the abolition of the English Department', that in Kenya one needed a syllabus that would incorporate all the elements that had shaped the literary life of the country as well as works from places that offered parallels and analogies.

FURTHER READING

Margaret Atwood, *Survival* (Toronto, 1972).

Anthony Conran, *The Cost of Strangeness* (Llandysul, 1982).

Anthony Conran, *Frontiers in Anglo-Welsh Poetry* (Cardiff, 1997).

Raymond Garlick, *An Introduction to Anglo-Welsh Literature* (Cardiff, 1970).

Michael Hechter, *Internal Colonialism: The Celtic Fringe in British National Development (1536–1966)* (London, 1975).

Bobi Jones, 'Anglo-Welsh: more definitions', *Planet*, 16 (Feb/March 1973), 11–23.

Bobi Jones, 'I'm your Boy – the four psycho-sociological positions of the colonised Welshman', *Planet*, 42 (April, 1978), 2–10.

Gwyn Jones, *The First Forty Years: Some Notes on Anglo-Welsh Literature* (Cardiff, 1957).

Saunders Lewis, *Is There an Anglo-Welsh Literature?* (Cardiff, 1939).

John Lovering, 'The theory of the internal colony', *Planet*, 45/6 (November 1978), 89–96.

Colin Partridge, 'Smouldering bush', *Planet*, 28 (August 1975), 2–7.

SPAN 41 (October 1995) (Waikato, New Zealand).

Ngugi wa Thiong'o, *Decolonising the Mind* (London, 1986).

M. Wynn Thomas, *Internal Difference: Writing in Twentieth-Century Wales* (Cardiff, 1992).

M. Wynn Thomas, *Corresponding Cultures: The Two Literatures of Wales* (Cardiff, 1999).

BIBLIOGRAPHIES

John Harris, *A Bibliographical Guide to Twenty-four Modern Anglo-Welsh Writers* (Cardiff, 1994).
Meic Stephens (ed.), *The New Companion to the Literature of Wales* (Cardiff, 1998).

SELECTED LIST OF PRIMARY TEXTS
(including sources of quotations in this volume)

Dannie Abse, *The View from Row G: Three Plays*, ed. James A. Davies (Bridgend, 1990).
Dannie Abse, *White Coat, Purple Coat: Collected Poems 1948–1988* (London, 1993).
Trezza Azzopardi, *The Hiding Place* (London, 2000).
Desmond Barry, *The Chivalry of Crime* (London, 2000).
Desmond Barry, *A Bloody Good Friday* (London, 2002).
Glenda Beagan, *The Medlar Tree* (Bridgend, 1992).
Ron Berry, *Hunters and Hunted* (London, 1960).
Ron Berry, *Flame and Slag* (London, 1968).
Ron Berry, *This Bygone* (Llandysul, 1996).
Ron Berry, *Collected Stories*, ed. Simon Baker (Llandysul, 2000).
Ruth Bidgood, *Selected Poems* (Bridgend, 1992).
Leonora Brito, *dat's love* (Bridgend, 1995).
Duncan Bush, *The Hook* (Bridgend, 1997).
Duncan Bush, *Glass Shot* (London, 1991).
Brenda Chamberlain, *The Green Heart* (Oxford, 1958).
Brenda Chamberlain, *Tide-race* (London, 1962).
Brenda Chamberlain, *The Water-Castle* (London, 1964).
Brenda Chamberlain, *Poems With Drawings* (London, 1969).
Gillian Clarke, *Collected Poems* (Manchester, 1997).
Tony Conran, *Blodeuwedd* (Bridgend, 1988).
Tony Conran, *Castles: Variations on an Original Theme* (Llandysul, 1993).
Tony Conran, *All Hallows: Symphony in 3 Movements* (Llandysul, 1995).
Tony Conran, *Visions and Praying Mantids* (Llandysul, 1997).
Tony Conran, *Eros Proposes a Toast* (Bridgend, 1998).
Tony Conran, *Theatre of Flowers: Collected Pastorals 1954–95* (Llandysul, 1998).
Tony Conran, *A Gwynedd Symphony* (Llandysul, 1999).

B. L. Coombes, *These Poor Hands* (London, 1939).

Sarah Corbett, *The Red Wardrobe* (Bridgend, 1998).

Alexander Cordell, *The Rape of the Fair Country* (London, 1959).

A. J. Cronin, *The Citadel* (London, 1937).

Tony Curtis, *Selected Poems 1970–1985* (Bridgend, 1986).

The Complete Poems of Idris Davies, ed. Dafydd Johnston (Llandysul, 1994).

John Davies, *Flight Patterns* (Bridgend, 1991).

Lewis Davies, *Work, Sex and Rugby* (Cardiff, 1993).

Rhys Davies, *The Withered Root* (London, 1927).

Rhys Davies, *Jubilee Blues* (London, 1938).

Rhys Davies, *A Time to Laugh* (London, 1969).

Rhys Davies, *Collected Stories* Vols. 1 & 2, ed. Meic Stephens (Llandysul, 1996).

Stevie Davies, *The Element of Water* (London, 2001).

W. H. Davies, *Autobiography of a Supertramp* (London, 1964).

W. H. Davies, *Selected Poems*, ed. Jonathan Barker (Oxford, 1992).

Hazel Walford Davies (ed.), *State of Play: Four Playwrights of Wales* (Llandysul, 1998).

[for John Dyer], *Minor Poets of the Eighteenth Century*, ed. H. I'A. Fausset (London, 1930).

Jean Earle, *Selected and New Poems* (Bridgend, 1990).

Alice Thomas Ellis, *The Sin Eater* (London, 1977).

Alice Thomas Ellis, *Unexplained Laughter* (London, 1985).

Caradoc Evans, *My People*, ed. John Harris (Bridgend, 1987).

Caradoc Evans, *Nothing to Pay*, ed. John Harris (Manchester, 1989).

Christine Evans, *Cometary Phases* (Bridgend, 1989).

Margiad Evans, *Country Dance* (London, 1932).

Margiad Evans, *Autobiography* (Oxford, 1943).

Margiad Evans, *A Ray of Darkness* (London, 1952).

Stuart Evans, *The Caves of Alienation* (London, 1997).

Richard Evans, *Entertainment* (Bridgend, 2000).

Peter Finch, *Selected Poems* (Bridgend, 1987).

Catherine Fisher, *Immrama* (Bridgend, 1988).

Menna Gallie, *Strike for a Kingdom* (London, 1959).

Menna Gallie, *Man's Desiring* (London, 1960).

Menna Gallie, *The Small Mine* (London, 1962).

Raymond Garlick, *Collected Poems, 1946–1986* (Llandysul, 1987).

Geraint Goodwin, *The Heyday In The Blood* (London, 1936).

Geraint Goodwin, *Collected Stories*, ed. Sam Adams (Tenby, 1996).

Iris Gower, *Copper Kingdom* (London, 1983).

Iris Gower, *Black Gold* (London, 1988).

Roger Granelli, *Dark Edge* (Bridgend, 1997).

Bryn Griffiths, *The Mask of Pity* (London, 1966).

Bryn Griffiths, *The Stones of the Field* (London, 1967).
Steve Griffiths, *Selected Poems* (Bridgend, 1993).
Niall Griffiths, *Grits* (London, 2001).
Paul Henry, *The Milk Thief* (Bridgend, 1998).
Douglas Houston, *With the Offal Eaters* (Newcastle, 1986).
Emyr Humphreys, *The Little Kingdom* (London, 1946).
Emyr Humphreys, *A Man's Estate* (London, 1953).
Emyr Humphreys, *A Toy Epic* (London, 1958).
Emyr Humphreys, *Outside the House of Baal* (1965).
Emyr Humphreys, *National Winner* (London, 1971).
Emyr Humphreys, *Flesh And Blood* (London, 1974).
Emyr Humphreys, *The Best of Friends* (London, 1978).
Emyr Humphreys, *Salt of the Earth* (London, 1985).
Emyr Humphreys, *An Absolute Hero* (London, 1986).
Emyr Humphreys, *Open Secrets* (London, 1988).
Emyr Humphreys, *Bonds of Attachment* (London, 1991).
Emyr Humphreys, *Unconditional Surrender* (Bridgend, 1996).
Emyr Humphreys, *The Gift of a Daughter* (Bridgend, 1998).
Emyr Humphreys, *Collected Poems* (Cardiff, 1999).
Emyr Humphreys, *Ghosts and Strangers* (Bridgend, 2001).
Emyr Humphreys, *Old People are a Problem* (Bridgend, 2003).
Siân James, *A Small Country* (London, 1979).
Siân James, *Storm at Arberth* (Bridgend, 1994).
Mike Jenkins, *Red Landscapes: New and Selected Poems* (Bridgend, 1999).
Nigel Jenkins, *Acts of Union: Selected Poems* (Llandysul, 1990).
David Jones, *In Parenthesis* (London, 1937).
David Jones, *The Anathémata* (London, 1952).
David Jones, *The Sleeping Lord* (London, 1974).
Glyn Jones, *The Valley, The City, The Village* (London, 1956).
Glyn Jones, *The Island of Apples* ed. Belinda Humfrey (Cardiff, 1992).
Glyn Jones, *The Collected Poems*, ed. Meic Stephens (Cardiff, 1996).
Glyn Jones, *The Collected Stories*, ed. Tony Brown (Cardiff, 1999).
Gwyn Jones, *Times Like These* (London, 1936).
Gwyn Jones, *Collected Stories* (Cardiff, 1998).
Jack Jones, *Rhondda Roundabout* (London, 1934).
Jack Jones, *Black Parade* (London, 1935).
John Sam Jones, *Welsh Boys Too* (Cardiff, 2000).
Lewis Jones, *Cwmardy* (London, 1937).
Lewis Jones, *We Live* (London, 1939).
Mary Jones, *Resistance* (Belfast, 1985).
Russell Celyn Jones, *An Interference of Light* (London, 1995).
T. Harri Jones, *Collected Poems*, eds. Julian Croft and Don Dale-Jones (Llandysul, 1977).

Joseph Keating, *Son of Judith* (London, 1900).
Stephen Knight, *Dream City Cinema* (London, 1996).
Alun Lewis, *Collected Stories*, ed. Cary Archard (Bridgend, 1990).
Alun Lewis, *Collected Poems*, ed. Cary Archard (Bridgend, 1994).
Gwyneth Lewis, *Parables and Faxes* (Newcastle, 1995).
Gwyneth Lewis, *Zero Gravity* (Newcastle, 1998).
Gary Ley, *Taking Ronnie to the Pictures* (Bridgend, 1998).
Richard Llewellyn, *How Green Was My Valley* (London, 1939).
Hilary Llewellyn-Williams, *The Tree Calendar* (Bridgend, 1987).
The Collected Arthur Machen, ed. Christopher Palmer (London, 1998).
Roland Mathias, *Collected Stories*, ed. Sam Adams (Cardiff, 2001).
Roland Mathias, *Collected Poems*, ed. Sam Adams (Cardiff, 2002).
Christopher Meredith, *Shifts* (Bridgend, 1988).
Christopher Meredith, *Griffri* (Bridgend, 1991).
Christopher Meredith, *Sidereal Time* (Bridgend, 1998).
Catherine Merriman, *Silly Mothers* (Dinas Powis, 1991).
Catherine Merriman, *State of Desire* (London, 1996).
Robert Minhinnick, *Selected Poems* (Manchester, 1999).
Clare Morgan, *An Affair of the Heart* (Bridgend, 1996).
Robert Morgan, *In the Dark* (Llandysul, 1994).
New Welsh Drama (Cardiff, 1998).
Leslie Norris, *Collected Poems* (Bridgend, 1996).
Leslie Norris, *Collected Stories* (Bridgend, 1996).
John Ormond, *Selected Poems* (Bridgend, 1987).
Malcolm Pryce, *Aberystwyth Mon Amour* (London, 2001).
Sheenagh Pugh, *Selected Poems* (Bridgend, 1990).
Allen Raine, *A Welsh Singer* (London, 1897).
Allen Raine, *Queen Of The Rushes*, ed. Katie Gramich (Cardiff, 1998).
Deryn Rees Jones, *The Memory Tray* (Bridgend, 1994).
Bernice Rubens, *Brothers* (London, 1984).
Bernice Rubens, *I Sent a Letter to my Love* (London, 1991).
Bernice Rubens, *Yesterday in the Back Lane* (London, 1996).
Oliver Reynolds, *Skevington's Daughter* (London, 1985).
Rhydderch, Samantha Wynne, *Rockclimbing in Silk* (Bridgend, 2001).
Alun Richards, *Home to an Empty House* (Llandysul, 1973).
Alun Richards, *Selected Stories* (Bridgend, 1995).
Lynette Roberts, *Poems* (London, 1944).
Lynette Roberts, *Gods with Stainless Ears* (London, 1951).
Lloyd Robson, *Cardiff Cut* (Cardiff, 2001).
Ian Rowlands, *A Trilogy of Appropriation: Three Plays* (Cardiff, 1999).
Owen Sheers, *The Blue Book* (Bridgend, 2000).
Steve Short, *Homo Sylvestris* (Salzburg, 1997).
Iain Sinclair, *Landor's Tower* (London, 2001).

Dylan Thomas, *Collected Poems 1934–1953*, eds. Walford Davies and Ralph Maud (London, 1988).

Dylan Thomas, *The Broadcasts*, ed. Ralph Maud (London, 1991).

Dylan Thomas, *Collected Stories*, ed. Walford Davies (London, 1995).

Dylan Thomas, *Under Milk Wood*, eds. Walford Davies and Ralph Maud (London, 1995).

Edward Thomas, *Three Plays* (Bridgend, 1994).

Gwyn Thomas, *Where Did I Put My Pity?* (London, 1946).

Gwyn Thomas, *The Dark Philosophers* (London, 1946).

Gwyn Thomas, *The Alone to the Alone* (London, 1949).

Gwyn Thomas, *All Things Betray Thee* (London, 1949).

Gwyn Thomas, *Sorrow For Thy Sons* (London, 1986).

Gwyn Thomas, *Selected Stories* (Bridgend, 1998).

Gwyn Thomas, *Three Plays* (Bridgend, 1990).

Ivor Thomas, *Unsafe Sex: New and Selected Poems* (Cardiff, 1999).

R. S. Thomas, *The Echoes Return Slow* (London, 1988).

R. S. Thomas, *Collected Poems* (London, 1993).

R. S. Thomas, *No Truce With The Furies* (Tarset, 1995).

R. S. Thomas, *Selected Prose*, ed. Sandra Anstey (1995).

R. S. Thomas, *Autobiographies*, ed. Jason Walford Davies (London, 1997).

R. S. Thomas, *Residues*, ed. M. Wynn Thomas (Tarset, 2002).

Chris Torrance, *Second Vector: The Book of Heat* (Heath, 1996).

Rachel Tresize, *In and Out of the Goldfish Bowl* (Cardiff, 2000).

John Tripp, *Selected Poems*, ed. John Ormond (Bridgend, 1989).

Henry Vaughan: *The Complete Poems*, ed. Alan Rudrum (Harmondsworth, 1976).

The Works of Henry Vaughan, ed. L. C. Martin (Oxford, 1957).

Richard Vaughan, *Moulded in Earth* (London, 1951).

Sarah Waters, *Tipping the Velvet* (London, 1998).

The Collected Poems of Vernon Watkins, ed. Ruth Pryor (Ipswich, 1986).

Harri Webb, *Collected Poems*, ed. Meic Stephens (Llandysul, 1995).

Charlotte Williams, *Sugar And Slate* (Aberystwyth, 2002).

Emlyn Williams, *The Corn is Green* (London, 1938).

Emlyn Williams, *George* (London, 1961).

Emlyn Williams, *Emlyn* (London, 1973).

Raymond Williams, *Border Country* (London, 1960).

Raymond Williams, *Second Generation* (London, 1964).

Raymond Williams, *The Fight for Manod* (London, 1979).

Raymond Williams, *Loyalties* (London, 1985).

Raymond Williams, *People of the Black Mountains* (London, 1989).

Penny Windsor, *Like Oranges* (Dinas Powis, 1989).

INDEX

Fox, Pamela 69
'Fox, The' (Chris Torrance) 299
Francis, Dick 5
'Francis Drake' (Idris Davies)121
Francis, Jo 5
Freud, Sigmund 106
From Hand to Hand see O Law i Law
Frontiers in Anglo-Welsh Poetry (Tony
  Conran) 321–3
Frost, Robert 110
'Fugue for Ann Griffiths' (R. S. Thomas)
  172–3
Full Moon see Un Nos Ola Leuad
'Funland' (Dannie Abse) 260
Fuse (Patrick Jones) 303

Gallie, Menna 51, 66, 75–7, 81, 84, 85,
  261–3
Garlick, Raymond 3, 7, 33, 178, 229,
  230, 234, 238–42, 311, 313–14, 319
Garthowen (Allen Raine) 36
Gay, John 29
*Gentleman's Tour through
  Monmouthshire and Wales* (Henry
  Penruddocke Wyndham) 34
'Gents Only' (Rhys Davies) 191
George (Emlyn Williams) 117
Georgian Poetry (ed. James Reeves) 115
Georgics (Virgil) 29
Germinal (Emile Zola) 52, 62, 69
Gerontion (T. S. Eliot) 174, 222
Ghosts and Strangers (Emyr Humphreys)
  198
Gibbon, Lewis Grassic 71
Gibson, W. W. 116
Gift, The (Emyr Humphreys) 195, 198
Gilbert and George 118
Gill, Eric 112, 118
Giraldus Cambrensis (Gerald de Barri) 34
Girl from Cardigan, The (Leslie Norris)
  269
Gissing, George 204
Glass Shot, The (Duncan Bush) 81, 87
Glastonbury Romance, A (John Cowper
  Powys) 106
Glyndŵr, Owain 173, 230
Gododdin, Y (Aneirin) 291
Gods with Stainless Ears (Lynette
  Roberts) 152, 155–7
'Gold' (Glyn Jones) 120
Golightly, Vic 59
Gollancz, Victor 56, 57, 75, 219, 301
Gomer Press 281, 302

Gone to Earth (Mary Webb) 105
Gone With the Wind (Margaret Mitchell)
  219
Goodbye, Mr Chips (James Hilton) 213
Goodwin, Geraint 2, 96–8, 105, 109,
  206, 223
Gower, Iris 62, 75, 78, 84, 220–1
Gower, M. G./M. G. J *see* Jones, Glyn
Graber, George Alexander *see* Cordell,
  Alexander
Granelli, Roger 84, 293
Graves, Robert 107, 115, 157
Great God Pan, The (Arthur Machen)
  40, 93
'Great Time, A' (W. H. Davies) 41
'Green Bridge, The' (Leslie Norris) 269
Green, Green My Valley Now (Richard
  Llewellyn) 74
'Green Heart, The' (Brenda
  Chamberlain) 188
Green Mountain (Dylan Thomas) 130
Greenwood, Walter 66
Gregson, Ian 183, 184
Gren 276
Griffith, Moses 34
Griffiths, Ann 174
Griffiths, Bryn 225–7, 228, 229–30, 237,
  238
Griffiths, Niall 301, 302
Grigson, Geoffrey 121, 140
Grits (Niall Griffiths) 301
'Grongar Hill' (John Dyer) 19, 20, 22,
  23, 24–7, 28, 30, 32
Gruffydd, Peter 228, 242
Guest, Lady Charlotte 39
Guild of Welsh Writers 225
Gurney, Ivor 110
Gurney, John 86
Gwalia Deserta (Idris Davies) 140, 141,
  142–3, 238, 322
'Gwen' (Lewis Morris) 38
Gwenallt 86, 230, 238
Gwynedd Synphony, A (Tony Conran)
  186, 292

Habington, William 13
Haines, Aldryd 83
Hallam, Arthur 151
Hamilton, Hamish 207, 214
Hamlet (William Shakespeare) 126
'Hand that signed the paper, The'
  (Dylan Thomas) 123
Hanley, James 5, 48